6 EDITION

FINANCIAL PLANNING

for the
Older Client

Dana Shilling, J.D.

P.O. Box 14367
Cincinnati, OH 45250-0367
1-800-543-0874
www.NationalUnderwriter.com

The **National Underwriter** Company
A Unit of Highline Media

The Leader in Insurance and Financial Services Information

ISBN: 0-87218-691-1

Copyright © 1992, 1994, 1997, 1999, 2001, 2006
The National Underwriter Company
P.O. Box 14367, Cincinnati, Ohio 45250-0367

6th Edition

Printed in U. S. A.

Table of Contents

About the Author

Dana Shilling, a member of the Harvard Law School class of 1975, has spent more than a decade researching and writing about issues of personal finance and law. Recently, she has concentrated on the study of elder law, and is co-author of a major legal treatise on this subject (and is co-author of almost two dozen other books on legal and financial planning topics). She has also produced a two-videocassette series on basic elder law concepts for professionals.

Introduction

Many things have changed since the publication of the Fifth Edition in 2001—and, from the perspective of the planner assisting older clients and their families, many things have changed for the worse!

Life expectancy continues to increase, and that's a good thing. The average age of the population, and the percentage of seniors in the population, also continue to rise. This will be good if it leads to greater opportunities, but it places strain on the economy because seniors consume a lot of medical services—and health care inflation is much more severe than other types of inflation.

The previous edition warned that the unprecedented bull market would have to come to an end sometime, and it did, with the dot.com crash. Many seniors lost a large percentage of their savings, and some had to defer retirement or return to the workforce post-retirement for financial reasons.

Demographic changes as well as economic factors have the Social Security and Medicare systems on the ropes. It's still unclear what steps will be taken to put the Social Security system on a sounder footing. Medicare has adopted new managed care rules (managed care plans are now known as Medicare Advantage plans, regulated as Medicare Part C) and a new prescription drug benefit (Part D).

The Part D program requires senior citizens who enroll to pay a monthly premium. The hope is that senior citizens, especially those who use a lot of prescriptions, will save money, but some estimates say that up to one-third of seniors will actually spend more after Part D than before, and this is a very costly program that will make the problems of the federal deficit even worse.

Investment choices for older investors have gotten a lot tougher: there are limited choices for safe income-oriented investments, and the stock market can be a scary place. For more and more working Americans, there is no employer-funded sure source of income in their future: their post-retirement security comes from the amount they can save in their 401(k) plans and IRAs, how well they manage their accounts, and what the financial market conditions are before and after retirement.

Another problem is that some employers, including major employers, are filing for bankruptcy protection, freezing their pension plans, or otherwise becoming unwilling or unable to make payments under the pension plans. It is very common for employers to eliminate or cut back on retiree health plans, so clients should not count on the former employer as an ongoing source of health care financing.

Housing prices remain strong—in fact, many observers say that the "housing bubble" is about to break. But in the meantime, many older people's net worth is bolstered by housing appreciation, and housing value can be accessed via reverse mortgages or otherwise to pay for necessary care.

Since the last edition, there have been few changes in Medicaid law, and the role of Medicaid in paying for long-term care has only increased. However, just as major bankruptcy legislation passed in 2005 after pending for many years; keep your eye on the horizon: there could be big changes, because the federal and especially the state governments need to save money in the expensive Medicaid program. That's a very good reason to discuss with your clients (at least those who are healthy enough to be underwritten) whether private long-term care insurance is a good idea.

There have been several rounds of tax cuts, and that's good news for many of your clients—although many of them will have to pay Alternative Minimum Tax. Under current law, few Americans will face estate tax, so estate planning is simpler than it used to be.

The more complicated the situation becomes, the more the older client needs sound advice from a trusted advisor—one who can view the situation from a 360-degree perspective, not a narrow one, and one who has the services and products, or the recommendations, needed to assemble an initial plan and review it periodically to see that it continues to meet the older person's needs vis a vis legal, economic, and personal changes.

Chapter 1

The Elder Care Perspective

Money isn't everything. That may seem like a strange way to kick off a financial planning book, but the fact is that although money is an important element in elder care planning, it cannot solve all problems single-handedly. A quality elder care plan will, in fact, be concerned with quality; the quality of life for the older client's remaining lifespan, which could be as short as a few months or as long as three decades.

One task of the family members and professional advisors involved in the planning team is to make sure that the pension and other post-retirement funds are chosen and deployed wisely. But that is not the end of the story. People over age 65 vary greatly in their physical and mental capacities and needs. Some need a few more nice days to perfect their golf swing, while others need constant hands-on care to perform even the most basic tasks of survival.

Health care is fairly peripheral to most financial plans, but it is crucial and central to elder care plans. With luck, very little medical care will be required and whatever care is necessary will be fully covered by Medicare (Chapter 5) and Medigap insurance (Chapter 3). Yet, for many senior citizens, Alzheimer's Disease or some other type of dementia will cause a gradual, but eventually severe, loss of cognitive power and ability for self-care. Or a chronic illness or a combination of several illnesses and conditions will call for home care assistance, a move to specialized housing, or a move to a nursing home. Even the affluent have concerns about how they will be able to meet health care expenses. PNC Financial Services Group said that 52% of a sample of wealthy people listed "providing for my health and wellness" as their number one financial concern, and 38% listed affording family health care their first financial planning priority. Nearly half thought that the financial instability of the Medicare system created risks to their family's wealth, and almost a quarter of those whose parents were still alive were worried because their parents did not have long-term care insurance. However, more than two-thirds of the study respondents did not own long-term care insurance themselves![1]

Therefore, sound planning for the post-retirement years requires: (1) a health care plan to ensure that quality care will be available when it is needed, and (2) a way to pay for the care. Care mechanisms could include treatment by physicians, hospitalization, skilled or custodial nursing homes, care at home, or a move from the community to specialized housing. Payment sources might include the retiree's own funds, contributions by family members, an employer's health plan, Medicare, Medigap insurance, long term care insurance, or Medicaid (although statutory changes that take effect in 2006 make Medicaid planning much more difficult). More to the point, the plan will probably evolve over time as the older person's needs change, and as the health care system and legal system also change.

DEPLOYING THE PLANNING TOOLS

In many ways, sound planning remains the same no matter the age or medical condition of the client. Certainly, the planner will want to make sure that the client can achieve lifestyle objectives: having the appropriate income level, taking reasonable planning steps to minimize the tax burden, and drafting any documents needed for transactions or transfers (including trust documents and a valid will).

Between the vast impact of retirement plans on the investment market and assets accumulated through non-retirement savings, older people's funds have a crucial effect on the U.S. economy. Robert L. Reynolds of Fidelity Investments projects that by 2010, 60-70% of all investment assets in the U.S. will be owned by people over 60. In 2005, 60% of the $1 trillion Fidelity had under management was in investment accounts. Fidelity's response was to roll out a service, Fidelity Retirement Income Advantage, to help pre-retirees make workable plans and to let retirees monitor their spending as compared to their various sources of income, with suggestions for making up any shortfalls.[2]

In many instances, financial planners work with married couples, or are consulted by a married man who takes the lead in planning for the family. A typical client is a mid-life male executive or professional. But elder planning also might involve an elderly widow or someone who has never been married. Many planning devices are tailored for married couples: for instance, the gift and estate tax marital deduction (see Chapter 13) and Medicaid protection for the community spouse (see Chapter 6). Of course, if the client is widowed or was never married these devices are inapplicable.

Good planning requires an unprejudiced mind. It is most common that in a married couple the husband will be older, earn more, have more assets, become sick first, and then die first, leading to a prolonged period of widowhood for his spouse. But this assumption may not necessarily pan out in a particular case. The younger spouse may die first, leaving a spouse suffering one or more serious physical or cognitive problems. This spouse may nevertheless survive for many years, requiring a large and ever-increasing amount of care each year.

Recent studies show that caregiving itself is so stressful that it is harmful to the caregiver, placing the caregiver at risk of health problems or even death shortly after the death of the person who received the care. An article published in the *New England Journal of Medicine* in early 2006 shows that the risk is lowest when the caregiver took care of someone with an acute illness, and highest if the care recipient had Alzheimer's Disease or a similar chronic illness. Widows and widowers had a 20% higher risk of dying prematurely than those who were still married. The risk was just as high for caregivers for a spouse with dementia. Those who had a hospitalized spouse had a 5% higher risk than those who had a healthy spouse. The most stressful illnesses are those that not only cause physical debilitation but also impair the victim's cognition. Caregivers were most likely to die within 100-200 days after bereavement or the onset of the spouse's serious illness.[3]

Not every senior citizen suffers from mental incapacity, and some will never suffer diminished capacity. Do not forget that senior citizens, just like their younger counterparts, are entitled to express generosity and romantic feelings. They are allowed to make mistakes about relationships or investments as long as they are not the victims of illness, fraud, duress, undue influence, or financial elder abuse.

The MetLife Mature Market Institute pointed out some interesting differences in the way men and women think about elderplanning. Among men who are married or have a partner, 88% think it is very or somewhat likely that their spouse will become their primary caregiver if they ever need assistance with daily tasks; 72% of women have this expectation. Seventy-seven percent of women, but only 61% of men, say it is very likely that they will become the primary caregiver if their spouse becomes disabled. For seniors who have children, 41% of men and 55% of women expect the children to become their primary caregivers if one is required. When they were asked if they had long-term care insurance, about one-fifth of the survey respondents said yes—but many of them were mistaken, believing that they had LTCI when in fact they were covered by a different kind of insurance or federal program. Furthermore, misunderstandings are common: 21% of both male and female respondents thought that Medicare would pay the bulk of their long-term care costs, and 7% of men and 9% of women thought that health insurance would take care of this. So an important part of the care plan is clearing up misconceptions.[4]

UNDERSTANDING THE ELDER COHORTS

In statistics, a "cohort" means a group of people born at about the same time. Perhaps the most famous cohort is the "Baby Boom" generation: an unprecedented large group that has dramatically affected the U.S. economy. However, it is not very accurate or helpful to think of senior citizens as a monolithic group. They vary greatly in their economic status, physical health, and need for care. That is why many analysts think of senior citizens as two or three groups: the "young-old" and the "old-old," with perhaps a middle group in between.

The oldest Baby Boomers will become senior citizens in 2011–and there will be Boomer centenarians in 2046. It is estimated that 19 million boomers will still be alive in 2050. At one point, 79 million members of the Baby Boom were still alive, but at the beginning of the twenty-first century, the Boomer cohort started to shrink as deaths exceeded immigration.

According to the Census Bureau, the number of senior citizens will increase two and a half times between 2000 and 2050. The working-age population will grow an estimated 35% in those fifty years—but the "oldest-old" (85 and over) will go from 1.5% of the population in 2000 to about 5% in 2050.[5]

The MetLife Mature Market Institute published some provocative figures in 2005. At that point, there were close to 36 million Americans born in or before 1939—12.6% of the population. The expectation was that in 2030 there would be 71.5 million senior citizens in America—and 86.9 million in 2050. In 1990, there were 37,306 centenarians, a number that had grown to 50,454 in 2003 and 88,289 in 2004.

The MetLife data paints an interesting picture of the living situations of the elderly. In 2000, 13.8% of men aged 65-74 lived alone; this was true of 21.4% of men over 75. Close to one-third of women 65-74 lived alone, as was also true of 49.4% of women 75 and older. About 3-4% of senior citizens went through life without ever marrying. However, 79.6% of men aged 65-74 were married and only 55.3% of women in this age group were married. The difference was even more dramatic among those over 85: 60.1% of men but only 13.2% of women in this age group were married—because of the tendency for women to marry men older than themselves, and to have longer life expectancies than their mates—leading to a high risk of widowhood.[6]

The Social Security Administration estimates that for people born in 1935, 88% of men and 92% of women could expect to survive to age 70; 74% of men and 82% of women to survive to 75; 56% and 69% respectively to live to 80; 36% and

51% to reach 85; 17% and 31% to live to be 90; and even 6% of men and 13% of women to live to be 95.[7]

In 2002, the life expectancy of a 65-year-old man was about 16 years, and for a 65-year-old woman, it was about 19 years.[8] In other words, if everybody retired at age 65 (and many people retire earlier),[9] the statistically average retirement would last for over 16 years. There would be nothing exceptional about a 25-year retirement, and even three decades of retirement would not be surprising.

The aging of the population has profound implications in many ways. Presently, a healthy person of 65 is really middle-aged, not old. However, an 85-year-old almost certainly suffers from at least one serious health problem. The odds are that the 65-year-old will have years of independent living in front of him, while the odds are that the 85-year-old will require assistance with at least some basic daily activities. This means that the demand for home care agencies, specialized housing, and nursing home beds will increase. Unless trends can be reversed, and costs brought under control, the economy will face a double whammy from elder health care needs: an expanding demand for care as well as constantly rising prices.

The Social Security system can be predicted to experience problems simply because the Baby Boom group is so large, with many in this group earning enough to receive maximum Social Security benefits. There are other, subtler effects that can be expected. As the population ages, there are fewer workers paying contributions into the Social Security system, while a larger retiree group draws benefits. This condition is known as being "upside down," referring to a large volume of retirees being supported by a small number of workers, rather than vice versa.

The Congressional Research Service (CRS) released a report in late 2005 analyzing income and poverty trends among senior citizens in 2004. They found that the median income (that is, the point at which half of seniors had higher income and half had lower) for 2004 was $15,199, and 28% of seniors had income below $10,000. Only 10% had income over $50,000. Nearly all senior citizens (88%) received Social Security benefits, and that program was the largest source of income for senior citizens. Over two-thirds of the senior cohort derived more than half of their income from Social Security, and close to a quarter had no income other than Social Security. The median private pension was only $6,720 a year. Although half of the seniors studied got some income from their assets, typically the amount of such income was quite small: in half of the cases, it was less than $1,000 a year.[10]

Because Baby Boomers have benefited by bull markets and housing booms, this is a highly affluent cohort. According to the Pew Research Center, the Baby Boomers transfer wealth within their families both to their aged relatives and to their children. Among Baby Boomers aged 41-59 in 2005, 29% provided financial help to a parent in 2004, and 57% did the same for an adult child. Close to one-fifth (19%) got financial help from their parents, and 14% got help from an adult child.[11]

Although some large cities have good public transportation, and a feature of some senior-oriented housing is van service or other transportation, most people in the United States are dependent on automobiles for transportation. To reduce this dependence among seniors who should not be driving, innovative programs are evolving: "dial-a-ride" van pools; services that make rides in cars and vans available at any time in exchange for a small fee; programs that allow seniors to trade in their cars for credits that can be used for transportation—in effect, a reverse mortgage for cars that would otherwise spend most of their time in the garage.

According to the Insurance Institute for Highway Safety, in 2000 there were 27.3 million senior citizens licensed to drive (14% of the total), a number that is expected to reach 65.4 million in 2030 (more than one-quarter of all drivers). But older drivers have problems caused by, for example, impaired vision and slower reflexes. There are also more than 300 "driver rehabilitation" specialists nationwide, who concentrate on retraining older drivers so they can drive safely despite impairments.

The 2005 federal transportation appropriations bill added coping mechanisms for the expected explosive growth in the number of senior citizen drivers such as making signs bigger and more reflective, changing the timing of traffic signals, adding pavement markings, and separate left-turn lanes (because older drivers have problems with intersections in general and left turns in particular).[12]

THE ECONOMIC IMPACT OF ALZHEIMER'S DISEASE

The latest statistics published by the Alzheimer's Association show that about 4.5 million Americans suffer from Alzheimer's Disease (more than twice as many as in 1980), and anywhere from 11.3 million to 16 million Americans could be in this category in 2050. One-tenth of seniors and almost half of persons over 85 have Alzheimer's Disease. Direct and indirect care costs for Alzheimer's Disease sufferers are at least $100 billion a year, and businesses spend and lose $61 billion a year between health care costs and lost productivity. The average lifetime cost of caring for an Alzheimer's sufferer is estimated to be $174,000.[13]

MetLife's Mature Market Institute released a 27-page guide for caregivers of Alzheimer's sufferers in October, 2005. "Since You Care: Alzheimer's Disease— Caregiving Challenges" was prepared in conjunction with the National Alliance for Caregiving to cope with the estimated 4.5 million cases of Alzheimer's; as the population ages, the number of Americans with Alzheimer's could be as high as 16 million by 2050.[14]

PRACTICE TIP: Call the Mature Market Institute at (203) 221-6580 for copies to distribute to your clients.

It is estimated that nearly one-quarter of all family caregivers take care of a person with dementia. Because of the advanced age of most Alzheimer's sufferers and the high need for care, Alzheimer's caregivers are usually older than other caregivers. These caregivers are also required to provide care over a longer period of time and to spend more time providing care. For more than one-quarter of Alzheimer's caregivers it is the equivalent of a full-time job, requiring 40 or more hours per week. Alzheimer's caregivers are twice as likely to experience physical strain and emotional stress as other caregivers. Over one in ten Alzheimer caregivers reports taking medication or alcohol to cope with caregiving stress.[15]

Although some caregivers are forced to quit their jobs or shift to a part-time schedule to meet their caregiving obligations, about four-fifths of employed caregivers work full-time. Approximately $26 billion of the cost to business comes from lost productivity among caregivers absent from work to cope with family needs. Replacing caregivers who are forced to quit their jobs costs over $3.5 billion. An estimated $1.3 billion is allocated to keeping up health insurance for caregiver-employees who take leave under the Family and Medical Leave Act, to heavy usage of Employee Assistance Programs by caregivers, and to fees for temporary agencies. Industry also spends an estimated $7.1 billion on health insurance and taxes that are allocated to senior citizens' health care and federal Alzheimer's Disease research.

Not all cognitive problems in elders are caused by Alzheimer's or other dementing diseases. The National Institute of Mental Health estimates that two million out of the current senior population of 35 million have a major depressive disorder, and another five million have symptoms that increase their risk of major depression in the future. This could be a frightening trend, but in a sense it's hopeful, because when properly diagnosed, depression is far more treatable than dementia.

PRACTICE TIP: For Web resources about depression in older adults, see the Positive Aging Resource Center, www.positiveaging.org; the Geriatric Mental Health Foundation, www.gmhfonline.org; and the National Mental Health Association's free online screening test for depression: www.DepressionScreening.org. A list of screening test centers can be found at www.mentalhealthscreening.org.[16]

CARE NEEDS

As it stands now, Baby Boomers are doing the bulk of the caregiving, but eventually they will be senior citizens and in need of care themselves. There are over 9.4 million Americans, many over the age of 65, who need help with ADLs (Activities of Daily Living; e.g., bathing, getting dressed, walking) and IADLs (Instrumental Activities of Daily Living, such as cooking, shopping, and paying bills). One out of nine female seniors, and one out of twelve male seniors, have serious limitations in one or more ADLs. For seniors over the age of 85, this is true of 31% of women and 21% of men.

However, nursing homes and other institutions provide only a small part of the care given to ADL- and IADL-dependent people. Almost 80% of the people who need long-term care are living in the community, not in institutions.[17]

The Government Accountability Office (GAO) estimated that between 2000 and 2040, the number of disabled elderly people requiring assistance with Activities of Daily Living (ADLs) could double. It was estimated that in 2000, about one-fifth of people in need of long-term care and who lived in the community (i.e., not in nursing homes) did not receive all the services they needed. In 1990, about 600,000 elderly people lived alone without having children or brothers or sisters they could call on for care—a number that was expected to double by 2020. On the bright side, the percentage of senior citizens having disabilities has been dropping—but the sheer number of elderly people will ensure that there will be heavy demand for long-term care.[18]

The majority of nursing home residents are members of the "old-old" cohort (i.e., they are 85 or older). Three-quarters of nursing home residents are women; 83% are single (either widowed, divorced, or never married); almost half suffer from cognitive impairments or other mental disorders; and nearly all (96%) have limitations in coping with Activities of Daily Living.[19]

A new study led by Professor Peter Kemper of Pennsylvania State University estimates that more than two-thirds of those who are senior citizens today will need some degree of long-term care at some point before they die. However, some of these care needs will be fairly modest, and can be met informally by family members and friends within the senior's own home. However, the study projects that more than one-third (37%) of today's senior cohort will need institutional care (in a nursing home or assisted living facility). The average stay will probably be less than two years, but 8% of the senior cohort will spend five years or more in a nursing home, at catastrophic expense, and 11% will need five years or more of home care. The Kemper study predicts that most elders will not use any significant amount of paid LTC, but 11% will have costs between $100,000 and $250,000, and 5% will incur costs over $250,000 (although these figures also include amounts paid by Medicare and Medicaid.) The researchers also found that, among seniors who sought to protect themselves by buying LTCI, 8% of those who had policies with a three-year term exhausted their policy benefits because their nursing home stay lasted longer. The study predicts that about 6% of senior citizens will enter nursing homes as private-pay patients, but shift to Medicaid coverage once they have exhausted their assets by paying for care.[20]

Another important financial planning problem for senior citizens is meeting the high and ever-burgeoning cost of prescription drugs. (See Chapter 5 for discussion of the Medicare Part D prescription drug program, which took effect at the beginning of 2006.)

2005 was the third year in a row in which, according to the AARP, the average price of brand-name drugs commonly prescribed to senior citizens rose more than twice as fast as overall inflation. When the CPI increased 3.1%, the average price increase for 195 popular drugs was 6.6%--but the cost of generic drugs (where there is extensive competition) went up less than 1%. The price of Lipitor, the best-selling cholesterol-reducing drug, went up 5%, to $2.17 for the 10 mg pill and $3.15 for the 20 mg pill—whereas the price of an older drug of the same type, Mevacor, remained stable at $1.18. The AARP estimated that a typical senior, who takes three brand-name prescriptions for chronic illnesses, would have faced price increases of $866 between 2000 and 2005. Although the Medicare program has added a drug benefit (see Chapter 5), the statute creating this benefit is complex and imposes new burdens on seniors.[21]

CAREGIVER ISSUES

The term "caregiver" is usually used to describe a family member or friend who provides informal, unpaid care. Caregivers differ in the amount of care they provide. Some live in the same home as the person receiving the care and are responsible for significant amounts of hands-on care. Others, especially those who live far away, have a role that may include emotional and financial participation, but not hands-on care.

The middle-aged children of elderly parents are often called the "sandwich generation," because they are caught between the financial demands of helping parents and paying for their own children's needs. However, intergenerational financial help moves in both directions. Many grandparents step in to take over raising grandchildren whose parents are dead or unable to care for them. Furthermore, there is an increasing trend for grandparents to provide financial assistance even to intact families (college and pre-college tuition; help with medical costs). Recent financial trends have made the senior citizen generation better off (because of government programs, the bull-market, and housing gains) but the middle generation worse off. Nowadays, education lasts longer and costs more than ever before, helping to create an indebted generation.

In 2005, the likelihood that a 20-year-old would have a living grandmother (91%) was greater than the percentage of 20-year-olds in 1900 whose mothers were still alive (83%).[22]

PLANNING TIP: Caregivers should be aware that a federal statute, the Family and Medical Leave Act (FMLA), 29 USC 2612, requires employers to grant up to 12 weeks unpaid leave per year (including full and partial days off) so that caregivers can deal with a parent's serious medical condition. However, the federal FMLA does not require employers to grant leave to care for a parent-in-law, although many caregivers are responsible for a mother- or father-in-law. Many of the states have their own family leave acts, which may be more generous toward "caregivers-in-law."

In many cases, the caregiver will also serve as an agent under a Durable Power of Attorney, as a trustee, or as a guardian for a mentally incapacitated senior citizen. The caregiver may also be named on the older person's joint accounts. Documents should set out exactly what powers the caregiver will have over the older person's finances, especially with regard to gifts. In some cases, "self-gifts" (gifts made by a caregiver to himself or to his spouse or children) are appropriate when they carry out the wishes of the older person and satisfy legitimate planning objectives, such as reducing the taxable estate. But in other situations they may be inappropriate, unfair to other family members, or possibly illegal as a violation of a fiduciary responsibility.

Mather LifeWays, a non-profit organization whose mission is the well-being of seniors, offers Powerful Tools for Caregivers, a six-week education program to improve caregivers' ability to cope with the stresses of caregiving and make practical plans for coping. The class is taught both live in churches, community centers, and Assisted Living Facilities and online.[23]

A recent *Wall Street Journal* article pointed out the significance of holidays to elder care: seeing older family members after an interval of months or even years can highlight the deterioration in their condition and ability to cope. That's why the Christmas holidays and the beginning of the year are the peak time for referrals to Geriatric Care Managers. Some signs of possible problems:

- Personality changes;

- Bills that go unpaid although the senior can afford to pay them;

- Withdrawing from contact with family and friends; and

- Deterioration in the condition of the home and/or personal appearance.

Sometimes (although not always) the fact that the senior citizen denies that there are problems is in itself a sign of dementia, and "I don't have the energy" to carry out suggestions from relatives and friends could hint at depression.

PLANNING TIP: Friends and relatives who are concerned that an older person is no longer a safe driver can contact the senior's physician, who can notify the DMV. That way, the anger is directed at the doctor or the agency, not at the caregiver.[24]

A federal statute, the Older Americans Act, which is instrumental in providing funding for the states to run programs for the elderly, was reauthorized on November 11, 2000. In December, 2000, Congress authorized additional funding for programs for the elderly.

Most programs, such as shared and home-delivered meals, received modest increases in appropriations. The reauthorization added a new National Family Caregiver Support Program, with $125 million in funding. The money will go to state and local Agencies on Aging and other organizations providing elder care, in order to create programs to assist caregivers. On January 4, 2005, House Concurrent Resolution 8 was introduced, calling for full funding of the National Family Caregiver Support Program so that the 52 million unpaid caregivers for the elderly and for children would continue to receive services to assist them in providing care at home and in the community.[25] The Federal Administration on Aging has conducted roundtable discussions with caregivers in over 30 cities to target their needs. As a result of these meetings, the programs will focus on information, assistance, counseling, training, and respite for caregivers.[26]

END OF LIFE ISSUES

It can confidently be predicted that all clients will die, sooner or later, as a result of one cause or another. Although nothing can alter this basic fact of existence, good planning can do a great deal to enhance the quality of life in a client's later years, including the time when the client is terminally ill or otherwise incapacitated.

The basic premise of our medical and legal systems is that health care is rendered based on a contract between the health care provider and the consenting patient. This model often breaks down at the end of life because the patient is unconscious, suffers from Alzheimer's Disease or another illness that impairs cognition, or is otherwise unable to make care choices or give informed consent to care.

The legal system has responded in several ways, principally by making provisions for Advance Directives. That is, an adult with mental capacity signs a document expressing his treatment wishes under various circumstances. The document can then be consulted if and when the patient is unable to express wishes directly. There are generally two kinds of Advance Directives: the Living Will, and the Durable Power of Attorney for Health Care. The Durable Power of Attorney for Health Care is also known as a health care proxy.

The Living Will is a written expression of the person's desire that treatment be either terminated or continued in the event the person ever becomes terminally ill and unconscious, or is otherwise unable to express treatment preferences. States differ in the extent to which Living Wills can be used to refuse care or direct that nutrition and hydration be provided if the person is also unable to eat. Most states do allow Living Wills to be used for this purpose, as long as the person's wishes are clearly and unequivocally expressed. Also, an advance directive can be used to express a preference for maximum as well as minimum treatment.

The health care proxy works differently. It designates a person, such as a spouse, adult child, or family friend, to make treatment decisions if the patient cannot make the decisions personally. This is broader than the Living Will, because it can come into play when the person who granted the proxy is mentally incapacitated but not terminally ill. Once again, it is probably possible to give the proxy decision-making power over nutrition and hydration decisions, but this is a matter of state law.

Certain health care providers that participate in Medicare, including hospitals and nursing homes, have an obligation under federal law to raise the subject of advance directives with their patients. While such a facility may not force a patient to sign an advance directive, if a patient does sign an advance directive, the facility is required to make it a part of the patient's medical record. If a patient signs an advance directive, the health care provider is not required to provide care that conflicts with the advance directive. The health care provider is not required to implement an advance directive if, as a matter of conscience, the provider cannot implement an advance directive and state law allows any health care provider or any agent of such provider to conscientiously object.

An increasing number of states have laws dealing with Do Not Resuscitate (DNR) orders. DNRs make it possible for an individual to say that he does not want CPR to be performed if he suffers a heart attack or respiratory arrest. Even in states that do not have specific statutes, it is worthwhile to discuss with the attending physician whether or not a "No Code" order should be placed in the medical record. If state law permits "out of hospital" DNR orders, and this is the client's wish, then local ambulance and EMS services should be notified and given a copy of the order so they will not perform an unwanted resuscitation.

Another trend in state law is the creation of "surrogate decision making" laws. These laws set out a hierarchy of people (usually, the spouse first, then if there is no spouse, an adult child, and so forth) who have a legal right to make medical decisions for an incapacitated patient who has not created an advance directive. Because the vast majority of people do not create advance directives, these statutes solve many problems. Without such a statute, the health care facility must obtain a court order appointing a guardian, and then approach the guardian for permission to carry out non-emergency health procedures, which is a cumbersome drain on both medical and legal resources.

The question of a guardian's powers over end of life issues is a very complex one. A California court held that the wife of a brain-damaged automobile accident victim, who was also his guardian (the California term is "conservator of the person"), might be able to obtain a court's permission to withhold life support (nutrition and hydration) from her husband, even though he was not in a coma. Under California law, the conservator is the only person who has the power to consent, or refuse to consent, to medical treatment for an incapacitated person.

The California Supreme Court held that to initiate the ending of life-sustaining treatment, the conservator must prove by clear and convincing evidence that the conservatee wished to refuse life sustaining treatment, or that withholding life sustaining treatment is in the conservatee's best interests. The court emphasized in its ruling does not affect permanently unconscious patients.[27]

The tragic case of Terri Schiavo, who died in 2005 after extensive litigation and involvement by Congress and the Florida State legislature, highlights the complexity of these issues. Ms. Schiavo was in a persistent vegetative state for 15 years. Her husband sought to have her feeding tube removed. There was no Living Will or health care proxy, although her husband, Michael, said that they had discussed the issue and his wife did not want to be kept alive by artificial means. Her parents, and their many supporters, opposed termination of life support. It is possible that the matter would have been just as controversial if Ms. Schiavo had left a Living Will, but her parents opposed termination of life support and challenged the validity of the document or whether Ms. Schiavo's condition fit into the specifications of the document.[28]

Opponents of termination of life support in this case spoke in terms of "starvation" and "dying of thirst," although doctors and researchers who specialize in end-of-life care say that patients who are comatose or in a persistent vegetative state no longer experience suffering. Termination of nutrition and hydration usually causes death within about two weeks as the kidneys cease to produce urine, toxins build up, and the patient becomes comatose and eventually suffers a fatal electrolyte imbalance.[29]

There is growing interest in providing palliative care for dying people—provision of pain relief and comfort care, but reduction or elimination of active treatment. Reducing the number of interventions also reduces costs and can be much more peaceful and less stressful for the dying and their families than frequently painful interventions in an uncomfortable hospital environment. Palliative care is related to but not identical to hospice. Usually hospice care is home-based and limited to the last six months of life. Palliative care can take place in a hospital, doctor's office, or a nursing home setting. Hospice care avoids active treatment interventions; palliative care may include them, but they are not the focus of the care team's work.[30]

The Central Massachusetts Partnership to Improve Care at the End of Life has published "A Guide for a Better Ending" with guidelines for the last phase. The organization urges health care agents to ask questions about the disease and what the patient can expect as death nears. The agent's job is to make sure that the patient's wishes are carried out, even if the health care agent disagrees about these decisions. Sample questions to be asked of health care providers:

- Can you explain the burdens and benefits of the treatment you suggest?

- Do you work with a hospice?

- Do you consult with a palliative care specialist to provide better symptom relief?

Health care proxies are automatically revoked by a subsequent proxy, or when the principal divorces or is legally separated from the agent. A principal should give this information to health care providers, who should also be notified if the principal revokes a proxy.

Some cities have a "File of Life" program that issues red folders with a magnetic strip that can be attached to the refrigerator (where first responders can find it). The folder contains emergency contacts and basic medical information. People who have signed a Do Not Resuscitate form should put the form into this folder and wear a medical alert bracelet.[31]

PRACTICE TIP: You can find the language of your state's advance directive statutes from a law school library (be sure to check the pocket-part in the back of the book to make sure you have the latest version). You can also contact the not-for-profit organization Choice in Dying, from which you can order state-specific documents for $5 a set by calling (800) 989-9455, or downloading the documents from www.choices.org. The National Hospice and Palliative Care Organization, www.caringinfo.org or nhpco.org, (703) 837-1500 and Aging with Dignity, www.agingwithdignity.org, (888) 594-7437 also have a complete library of state forms. Make sure that designations of a health care proxy include (or that older forms are amended to include) giving the agent the right to access the patient's medical records that would otherwise be shielded by the federal Health Insurance Portability and Accessibility Act (HIPAA) privacy rules.

If the client wishes to become an organ donor, it is important to sign the necessary forms ahead of time, to carry organ donor identification, and, most importantly, to let close family members know of this intention. Otherwise, it is unlikely that the donation will take place, because the intention to donate will not be discovered in time.

THE PLANNING PROCESS AND THE PLANNING TEAM

The optimum elderplan reflects the wishes of the senior citizen and family (to the extent that these wishes can realistically be carried out). It provides for quality care in the optimum setting. It can also provide for different settings as needs change, because needs typically increase rather than decrease. The plan balances strictly financial issues such as investment and tax planning against medical, social, and psychological needs. It deploys financial products and services, as well as health care products and services, to meet these objectives.

You would not expect the average senior citizen to have access to one person who combines the skills and perspectives of half-a-dozen professionals. The obvious solution is to create a planning team, each of whose members brings a set of skills and a professional perspective to the project of creating and monitoring the elderplan.

Depending on the facts of the situation, the preferences of the senior and family, and the size and complexity of the plan, the team might include:

- An attorney, preferably an attorney with current information about elder law. Certain states have a program that allows an attorney to become a Certified Elder Law Attorney (CELA).[32] Becoming a CELA is evidence of commitment to elder law and of having achieved status within the field, although there are fine elder law attorneys who are not CELAs;

- A Geriatric Care Manager (GCM), usually trained in nursing or social work, with practical expertise not only with services available to the elderly, such as how to coordinate a service plan and how to apply for public benefits, but also day-to-day knowledge of, and contacts with, local service providers;

- An accountant to deal with tax and financial matters (e.g., valuation of a closely held business when the founder retires);

- A financial planner, whether fee- or commission-based;

- An insurance professional; and

- A broker or investment advisor, or both (the number and qualifications of the people involved will depend on the size and complexity of the portfolio).

The field of financial gerontology continued to expand. From 2004 to mid-2005, about 100 people were designated as "registered financial gerontologists" by the American Institute of Financial Gerontology, a designation created in 2003 by Widener University in collaboration with the American Society on Aging. The Society of Certified Senior Advisors (Denver) also granted designations, and the American College (Bryn Mawr) designated "chartered advisors for senior living."[33]

The number of financial advisors is hard to quantify, because various kinds of licenses are used, but not all advisors are required to be licensed, and there are dozens of titles in use. According to the National Association of Securities Dealers, in the first quarter of 2005, there were 190,468 people holding the Series 7 license (required to sell securities) working in 5,191 brokerage firms. The number of brokerage branch offices expanded from 88,168 in 2001 to 103,307 in 2004.

As of August 2005, 487,754 people had been granted the Certified Financial Planner designation. There were over 40,000 Chartered Financial Consultants (ChFCs) (issued by The American College) and the National Association of Personal Financial Advisors (NAPFA) had 943 members.[34]

PLANNING TIP: Early in 2006, the SEC tried to make it easier to find a qualified adviser by introducing a rule that stockbrokers must clarify whether they are acting as brokers (i.e., selling a product) or advisers (giving neutral advice in the best interests of the client). The Consumer Federation of America warned against inflated titles that reflect nothing more than the holder's attendance at a proprietary seminar. The CFP and ChFC designations are respected because they require a broad range of knowledge and experience and require the holders of the designations to take a number of intellectually challenging courses.[35]

Forming the Team

Professional ethical standards mandate that not only must a professional avoid practicing in professions for which he is not licensed, but he should suggest the involvement of other professionals whenever he encounters a situation that he is not trained or equipped to deal with.

It should be made clear to the client that he can assemble the team personally, but that the professional initially consulted is willing and able to make referral suggestions. (Consult the various codes of ethics for the extent to which fees can be shared, or if referral fees are appropriate.) In many instances, the client will not be aware of the full scope of services available, or of the division of labor among professionals. (For example, few people outside the elderplanning community even know that GCMs exist, and of those who are aware of GCMs, even less know how to work with them effectively.)

The planner will want to develop a network of other elderplanning professionals to work together on complex projects and to make referrals for simple tasks that fall into only one professional domain. An excellent way to do this is by attending multi-disciplinary continuing education programs. Not only will this hone the planner's skills, the planner will be able to observe local members of other professions.

In fact, it makes sense for a planner to offer his services as a speaker at single-profession or multi-disciplinary seminars, or to offer his own seminars (e.g., to employee groups, at senior centers, or to a congregation), because individuals who have seen the planner offering useful professional advice are more likely to want to retain his services or purchase financial products from him.[36]

Standards for making referrals, or adding a person to the team the planner recommends, include:

- Where and when did the person obtain basic education about elderplanning?

- How does he stay current on elderplanning issues? (e.g., from continuing education programs, committee activities, reading journals and newsletters, consulting Web sites that deal with planning issues)?

- If professional specialty or certification programs are available, has the person obtained certification?

- Is elderplanning central to the person's professional practice, or is it an afterthought?

- Is he aware of the functions of other professionals on the team, and does he know when to refer the case or bring in another team member?

- Is he aware of potential legal pitfalls (so he will not give dubious advice) and sensitive to Medicaid and tax consequences of transactions? This is especially important in the wake of the major changes made by the Deficit Reduction Act of 2005.

- How much time will the person be able to devote to this case?

- Will the person handle the case personally or delegate it to assistants? If it is delegated, how knowledgeable and skillful are the assistants?

- Does the person belong to important professional associations? Some professional associations are about as intellectually fruitful as a fraternity party, but others offer a year-round program of services, publications, and continuing education. On the other hand, some people just are not joiners, or they need to spend money that would otherwise go to dues on building a library or automating their practice; and

- Is the person easy to work with, and comfortable with older people and their families? How is his equivalent of a doctor's "bedside manner?"

As a 2005 *New York Times* article shows, elder planning is not easy—even for experts, when they encounter planning problems within their own families. Professors Robert and Rosalie Kane, both elder care experts, often found themselves baffled when they had to provide care for their own parents. What they gleaned from their experience is that adult children need to create and stick with a structured process for making decisions, especially when they are under pressure to find a care setting for a parent facing discharge from a hospital. They recommend getting a consultation from multiple physicians, not just relying on a primary care physician or a specialist who has not studied the special problems of the elderly. They warn that sometimes the elder's wishes must be honored, and his or her previously lifestyle observed as much as possible—even if it adds some risks that might be avoided in a more restrictive institutional placement, but where quality of life is lower.[37]

ETHICAL ISSUES

In practical terms, when a planner takes on an elderplanning case he is working for the entire family. The plan that is created may have implications that carry on for generations. The classic ethical issue for elderplanners is "who is the client?" In the ideal case, everyone is "on the same page" and agrees what should be done. In the real world, it is far more likely that there will be disagreements and hard choices will need to be made. For example, it may cost more for a frail senior citizen to be cared for at home (with three shifts of attendants, plus professional care) than in a nursing home. If home care continues for years, and little or none of the cost is reimbursed by Medicare or insurance, there probably will be less for the senior citizen's heirs to inherit. Similarly, the decision of whether to discontinue life support may be colored by financial as well as religious and compassion-related motives.

Sometimes the older-generation member realizes greater tax benefits from a lifetime gift, but the potential donee prefers an inheritance. Sometimes the potential recipient wants a gift now, but the potential donor wants to hang on to the money. If a son or daughter is named as agent under a Durable Power of Attorney (see Chapter 13 for a discussion of a Durable Power of Attorney), the question becomes whether the agent is allowed to make gifts of the senior citizen's money to himself or his family, and how this will affect the rest of the family.

As can be seen, there may be many interests and many opinions involved in creating a plan. The planner must decide who is the client and whose interests he must protect in case of a conflict. Sometimes it is necessary for individuals with seriously conflicting interests to have separate representatives, or at least to sign a waiver indicating that they are aware of the potential conflict but choose to employ the same attorney, accountant, or other advisor. It also matters who writes the check to pay the fee (if the planner is a fee-based planner). That person may technically be the client, even if the planner was hired to make a plan for someone else.

No matter who is technically the client, make sure that the planner receives the honest, unbiased, and uninfluenced opinion of the senior citizen who is the subject of the plan. It is often necessary to remove the children and in-laws from the room, and perhaps repeat the inquiries several times to find out what the senior citizen wants and not just what he thinks the children or in-laws want, or what an ideally unselfish parent would want.

PRACTICE TIP: Check with an experienced elder law attorney, or the local government agency that protects the elderly, for clues on how to spot physical or financial elder abuse and the scope of the legal duty to report suspected abuse. Most state laws provide that professionals have a legal duty to report suspected abuse that they observe as part of their professional practice. These laws provide that there is no penalty for making a good-faith report that turns out to be unfounded.

Another important ethical issue is how to handle a client who definitely would benefit by a particular transaction, but perhaps lacks the legal capacity to engage in the transaction. It is possible to reassure yourself, by taking extra time and trouble, that the older person finally understands the transaction and gives informed consent to engage in it. See if the family or attending physician can suggest times when the older person is especially alert. But if capacity is permanently lacking, then it may be necessary to have a guardian appointed, to use a Durable Power of Attorney already in existence, or to have a guardian appointed for the specific and limited purpose of carrying out the necessary transaction.

Psychological Issues

The families the planner meets in his elderplanning efforts will certainly be facing up to hard facts. Many of them will be going through a crisis. That means that sometimes the planner sees people at far from their best. Elderplanning puts us in touch with some very frightening realities: chronic illness, debilitation, loss of physical and mental capacity, loss of independence, confrontation with death, and the loneliness and anguish of survivors.

Many families encounter predictable problems in dealing with elder care financial planning. Often, the older generation are secretive about their assets and debts, and suspicious about their children's motivation for asking. The younger generation can ignore clear signs that a parent is floundering and needs help. Whenever possible, plans should be made while the parent still has capacity; once capacity is lost, a time-wasting, expensive, contentious guardianship proceeding is likely to be required.

One important role the financial planner can play is to be an objective third party who can bring up subjects that would be too touchy for a family member to raise. Financial planners can also give the younger generation some hints about how to start the discussion and use helpful language like "How can we make sure your wishes are honored?" rather than "Get out of the way, we're taking over."

Paul Malley, president of Aging With Dignity, identified four levels of elder care planning. At the simplest level, adding children to joint checking accounts is an inexpensive way to provide money management for seniors, but with the risk that the children will misuse the funds. Joint accounts also have Medicaid consequences (see Chapter 6). Direct deposit, automatic bill payment, and computer financial tracking programs like Quicken have greatly simplified basic daily money management. The next step is to create a Durable Power of Attorney, and then a revocable living trust. For large estates ($1 million or over) the family's tax professional may suggest implementing a family Limited Partnership or Limited Liability Company.[38]

To be an effective elderplanner, a planner needs to understand how this work will affect him psychologically. On the good side, he may be "adopted" as a surrogate child by a really nice family who is grateful for the help he can give them. The flip side? He may become caught in a swirling maelstrom of emotions in a family that is still angry and resentful about decades-old, half-forgotten events. He may be blamed for things that are not his fault and that he is not able to change: he cannot bring back a lonely widow's beloved husband, he cannot reverse a lifetime of bad financial choices by drafting a few documents, or he cannot cure an inoperable cancer or restore capacities eroded by Alzheimer's Disease.

The planner must be able to separate his professional skills from feelings about clients. He will also need to sort out feelings about his own family from feelings about his clients and their families. If this professional work inspires the planner to be a more thoughtful, sensitive, and effective son, daughter, or parent, then that is all to the good.

COMPUTERS AND ON-LINE ISSUES IN ELDERPLANNING

For the professional involved in elderplanning, desktop and laptop computers, and especially Internet access, have an important part to play in creating and communicating the care plan. In many instances, carrying a laptop computer is key to the sales process, especially for complex products such as long term care insurance and equity indexed annuities.

Using a laptop computer, the planning professional can provide current information about the entire category of products, as well as extremely detailed information about specific products that the client might purchase. Not only can the professional retrieve text, but he can retrieve or create graphics or use multi-media such as sounds, music, and video. Furthermore, complex calculations involving the client's own financial situation can be performed almost instantly. So instead of having an unwieldy pile of brochures, the client sees an easy-to-understand presentation that is perfectly tailored to his needs.

For the planning professional, the Internet is a wonderful source of current information on almost any topic. However, some of this easily accessible information should be taken with a grain of salt. It is just as easy to post outdated, incomplete, inaccurate, or even completely fraudulent information as it is to provide a real service.

"E-commerce" is still developing. It is easy to use the Internet to deliver information to clients who have computer access, or to obtain information and communicate it to the client verbally or in writing. Consumers can gather information on-line, then "sign on the dotted line" with an agent, or they can both find information and make credit card purchases on-line. However, it is not yet common to carry out an entire insurance sales transaction on-line, because on-line "signatures are still evolving."[39]

The Internet makes it just as easy to send information 10,000 miles away as it is to send it across the street. Insurance products, though, are still regulated by the states that decide who is licensed to sell what. The National Association of Insurance Commissioners (NAIC) is working on a simple, uniform license application for agents outside a particular state who want to sell within the state. The NAIC is also working on a Producer Information Network to centralize the process of applying for multiple licenses.[40]

An Internet Tour for the Planning Professional

Some important sites for the insurance professional, financial planner, attorney, broker, accountant, or other member of the elder planning team:

- AARP: www.aarp.org.

- Administration on Aging (federal): www.aoa.dhhs.gov.

- The Administration on Aging runs a decision-support site with information about eligibility and cost-benefit analysis for Medicare Part D and other programs for drug assistance: ssl3.benefitscheckup.org (no www).

- Alzheimer's Association: www.alz.org.

- American Bar Association Commission on Legal Problems of the Elderly: www.abanet.org/elderly/home.html.

- Center for Medicare Advocacy Inc., a not-for-profit organization that provides information and advocacy, including tips on maintaining Medicare home care: www.medicareadvocacy.org.

- Elder Law at Georgetown University Law School: www.ll.georgetown. edu/guides/health.cfm.

- Elder Web (site of CPA Karen Stevenson Brown): www.elderweb.com.

- Kansas Elder Law Network (KELN): www.keln.org.

- Medicare and Medicaid information: cms.hhs.gov and www.medicare.gov (See especially www.medicare.gov/NHCompare/home.asp for information about local nursing homes). In November, 2000, the HCFA (now known as CMS) announced new features for www.medicare.gov, including a directory of doctors participating in Medicare, a Spanish-language version of the Medicare Compare site, more information about nursing homes, and a guide to prescription drug assistance programs. The Medicare Compare database can also be accessed by calling (800) 633-4227.

- National Academy of Elder Law Attorneys: www.naela.com (includes a directory so other professionals and consumers can locate member attorneys in their geographic area).

- National Senior Citizens Law Center: www.nsclc.org.

- Senior Law (from the elder law firm of Goldfarb & Abrandt): www.seniorlaw.com.

- Social Security Administration: www.ssa.gov.

- United States Senate Special Committee on Aging: www.senate.gov/7Eaging.

This is by no means a complete listing of on-line elder law resources, and no implication is intended that sites that do not appear here are inferior. If a site is not included it just means that the author did not know about them. For a more extensive list, many of the sites listed above include a section of links to other elder law and related sites.

Seniors On-line

Senior citizens tend to fall into two categories when it comes to using computers and especially going on-line. There is a small group of enthusiasts, and then there is a much larger group of people who are afraid of the technology and feel incapable of learning how to use it. There do not seem to be too many older people in between, who feel that they can use computers and on-line tools, but are emotionally indifferent to them.

Becoming comfortable with computers is an important step for people who want to remain intellectually active and maintain family and friendship relationships (or create new ones), but who have budget or mobility limitations. Even a modest modem-equipped computer, and free or low-cost Internet access, will permit the older person to do health and financial research, shop and compare prices for almost any kind of goods, play games, "talk" to someone, or participate in a broad and free-ranging chat environment. Hobbyists can get in touch with people from all over the world who share an interest that might have made them feel isolated if nobody in their social circle shared it.

Older people who cannot afford or do not want to maintain their own computers can find access to computers in public places, such as libraries. The Department of Health and Human Services also has a project to place computers in senior centers so older people can access sites of interest to the elderly. See www.cms.hhs. gov/apps/media/press/release.asp?Counter=25 for information about this program and locations of the participating senior centers.

INCOME TAX ISSUES

Under our current system, where there are few tax brackets and the brackets are fairly close together, there is not much significance to the fact that many people drop into a lower tax bracket after retirement. For most purposes, senior citizens face the same income-tax planning issues as any other taxpayer. See the various substantive chapters for income tax issues of, for instance, Social Security benefits, annuities, and retirement planning.

Persons over 65 are entitled to have approximately $1,000 more income than non-senior citizens before the need to file an income tax return at all is triggered. A senior citizen is entitled to a larger standard deduction than a non-senior citizen; an additional enhancement to the standard deduction is available to those who are legally blind. (These additional standard deductions are reduced if the senior citizen can be claimed as someone else's dependent.)

For 2006, a married senior citizen or blind person can claim an additional standard deduction of $1,000. If the taxpayer is single, the additional standard deduction is $1,250 for either a senior citizen or a blind person. The ordinary standard deduction is $10,300 for married persons filing joint returns and surviving spouses, $7,550 for heads of households, $5,150 for single persons, and $5,150 for married persons filing separate returns.[41]

The Economic Growth and Tax Relief Reconciliation Act of 2001 (EGTRRA 2001)[42] provided tax relief that is aimed at both higher-income and lower-income taxpayers. EGTRRA 2001 added a new, 10% income-tax bracket and phased in higher income limits for the lower tax brackets, so that most taxpayers achieved at least some tax savings.

Also for 2006, the gift tax annual exclusion rises from $11,000 to $12,000. It is expected that taxes on a joint return with taxable income of $100,000 will be $215 lower in 2006 than in 2005. However, unless Congress takes action, the number of taxpayers subject to the Alternative Minimum Tax is expected to rise from 3.8 million in 2005 to 20 million in 2006.

For 2006, the tax brackets were 10% for joint income up to $15,100 and a single return of half that much; 15% on income up to $61,300/$30,650; 25% up to $123,700/$74,200; and 28% $188,450/$158,800. The 33% bracket is expected to apply to income (for either joint or single returns) up to $336,550.

Low-income persons over 65 (and persons who have retired because of a permanent and total disability) may also qualify for a tax credit. The maximum amount of the credit is $1,125. The maximum credit may be reduced by non-taxable pension and Social Security benefits, and is phased out at higher income levels. For a married couple filing jointly, where both spouses qualify for the credit, the phase-out level starts at an Adjusted Gross Income (AGI) of $10,000 and completely phases out at an AGI of $25,000.[43]

See IRS Publication 524 for details. (A credit reduces the actual amount of tax due, while a deduction reduces the amount of taxable income that is used to calculate tax liability.)

PRACTICE TIP: Note that the Credit for the Elderly can be claimed on either Form 1040 or 1040A, but not Form 1040EZ.

In some instances, the senior citizen is considered, for tax purposes, as a dependent of a caregiver child, or of several children who have combined to provide a "multiple support agreement" covering the senior citizen. Five tests are used to determine whether a deduction may be taken:

- Whether the elderly person lives in the taxpayer's home for the entire year, or is a relative of the taxpayer;

- The elderly person is either a U.S. citizen or a legal resident of the U.S. or a country contiguous to the U.S.;

- The senior citizen's gross income does not exceed $3,300 (in 2006 – this amount is indexed for inflation); non-taxable Social Security benefits are not counted in gross income;

- The senior citizen does not file a joint return; and

- The taxpayer provides at least half of the senior citizen's support (or at least half of the senior citizen's support is provided under a multiple support agreement).

Also, for 2006, a person who is claimed as a dependent on someone else's return may not take a standard deduction over $850 (or $300 plus the individual's earned income, if that sum is larger than $850), even if she would otherwise be eligible for an additional standard deduction.

If there is a multiple support agreement, it should be drafted to specify which contributor will take advantage of deductions arising out of the senior citizen's dependent status. The taxpayer claiming the deductions must personally provide at least 10% of the senior citizen's support.

An unmarried caregiver whose dependent parent lives in his household can pay taxes at head-of-household rates, which are lower than rates for single persons. Head-of-household status may also be claimed by an unmarried person who pays more than one-half the cost of maintaining a separate household in which the parent lives. The child is deemed to maintain the household even during the parent's health-related absences (e.g., while hospitalized).

A caregiver child can claim a medical-expense deduction for expenses actually paid on behalf of a dependent parent. Even if the child is not able to take a dependency deduction (because the parent's income is too high, or because the parent files a joint return), the child can claim a medical expense deduction for amounts paid toward the parent's medical expenses. If there is a multiple support agreement, only the child who is entitled to claim the dependency deduction is allowed to deduct the parents' medical expenses. Other contributors to the multiple support agreement cannot, even if they actually paid the expenses.

Of course, the parents' medical expenses can be deducted only if they were not reimbursed by insurance or otherwise, if they are legitimate medical expense deductions, and only to the extent that, in conjunction with all other medical expense deductions, they exceed 7.5% of the taxpayer's adjusted gross income.

Not all health-related expenses are deductible. Unreimbursed costs of prescription drugs and insulin are deductible, but costs of over-the-counter drugs are not. If an individual enters a nursing home primarily in order to receive medical care, all of the costs (including those that substitute for ordinary living expenses) are deductible. But if the primary motive is the convenience of the resident and the resident's family, then only the portion of the bill that is allocated to medical and nursing care is deductible; the portion allocable to room and board is not.

In a 2004 Tax Court case, the taxpayers paid monthly service fees to live in an independent living unit within a retirement community. Their agreement with the facility provided some health-related services, such as having a nurse on duty at all times to handle emergencies, and access to the pool, spa, and exercise equipment. The Tax Court ruled that part of the monthly fee qualified for deduction under IRC Sec. 213. Either the traditional percentage method or the actuarial method favored by the IRS could be used to determine the deductible part. However, the exercise and pool component of the fee could not be deducted, because the taxpayer failed to establish what portion of the usage was medical rather than recreational—and failed to show that the money would not have been spent if the taxpayer had been in good health.[44]

One of the exceptions to the 10% penalty for premature withdrawal from a retirement plan is to pay medical expenses. An IRS information letter says that the definition of medical expenses for this purpose is the same as for Schedule A of Form 1040: unreimbursed expenses, deductible under IRC Sec. 213, in excess of 7.5% of Adjusted Gross Income. Relief from the 10% penalty applies even if the participant does not itemize deductions.[45]

For 2004 and the first eight months of 2005, the standard mileage rate for using an automobile to get to the place of medical treatment was 15 cents a mile. For the last four months of 2005, the IRS, in response to higher gas prices, raised the rate to 22 cents a mile. In 2006, this rate is 18 cents a mile.[46]

Under appropriate circumstances, long term care insurance premiums may give rise to a tax deduction (see Chapter 4). Long term care insurance benefits can be received tax-free, within statutory limits. The same limits apply to accelerated death benefits or viatical settlements that are received by a chronically (but not terminally) ill person who applies the benefits to the costs of health care. Tax advantages are not available to a healthy elderly person who chooses to enter into a viatical settlement for purely financial reasons.

CHAPTER ENDNOTES

1. Rebecca Moore, "Wealth Is No Buffer to Health Care Cost Concerns," www.plansponsor.com/pi_type10_print.jsp?RECORD_ID=32182 (January 23, 2006).

2   Riva D. Atlas, "Helping Retired Baby Boomers Manage Income and Expenses," *New York Times,* June 10, 2004, p. C7.

3. Benedict Carey, "Study Details Risk of Death for Those Caring for Elderly Spouses," *New York Times,* February 16, 2006, p. A27; Suzanne Sataline, "Caring for Ill Spouse Can Take Toll on Your Health," *Wall Street Journal,* February 16, 2006, p. D6.

4. MetLife Mature Market Institute, "Gender Differences: Do Men and Women View Long-Term Care Differently?" (November 2004).

5. Testimony by CBO director Douglas Holtz-Eakin, "The Cost and Financing of Long-Term Care Services," (House Subcommittee on Health April 27, 2005, www.cbo.gov/ftpdocs/63xx/docs6316/04-27-LongTermCare_testimony.pdf.

6. MetLife Mature Market Institute Demographic Profile, www.metlife.com/WPSAssets/78466792201110468360V1F65+Profile-10-10-04.pdf

7. Alicia H. Munnell and Steven A. Sass, *401(k) Plans and Women: A "Good News/Bad News" Story*, Just the Facts on Retirement Issues (Center for Retirement Research) January 2005; www.bc.edu/centers/crr/facts/jtf_13.pdf.

8. These figures come from the Statistical Abstract of the United States, 125th Edition (2006), Table 98.

9. In 2004, only about 19% of males over 65 were still in the work force; only about 11% of female senior citizens were still in the work force. Statistical Abstract of the United States, 125th Edition (2006), Table 577.

10. Debra Whitman and Patrick Purcell, "Topics in Aging: Income and Poverty Among Older Americans in 2004," benefitslink.com/articles/RL32697.pdf.

11. Hubert B. Herring, "Boomers Hit 60, Supporting Both Young and Old," *New York Times*, January 8, 2006, Business p. 2.

12. Kelly Greene, "Coaxing Seniors Out From Behind the Wheel," *Wall Street Journal* January 12, 2005 p. D2; "Keeping Elderly On the Road, But Not Behind the Wheel," *New York, Times* January 20, 2006, p. A15; Jennifer Saranow, "Bill Orders Safer Roads for Seniors," *Wall Street Journal*, September 1, 2005, p. D8.

13. These figures come from "Statistics about Alzheimer's Disease," www.alz.org/AboutAD/statistics.asp.

14. "Insurer Issues Alzheimer's Guide," NU Online News Service Breaking News, October 4, 2005.

15. "Who Cares?: Families Caring for Persons with Alzheimer's Disease" (1999), published by the Alzheimer's Association and the National Alliance for Caregiving.

16. Laura Landro, "Offering Help to Depressed Seniors," *Wall Street Journal*, October 5, 2005, p. D13.

17. Agency for Healthcare Research and Quality (AHRQ) Research Alert, "Long-Term Care Users Range in Age and Most Do Not Live in Nursing Homes," www.ahrq.gov/news/press/pr2000/ltcpr.htm (11/8/00); William D. Spector, John A. Fleishman, Liliana E. Pezzin, Brenda C. Spellman, "The Characteristics of Long-Term Care Users," from AHRQ Publications Clearinghouse.

18. Testimony of Kathryn G. Allen, "Long-Term Care Financing: Growing Demand and Cost of Services Are Straining Federal and State Budgets," April 27, 2005, GAO-05-564T, www.gao.gov/cgi-bin/getrpt?GAO-05-564T.

19. Kaiser Family Foundation Issue Paper, "The Distribution of Assets in the Elderly Population Living in the Community," www.kff.org/medicaid/loader.cfm?url=commonspot/security/getfile-cfm&PageID=53591.

20. "Study Assesses LTC Risk," NU Online News Service March 2, 2006; Jonathan Clements, "Long-Term Planning: How to Protect Against the High Cost of Nursing Homes," *Wall Street Journal*, February 22, 2006, p. D1.

21. Milt Freudenheim, "Prices of Drugs for Elderly Said to Far Outrun Inflation," *New York Times*, August 16, 2005, p. C3.

22. Tamar Lewin, "Financially Set, Grandparents Help Keep Families Afloat, Too," *New York Times*, July 14, 2005, p. A1.

23. Angelas Maas, "Online Education Program Helps Employed Caregivers," Employee Benefit News, February 2005, www.benefitnews.com/pfv.cfm?id=7057.

24. Hilary Stout, "Hard Holidays: Facing Aging Parents' Decline," *Wall Street Journal*, December 2, 2004, p. D9.The Association of Professional Geriatric Care Managers (PGCM) can be reached at www.caremanager.org or (520) 881-8008; the National Association of Elder Law Attorneys at www.naela.org or (520) 881-4005; and The American Association of Daily Money Managers at www.aadmm.com.

25. See thomas.loc.gov/cgi-bin/bdquery/z?d109:h.con.res.00008.

26. Howard Bedlin, "OAA Programs Receive $170 Million Increase in Funding", located at www.ncoa. org/news/oaa_2001.html; "AoA to Release Funds to Support Family Caregivers," located at www. aoa.gov/pr/PR2000/nfcsp011101.html.

27. *Wendland v. Wendland*, 28 P.3d 151 (Cal. 2001).

28. See, e.g., Robin Toner and Carl Hulse, "A Family's Battle Brings Life's End Into Discussion," *New York Times* March 20, 2005 p. A1; Carl Hulse, "The Medical Turns Political," *New York Times*, March 19, 2005, p. A20.

29. John Schwartz, "Experts Say Ending Feeding Can Lead to a Gentle Death," *New York Times*, March 20, 2005, p. A29.

30. Gautam Naik, "Unlikely Way to Cut Hospital Costs: Comfort the Dying," *Wall Street Journal*, March 10, 2004, p. A1.

31. www.betterending.org/downloads/guideforabetterending.pdf.

32. Andrew H. Hook describes the process in "How to Become a Certified Elder Law Attorney," XII *The ElderLaw Report* No. 3 (October, 2000), p. 1.

33. Colleen DeBaise, "Financial Planners Target Boomers," *Wall Street Journal*, August 16, 2005, p. D2.

34. Julie Bennett, "Jobs Are Aplenty for Those Who Can Help People Manage Their Money," *Wall Street Journal*, September 20, 2005, p. B9 (special advertising s section).

35. Lingling Wei, "Brokerage Firms Encourage CFP Title for Financial Advisers," *Wall Street Journal*, February 28, 2006, p. B6; Jeff D. Opdyke, "Wait, Let Me Call My ChFC," *Wall Street Journal*, January 28-29, 2006, p. B1.

36. For seminars as a marketing tool in the elder planning market, see Linda Koco, "LTC Specialists Offer LTC Sales Tips," *National Underwriter*, Life and Health/Financial Services Edition, December 7, 1998, p. 23.

37. Jane Gross, "When Experts Need Experts," *New York Times*, November 10, 2005, p. F1.

38. Hilary Stout and Andrea Petersen, "The Parent Trap," *Wall Street Journal*, August 15, 2005, p. R1.

39. The *National Underwriter*, Life and Health/Financial Services Edition, issue of January 25, 1999 includes several articles about the Internet in insurance marketing, including Hal Stucker, "Term Life Sales on the Internet are Seeing Rapid Growth" (p. 7); Steven Aldridge, "Web Challenges Service Cos" (also p. 7); Trevor Thomas, "Study: Women Buying More Insurance Online," p. 8; Darrell Ticehurst and Kevin Keegan, "Planning, Branding Are Keys to Online Sales" p. 10, and Dennis M. Groner, "Agents, How Compliant Is Your Web Site?" p. 18. Also see Sam Friedman, "Web-Savvy Agents Get Competitive Edge," *National Underwriter*, Life and Health/Financial Services Edition, November 9, 1998, p. 28. However, poor design and operation of insurance sites may create customer dissatisfaction; see Alex Maurice, "Insurance Frustrates Online Shoppers," *National Underwriter*, Life and Health/Financial Services Edition, December 7, 1998, p. 40.

40. Joel V. Volker, "Selling on the Internet May Not Be as Different as It Seems," *Best's Review*, Life/Health edition, October 1998, p. 97.

41. Rev. Proc. 2005-70, 2005-47 IRB 979.

42. P.L. 107-16.

43. IRC Sec. 22.

44. *Baker v. Comm.*, 122 TC 143 (2004).

45. IRS Information Letter 2005-0009 (Released March 31, 2005), www.irs.ustreas.gov/pub/irs-wd/05-0009.pdf.

46. Rev. Proc. 2005-78, 2005-51 IRB 1177.

Chapter 2

Life Insurance in the Elder Care Plan

INTRODUCTION

Odds are, if you're reading this, you are aware of the central role that life insurance plays in financial planning. In the early stages of an individual's, couple's, or family's planning cycle, life insurance creates an "instant estate" at a time when there may be few other resources available for the family if a breadwinner dies. It is typical for older clients to have completed the accumulation phase of their financial plan and to look for tax-wise ways to transmit assets to a surviving spouse or to other heirs. Once again, life insurance plays a valuable role. Congress considers life insurance a worthwhile purchase, so it qualifies for favorable tax treatment.

However, in the post-EGTRRA 2001 environment, where fewer estates will face federal taxation, it is possible that some clients will scale down their life insurance purchases because they believe their estates will not be large enough to be taxed under the law prevailing at the time they predict that their deaths may occur.

In a small-to-medium size estate, where the surviving spouse is incapable of personally managing large sums of money, a life insurance policy paid out under a settlement option is an efficient, low-cost, low-maintenance way to provide additional income without subjecting the survivor to unwanted investment management tasks. In a large estate, life insurance, particularly second-to-die insurance, is often used to provide funds to pay estate taxes, thus preserving the entire estate for transmission to the heirs. In any size estate, life insurance furnishes liquidity: cash that can be used for daily expenses pending the settlement of the estate. It is sensible to add other liquidity features to the plan: each spouse should have a separate account containing enough funds to pay living expenses for several months because joint accounts are typically frozen when one joint owner dies.

No matter how valuable life insurance is to the elder care plan, it must be viewed in context. Sometimes life insurance represents too large a percentage of the overall insurance program, or the plan as a whole. In some circumstances, a healthy senior citizen with an ample, diversified portfolio, and a spouse with significant personal assets such as investments or pension rights may have too much life insurance. In this instance, it may make sense to reduce the life insurance coverage (or to borrow against its cash value) and use the premium dollars that are freed up to purchase long-term care insurance. As illustrated throughout this book, the high cost of long-term care is a major peril to the financial security of older individuals. Once the survivor's needs are taken care of, it often makes sense to add long-term care insurance to the insurance portfolio or even increase the long-term care coverage, if possible.

Older insured individuals run a greater risk than others of losing insurance coverage simply because they are more likely to forget to pay the premiums. Several states have passed laws requiring additional protection against an involuntary lapse (such as an additional grace period for senior citizens), and allowing the insured to designate someone else (typically, a son, daughter, or family friend) to receive notice of a potential lapse and make sure that the payment is made. This valuable feature, which is offered voluntarily by some insurers, could be the deciding factor in choosing a policy. It is probably a good idea to maintain a "tickler" in the client files of older clients to make sure payments are made on time.

LIMRA figures from 2004 show that over a 20-year period, the proportion of Americans owning individual life insurance fell from 63% to 53%. Sales of individual policies in the second quarter of 2004 were 2% lower than those of a year before. However, in 2004 the total annualized premium (amounts paid by insured persons) and face amount of coverage purchased rose 10% and 9% respectively over 2003 levels. Universal life was the most popular type of coverage, earning 36% of aggregate premiums for the first half of 2004. Sales of variable and variable-universal life insurance were up 3% for the year and 15% for the second quarter of 2004. Term insurance premiums paid were 7% higher in 2004 than 2003, but whole life premiums fell 6%.[1]

The National Underwriter Company's Linda Koco reported in 2004 that life insurance sales in general were flat but there were areas of strength. Many companies improved their universal life products by extending maturity provisions and adding guarantees against lapse, creating opportunities for clients to upgrade their policies. In response to customer dissatisfaction in the 2001-2003 bear market, many insurers developed universal life benefits with death benefits guaranteed to age 100—an important feature as life expectancies increase. Some companies did well with equity index universal life products—universal life insurance with a minimum interest guarantee and excess interest crediting linked to an index such as the S&P 500.[2]

There are obvious opportunities for new sales and new markets. According to LIMRA, 22% of U.S. households (24 million households) do not have any life insurance. More than a quarter (29%) of survey respondents said they would like to discuss life insurance with a financial professional, and 70% agree that reviewing existing life insurance coverage periodically is a good idea. Less than one quarter of the households surveyed had a life insurance agent/broker or a personal financial advisor or planner, showing that there is a strong market for helpful advice.[3]

Financial planners often incur cost-based objections from older clients, who say that they do not need life insurance because their children are grown up and their mortgages are paid off. In that situation, The National Underwriter Company's Mark Levy suggests low-cost universal life products, which can be much less costly than whole life insurance. However, permanent life insurance is useful in many elder financial plans: to provide a legacy that will not be subject to probate costs and perhaps estate taxation; to provide long-term care for the surviving spouse after the first spouse's death; or to help adult children with their financial problems (e.g., caused by divorce, poor health, or unemployment). Life insurance can also be used to bolster the survivor's financial position if one spouse's pension is not paid as expected, or if the couple chose to take a single-life pension that dies with the first spouse. Some financial plans call for placing highly appreciated assets in Charitable Remainder Trusts, to generate income during life (see Chapter 13). Life insurance can be used to replace assets that the younger generation might expect to inherit.[4]

Increases in longevity required the insurance industry to revise its mortality tables in 2004—the first revision since 1980, and only the fourth since 1958. The new tables go up to age 120, while previously they went up to only age 100. In 2000, there were about 50,000 centenarians in the United States—and tax law provides that a person has taxable income when he or she is cashed out at age 100 on the grounds of having no remaining life expectancy, so the new tables will help this group. The new table says that the "mortality rate" (i.e., the probability that a person will die within that year) is 1.0% for men and 0.8% for women at age 60; 2.6% and 1.8% for men and women respectively at 70; 7.0% and 4.4% at 80; 18.8% and 12.2% at 90; and 36.3% and 27.6% at age 100, when the earlier tables ran out.[5]

NOTE: See www.naic.org for NAIC rule-making on topics such as viatical settlements, product suitability, and accelerated death benefits.

TYPES OF LIFE INSURANCE PRODUCTS

The balance of this chapter discusses life insurance issues specific to the elder insured, beginning with a summary of general life insurance principles.

A life insurance policy can be pure insurance with a limited duration, such as term insurance, or permanent insurance that accrues cash value, such as whole life insurance. Some products are limited to providing insurance coverage; others, such as universal life, variable life, and variable universal life, combine insurance and investment aspects. The various types of life insurance are discussed in greater detail later in this chapter.

If the policy is "participating" rather than "non-participating," the insurer issues policy dividends out of its surplus earnings, and these dividends reduce the effective net cost of life insurance. However, a number of "mutual" companies that pay dividends have "de-mutualized" and reorganized as "stock" companies that do not pay dividends to policyholders.

The actual ownership of the policy is also significant. A group policy, typically purchased by an employer or organization, has only one master policy which belongs to the purchaser. The individuals covered under the policy are known as "certificate holders," and receive certificates evidencing their coverage rights. An individual policy is purchased by an individual (often, but not always, the insured), who can choose the policy terms, options, and riders. To purchase a policy on the life of someone else, the purchaser must have an "insurable interest" in that person's life, for example, a family or business relationship.

A policy can be purchased by one individual and then ownership can be transferred to another individual, or to a trust or some other entity. This might be done to keep the policy proceeds out of the estate of the original owner/insured, as part of a charitable giving program, or for other practical or tax reasons.

On March 6, 2001, the NAIC released its draft of the Life Insurance and Annuities Suitability Model Regulation. The Model Regulation seeks to ensure that life insurance producers will ask the right questions and get relevant information so that they can recommend life insurance products that are suitable for the client's ability to pay, family situation, risk tolerance, and tax and estate planning needs.

Term Insurance

Term insurance is pure insurance, with no investment element. It extends either for a term of years or until the insured reaches a particular age (typically, age 65). The death benefit under a term policy can be level, increasing, or decreasing, depending on the purchaser's needs and financial condition. For instance, decreasing term is often used to secure the payment of a mortgage or other financial obligation. As continuing payments are made, the balance declines, and so does the need for coverage. Increasing term insurance goes up either by a specified amount or based on an economic index. It might be selected by someone who feels that inflation will increase the financial needs of beneficiaries.

Term insurance is not always suitable in an elder care plan, because any term insurance obtainable on a senior citizen is likely to be quite costly. Middle-aged and healthy "young-old" clients might prefer convertible term insurance, which can be converted to whole life insurance at the point where term insurance becomes hard to get or prohibitively expensive.

A renewable term policy permits the insured to renew the policy at the end of the term. The renewal is usually made on the same or less favorable terms, rather than for a longer term and/or greater amount of coverage. However, proof of continued insurability is not required before renewing.

A re-entry term policy lets the insured submit proof of insurability in exchange for a lower premium rate. Typically, term policies either set an age (such as 65) after which further renewals will not be permitted, or limit renewals to a certain number (e.g., only three renewals). At renewal, the premium can be adjusted based on the insured's attained age at the renewal date, but not based on medical condition. Term premiums are usually level throughout the term, so the renewal premium is often significantly higher than the premium for the previous term.

A conversion privilege allows a switch from term to permanent coverage without proof of insurability. The permanent life insurance premium is usually set based on the insured's age at the time of conversion. A few policies permit "original age conversion" where the premium for the post-conversion whole life policy is calculated based on the insured's age when the original term policy was purchased. Common provisions limit conversion either in time (e.g., not after 55, not after 65, or not after the first five years of a ten-year term) or amount (e.g., only 50% of the face amount of the original term policy).

If the policy does not include renewal or conversion provisions, it will simply expire at the end of its term and there will be no further insurance coverage. The renewal and conversion privileges offer flexibility and greater access to insurance, so they add to the cost of the policy.

For Medicaid purposes, insurance cash value in excess of $1,500 is considered an available asset. A term policy, of course, has no cash value and thus is not included in the calculation. As a general rule, the purchase of term insurance is not a transfer, because there is no gratuitous element: it is an ordinary arm's length commercial transaction. However, at least one state has taken the position that the purchase of term insurance during the "look-back" period can be a transfer if the death benefit adds up to less than twice the sum of the premiums. See Chapter 6.

The purchase of a pre-need funeral policy is not considered a transfer, but if the policy provides benefits greater than the actual cost of the funeral, the state Medicaid agency is entitled to recover the excess.

Whole Life Insurance

Term insurance provides nothing but insurance coverage for a limited time. In contrast, whole life insurance combines pure insurance with a savings element. This type of policy generates cash value, which can be borrowed against, although any loan amounts outstanding at the insured's death will reduce the death benefit paid to the beneficiary.

As described below, in some circumstances whole life benefits can be used during the insured's lifetime, especially to pay expenses of a terminal illness. Since 1996, such benefits are treated more or less like long-term care insurance for tax purposes.

The basic whole life policy's premium is level, based on the age of the insured person at the time of purchase. The premium on a whole life insurance policy is due each year for the remainder of the insured person's life. This mode of payment is known as "straight life" or "continuous premium." However, whole life insurance is also available as a "single premium" coverage or via payments over a shorter duration (e.g., "20 pay" or "30 pay" or payments until a certain age) that result in a paid-up policy.

Investment-Oriented Insurance

Some clients want to combine life insurance with an investment product that offers potential for gain. Naturally, along with the potential for gain comes the risk of loss of value. Given low interest rates paid on bonds and other yield-oriented investments, these products are probably not suitable for clients who have enough money to separate their insurance needs from their investment portfolios. However, a client who does not have much money to invest, or who is financially impulsive and might benefit from a forced saving element, might find these products useful. So might a cautious client fleeing stock market chaos.

A "universal life" policy is more flexible than a conventional whole life policy in that the cash value, the premium, and the face amount can be altered at the insured's option. The insurer sets limits, but within these limits the insured decides how much premium will be paid. The larger the premium, the higher the cash value, given a steady death benefit. It should be noted that the Internal Revenue Code (IRC) limits the ratio between the cash value and face value of the universal life policy in order to preserve its nature as an insurance contract rather than a pure investment.

As each universal life premium is paid, the insurer deducts charges for administrative expenses and predicted mortality costs. Because mortality risks are higher for older insureds, the deductions will also be greater. The rest of the premium is credited to the cash value of the policy. Interest is accrued at a market rate; the insurer guarantees a minimum interest rate (e.g., 4 percent). Universal life insurance works best when interest rates are high and thus cash value grows quickly.

If the insured wishes to increase the face amount, the insurer will probably demand proof of continued insurability. To decrease the face amount, it may be necessary to withdraw part of the cash value to stay within IRC criteria for insurance contracts. Universal life is not a suitable product for older clients who are unable or unwilling to monitor the policy and decide when changes should be made in the policy parameters.

Variable life insurance is the insurance counterpart of the variable annuity (see Chapter 12). It can be purchased either with a single premium or with a continuing premium stream. The insurer provides life insurance whose face amount and cash value are both dependent on the investment results of one or more mutual-fund-like funds offered by the insurer and reflecting differing investment philosophies. The policy determines when and how often the insured will be able to move funds between the accounts.

The original face value of the policy, or other amount defined by the policy, operates as a floor beneath which the face amount will not fall. Therefore, the insured always has at least a defined minimum of life insurance protection, but the policy's cash value is not guaranteed and can fluctuate or even disappear. Variable life insurance is considered a security, so only individuals with a securities license can sell it.[6]

Combination policies known as variable universal life or flexible premium variable life are also available, permitting the insured to control the investment of the premium funds, as well as the amount of the premium and the face amount of the policy. Once again, these products are only suitable for older individuals who have the capacity and desire to monitor market conditions on a regular basis and make decisions about the policies.[7]

In June 2004, the *Wall Street Journal*'s Kathy Chu noted a trend toward offering variable universal life with anti-lapse guarantees providing protection against economic downturns. In a strong market, the market gains applied toward the VULI premium meant that the policy could pay for itself. Recently, however, stock market drops required insured persons to make large contributions to maintain the policy. A no-lapse feature promises that as long as the policyholder continues to make at least minimum premium payments, the policy will remain in effect and will pay a death benefit to the insured person's designated beneficiaries.

Overall, LIMRA figures show that new premiums on VULI policies were 33% lower in 2003 than in 2002, and new premiums for other variable life products fell 40%. However, companies that added anti-lapse features showed strong premium growth in VULI.[8]

Second-to-Die Insurance

If a married couple's assets are greater than the amount that can be sheltered from estate tax by the unified credit (see Chapter 13), then clearly there is some risk of federal estate taxation. What usually happens is that the marital deduction, perhaps in conjunction with a qualified terminable interest property (QTIP) trust and/or credit shelter trust, reduces the first estate below the taxable level. However, the estate of the surviving spouse is then large enough to encounter an estate tax bill. Funds provided by second-to-die life insurance become especially important if the estate is illiquid (e.g., contains a high proportion of stock in a closely-held corporation), because there will be few other available sources of ready cash and assets must otherwise be sold on unfavorable terms to pay the taxes.

Second-to-die life insurance, also called survivorship insurance, covers a couple, but does not pay benefits until both of the spouses have died. At this point, if the second estate is taxable, the second-to-die policy will provide cash that can be used to pay the estate taxes without depleting the property intended for children and other beneficiaries. In effect, the premiums are used to add a new asset to the estate, earmarked for tax payments. Some plans are written with a "double death benefit" to cope with the unusual case of spouses both of whom die during the first four years a policy is in force, requiring two expensive and cumbersome estate administrations.[9]

It is often worthwhile to place the second-to-die policy in an irrevocable life insurance trust (ILIT, discussed below), so that the proceeds will be kept out of the estate of the second spouse to die. However, this trust must be separate from the ordinary ILIT which benefits the surviving spouse, for the simple reason that there will be no second-to-die benefits until both spouses have died. It makes sense to draft the second-to-die ILIT so that it is allowed to (but not forced to) purchase assets from the estate, or lend money to the estate, thus creating flexibility to assist the estate without making the policy proceeds part of the taxable estate.

Employment-Related Life Insurance

For some older individuals who are still employed, life insurance is offered by their employer. The most common form of employer-related life insurance is group term life insurance. Basically, the premium for the coverage is paid by the employer and the death benefits are paid, in the event of the employee's death, to a beneficiary named by the employee.

The cost of up to $50,000 of group term life insurance coverage is not taxed to the employee. However, the cost of coverage in excess of $50,000 is taxable. The cost of the excess coverage is measured using a set of rates generally referred to as the "Table I" rates. Table I rates are found in regulations issued by the Treasury Department that accompany Section 79 of the Internal Revenue Code.[10]

In 1999, the Bureau of Labor Statistics' figures showed that 56% of workers had employment-related group life insurance, a percentage that declined to 48% in 2004. Furthermore, many employers stopped paying for group insurance and made it an employee-pay-all optional benefit. In 2004, 43% of policies sold were term and 37% were whole life policies. See www.life-line.org for the Life and Health Insurance Foundation for Education's life insurance calculator.[11]

Revenue Procedure 2005-25[12] provides guidance for calculating the fair market value of life insurance products (life insurance contracts, retirement income contracts, and endowment contracts) held in retirement plans. Springing cash value life insurance products will no longer be permitted in retirement plans. The date for determining the fair market value of a policy is its date of sale or distribution. Safe harbors are provided for variable and non-variable contracts.[13]

Retiree Health Benefits

A qualified retirement plan is authorized, under Internal Revenue Code section 401(h), to provide benefits for the sickness, hospitalization, or medical costs of retirees and their spouses, as long as the retiree health benefits are "subordinate" to the plan's retirement benefits. The requirement is that the aggregate cost of both incidental life insurance and retiree health benefits must not exceed 25 percent of the employer's total actual contributions to the retirement plan. Unlike most tax calculations, this is not performed on an annual basis; the test is the total amount involved over the entire period for which the plan provided retiree health benefits.

Split Dollar Arrangements

In a split-dollar arrangement, a business, employer, or charity pays part of the insurance premium; the insured person, or perhaps a life insurance trust created by that person, pays the rest of the premium. When the insured person dies, the employer or other payor receives part of the death benefit in reimbursement for the premiums advanced and the rest goes to the trust or the beneficiary designated by the insured person. The IRS' definition of split-dollar is joint purchase of life insurance on an employee's life, under a contract allocating the division of policy benefits.

In a conventional split-dollar plan, the employer pays the premiums and receives the cash value of the policy when the employee dies. In an equity plan, the employer is merely entitled to reimbursement for premiums paid.

The IRS began regulating split-dollar plans in the 1950s. Starting in 2001, the IRS has made it increasingly difficult to gain any tax advantage from split-dollar plans, whether in the employment or the charitable context. The IRS began to tax these arrangements either under IRC Sections 61 and 83 (certain forms of employee compensation) or under IRC Section 7872 (below market-rate loans).

In 2001, a new premium rate table was issued for valuing the current life insurance protection under a split-dollar plan. In 2002, the IRS required split-dollar arrangements to be characterized as either transfers of property or as below-market loans. If the endorsement method is used (the employer owns the policy), the transfer rules apply. Under the collateral assignment method (the employee owns the policy), the arrangement is taxed as a below-market loan. Finally, in 2003, the IRS issued final regulations making it impossible to use split-dollar as a tax-free compensation method. A further complicating factor is that if the employer company is publicly traded, split-dollar arrangements with key executives may be considered loans that violate the SEC's rules under the Sarbanes-Oxley Act (the statute that attempts to reform corporate governance).[14]

BASIC TAX RULES FOR LIFE INSURANCE

Internal Revenue Code section 101 has favorable rules for life insurance. Life insurance death benefits are not taxable income for any beneficiary whether or not the beneficiary paid any of the policy premiums. Thus, the entire amount of the proceeds can be used to support the beneficiary and the beneficiary's family.

There are several exceptions to this basic rule. The "transfer for value" rule under Code section 101(a)(2) provides that the proceeds of a policy that is sold or otherwise transferred for value (i.e., is not the subject of a gift) escapes income taxation only to the extent of the consideration paid by the individual purchasing the policy, plus premiums paid by this individual after the transfer. All other proceeds are taxed to the purchasing individual. This rule is not applied if the policy is transferred to the insured, a partner of the insured, a partnership in which the insured is a partner, or to a corporation in which the insured is an officer or stockholder.[15]

Life insurance death benefit proceeds paid under settlement options are also not completely free of income taxation. The portion of the proceeds representing the death benefit is received tax-free, but the portion that represents appreciation during the time the funds are under the insurance company's administration is taxable. Generally, unless the amount paid out is defined so that it cannot exceed the amount payable at the death of the insured, each payment to the beneficiary must be prorated into a tax-exempt and a taxable portion.

The Medicaid implications of settlement options must also be considered. In a "medically needy" state, the income paid out under the option will affect the amount that must be spent down, but will not preclude Medicaid eligibility; but in a "cap" state, the consequences of additional income are more serious. See Chapter 6.

Internal Revenue Code section 1035 allows the tax-free exchange of a life insurance contract for another life insurance contract, an endowment contract, or an annuity contract. One endowment contract can be exchanged for another endowment contract that begins payments no later than the first one or for an annuity contract. Annuity contracts, however, can only be exchanged tax-free for other annuity contracts, not life insurance policies or endowment contracts. See Chapter 12 for more information about annuities.

The tax rules discussed in this section apply to amounts paid under a "life insurance contract." Clearly, a conventional whole life policy will qualify, but certain investment-oriented policies (as discussed earlier in this chapter) may fail to satisfy the requirements of Internal Revenue Code section 7702. This section sets forth the requirements that a policy must meet in order to be considered a life insurance policy for tax purposes. Variable life policies based on a segregated asset account must meet further requirements, including a diversification requirement. A portion of the death benefits of a policy that fails to meet the Section 7702 requirements will be taxable income.

ILITs: IRREVOCABLE LIFE INSURANCE TRUSTS

The general rule is that life insurance is not included in the estate of the person on whose life the benefits are payable, provided that the insurance is not payable to the estate of the deceased insured. However, insurance will not be included in the estate, no matter who it is payable to, if the insured never had incidents of ownership in the policy (e.g., the right to designate the beneficiary) or if the insured once had incidents of ownership but transferred the policy more than three years before death.

Spouses have an insurable interest in one another, so the immediate problem can be solved by having each spouse purchase insurance on the life of the other (so that neither ever has incidents of ownership in the policy on his or her own life). But this can create a second estate problem, if the surviving spouse does not spend the proceeds of the policy on the life of the first spouse to die, thus enhancing the survivor's taxable estate. If the older client's children are financially responsible, it might make sense to transfer ownership of the policies to the children, again to prevent estate inclusion. However, once they own the policies the children gain access to incidents of ownership. For instance, the children can take loans against the policy cash value and use the funds for their own purposes rather than for the benefit of the insured parent.

A clear alternative is to have an irrevocable trust purchase the policy, or accept transfer of a policy, in the hope that the three-year rule can be avoided. If the trust were revocable, the grantor's power to modify or revoke the trust would operate as an incident of ownership, throwing the proceeds right back into the estate. The downside of irrevocability is that the grantor may later have second thoughts about having placed a valuable policy into trust. For instance, if the spouses divorce and the grantor is no longer pressingly interested in the financial well-being of the ex-spouse.

But when an irrevocable trust is used, the insurance stays out of the estate, and the surviving spouse receives income from the trust, and may be able to invade the principal of the trust, if necessary.

If the surviving spouse is given the power to invade the trust principal, it probably makes sense to limit this power to "five or five," that is, no more than five percent of the principal or $5,000 a year, whichever is greater. "Five or five" powers are frequently used because they avoid unfavorable tax consequences.

Usually, ILITs are drafted so that the trustee is both the owner of the policies on the life of the insured and the beneficiary of these policies. The trust documents should provide that the trust cannot give the proceeds to the insured's estate (because this would result in estate inclusion), but it should be permissible for the trustee of the ILIT to lend money to the estate or buy assets from the estate (if it needs immediate cash).

PRACTICE TIP: A client who insists on setting up a life insurance trust for a person whose insurable interest is doubtful could transfer an existing policy to the trust (which, however, would constitute a taxable gift). If the client dies within three years of the transfer, the funds will be returned to his estate as a gift in contemplation of death.

Many ILITs are unfunded; they are drafted but do not contain any assets (a life insurance policy will be deposited later) or contain only a life insurance policy. If a paid-up policy is deposited, there is no need to make further premium payments. Otherwise, there needs to be some arrangement for the payment or a funded trust (containing income-producing assets that throw off enough income to pay the premiums) will need to be used instead. It is permissible for the insured person to lend money to the trust for payment of the premiums. This is not considered an incident of ownership.[16]

If practical, it is usually better for the trust to purchase the insurance policy. But it is not always practical. The insured is probably elderly and may be in poor health, making the policy unaffordable. The insured may also have life insurance policies that are not really needed for the immediate financial support of the surviving spouse and could better be transferred to the ILIT.

In the Medicaid context, cash value life insurance is an asset, but term policies are not. So transferring term insurance into an ILIT is not a "transfer" for Medicaid purposes and does not generate a penalty period (see Chapter 6). But a Medicaid applicant who continues to own a cash value policy with more than nominal cash value will have an excess asset that may limit eligibility. So it could make sense to place the cash value policy into the ILIT and hope that the penalty period generated by the transfer will run before it is necessary to apply for Medicaid.

It pays to remember that making contributions to a life insurance trust or paying premiums on a policy owned by a trust is considered a gift to the trust. However, the gift does not qualify for the gift tax annual exclusion because it is not a gift of a present interest. Therefore, the person who makes such contributions will be using up part of the unified credit. (See Chapter 13.) A way around this problem is to include a "Crummey" power (named after the tax case that authorizes the strategy) in the ILIT. By giving beneficiaries of the trust the right to make a "five or five" withdrawal once a year for a short period (usually 30 to 45 days) gifts to the trust become present interest gifts that qualify for the gift tax annual exclusion. This is true even if nobody ever does make a withdrawal. In fact, Crummey powers are almost never exercised.

Prosperous senior citizens who would otherwise keep their Roth IRA accounts intact, or would make only minimum withdrawals from a conventional IRA, might wish to make slightly larger withdrawals to pay insurance premiums or to purchase second-to-die insurance that will pay estate taxes.

One estate administration problem is that trustees do not always manage life insurance as actively as other assets. The premiums for trust-owned life insurance could prove larger than expected, or there could be financial problems that prevent the grantor from continuing to contribute to the trust to pay the premiums.

In 2004, when *Trusts and Estates* magazine surveyed professional trustees, 83.5% said they did not have guidelines and procedures for handling life insurance owned by the trust. Almost three-quarters of non-professional trustees (e.g., trust grantors, spouses, family members, and friends of grantors) said they had not reviewed the life insurance policies in the trust for the past five years. About 95% of both professional and non-professional trustees did not have guidelines for allocating the assets of variable life policies held in trusts.

Other surveys say that at least 75%, and perhaps up to 95% of life insurance policies owned by trusts are not serviced by a life insurance agent. (It is appropriate for fiduciaries to delegate duties to outside professionals—as long as they are carefully chosen and their performance is monitored.) A professional service firm that handles trust-owned life insurance predicts that up to 92% of existing trust-owned policies could be restructured to provide up to 20% more value. In fact, at least 75% of the contracts could be restructured to provide a 40% premium reduction, or an equal increase in the death benefit.

The Uniform Prudent Investor Act, which has been adopted in 43 states, requires trustees to use the same standard of care, skill and caution that a prudent investor would use with respect to his or her own funds. Trustees do not necessarily need to remove or replace the policy held in the trust on a regular schedule, but they must exercise care in selection and must maintain only policies that continue to be appropriate. Trustees must tailor the risk profile of the trust's investments to the purposes of the trust and the beneficiaries' circumstances, general economic conditions, diversification of trust assets, and tax planning.[17]

ARRANGING THE LIFE INSURANCE POLICY

Designating the Beneficiary

The simplest situation is that of the person who buys a policy on his or her life, makes all the premium payments, always has access to any cash value the policy possesses, and always controls any investment decisions to be made about the policy.

This insured names a beneficiary and contingent beneficiary (who will receive benefits only if the initial beneficiary dies before the insured) and never changes the beneficiary. The designated beneficiary might be an individual, a corporation, a charitable organization, or an estate.

Even this simplest case can give rise to some problems. For instance, naming "my wife" or "my children" as beneficiaries creates problems if there has been a divorce and remarriage or if children are born after the policy is purchased. Therefore, it is better to name beneficiaries as well as identify them by title. Part of the divorce process should be to check state law to see how a divorce affects beneficiary designations and to make any necessary modifications. However, it is a fairly common separation agreement provision to require maintenance of life insurance to protect the children of the marriage, and sometimes to ensure that the ex-spouse will receive at least the amount of property and income provided under the agreement.

If a beneficiary or contingent beneficiary is a minor at the time he or she becomes entitled to insurance proceeds, ownership of funds is likely to be subject to legal limitations. To avoid the need for the appointment of a guardian, the better strategy is to name an adult to be the beneficiary in the capacity of guardian or custodian for the minor or to direct payment of the funds to a trust benefiting the minor.

In many cases, however, the spouse will be designated as the beneficiary. In this situation, selection of contingent beneficiaries becomes vital because it is not unlikely that the beneficiary-spouse will die before the insured-spouse or will have impaired mental capacity. Furthermore, if the surviving spouse is already a Medicaid beneficiary, or is likely to become so in the near future, receiving insurance proceeds will be detrimental. In this situation, it is better to name a child, grandchild, or charity as the beneficiary. At the other end of the financial continuum, the survivor may not need the insurance funds if personal funds and other inheritances from the deceased spouse are ample. If the life insurance proceeds are not needed, then terminating the policy, borrowing against its cash value, or shifting some premium dollars to long-term care insurance may make sense.

Changing the Beneficiary

The beneficiary designation under most life insurance policies is revocable. That is, the owner of the policy can change the beneficiary at will. The person originally named as beneficiary has no right to protest a change of beneficiary or the policy owner's borrowing against the cash value, even if it reduces the amount actually paid to the beneficiary.

However, changing the beneficiary of the policy is a business transaction that requires contractual capacity. A person who is unconscious, mentally ill, or suffers from Alzheimer's disease or other similar illness is not able to change a beneficiary designation. Thus, the appropriateness of current beneficiary designations should be carefully considered given the fact that it may be impossible to change them in the future.

Another possibility is an irrevocable beneficiary designation which, in effect, makes the beneficiary a co-owner of the policy whose consent is required before exercising incidents of ownership, including changing the beneficiary designation.

Policy Ownership

The insured is not the only possible owner of the policy. Indeed, it is often better for the policy to be owned by someone other than the insured for estate tax purposes. Anyone with an insurable (i.e., a legitimate financial) interest in someone else's life can purchase a policy on that person's life.

Because a life insurance policy is an item of property, it can be sold, assigned, or given away by its owner. Annual exclusion gifts (i.e., gifts of present interests of up to $10,000 per year as adjusted for inflation, or $20,000 a year as adjusted if the donor's spouse joins in the gift; $12,000 and $24,000 in 2006) can be made to children to permit them to purchase insurance on the donor's life. Or insurance gifts can be used to benefit a favorite charity.

For Medicaid purposes, life insurance cash value in excess of $1,500 is an available resource. Transfer of a policy to the spouse will not give rise to a penalty (no interspousal transfer is penalized), but the cash value will become part of the "snapshot" that determines the amount of resources that the couple owns.

DEATH BENEFITS PAID BEFORE DEATH

Accelerated Death Benefits

A common life insurance benefit, either drafted as part of the original policy or offered as a rider at no additional cost, is the ability to accelerate the death benefit. Accelerated death benefits (ADB) may be made available on the basis of a diagnosis of terminal illness, or for either a terminal illness or chronic illness requiring long-term care. In a sense, this is an extremely logical development. Cash value life insurance always gives its owners the potential to tap the cash value by policy loan, so why not let them have access to the value during life?

If an older person can afford $50,000 or so, a single-premium life insurance policy with a death benefit that can be accelerated by a chronically ill person can be used as an estate planning hedge. A 65-year-old female non-smoker might be able to purchase a single-premium policy with a $110,000 death benefit in exchange for a one-time deposit of $50,000. The death benefit can be accelerated up to $150 a day for nursing home or home care, or $75 a day for adult day care. After the death benefit is used up, the insured has access to a long-term benefit fund of $220,000. However, if the insured dies without using any accelerated benefits, the policy operates like a conventional life insurance policy and pays the death benefit to the designated beneficiary.[18]

In fall 2005, the New York State Insurance Department proposed updates to the regulations for accelerated death benefits. These proposed regulations affect individual life, group life, and fraternal life insurance companies doing business in New York and offering early benefit payments on the basis of serious health problems, especially when payments are used for long-term care (LTC). Consumers must be notified that they are receiving only limited access to life insurance benefits, and not full-scale long-term care insurance. Under the proposal:

- Accelerated death benefits must meet the IRS standards for qualified LTCI (see Chapter 4);

- The application for a life insurance policy with LTC benefits must contain a prominent disclosure that accelerating benefits could affect eligibility for public benefits;

- Sellers of life policies with ADB features must follow strict guidelines in giving policy illustrations;

- If the ADB has a discounting feature, the illustration must assume that death will occur within a year, and must use an 8% interest rate assumption (or other mortality basis filed with the Superintendent of Insurance); and

- The present value of the amounts to be accelerated must not exceed the policy death benefit, and ADB payments must be deducted from the value of the ultimate death benefit. Additional death benefits can be paid, but only if there are no premium requirements for the benefits once they are paid. It is also permissible for an insurer to pay a "residual death benefit" up to 10% of the original death benefit, subject to a maximum of $25,000.[19]

Viatical Settlements

Instead of turning to the insurer to provide liquidity, another possibility is a viatical settlement. A viatical settlement is a contract with a third party. The third party collects funds from investors. The investors then, in effect, purchase life insurance contracts at a discount, generally from insureds who are terminally ill. (The viatical settlement company takes over premium payments subsequent to the purchase.) The longer the life expectancy of the insured person, the greater the discount. The financial risk for the investor and viatical settlement provider is that a person diagnosed as terminally ill will, in fact, live longer than anticipated.

In general, viatical settlement payments are made in a lump sum, which the viator can use to settle debts, pay for medical treatment, or simply pay expenses. It is permissible for the viatical settlement provider to buy an annuity for the viator instead of paying a lump sum. Generally, no one involved on the business side of viatical settlements is allowed to offer or pay a commission or finder's fee to doctors, lawyers, or financial advisers of potential viators.

The NAIC's approach to the regulation of viatication concentrates on state regulation of settlement providers and creating a standardized approach to the disclosures to be made to potential viators (policy sellers).

In mid-2005, the Eleventh Circuit ruled that a viatical settlement is an "investment contract" subject to federal securities laws, because the settlement company promised its investors fixed returns of 12-72%, depending on the length of the investment. The SEC charged the promoters with failing to disclose that 65% of the policies sold used fraudulent life expectancy factors, and 90% of the insured persons selling policies had already survived their "life expectancy."[20]

After the SEC sued in May 2004 for securities fraud, a receiver was appointed for viatical settlement provider Mutual Benefits Corp. The receiver wanted to sell the company's portfolios, but the investors persuaded U.S. District Judge Federico Moreno to permit the investors to control the disposition of the policies—a decision that should reassure potential investors who are concerned with possible instability in the sector. In December 2005, the SEC and Mutual Benefits negotiated a settlement under which the former principals of Mutual Benefits Corp. agreed to disgorge wrongful profits and pay civil penalties. The settlement as a whole was valued at $25 million.[21]

Taxation of Accelerated Death Benefits and Viatical Benefits

The Health Insurance Portability and Accessibility Act of 1996 (HIPAA) addressed the taxation of accelerated death benefits and viatication at the same time that it clarified the tax treatment of long-term care insurance (see Chapter 4). Many of the same rules and concepts apply. Any funds that a terminally ill person (one with a life expectancy under 24 months) receives through an accelerated death benefit payment or a viatical settlement will be free of income tax. But if the recipient fits the definition of "chronically ill" but is not "terminally ill," then only amounts that represent the actual cost of care or do not exceed $250 per day (as indexed for 2006) can be received tax-free.[22] Furthermore, funds from a viatical settlement are income-tax free only if the investor in the contract meets NAIC standards or has a state license.

Planning Strategies for Viatication

One theme that emerges is consideration of estate tax consequences. For instance, a person who is seriously ill and is at risk of dying with a large insurance policy in the estate (and unlikely to live for three years, so even an immediate transfer would run afoul of the three-year rule) has a good estate planning reason to viaticate even if cash is not needed for last-illness expenses. Viatication is considered a sale for value, not a donative transfer, and thus does not trigger the three-year rule.

Viatication can also be done by a third-party owner, such as the trustee of an ILIT. The seriously ill owner of a closely held business might be at risk of heavy taxation on his or her estate. If the ILIT includes life insurance on the business owner's life, it might make sense for the trustee to viaticate the policy and use the funds to buy a minority interest in the business from its owner. A significant discount would probably be available, because the closely held business interest is a minority interest with little marketability. And, of course, the interest purchased by the trust is removed from the business owner's estate as is any appreciation between the date of sale and the owner's eventual death.

Some insurance policies can be viaticated based on the insured having reached age 70 or 75. A healthy but aged business owner might want to use viatication in a similar way. This is especially true because the owner might survive for five or even ten more years, allowing a significant amount of appreciation to be kept out of the estate.

Viatication can also be done in conjunction with charitable gift planning. From the estate planning perspective, the best charitable gift is a highly appreciated asset, because the income tax deduction is based on the fair market value, not the donor's (typically much lower) basis. However, highly appreciated assets usually throw off income that can be useful to the potential donor. One planning option is to give the highly appreciated asset to charity, then viaticate and either use the settlement proceeds to replace the income from the donated asset or give away the income as well, powerfully reducing the potentially taxable estate.

Selling an insurance policy can also be a good strategy for the "borderline" estate, one that is not much greater than the current break point for estate taxation. If the life insurance policy is the most expendable asset, getting it out of the estate could tip the balance away from taxation.

Life Settlements

Unlike a viatical settlement (made by a terminally ill person), a life settlement is made by a senior citizen who owns a policy with a face amount of $200,000 or more, and who is willing to sell the policy to a third party. For example, a policy with a death benefit of $1.5 million could yield a life settlement of $450,000. This is a fast-growing market. In 2002, the overall market for life settlements was about $2 billion in life insurance policy face amounts, rising to $3.3 billion in 2004 and $5.5 billion in 2005.[23]

In 2004, the NAIC, disagreeing with a number of states, decided that insurance agents do not require separate licenses to broker life insurance policy sales. The Viatical and Life Settlement Association of America expected this development to lead to a significant expansion of the market. At that point, the value of life settlements already sold had reached $2 billion, and the industry grew at a rate of almost 20% a year. Life settlements are becoming more popular among senior citizens who are short of cash, do not need the coverage, and do not want to pay any more premiums.

Doug Head, the executive director of the Viatical and Life Settlement Association was quoted as saying that the value of a Universal Life policy for life-settlement purposes is at least three times the underlying cash value, and even term policies have a value of 10-30% of the face value. One settlement company paid a 66-year-old $248,947 for a $1 million term policy, and paid a couple in their eighties over $232,000 for a $2 million Universal Life policy carrying a cash value of $54,300.[24]

Nat Shapo of the life settlement company Coventry First LLC told The National Underwriter that new regulations are needed to regulate life settlements—an area where a number of states lack regulations. To Shapo, viatical settlements (which many jurisdictions regulate) are unique and have a limited reach, whereas life settlements are a basic financial planning tool. The average participant in a life settlement survives the transaction by about 10 years, so is able to make a more leisurely and sophisticated judgment about the value of the transaction. To Shapo, the life insurance industry and the settlement industry have more shared interests than they have rivalry, and potential purchasers will be more inclined to buy insurance they might otherwise pass up if they know there is a strong secondary market for policies they will not need any more.[25]

A study performed by Deloitte Consulting LLP and the University of Connecticut shows that for older policyholders with some health problems (the target market for life settlements), keeping life insurance is often a better financial bargain than selling it to an investor or surrendering the policy for its cash value. The researchers described the typical life settlement candidate as a person over 65, with $250,000 or more insurance, some health problems, and a life expectancy between two and 15 years.

To maximize the estate for heirs or for charity, retaining the policy is probably the best move because commissions and transaction costs have already been absorbed. An insured person who needs cash is probably better off retaining the policy and selling other assets, such as stocks. Another factor is that a person in poor health is very unlikely to be able to purchase insurance coverage later if it is determined that the sale was imprudent or if coverage is needed for other reasons (e.g., a later marriage).

However, the study found that selling the policy to an investor was more lucrative than surrendering it. Life settlement companies paid an average of 20% of the face amount, whereas the researchers estimated the payout on the policy minus future premiums was about 64% of the face amount. And life settlement companies can pay as much as eight times surrender value.[26]

Yet another variation on the theme is "nonrecourse premium financing," a new strategy pitched to wealthy senior citizens (70 or over; able to qualify for at least $5 million in insurance). A financing company lends money to the affluent elder or a family trust; the loan lasts two years or more. (The two-year period was chosen to get around insurers' incontestability rules.) A large policy is purchased on the senior citizen's life. If he or she dies during the loan term, the estate pays back the loan plus interest and fees; the heirs keep the rest of the insurance.

If the senior lives through the term, the older person can either keep the policy and repay the loan, or transfer the policy to the lender to satisfy the loan without making a cash repayment. The older person gets an inexpensive or free source of short-term insurance. Hedge funds and other institutional investors looking for new revenue sources are promoting such transactions, which are usually packaged into a pool that gives steady returns (sometimes as high as 8-12%) rather than uneven payments when an insured person dies.

However, critics say that nonrecourse premium financing distorts the purpose of insurance in providing for those with a genuine financial interest in the insured. Insurance companies are opposed to this development, because it disrupts their calculation of lapse rates, and because they are concerned that Congress will cut back on the tax advantages of life insurance if it becomes too much of an investment product rather than a family financial planning device. The NAIC is considering making state insurable-interest laws tougher, to make it harder for investors with no real connection to the insured to get involved.[27]

Under the Internal Revenue Code transfer for value rule, investors probably pay income tax on the death benefit they receive, minus the premiums and transaction costs paid. The policyholder who transfers a policy under one of these arrangements is probably taxable on accrued interest that would otherwise have been charged, and cash advances are probably taxable income.[28]

CHAPTER ENDNOTES

1. Online with LIMRA, "Life Insurance Industry Seeks to Reverse Declining Sales Trend," www.limra.com/Pressroom/PressReleases/pr090204.aspx (September 2, 2004).

2. Linda Koco, "Life Insurance is Revving Up Again," NU Week in Life & Health 2004 Issue #26.

3. "Facts About Life 2005," www.limra.com/pressroom/pressmaterials/factsaboutlife2005complete.pdf.

4. Mark Levy, "Aging America Still Needs Permanent Life Insurance," NU Week in Life & Health 2004 Issue #40.

5. Dylan Loeb McClain, "Now Only Death Is Certain After 100," *New York Times,* April 25, 2004, Week in Rev p. 2.

6. For recent sales statistics, see Geraldine Murtagh, "3rd Qtr VL Sales Increased 27% Over Last Year," *National Underwriter,* Life and Health/Financial Services edition, January 11, 1999, p. 4.

7. See Linda Koco, "New Approaches Needed for VUL Sales Success," *National Underwriter,* Life and Health/Financial Services edition, November 9, 1998, p. 1.

8. Kathy Chu, "Protected for Life: New Policies Cover Downturn," *Wall Street Journal,* June 29, 2004, p. D2.

9. See Chris Kite, "The Ins and Outs of Second-to-Die Life Insurance," *Trusts & Estates,* February, 1998, p. 63.

10. See Treas. Reg. §1.79-3(d)(2).

11. Kathy Chu, "Survey Finds Rise in Demand for Life Insurance," *Wall Street Journal,* April 12, 2005, p. D3.

12. 2005-17 IRB 962.

13. McKay Hochman Co., Inc. Commentary, "Life Insurance in Retirement Plans" (April 28, 2005), www.mhco.com/Commentary/2005/Life_Insurance_In_Retirement_Plans_042205.htm.

14. See, e.g., Notice 2001-10, 2001-1 CB 459; T.D. 9092, 2003-46 IRB 1055.

15. Code section 264(a)(4) disallows interest deductions for indebtedness that relates to life insurance. However, for life insurance contracts issued after June 8, 1997, interest that would be disallowed under Section 264(a)(4) can be added to the exempt amount of a policy that was transferred for value.

16. Let. Rul. 9809032.

17. Mark A. Teitelbaum, "Trust Owned Life Insurance: Is It An Accident Waiting to Happen?" NU Week in Life & Health 2004, Issue #19.

18. This strategy is suggested by Jeffrey Baskies and Neal Slafsky, "A Deposit-Based Approach to Long-Term Care Insurance Planning," *Trusts & Estates*, June, 1997, p. 41.

19. See www.ins.state.ny.us/rproindx.htm.

20. *SEC v. Mutual Benefits Corp.*, 408 F.3d 737 (11th Cir. 2005).

21. "Judge Lets Viatical Investors Control Asset Sale," NU Online News Service, September 30, 2005. See also "SEC Accepts Viatical Firm Settlement," NU Online News Service, December 2, 2005.

22. See IRC Sections 101(g), 7702B.

23. These figures come from Conning Research and Consulting Inc.; see Trevor Thomas, "Life Settlements Hit $5.5 Billion Last Year: Conning," NU Online News Service, January 16, 2006.

24. Jeff D. Opdyke, "Selling Your Life Insurance to a Stranger," *Wall Street Journal*, September 21, 2004 p. D3.

25. Steve Tuckey, "Shapo Says Life Settlement Market Needs Better Rules," National Underwriter Life & Health Online News Service, September 2, 2005.

26. Rachel Emma Silverman, "Recognizing Life Insurance's Value," *Wall Street Journal*, May 31, 2005, p. C2.

27. Matt Brady, "Groups Push for Changes in Viatical Model," NU Online News Service, February 23, 2006.

28. Rachel Emma Silverman, "Letting an Investor Bet on When You'll Die," *Wall Street Journal*, May 26, 2005, p. D1.

Chapter 3

Medigap Insurance

The Medicare system includes a variety of deductibles and coinsurance requirements. Medicare Supplementary insurance (Medigap) helps the elderly with these payments. The Medicare system also excludes various services and medically-related items. With one prominent exception, coverage of prescription drugs, Medigap insurance does not cover items that are excluded by the basic structure of Medicare. Therefore, Medigap insurance does not provide custodial nursing home or home care, although long-term care insurance does (see Chapter 4).

Medigap insurance is essentially a commodity product, like flour or sugar. Insurers are allowed to offer only 12 basic plans of Medigap insurance, known as Plans A-L. (Plans F and J can be adapted for coordination with Medical Savings Accounts (see Chapter 5).)[1]

Medigap policies have certain coverages that are shared by all plans. Plan A provides certain basic benefits, with the other plans adding further benefits. In particular, all the other plans cover the Part A deductible. (Only a few cover the Part B deductible, but that is a comparatively minor $124 per year.) Plans C-J include coverage of coinsurance for Days 21-100 of a stay in a Skilled Nursing Facility covered by Medicare.

Although generally Medigap insurance is standardized nationwide, there are some state-to-state variations. The standard Medigap policies are available in 47 states. Massachusetts, Minnesota, and Wisconsin have their own standards for supplementary policies.

Insurers that want to sell Medigap insurance within a state must offer Plan A, the basic package. In most states, they decide which of the other plans they will offer. However, certain states do not allow all the plans to be sold in that particular state.[2]

As a general rule, people who are enrolled in a Medicare managed care plan do not need Medigap insurance, because they are not liable for copayments and have coverage broader than fee-for-service Medicare. In fact, in certain circumstances, it is illegal to sell a Medigap policy to someone who the seller knows to be enrolled in Medicare managed care.

It should be noted that most Medicare Part B claims are assigned, meaning that the service provider has agreed not only to bill the Centers for Medicare & Medicaid Services (CMS) directly for 80 percent of the schedule amount (with the patient paying the 20 percent coinsurance), but has agreed to accept the schedule amount in full payment. Even for non-assigned claims, in most instances it is illegal for the provider to charge more than 115 percent of the schedule amount. (Sometimes even tougher limitations on such "balance billing" apply.) Therefore, the role of Medigap in reimbursing Medicare beneficiaries for their Part B copayments has lessened, because the possible amount of the co-payment obligation has been reduced.

THE MEDIGAP MARKETPLACE

In 2005, the latest figures analyzed by America's Health Insurance Plans Policy Institute related to the year 2002. At that time, 23% of Medicare beneficiaries who were not institutionalized owned Medigap insurance. One-third of Medigap policyholders had income between $10,000 and $20,000; two-thirds had income below $30,000 a year.

In 2002, the comprehensive Plan F was the most popular, owned by 38% of policyholders. Plan C was the next most popular, owned by 20%. The bare-bones Plan A and extra-comprehensive Plan J each were owned by 7% of policyholders; Plans B and D each had an 8% market share.[3]

National Underwriter's Jonathan Neal pointed out that few sellers of annuities and LTCI also sell Medigap, and vice versa, although the products share a targeted group of customers. Although many Medigap buyers can't afford annuities or long-term care insurance, they can still be a valuable source of referrals to more affluent senior citizens. Neal suggests that sales of Medigap can pay for the expenses of prospecting for LTCI and annuity sales.[4]

The part D program is likely to hurt Medigap insurers. Up to 1.9 million potential Part D beneficiaries have prescription drug coverage under Medigap. According to NAIC, total 2002 revenue for the Medigap sector was $17 billion. CMS estimates that revenues could fall by $2.5 billion in 2006 and as much as $3.2 billion. However, insurers have some new revenue opportunities under the Part D program (as well as the latest version of Medicare managed care, now enacted as Part C).[5]

WHAT MEDIGAP COVERS

The basic, bedrock Plan A provides the following benefits, which are also available under all the other Medigap plans:

- Coverage of Part A coinsurance for in-patient hospital days 61-90 in each benefit period (see Chapter 5 for a discussion of Medicare coverage of inpatient hospitalization);

- Coinsurance for the Part A lifetime reserve days;

- One hundred percent coverage of hospital costs that would be eligible for Part A coverage if it were not for the fact that the person has used up all 90 coverage days in the benefit period and has also used up all 60 lifetime reserve days (this Medigap benefit is limited to 365 days beyond what Medicare will pay);[6]

- Three pints of blood or packed red blood cells per year; and

- Coverage of Part B coinsurance (generally 20 percent of the approved charge, after satisfaction of a $100 annual deductible for physician services; other services may have different coinsurance amounts).

Plan B covers the basic services of Plan A, plus the Part A deductible.

Plan C covers:

- The same services as Plan B;

- The Medicare Part B deductible;

- The Skilled Nursing Facility (SNF) coinsurance; and

- Emergency care during travel outside the U.S., subject to a $250 deductible and 20 percent coinsurance up to a lifetime maximum benefit of $50,000 ("foreign emergency care").

Plan D covers:

- The same services as Plan B;

- The SNF coinsurance;

- Foreign emergency care; and

- "At-home recovery"–a benefit of up to $1,600 a year for short-term home care assistance with activities of daily living (ADLs) (e.g., bathing, dressing, personal hygiene), as part of the process of recuperating from injury, an operation, or an illness.

Plan E covers:

- The same services as Plan B;

- The SNF coinsurance;

- Foreign emergency care; and

- Up to $120 a year for preventive care and screening.

Plan F covers:

- The same services as Plan C; and

- One hundred percent of "excess charges" under Part B (excess charges are amounts greater than the schedule amount for the service, but within the permissible 15 percent limit over and above the schedule amount that providers are allowed to charge).

Plan G covers:

- The same services as Plan D; and

- Eighty percent (not 100 percent) of Part B excess charges.

Plan H covers:

- The same services of Plan B;

- SNF coinsurance;

- Foreign emergency care; and

- An outpatient prescription drug benefit covering 50% of prescription drug charges after a $250 deductible, with a $1,250 annual limit on benefits.[7]

Plan I covers:

- The same services as Plan C;

- One hundred percent of Part B excess charges; and

- The prescription drug benefit of Plan H.

Plan J covers:

- The same services as Plan F;

- At-home recovery;

- Up to $120 a year for preventive care and screening; and

- A prescription drug benefit like that of Plan H but with a $3,000 annual limit.

Plans F and J can also be issued in high-deductible form to coordinate with Health Savings Accounts and MSAs. In 2006, the deductible for such plans was $1,790 a year.[8]

The Medicare Prescription Drug Improvement and Modernization Act (MPDIMA; P.L. 108-173) altered the Medicare and Medigap landscape by adding the Medicare Part D prescription drug benefit. Under MPDIMA, new policies in forms H, I and J will no longer be issued after January 1, 2006. Persons who already have these policies will be permitted to continue to renew them, although they will have to pay the premium charged by the insurer, which CMS notes often exceeds $120 a month. The Part D premium for 2006 will only be approximately $37 a month. Furthermore, Medigap prescription drug coverage is subject to annual limits, whereas there is no limit on the amount of prescription drug spending that can be covered by Part D.

PLANNING TIP: Once Part D becomes operational, Medigap insurance can be used to fill the gaps in Part A and Part B coverage—but NOT to pay Part D co-payments. The theory is that having to pay out of pocket will make seniors better prescription drug consumers. Nor do Medigap policies cover cost sharing under Part C (Medicare Advantage managed care plans): see 70 Fed.Reg. 15399 (March 25, 2005).

A person who owns a Medigap policy and wishes to enroll in Part D is allowed to renew the policy, without drug coverage, and with a reduced premium to compensate for the obligation to pay the Part D premium. However, the insured person must make a choice: either enroll in Part D or renew the drug benefits under the Medigap policy.[9]

MPDIMA also adds two new forms of Medigap policy, K and L.

Plan K covers:

- Basic services;

- 100% of Part A hospital coinsurance for days 61-90 of a hospital stay;

- 100% of Part A coinsurance for lifetime reserve days;

- 100% of Medicare-eligible expenses once lifetime reserve days have been used up;

- 100% of Part B cost sharing (but not the annual Part B deductible); and

- 100% of Part A and Part B cost sharing once the insured person has made out of pocket payments of $4,000 for the year. The payments that count are half the cost sharing for certain services.

Plan L is the same, except that the out of pocket limit is only $2,000, making the insured person responsible for 25% of the Part A deductible, 25% of the SNF copayment, and 25% of the patient's responsibility for copayments for services such as blood and hospice care. (These are 2006 figures; they will be indexed each year for inflation.)

It is important to note that "excess charges" are not included in the $2,000 or $4,000 limit. Excess charges are amounts charged over and above the Medicare approved amount for a service or procedure by a provider who does not accept assignment. The beneficiary is personally responsible for paying the excess charges without insurance.

PREMIUMS

All post-1992 Medigap policies must be guaranteed renewable, meaning the insurer must allow the renewal of a policy unless a material misrepresentation has been made or if premiums are not paid. Some pre-1992 policies, which allow non-renewal for other reasons, still remain in force.

Although benefits are highly standardized, insurers are given discretion to determine how they will set the Medigap premium, whether it be by issue age, attained age, or a "no-age rating." Premiums set via the issue age method are set based on the age at the time of purchase, and remain the same as long as the coverage is retained. Attained age premiums increase each year, as the insured grows older. No-age rating sets a single, uniform premium irrespective of age at purchase or attained age. Medigap premiums may increase due to inflation.

Community-rated premiums are the same for everyone in the whole book of business, which is beneficial to older and sicker purchasers who would otherwise pay more—but probably means that younger and healthier purchasers will pay more than they would under other systems. Entry age premiums are based on anticipated claims throughout the policy life of customers who are the same age at purchase, which tends to favor younger purchasers. Attained age premiums are adjusted every year for the expected higher utilization. This can be attractive to young purchasers who plan to switch to a cheaper plan later on—but that strategy can backfire if their health has deteriorated so that they do not qualify for another policy later on.

PLANNING TIP: It is usually wise strategy to purchase the most comprehensive plan that the senior can afford when he or she first enrolls in Medicare and purchases a Medigap policy. That's because the rules guarantee the right to maintain the same level of coverage, even if there is a deterioration in health status. The right to change to another policy (as long as there is never a 63-day gap in coverage) also has some legal protection. But in general, insurers are only required to offer the same form as the original coverage, or one with less coverage; there is no protected legal right to upgrade coverage, and it is lawful for insurers to turn down an application for greater coverage based on the applicant's health status.

In 2001, a comprehensive Medigap policy with prescription coverage cost an average of $174 a month. Premiums increased more than 10% a year (in constant dollars) in 1999, 2000, and 2001.[10]

In 2004, Weiss Ratings found that premiums for the same form could be much higher depending on the insurer and the location. For example, the nationwide average cost of Plan C for a 65-year-old female purchaser was $1,689 a year, but the lowest premium was $616 a year and the highest $6,270. In New York, a 65-year-old woman could pay $927 or $1,463 for Plan A, depending on insurer; the same purchaser could be charged anywhere from $1,087 to $2,894 for Plan C in Nevada. TIP: A quick source of information on Medigap pricing within a client's Zip Code is the "personal plan finder" at the medicare.gov site. The Medicare site also has contact information for State Health Insurance Programs (SHIPs) that have information for health insurance consumers, including current rates for insurers selling Medigap plans in that market.[11]

The Arizona Department of Insurance's Website, http://www.id.state.az.us, noted that a 65-year-old's premiums for Plan B could be anywhere from $87 to $239 a month; Plan F premiums for an 80-year-old could be anywhere from $149 to $455 a month. The general range was a highest-price policy costing three to four times as much as the lowest-price. In some cases, higher premiums bought additional services such as 24-hour customer service and access to speedy and convenient automated online claims processing.

LOSS RATIOS

Federal law requires Medigap policies to have an overall loss ratio of at least 65 percent (i.e., at least 65 percent of premiums taken in must be returned in the form of benefits). The mandated loss ratio for group policies is 75 percent.

According to the General Accounting Office, the average loss ratio for 1995 was well above the requirement: 86 percent.[12] But there were some significant geographical differences, differences among insurers, and especially differences among the various plans. Plan G, at 73.8%, had the lowest average loss ratio, while Plan A, at 102.3%, had the highest loss ratio (i.e., insurers lost money on this plan, but could not stop offering it because of federal mandates). Plan F is the most popular plan, even though it typically costs more than Plan C and has a lower loss ratio (an average of 75.5% for Plan F, versus 89.3% for Plan C). The only difference between the two is that Plan F provides coverage of physician's excess charges. However, few insureds ever collect on these charges, because more than 95% of Medicare claims are assigned, resulting in no excess charges.

MEDIGAP OPEN ENROLLMENT

Individuals who become eligible for Medicare have a six-month open enrollment period, during which they have an absolute right to buy any Medigap plan offered by the insurer of their choice. An individual cannot be turned down (or charged a higher premium) on the basis of health or claims experience, although coverage of preexisting conditions (those in existence as of six months prior to the effective date of the policy) may be excluded or limited until the policy has been in effect for six months. Generally, the open enrollment period begins on the first date that the individual has both enrolled in Medicare Part B and attained the age of 65.

There is a special open enrollment period for Part D, which will affect Medigap policy renewals. This IEP (Initial Enrollment Period) runs from November 15, 2005 to May 15, 2006. During the IEP, the owner of a Medigap policy will be able to buy another policy from the same issuer. If the insurer offers the plan and is selling it to new purchasers, issue of Forms A, B, C, F (in regular or high-deductible form), K, and L is guaranteed. Insurers are also allowed to issue the other Medigap forms on a guaranteed issue basis, but this is not a legal obligation.

The guaranteed issue period is 63 days, starting on the effective date of the policyholder's Part D coverage. But if the owner of a Medigap policy fails to enroll in Part D before May 15, 2006 (the end of the IEP), he or she will not be entitled to guaranteed issue of a Medigap policy that does not have drug benefits, although he or she will be allowed to renew an existing policy without drug coverage.

PLANNING TIP: Federal law imposes Medicare secondary payor provisions, which provide that Employer Group Health Plans (EGHPs) are generally the primary payor for persons (such as over-65 employees and their dependents) who are covered by both Medicare and the EGHP. That is, the senior citizen can choose to be covered primarily by Medicare, secondarily by the EGHP, but the employer cannot draft its plan to make Medicare the primary payor. The secondary payor provisions do not apply to employers with less than 20 employees.

People covered by an EGHP are usually better off if they delay enrolling in Part B until they are no longer covered by the EGHP. Those with EGHP coverage probably do not need a Medigap policy. The open enrollment period for Medigap runs from the date of Part B enrollment, so those who defer their Part B enrollment until they leave the EGHP can also delay their Medigap open enrollment period.

TRANSITIONS BETWEEN POLICIES

It should not be necessary for the same person to have more than one Medigap policy. In fact, NAIC rules and federal law require a pre-sale inquiry as to whether the potential purchaser already has Medigap insurance. If so, the old policy must be dropped in order to purchase a new one. In general, if the old policy was held for more than six months, no new waiting period can be imposed to bar claims on the basis of pre-existing conditions. However, a second waiting period is legitimate if the purchaser of the second policy voluntarily chose to switch to a policy plan offering greater benefits.

Guaranteed Issue

Older individuals may be disadvantaged if they belong to an EGHP and the EGHP stops offering benefits that supplement Medicare, or if they own a Medigap policy and their Medigap insurer becomes insolvent. Problems have also arisen for people who signed up for the current incarnation of Medicare managed care, only to find that the plan was being discontinued or would no longer be available in their area. Without a protective provision under federal law, they might find it difficult or impossible to find a Medigap carrier to insure them.

Under this protective provision, an insurer must allow the guaranteed issue of Plans A, B, C, or F.[13] Any Medigap insurer must sell Plan A on request, and it must sell B, C, or F if it normally sells that plan.

Federal rules do not allow Medigap insurers to deny guaranteed-issue applicants or charge them a higher premium on the basis of health status, health history, or claims history. (However, if the insurer otherwise charges age-based premiums, it can properly take age into account.) Pre-existing condition exclusions cannot be applied to anyone who had six months of continuous health insurance. For persons with under six months of continuous insurance, the term of any prior insurance reduces the pre-existing condition waiting period.

Note: Because Massachusetts, Minnesota, and Wisconsin have opted out of the ordinary regulation of Medigap insurance, these states have special transition rules.

For the NAIC guaranteed-issue rules, see www.naic.org.

MEDIGAP, MEDICAID, AND BUY-INS

Under federal law, it is unlawful to sell a Medigap policy to a person who is a Medicaid recipient. If a person who owns a Medigap policy later becomes eligible for Medicaid, he has the option of having both premiums and benefits suspended for up to two years while Medicaid covers the cost of care. If that person later loses Medicaid eligibility (e.g., as a result of receiving an inheritance), he can demand reinstatement of the policy up to 90 days after losing Medicaid eligibility, but must then resume premium payments. States have the option of coordinating Medicaid with Medigap by purchasing Medigap insurance on behalf of Medicaid beneficiaries.

CRITICAL ILLNESS INSURANCE

Critical illness (CI) insurance is an emerging form of health insurance that serves some of the same objectives as Medigap insurance. CI insurance first emerged in South Africa about 20 years ago, and was first offered in the United States in the mid-1990s. As of late 2000, there were about two dozen CI sellers in the U.S. marketplace, with another dozen or so evaluating whether to offer CI coverage.

CI insurance covers a specific group of named illnesses (e.g., stroke, cancer, heart attack). The policy pays a lump sum if and when the insured is diagnosed with one of these ailments. According to the American Heart Association, stroke (an ailment that usually strikes senior citizens) is the leading cause of serious long-term disability in the United States. About two-thirds of critical illness patients survive their particular illness, and about two-thirds of the costs associated with one of these illnesses are indirect. Even a person who has a complete, integrated package of health care coverage may encounter expenses (such as copayments, a caregiver's lost income, and home modifications) that are not covered by any of the policies within the package.

CI proponents say that this coverage supplements other parts of a person's insurance package. Accelerated Death Benefits (See Chapter 2) are made available in the case of a terminal illness. Health insurance pays medical bills, and disability insurance replaces lost employment income. CI covers the extra cost of keeping a household going during an illness. Most long-term care insurance policies (other than a few that use a disability model) link their benefits to specific health care services, whereas CI provides a lump sum that can be used for all household needs, not just health care bills.

Relevant issues in assessing a CI policy include:

- How many illnesses are covered;

- How precisely the illnesses are defined;

- If premiums are refunded should the insured die without making a claim;

- If a refund is available in cases of accidental death not related to a named illness; and

- Criteria for issuing the policy.[14]

CHAPTER ENDNOTES

1. Social Security Act §1882 makes it unlawful to sell Medigap policies that do not conform to federal regulations. On December 4, 1998, HCFA issued a Notice, published at 63 FR 67078, announcing that the NAIC Model Regulation as of April 29, 1998 determines which policies conform to federal regulations. A policy will also be in compliance if it satisfies a state standard that is at least as stringent as the April 29, 1998 NAIC rule. See 65 Federal Register 890442 (December 21, 2000): options F and J coordinated with MSAs have a $1580 out-of-pocket deductible in 2001.

2. This information comes from the Centers for Medicare and Medicaid Services Web site: www. medicare.gov/publications.html.

3. "Low-Income and Rural Beneficiaries With Medigap Coverage," http://www.ahipresearch.org/pdfs/medigap01/005_full.pdf.

4. Jonathan Neal, "Make Medigap Marketing an LTCI Profit Center," National Underwriter The Week In Life & Health 2005, Issue #5.

5. Arthur D. Postal, "Medigap Revenue Could Drop $2.5 Billion," National Underwriter Life & Health Week in Life & Health (September 27, 2004).

6. After Part A benefits are exhausted, a Medigap insurer is only required to pay hospitals the Medicare rate for the rest of the days in the hospital stay, not the hospital's regular rate (which is three or four times the Medicare rate): see *Vencor Hospitals v. Blue Cross/Blue Shield of Rhode Island*, 86 F.Supp.2d 1155 (S.D. Fla. 2000). The policy covered 90% of "Medicare eligible expenses," so insured persons could be required to copay 10% of the Medicare rate but could not be required to pay the difference between 90% of the Medicare rate and the hospital's regular rate.

7. The Court of Appeals for the First Circuit struck down a Massachusetts law requiring all Medigap insurers to offer at least one plan that provides unlimited coverage of outpatient prescription drugs, on the grounds that only the federal government and not the states can regulate benefit and coverage requirements for Medigap plans. *Massachusetts Ass'n of HMOs v. Ruthardt*, 194 F.3d 176 (1st Cir. 1999).

8. See 70 Fed.Reg. 15413 (March 25, 2005).

9. Medicare Fact Sheet "Final Rules Implementing the New Medicare Law," January 21, 2005 http://www.cms.hhs.gov/medicarereform/pdbma/fs-pdbmafinalrules.pdf .The federal rules for coordination between Medigap and Part D were published at 70 Fed.Reg. 15394 (March 25, 2005].

10. Richard W. Johnson and Rudolph G. Penner, "Will Health Care Costs Erode Retirement Security?" CRR Issue in Brief #23 (Oct. 2004), http://www.bc.edu/centers/crr/issues/ib_23.pdf.

11. Jeff D. Opdyke, "Medigap Premiums Vary Greatly Among Insurers," *Wall Street Journal*, September 8, 2004, p. D4.

12. GAO/HEHS-98-66, supra.

13. A Notice appearing at 63 FR 67078 (December 4, 1998) clarifies that guaranteed issue of plans A, B, C, and F becomes effective July 1, 1998, and continues even after 2002 if a Medicare+Choice plan terminates or the enrollee moves outside the plan's service area.

14. Linda Koco, "Critical Illness Insurance: Real or Gimmick?" *National Underwriter* Life and Health/Financial Services Edition January 2, 2001, p. 11; Wade V. Harrison, "CI Plans Meet Needs Other Coverages Don't," *National Underwriter* Life and Health/Financial Services Edition, December 4, 2000, p. 26.

Chapter 4

Long-Term Care Insurance

It is obvious that Medicare cannot meet all the medical and care-related needs of senior citizens, because Medicare excludes precisely the kind of custodial care that so many seniors need. It is also obvious that Medicaid planning has many deficiencies, both for individuals and for society as a whole. Given this situation, one might expect the private sector to step in, and that's exactly how long-term care insurance (LTCI) came about: as a means for people to purchase affordable coverage for their own future care.

Although the Economic Growth and Tax Relief Reconciliation Act of 2001 (EGTRRA 2001) does not contain provisions directly affecting long-term care insurance, it may have an indirect effect, especially on clients who acknowledge that they want to buy this coverage but have concerns about affordability.

Lower income tax rates provide more after-tax, spendable income that can be used to pay LTCI premiums. Lower income tax rates may also affect the timing of retirement if clients believe that their post-retirement income will be taxed at an affordable rate if they retire at a desired point in time. Some clients will reduce their life insurance portfolios because they believe their estates will not be taxed under the EGTRRA 2001 rules, and therefore can shift premium dollars within the insurance portfolio.

A person with LTCI coverage who needs nursing home care or home care can enter the best available facility or sign up with the best local agency without worrying about whether the facility or agency participates in Medicaid or has openings for Medicaid patients. Insured persons can plan their own financial lives, dispose of their assets, and make their own estate plans as they choose, with no need to fit into Medicaid requirements or explain their transfers. Many people find this freedom and flexibility extremely worthwhile.[1]

According to calculations by Ralph D. Leisle,[2] over a 30-year planning horizon for a married couple's estate, a hypothetical couple aged 59 and 57 would pay $235,000 for long-term care and LTC insurance. This assumes that they pay LTCI premiums of $4,600 a year and also pay the cost of care during a 90-day policy elimination period. The husband is assumed to need five years of care starting 16 years from now, and it is assumed that the wife will survive him by 10 years. But if long-term care costs are $180/day (based on an assumption that long-term care costs $65,700 a year per year, plus inflation at a rate of 5% annually), and if they do not have long-term care insurance, the cost of their care will be $2 million. If the couple chooses simple rather than compound inflation protection and elects a three-year rather than a lifetime benefit period, the premium expense will be reduced by 50%–but the net cost of long-term care will be $1 million, thus reducing the wealth in the estate by nearly $800,000.

While peace of mind can be priceless, LTCI is often expensive. So, the older client should shop carefully and select the right policy. The right policy is one provided by an insurer of top-flight financial soundness and reputation for service. It should also be provided by a company that plans to be in the LTCI market for the long haul. The older client must determine a basic financial objective (i.e., payment of the first dollar of expenses or of catastrophic expenses only) and select the desired benefits. The list of benefits available includes nursing home and home care as well as innovative benefits such as adult day care, caregiver training, and assisted living facility housing.[3]

One of the most important determinants of premium is the age of the insured individual at the time of purchase (because premiums usually remain level after purchase). The premium also depends on allocation of risk. The more risk the insured accepts (in the form of lower daily benefit levels, longer waiting periods, or shorter duration of benefits), the lower the premium will be. However, there is a meaningful possibility that the insured will have to make significant copayments once coverage is triggered.

As discussed in Chapter Three, Medigap insurance must conform to strict federal requirements. LTCI insurers are given more leeway in designing policies. However, certain LTCI policies are designed to meet certain tax requirements and thus be "tax-qualified." Purchasers may be entitled to a tax deduction for part of the premium and probably will get favorable income tax treatment when they collect benefits. It is perfectly acceptable to sell non-qualified policies (as long as they satisfy state licensing requirements) and, in fact, sometimes a non-qualified policy is the best choice for an individual purchaser.

This discussion revolves around the rules promulgated by the National Association of Insurance Commissioners (NAIC), especially the Long-Term Care Insurance

Model Act and Model Regulation. However, because the states play an important role in regulating long-term care insurance policies it is important to check what each individual state has done in this field as well as to keep up with developments in the NAIC's thinking.

Traditionally (if a fairly new product can be said to have a tradition) LTCI policies have paid on a "reimbursement model." That is, when an insured person triggers the policy by satisfying the criteria for coverage, a payment (typically somewhere between $50 and $300 a day) is made for each day that the insured person uses covered services such as a nursing home or paid, formal home care. The reimbursement model provides both lower limits (the insured person will receive less than the daily limit if he or she spends less than the limit on care) and upper limits (reimbursement is limited to a defined daily amount, even if actual expenditure is greater on a day when several services, such as skilled nursing, physical therapy, and homemaker services are used on the same day).

This model is now being supplemented by a "disability model," similar to disability insurance policies that replaces lost income. Under the disability model, if the insured person satisfies the criteria for coverage, he or she is entitled to a payment. And while reimbursement-model funds must be used for covered care, disability-model funds can be used for household expenses, payments to family or other unlicensed caregivers, travel, or the insured person's general family needs, making this type of policy is more flexible.

The downside is that, because claims are more likely under a disability-model policy, premiums are also higher: generally 30-50% greater than premiums for a comparable reimbursement-model policy.[4]

POLICY STRUCTURES

The central coverage of LTCI is nursing home coverage, typically expressed as a set dollar amount per day, with a usual range of $50 to $275 per day. It is permissible to sell policies covering only nursing home treatment, but selling a policy that is limited to skilled nursing home treatment is not allowed. Given the preference of most elders for staying at home, coverage of home care, by policy or rider, is popular. At one time, a typical policy might be designed to pay half as much for home care as for nursing home coverage: for example, $100 per day institutional benefit and $50 per day home care benefit. The current trend is toward benefit parity. To an increasing extent, LTCI policies are adding coverage of other types of benefits, such as adult day care. Some policies blur the distinction between housing and health care by offering coverage for stays in assisted living facilities and continuing care retirement communities.

NAIC rules (see below) and state law usually require LTCI policies to provide at least one years' coverage and many state laws do not permit LTCI policies covering less than two years. Instead of a deductible, LTCI policies may have a waiting period (typically, 10, 21, 30, or 100 days), although "first-day" policies are also available. Naturally, the longer the waiting period, the lower the premium.

By and large, LTCI policies are guaranteed renewable, so the age at purchase and the benefit package selected are the major determinants of premium. Further, premiums can usually be increased only on a class-wide basis, not for the individual. Creative options are also available in payment terms. For example, in 1998, one insurance company began to offer two new payment options. Under the "age 65" option, the policyholder makes larger annual payments and owns a paid-up policy at age 65. Similarly, the "10-year" option calls for only 10 years of premium payments to receive a paid-up policy. Obviously, premiums for these two payment options will be higher than conventional premiums.[5] Target purchasers include mid-life executives who can pay premiums out of their salary during high-income working years and have a fully paid-up policy at or shortly after retirement.

One of the most controversial LTCI issues is whether the individual purchaser should elect inflation protection. If elected, the question is whether the purchaser should select the 5% simple inflation protection (which will increase the premium about 50%) or the 5% compound (which will nearly double the premium).[6] The younger the insurance buyer, the greater the significance of inflation protection. Affluence cuts both ways. The larger the individual's assets, the greater the ability to purchase even more expensive coverage, but also the greater the ability to use those assets to pay for private care. A possible option is to increase the size of the policy benefit initially purchased and hope that it will continue to be adequate.

The question of benefit triggers is also significant. Some of the first generation of LTCI policies used a "medical necessity" trigger under which certification of medical need for the care was a prerequisite for insurance reimbursement. However, many elderly people suffer from many ailments at once, or from generalized frailty but not from a specific, identifiable ailment, and thus might not qualify for benefits under this trigger.

Qualified policies (see below) must have both an ADL trigger and a cognitive impairment trigger. That is, benefits must be available on the basis of the limitation of the insured individual to perform a certain number of the activities of daily living (ADLs) such as eating, dressing, and bathing. Benefits must also be available to cognitively impaired individuals, even if they retain a high degree of physical capacity. Insurers who sell non-qualified policies have greater flexibility and can use any trigger, or combination of triggers, permitted by state law.

Because nine-tenths of consumers want to stay home for care, home care provisions are being expanded: for example, policies that do not impose an elimination period for home care, and that allow some payments to be made to caregiver family members. Features that once were riders are being incorporated as standard features: for example, restoration-of-benefits provisions that allow months of benefits that were used to be gradually added back to coverage if a period of time elapses with no covered care. Some policies include limited worldwide benefits, offering care overseas until the patient is healthy enough to return to the United States for treatment of a long-term illness.

The new LTCI policies have many useful features that older policies lack. However, a number of the older policies remain in force, and are limited to nursing home benefits (perhaps requiring hospitalization before nursing home benefits are available) and/or lack inflation protection. The problem is that it's not always feasible to transfer clients to the newer and superior policies, because they will cost much more. Perhaps if the client is going to drop the policy altogether for cost reasons, a switch to a bare-bones policy will be possible—but only if the client is healthy enough to be underwriteable by another insurer.[7]

The current trend is to expand "informal care" benefits (permitting payments to friends and relatives who provide home care that keeps an impaired elder out of a nursing home) and add benefits for home modification and durable medical equipment. A "shared care" benefit allows transfer of unused LTCI benefits to the surviving spouse after one insured spouse's death.[8]

Insurers are adopting features aimed at improving group sales and sales to customers when they are middle-aged rather than senior citizens. The double indemnity rider provides twice the benefit if long-term care is needed as the result of an accident occurring before age 65. A very popular feature is to handle inflation adjustments by tying the benefit level to the consumer price increase for urban areas, instead of using a simple or compound interest rate that does not reflect actual costs. Group insurers are giving employers more options for customized plans that fit their employee profiles.[9] Another policy design frontier is the policy dividend. In February 2005, for example, New York Life Insurance approved a dividend for people who had held an LTCSelect Premier LTC policy for three years; the dividend was used to reduce the next premium. Although dividends are not guaranteed, the company announced that it would provide dividends to both new purchasers and existing holders; 40 states had already approved the change.[10]

NAIC: DEFINING LONG-TERM CARE INSURANCE

The National Association of Insurance Commissioners (NAIC) defines long-term care insurance as a policy or rider that covers at least 12 consecutive months of "necessary or medically necessary diagnostic, preventive, therapeutic, rehabilitative, maintenance or personal care services" in any setting outside an acute care hospital.[11] Therefore, LTCI definitely covers custodial care, not just acute care that is eligible for Medicare reimbursement. LTCI policies also have the potential to cover care rendered at home or in a community setting such as an adult day health center, not just institutional care in a nursing home. Although the most common method of providing benefits is indemnity, the Model Act also permits benefits to be made on an expense incurred, prepaid, or other basis.

Long-term care coverage can come from a stand-alone policy or a rider, either "qualified" for tax purposes or non-qualified. Annuities and life insurance that provide incidental long-term care benefits fall under the NAIC definition, but Medigap, hospital, major medical, disability, and accident insurance do not. Life insurance death benefits that can be accelerated based on terminal illness or institutionalization are not considered long-term care insurance.

A group policy is issued to one or more employer, labor organization, or professional or trade organization.[12] In such a circumstance, the entity holds the policy and the individuals who are covered under it receive certificates. However, because most LTCI policies are sold to individuals, the discussion in this chapter largely centers upon the individual policy, with references to the policy-holder rather than the certificate-holder.

NAIC standards permit state commissioners to adopt disclosure regulations, dealing with issues such as:

- Terms of renewability;

- Eligibility;

- Non-duplication of coverage with other insurance;

- Dependent coverage;

- Treatment of preexisting conditions;

- Continuation, conversion or termination of policies;

- Waiting periods; and

- Limitations on coverage.[13]

A 2003 paper by the Kaiser Family Foundation looks at the history of state regulation of LTCI. The authors note that LTCI was introduced as a product in 1974 but was not widely marketed until the 1980s. NAIC's first Model Act was drafted in 1987 with the most recent amendments in 2000, and the first Model Regulation in 1988.

In 1989, the NAIC prohibited post-claims underwriter (see below); in 1990, the suitability requirement was added; minimum benefit triggers were defined in 1995, and the rules for applying for rate increases were set out in 2000. Although all the states now have at least some laws regulating LTCI, and some of them impose stricter consumer protection than the NAIC, only 12 states cover all four of the major consumer protection topics (replacement, suitability, post-claims underwriting, and benefit triggers). Twenty-one states regulate in three of these areas, 10 in two areas, and five in only one. The standard for replacement of policies is the most popular, having been adopted by 47 states. Thirty states have adopted the NAIC suitability standards, 42 the post-claims underwriting standard, and 18 have adopted the benefit triggers standard.[14]

Banned Practices

The NAIC Model Act forbids certain insurer practices:[15]

- Using the insured's age or deterioration of mental or physical health as a reason for canceling, non-renewing, or otherwise terminating a policy;

- Imposing a new waiting period when coverage is converted or replaced within the same company–except if the insured has voluntarily chosen to increase the benefits under the policy; and

- Limiting coverage to skilled nursing facilities or providing significantly more coverage for institutional skilled care than custodial care.

The most restrictive definition of "preexisting condition" that the NAIC will allow for an individual policy is "a condition for which medical advice or treatment was recommended by, or received from a provider of health care services, within six (6) months preceding the effective date of coverage of an insured person." Furthermore, the preexisting condition limitation can only be applied to losses and institutional confinements occurring within six months of the effective date of coverage.[16] The NAIC makes it clear that insurers can do medical underwriting based on their own standards and can legitimately use the application form to collect the applicant's complete medical history.

The NAIC forbids prior hospitalization and step-down requirements in LTCI policies. That is, benefits must be made available to individuals who live in the community, even if they have not been hospitalized, and even if they have not received a higher level of care before receiving a lower level of care.[17] This is an important advantage of LTCI over Medicare and is a better fit with the usual pattern of care in which senior citizens start out reasonably healthy and functional but require more and more care over time.

However, a prior institutionalization requirement can be imposed in certain limited contexts: waiver of premium; recuperative benefits; and benefits for post-confinement and post-acute care. Any such requirement must be clearly disclosed and benefits cannot be conditioned on a prior institutional stay of more than 30 days.[18]

The Model Regulation requires all policies (whether qualified or not) to include both cognitive impairment and activities of daily living (ADL) triggers.[19] The most restrictive permissible provision is dependency in three ADLs. The insurer must consider bathing, continence, dressing, eating, toileting, and transferring to be ADLs and can add more ADLs to the policy definition. But, a person dependent in three ADLs must be entitled to coverage. Dependency is defined as a need for the hands-on assistance of another person to perform the ADL.

Consumer Protection

LTCI buyers have the right to return their policies within 30 days of delivery for a full refund of premium no matter why the applicant is dissatisfied. This right must be disclosed on the first page of the policy.[20]

When the initial solicitation is made to a potential buyer, he or she must be given an outline of coverage in the standard format prescribed by the local commissioner. If the policy is solicited by an agent, the agent must provide the outline of coverage before offering an application or enrollment form. With direct response solicitations, the outline must be presented together with the application or enrollment form.

The Model Act requires the outline of coverage to include:[21]

- A description of the policy's principal benefits and coverage;

- The policy's principal exclusions, reductions, and limitations;

- The insurer's terms for continuing the policy, including any reserved right to change the premiums;

- Terms for returning the policy and obtaining a premium refund;

- A brief description of the relationship of cost of care and benefits; and

- Disclosure that the outline is only a summary and that the full terms can be found in the policy itself.

Certificate-holders under a group policy receive a briefer summary, describing the principal benefits and coverage, exclusions, reductions, and limitations. This summary discloses that the group master policy contains the actual contract terms.[22]

When a policy is delivered, a policy summary must also be delivered for an individual life policy that provides long-term care benefits, either within the policy or through the use of a policy rider.[23] Some of the items that the summary must explain are:

- How the long-term care benefits interact with other aspects of the policy;

- The amount and duration of benefits and any guaranteed lifetime benefits;

- Any exclusions, reductions, or limitations on the long-term care benefits;

- Any guarantees as to the costs of insurance charges; and

- Current and projected maximum lifetime benefits.

Disclosure must also be made if inflation protection is not applicable. Purchasers must be informed of the effect of exercising their other rights under the policy.

The Model Act requires a monthly report to the policyholder if and when accelerated death benefits are in pay status.[24]

A new §9 of the Model Act has been proposed requiring eight hours of training before an agent will be permitted to solicit individual LTCI purchases, and supplemented by eight update hours every two years. Training may not be company-specific. The instructional topics include federal and state rules, the types of long-term care services available, the tax consequences of buying a qualified policy, the importance of inflation protection, and the standards and guidelines for determining the suitability of a policy.[25]

Suitability

In 2000, the NAIC adopted Model Regulation provisions on suitability, requiring insurers to develop their own standards for suitability (e.g., types of coverage and premium levels appropriate for persons in various situations) and train their agents not to make unsuitable sales. Applicants must be asked for significant amounts of information about their financial needs, LTC goals, existing coverage, and ability to pay (involving discussion of assets, income, and investments).[26] Clients must be given a personal finance worksheet to fill out.

Incontestability

During the first six months an LTCI policy is in force, the insurer has the right to rescind the policy or deny a claim that would otherwise be valid, if it can show that the insured engaged in misrepresentation that was material to acceptance of the application. Once the policy has been in force for six months, but for less than two years, the policy can be rescinded and claims can be denied on proof of misrepresentation by the insured that was both material to acceptance of the application and also related to the actual condition for which the insured has applied for benefits. In other words, in this situation, a misrepresentation about the insured's cardiac condition will not affect an application for benefits required by a hip fracture, although the insurer would be justified in rejecting a claim for home care after an episode of heart failure.[27] The draft under consideration in mid-2005 would also permit the policy to be contested on the basis of intentional, knowing misrepresentation about health.

The 2005 draft makes policies incontestable after two years.

The Model Act also forbids "field underwriting" based on medical or health status unless the LTCI producer is not compensated based on the number of policies sold.[28] This means that the agent or third-party administrator is not allowed to issue a policy, only to have it rescinded later by the home office, once the applicant's true health status becomes known. In contrast, it is quite legitimate for the agent to accept applications that are contingent on satisfactory health underwriting.

Once benefits have actually been paid under the policy, the insurer may be able to rescind the policy (if the appropriate conditions are met), thus preventing future obligations, but the insurer may not recover benefit payments that have already been made.

Nonforfeiture Provisions

Whether long-term care insurance policies should include nonforfeiture provisions is one of the most controversial areas in LTCI regulation. It is not known for certain what percentage of people in a particular age range will ever use home care or go to a nursing home, and it certainly is not known which individuals within the group will do so. Generally, at any given time about 5% of senior citizens live in a nursing home and about 45% will spend time in a nursing home at some point. Certainly one reason for consumers reluctance to purchase LTCI is the belief (whether rational or not) that they will never need this coverage.

On one side of the controversy, it can be argued that it is unfair for insured persons who do not use the long-term care coverage to pay premiums and receive no return. It can also be argued that nonforfeiture features are an incentive to purchase. On the other side, it can be argued that insurers cannot stay in the LTCI market unless they can earn a reasonable profit, which they will not be able to do if they must turn over a large percentage of their premium base.

The way the NAIC has resolved the debate is to require insurers to offer their customers the option of purchasing a policy or rider providing nonforfeiture benefits. That is to say, the benefit must always be offered, but need not be included in every policy. Policies that include nonforfeiture benefits must have the same coverage elements, eligibility rules, benefit triggers, benefit lengths, and loss ratios as policies purchased by individuals who have declined the nonforfeiture benefit.

The NAIC Model Regulation defines the required nonforfeiture benefit as a "shortened benefit period providing paid-up long-term care insurance coverage after lapse."[29] The amount and frequency of benefits must continue the same as prior to the lapse (but will not increase), but the maximum amount to be paid or days of benefits will be set to equal 100% of the premiums already paid. The standard nonforfeiture credit is 100% of premiums paid, but not less than 30 days' nursing home benefit (measured as of the time the policy lapses). Insurers can provide other shortened benefit period options, as long as they are at least as generous as the standard. Nonforfeiture credits can be applied to any covered services, not just nursing home care. However, the total of benefits provided while the policy was in premium-paying status, plus those offered when it is in paid-up status, should not exceed the maximum benefits that would have applied if the policy had remained in premium-paying status.

Policyholders who decide not to purchase this protection must be offered a contingent benefit upon lapse that can be used during a specified period after a "substantial" increase in the premium.[30] The younger the policyholder, the larger the premium increase that will be deemed substantial, ranging from 200% at ages 29 and under to 10% over age 90. That is, they must be given a chance to reduce their policy benefits or convert to reduced paid-up insurance so that coverage will continue, albeit at a lower level, without the need to pay the increased premium for full coverage.

The current draft of the Model Regulation requires insurers to inform policyholders within 12 months when a new policy series is made available in the state covering a new and innovative kind of care (unless the policyholder is or previously has been in claim status, or would not be eligible to apply for the coverage). Insurers are permitted to require underwriting to elect the new coverage. The new services can be covered via riders (with a separate premium based on attained age), by exchanging the existing policy for a new one, or by another program that has been approved by the state's insurance commissioner. But notice is not required for new proprietary policy series that are intended for limited distribution channels.[31]

Section 27 of the Model Regulation requires insurers to allow insureds to reduce their coverage (and lower their premiums) in at least three ways: by cutting back on the lifetime maximum benefit, by reducing the nursing home per diem and the home care benefit, or by converting a comprehensive policy into one that covers only home care or only nursing home care. If a policy is about to lapse, the insurer must disclose the option of maintaining the policy in more limited form. Insureds facing a premium increase must also be given the chance to cut back in these ways.

Rate Stability

Although individual rate increases are seldom a possibility in LTCI, class-wide premium increases can occur, and there have been some instances of very high increases, either causing the policies to be dropped because they are no longer affordable, or requiring financial sacrifices on the part of insureds to maintain the policies. A class action lawsuit in the District of North Dakota was settled in 2000 on this issue.[32]

In 2004, an AARP Bulletin profiled a senior couple who had owned LTCI since 1995. In August 2003, they were hit with a 50% rate hike: premiums for the two rose from $3,245 a year to $4,862. When they purchased the policy, they were told "premiums can never go up," but that referred to individual increases; the insurer got approval for a class increase. The AARP Public Policy Institute's research showed that in 2003, seven of the top ten LTCI companies had fairly significant premium increases, and that rate increase requests are usually approved by state regulators.[33]

However, there may be a trend away from automatic approval of all requested increases. Late in 2005, Delaware's insurance commissioner rejected several LTCI insurers' requests for 25-43% increases, on the grounds that the increases reached far above the maximum annual increases that, in obedience to Delaware law, they disclosed in their marketing materials. Commissioner Matt Denn said that his agency's financial analysis showed that the increases were excessive and could not be justified by actuarial or market conditions. Delaware law also penalizes overcharges by fines of up to $10,000.[34]

LTCI premiums vary widely: for instance, among 10 companies selling LTCI, the average annual premium for purchase at age 60 ranged from $604.08 to $1070.21; at 70, the range was from $1462.32 to $2191.38. In other words, some policies cost about 50% more than comparable policies. But it is hard to say which policy has the "right" premium. A high premium could be exploitive–but a low premium could be inadequate in the long run, requiring a later rate increase or a spiral of rate increases. Inadequate premiums, in turn, could be due to deliberate manipulation or simply lack of adequate actuarial information to make pricing decisions. In short, not only is it important for insurers to select the right premium, but that consumers rely on premium stability when they choose a policy.

Model Regulation, §20 imposes a rating process that encourages the setting of initially adequate premiums (rather than unrealistic "lowball" premiums that will have to be raised frequently or significantly). Insurers that apply for a rate increase must show why the increase is required. If an increase is later found to be unnecessary, the insurer must pay refunds to policyholders. Insurers are also obligated to issue replacement policies with lower benefits, without underwriting, if customers are unwilling to pay the increased cost of their current policies.

The prior versions of the Model Regulation imposed a loss ratio requirement of 60% on a company's initial rate filing: that is, at least 60% of the premiums collected must be paid out in the form of benefits. This requirement is removed by the August 17, 2000 amendments.

However, the amendments say that when state regulators grant a class-wide rate increase, the insurer must satisfy a loss ratio of 58% of initial premiums and 85% of the increased portion of the premium. An even higher–70%–loss ratio is imposed on a company that is granted an exceptional increase in response to changes in state law or unexpected increases in utilization. Furthermore, the amendments provide new enforcement power to state insurance regulators. A company that persists in deliberately setting inadequate initial premiums (to motivate consumers to buy policies that will become the subject of "bait and switch" tactics) can be banned from the LTCI market for up to five years.

The amendments also increase an insurers' disclosure obligations for LTCI policies (other than noncancellable policies, whose premiums cannot be increased under any circumstances):

- The insurer must disclose its history of rate increases going back 10 years;

- The insurer must disclose that rate increases may be granted in the future, and what the policyholder's options are if they are granted;

- The applicant must sign a statement acknowledging an awareness that premiums may increase;

- Agents and brokers must be trained to explain the potential rate increases;

- Whenever a policy is sold, the agent must provide copies of the disclosure forms and explain the contingent benefit on lapse; and

- The outline of coverage must give contact information for someone who can be reached if the applicant purchaser has questions about the policy.

As of 2003, only 21 states had adopted this NAIC standard, but several more states indicated an intention to do so in the future.[35]

LTCI UNDERWRITING

Theoretically, healthy senior citizens should find it easy to understand the benefits of buying LTCI. In practice, consideration of LTCI (and other potentially distressing topics) tends to be deferred, often until the individual's health has deteriorated enough to make long-term care a topic of increasing personal relevance. At that point, it might seem a waste of time even to try to purchase LTCI coverage. However, although detailed insurer-specific information is hard to find,[36] there seems to be a wide variation in acceptance rates. In one survey, the average survey respondent accepted 47% of LTCI applications at the preferred rate, but the range within the respondents was from 3% to 74%.

A review of underwriting guidelines from 23 companies found that AIDS, cirrhosis of the liver, multiple sclerosis, muscular dystrophy, and Parkinson's Disease were considered grounds for rejection of an application. However, companies varied widely in their attitude toward selling LTCI to diabetics. Some declined insulin-dependent diabetics while others declined only those requiring large insulin dosages or already suffering diabetes-related complications. Areas of increasing concern in underwriting are osteoporosis and cognitive decline in applicants.[37]

In mid-2005, the *Wall Street Journal* reported that underwriting had gotten much stricter over the previous five years: in 2000, the majority of insurers would accept an applicant who was an insulin-dependent diabetic; by 2005 the majority would decline the application.[38] However, after the Deficit Reduction Act of 2005 (DRA '05), as insurers seek to expand the number of policies sold, perhaps they will relax standards somewhat.[39]

It has been said that LTCI underwriting is still more of an art than science, because insurers do not yet have disease-specific actuarial data available to them. Companies also do not have the claims experience to predict which applicants are likely to suffer functional or cognitive impairments that will trigger claims in the future.

However, insurers recognize that it is important to develop this information (for instance, using the company's own records of its experience in LTCI sales and claims) and create valid risk classes that evaluate the applicant's medical status and how "co-morbidity" (presence of more than one disease or condition at once, e.g., diabetes and heart disease) affects the insured person.

It has been estimated that about 20% of applicants are denied for health reasons. Hypothetically, if all Americans applied for LTCI at age 65, 12-23% would probably be rejected; rejections would probably increase to 20-31% of applicants at age 75.

Insurers have two main motivations for creating risk classes for LTCI, instead of having a simple "accepted/denied" model. First, the ability to offer attractive discounted preferred rates can improve policy sales to healthy applicants. Also, it may be more economical to broaden the base of potential purchasers by adding higher-price substandard risk classes, amortizing the agent's time investment and the company's administrative expenses over a larger group of purchasers.[40]

Data is emerging that insurers wanting to control their claim costs should control their underwriting practices. "Loose" underwriting companies seldom do face-to-face appraisals, and might not even ask applicants for medical records. Companies with "tight" underwriting practices obtain medical records even from young (under-50) applicants, and usually require face-to-face assessments from applicants over 71, whereas moderate companies do not require face-to-face interviews until age 80, and only require medical records from half the under-80 applicants.

According to the actuarial firm Milliman & Robertson Inc., tightening underwriting standards results in lower claim costs. For all LTCI policies in force for three years, the average claims ratio is 38%. For policies in force between five and nine years, the overall average claims ratio is 57%, but loose underwriters had a claims ratio of 77%, and tight writers only 49%.[41]

In short, giving clients accurate advice about LTCI requires an individualized inquiry into the availability of insurance at premium, standard, or sub-standard rates. Unless the client is already severely ill, it should not be assumed that insurance is unavailable.

The Lewis, Wilkin and Merlis research cited above looks at the effect of underwriting assumptions on premiums. They contrasted "optimistic" and "conservative" companies. The optimistic company assumes that its underwriting process has kept out most of the unduly bad risks. The conservative company charges a 6% higher premium because it assumes that its underwriting had a weaker effect.

The optimistic company assumes that 5% of policyholders will let their policies lapse; the conservative insurer expects only a 2% lapse rate—and furthermore expects the sickest policyholders, those who will make the largest claims, will be the most likely to retain their policies rather than letting them lapse. Assuming the lower lapse rate will require the premium to increase by 26%, with a further 8% adjustment based on the assumption that the healthier customers are more likely to lapse. The optimistic insurer sets its pricing based on a belief that policyholders will use 30% less long-term care than the population in general, whereas the conservative insurer assumes the utilization rate will be the same—so its premiums will be 42% higher for this reason than the optimistic insurer. The optimistic company projects earning 7% interest on its reserves. The conservative company expects only a 5% return, and therefore charges an 11% higher premium for this reason. The optimistic company expects a loss ratio of 66% (that is, two-thirds of premiums earned will be paid out in the form of claims). The conservative insurer anticipates a 58% loss ratio, which adds another 7% to the premium. The aggregate result is that, if the optimistic company charges $840 a year for its policy, the conservative company would charge 149% more—$2,088 a year.

The researchers point out that if the first insurer's optimism is misplaced, it could need to apply for rate increases over time—and the longer it takes to reach this conclusion, the larger the rate increase that will be required.

LIFE INSURANCE LTC BENEFITS

Any life insurance policy or rider that is sold as long-term care or nursing home insurance must comply with the NAIC Long-Term Care Insurance Model Act as well as with applicable life insurance regulations. The Model Act also deals with individual life insurance policies that provide long-term care coverage within the policy or by rider.

When the policy is delivered, it must be accompanied by a policy summary that explains the relationship between long-term care benefits and other components of the policy (e.g., by deduction from the eventual death benefits). The summary must show the amount of benefits, length of benefits, and any guaranteed lifetime benefits, as well as exclusions, reductions, and limitations of benefits.

If it is appropriate for the policy type, the summary must disclose the effect of exercising other rights under the policy, disclose guarantees affecting the long-term care costs of insurance charges, and the current and projected maximum lifetime benefits. Further, the summary must note that inflation protection is not available under the policy.

If and when the long-term care benefit is triggered and is in payment status, the policyholder must be given a monthly report explaining the LTC benefits paid during the month, any changes in the policy (typically, reduced cash values or death benefits) resulting from the payment of these benefits, and the remaining LTC benefits still available for future use.[42]

Another option is a life insurance policy that creates a "reservoir" of twice the death benefit to pay for long-term care expenses. Such a policy can be purchased with a single premium, on a 10-pay basis, or with ordinary recurring premiums. A single premium policy might be financed by using money from a certificate of deposit, money market account, annuity, or IRA, or by converting another life insurance policy pursuant to IRC section 1035. If the long-term care benefits are accessed shortly after purchase, four years of benefits, with a monthly benefit of 2% of the reservoir, would be available; if benefits are used later, additional benefits will accrue.

A late-2004 article describes the appeal of such "linked" (also called "combination" or "hybrid") policies as the chance to reduce risk by collecting at least something under the policy under either the scenario that the insured person needs long-term care, or that he or she dies without needing such care.

This article notes that linked policies are usually whole life or universal life policies with long-term care riders providing benefits for a term such as two to six years. They are often sold for a single premium, which often exceeds $50,000, making this an option for those with a substantial amount of cash. (However, people who are not rich might inherit a lump sum, or receive a distribution from a pension plan, or might sell a large family home and move into a less-expensive, easier-to-manage condominium unit; they might also free up funds from low-interest savings accounts.) Hybrid policies "accelerate" payment of the death benefit if long-term care is needed; if it is not, the policy pays off like a regular life insurance policy when the insured person dies.

Linked policies have not attained great popularity. LTCI as a whole is not widely purchased, and through 2002, only 3% of LTCI policies were hybrids.[43]

QUALIFIED POLICIES

The Health Insurance Portability and Accountability Act of 1996 (HIPAA) cleared up some important tax questions about long-term care insurance and enacted a new Internal Revenue Code Section, 7702B, to provide favorable tax treatment for "qualified" policies. Under Section 7702B, all qualified policies must meet certain standards for benefits and consumer protection as set forth in the NAIC Model Act and Model Regulation.

Nevertheless, insurers have fairly broad discretion in designing their policies. Congress did not use HIPAA to impose the same kind of standardization that it earlier imposed on Medigap policies. The Taxpayer Relief Act of 1997, IRS Notice 97-31, and long-term care regulations clarify the HIPAA rules and provide some guidance in applying them.[44]

A qualified policy is an individual or group policy that offers coverage of qualified long-term care services, but nothing else; it can also be a life insurance policy that has an LTCI rider. Qualified contracts must be guaranteed renewable. They may not have cash value. Any dividends or premium refunds must be used to increase future benefits or reduce future premiums, but refunds can be made when the insured person dies or the contract is surrendered or canceled.[45]

The purpose of an LTCI policy is to provide "qualified long-term care services" to a "chronically ill individual" (as defined under an ADL test, a severe cognitive impairment test, or other tests grandfathered in or allowed by statute). That is, all qualified policies must have both an ADL trigger and a cognitive impairment trigger, but may not impose other requirements, such as medical necessity, on benefits.[46]

Qualified long-term care services are "necessary diagnostic, preventive, therapeutic, curing, treating, mitigating and rehabilitative services, and maintenance or personal care services" furnished to a chronically ill individual under a health care professional's plan of care.[47] Note that there is no requirement that the services be able to cure or even improve the condition–maintenance and custodial care are covered.

A chronically ill individual is one who has suffered a loss of functional capacity so that, for a period of at least 90 days, he or she is unable to perform two or more ADLs without substantial assistance.[48] (The 90-day period is not a policy waiting period; it is intended to draw a distinction between temporary changes in ability that are within the domain of acute health insurance, and lasting or permanent changes that fall under LTCI.)

HIPAA includes a list of six standard ADLs (eating, toileting, transferring, bathing, dressing, and continence). Qualified policies must either refer to all six of these or pick five of them to determine whether or not a person is ADL-impaired.[49] Insurers that sell qualified policies cannot define their own ADLs. It should be noted that bathing is usually the first ADL with which older people experience difficulty, so excluding bathing from the list of covered ADLs would have the effect of significantly limiting claims. Substantial assistance means either the physical assistance of another person or having another person nearby in case of need for assistance.

A chronically ill individual is also one who suffers from severe cognitive impairment,[50] which is defined as Alzheimer's disease or other condition causing a comparable loss or deterioration of intellectual capacity, leading to impairment in memory or orientation that can be measured by scientific tests. Ability to perform ADLs is irrelevant to this test.

Qualified policies are not allowed to pay or reimburse any expenses that could be covered by Medicare (or that would be covered except for co-payment responsibilities). However, qualified policies are allowed to cover expenses for which Medicare is a secondary payor. Medicare-eligible amounts can be covered by qualified policies that make periodic (e.g., per diem) payments that are not tied to actual expenses.

BENEFIT TRIGGERS

The Model Regulation has two sections dealing with benefit triggers: one addressing the topic in general[51] and a second for qualified policies.[52] The general section requires both cognitive impairment and ADL triggers. The ADL trigger must not require deficiencies in more than three ADLs. Bathing, continence, dressing, eating, toileting, and transferring must be treated as ADLs. The insurer can add additional ADLs as long as they are defined in the policy. A person is deemed to be deficient in an ADL if the hands-on assistance of another person is needed to perform the activity. For the cognitive impairment trigger the test is whether verbal cueing from, or supervision by, another person is needed to perform the activity. ADL and cognitive impairment assessment must be made by professionals. The policy must clearly describe the appeals procedure for benefit determinations.

The section of the Model Regulation dealing with qualified policies adopts the HIPAA requirement of a cognitive trigger plus an ADL trigger, this time defined as inability to perform one or two ADLs for an expected period of at least 90 days, resulting from loss of functional capacity. Generally, an insured will be considered to have met the requirements if, within the preceding 12-month period, a licensed health care provider has certified that the insured has met the requirements and the provider has prescribed the qualified long-term care insurance services under a plan of care.[53] Only the statutory ADLs (bathing, continence, dressing, eating, toileting, transferring) can be used; the insurer cannot use different or additional ADLs to determine access to benefits under a qualified policy.

THE LTCI MARKETPLACE

According to the NAIC, in 1992 about 1.7 million elderly persons owned LTCI–a number that grew to approximately 4.1 million in 1998. But in 1998 Medigap insurance was a much more popular product, with about 23 million elderly persons–some two-thirds of the senior citizen population–owning a Medigap policy.

By the early 2000s, the number of Medigap owners had declined significantly—to less than one-quarter of seniors. By the end of 2002, 9.16 million LTCI policies had been sold overall, and 6.4 million were still in force. In 2002, to purchase a policy with a $150/day benefit, four years' coverage, and a 90-day elimination period would cost an average of $564 at age 50 (or $1,134 for the same coverage plus compounded inflation protection). At 65, the same policy would cost $1,337 a year without inflation protection, $2,346 a year with it; at 79, the corresponding figures are $5,330 and $7,572.

According to LIMRA, LTCI policy sales dropped 24% between 2003 (when 585,000 policies were sold) and 2004 (362,000 policies sold) and the beginning of the twenty-first century was marked by a consolidation within the LTCI market where a number of insurers exited the field and others were forced to raise their premiums (often, by 20-40% over a three-year period) to cope with investment losses, policyholders who lived longer than expected, and lapse rates that were much lower than predicted.[54]

About 60% of the users of long-term care are senior citizens; the rest are younger people with disabilities. In 2002, only about 5% of the senior citizens enrolled in Medicare lived in nursing homes (the rest lived in the community)—but the senior population is large enough that only 5% added up to about 1.6 million people. Although only a small part of the senior population lives in a nursing home at any given time, it is estimated that 44% of seniors will spend at least some time in a nursing home. About 1.3 million seniors living in the community received paid home care (from caregivers at all levels of skill) and another 5.5 million received unpaid home care from family members and friends.

One paper gives the average 2004 daily private-pay rate in nursing homes as $192, which adds up to $78,100 a year, and a semi-private rate of $169/day, or $61,700 a year. The average hourly charge for home health aides was $18, so each year of receiving three hours of care a day, five days a week would cost $14,000.[55]

Johnson and Uccello's paper, cited above, says that in 2002, 9% of adults aged 55 or older owned LTCI, but only 7% of the "near-elderly" (aged 55-64) did. Understandably, the more income and wealth a senior had, the more likely he or she was to own LTCI. In 2002, 3% of older adults with income below $20,000 a year, and 4% of those whose financial assets (i.e., savings and investments other than their home) were under $20,000 had LTCI. The proportions of wealthier older adults owning LTCI were much higher—but were still low (14% of those with income over $50,000 a year; 18% of those with financial assets of $100,000 or more).

Johnson and Uccello identified some reasons why LTCI is not a complete solution to the problem of financing quality long-term care for everyone who needs it. They quoted studies showing that in 2000, 12% of married couples and 62% of single people in the 55-61 age bracket (prime ages for purchasing LTCI) had income under $25,000 a year. In the 70-74 age group, this was true of 29% of married couples and 62% of single people. For these reasons, some studies suggest that only 10-20% of older adults can afford long-term care insurance. An additional 15% of applicants are denied for health reasons.

Group long-term care insurance came into the market in the late 1980s. As of mid-2005, about 6,600 employers (including the federal government) offered group LTCI coverage. That's twice as many as offered the coverage in 2000. Many employers like this benefit because it is typically paid for 100% by the insured, so the employer's costs are minimal.

America's Health Insurance Plans (a trade association) estimated that in 2002, almost 280,000 LTCI policies—approximately one-third of the total sales for the year—were purchased in the workplace. Other estimates, however, show that about four-fifths of LTCI policies are purchased in the individual rather than the group market. Typically, workplace purchasers are much younger than individual purchasers (an average age of 45 versus one of 60). Workplace plans often make it possible for the employees to purchase LTCI covering their parents—an attractive option for middle-aged members of the "sandwich generation" worried about their future obligations to care for sick elderly parents.

According to the American College of Life Insurance (ACLI), more than one-third of companies with 5,000 or more employees offer LTCI. So do about a quarter of mid-sized firms and at least 22 state governments. Penetration is low: typically, only about 2-10% of the eligible employees, for reasons of cost, lack of understanding about the need for the coverage, or psychological unwillingness to confront depressing issues head-on.[56]

Group policies often make provision for future health care cost increases by giving purchasers a choice between automatic benefit increase (ABI), also known as automatic inflation protection, and the option to add more coverage in the future (Future Purchase Option or FPO). Eighty percent of new group plans offer policies with automatic benefit increase provisions.

At the outset, ABI means a higher premium than FPO, but once the purchaser reaches age 67, FPO premiums are higher than ABI premiums, and become much higher at older ages. The example cited in the article is a 55-year-old government employee who would pay either $50 a month for an FPO policy or $140 a month for an ABI policy, where both provided a daily benefit of $150. If the buyer added more coverage whenever it became available, at age 75 (assuming no class increases in premium) the ABI policy would still cost $140 a month, but the FPO monthly premium would be $300. At age 79, the premium would be more than $500 a month, with the age-based increases concentrated post-retirement, when the buyer's income would probably be lower than it was pre-retirement.

FPO policies are more popular than ABI policies: 70-80% of buyers who can choose either take the FPO policy. Some consumer advocates are concerned that buyers are not fully informed about the alternatives, and opt for the policy that is initially cheaper because they don't understand the full risk of cost increases.[57]

The ACLI points out that someone who is 45 years old in 2001 could expect to spend $489,446 to spend two years in a nursing home in 2041. To fund that stay out of personal resources, he or she would have to save and invest $3,557 a year. That is about eight times the average premium for an LTCI policy with two years of coverage ($417). What about someone who might enter a nursing home at age 85 in 2023? ACLI estimates that two years in a nursing home would cost $235,432 at that time, requiring annual savings of $4,481 to pay out-of-pocket—about five times the $824 LTCI premium. Once again, the earlier the policy is purchased, the greater the savings.[58]

A 1998 survey containing details of 111 long-term care insurance products offered by 58 insurers found that, in addition to the conventional nursing home and home care coverages, most long-term care insurance policies cover assisted living, hospices, respite care (for relief of family caregivers), case management and care coordination, durable medical equipment, and bed-holds (paying to maintain a nursing home bed while the nursing home resident is temporarily hospitalized).[59]

The same survey showed a long-term care insurance annual premium range of about $700 to $1,560 for $120 per day lifetime coverage, no waiting period, including home health care, purchased at age 60. For age-70 purchase, the range was from $1,790 to $3,864 per year. In other words, the most expensive policy at a particular age range cost more than twice as much as its least expensive counterpart. However, a simple price comparison does not tell the whole story, because LTCI policies vary quite a bit in the non-core benefits they offer and insurers also vary significantly in reputation, financial soundness, and claims management.

It is interesting to note that, although the incidence of most employee benefits increases with the size of the firm, most employment-related LTCI plans are offered by small (under 500 employees) or very small (less than 100 employees) companies. Of the approximately 1500 plans in place in 1996, 432 plans had some degree of employer involvement in paying for the plan while the others were "employee-pay-all" plans. However, because the average age for purchasers under these group plans was 43, the premium was probably quite low. Employer-sponsored LTCI plans often permit employees to cover their spouses or their parents and parents-in-law. Thus, an older client who wants LTCI but feels unable to afford it may be able to find coverage through a child's (or child's spouse's) work-related policy.

INCOME TAX TREATMENT OF LTCI

Under appropriate circumstances, someone covered under a qualified LTCI policy can receive part or all of the benefits under the policy without encountering income tax liability. The amount received will be free of tax if the benefit paid to a chronically ill individual does not exceed a daily indemnity amount of $250. These figures are for 2006 and are adjusted for inflation. The Internal Revenue Code makes it clear that benefits paid under qualified policies are tax-free (subject to these limits). However, the Code does not specifically say how benefits paid from a non-qualified policy are treated for income tax purposes.[60]

There is also the potential for an income tax deduction for the purchase of a qualified LTCI policy. The Internal Revenue Code sets forth premium amounts, keyed to the taxpayer's age. LTCI premiums may be deducted up to these amounts. In 2006, the premium amounts are $280 for persons age 40 or less; $530 for ages

41 through 50; $1,060 for ages 51 through 60; $2,830 for ages 61 through 70; and $3,530 for over age 70.[61] Like the benefit limitation amounts above, the premium amounts are indexed for inflation.

Unfortunately, these amounts are not deductible per se. Instead, they are treated as potential medical expense deductions. That is, they are aggregated with all other allowable medical expenses and the actual deduction is the difference between total allowable medical expenses and 7.5% of the taxpayer's adjusted gross income.[62] For example, assume that Donald and Jennifer Platt's adjusted gross income is $109,487 for 2005, a year in which they pay LTCI premiums of $3,000 each. Donald is age 71 while Jennifer is age 67. Therefore, Donald can treat $3,400 as a potential deduction; Jennifer can treat $2,720 as one. Ironically, neither of them can take full advantage of the tax deduction: Donald, because he pays less than the potentially deductible amount, Jennifer because she pays $3,000 a year, but only $2,720 is potentially deductible. Donald and Jennifer must calculate their deduction by first finding the "floor" amount for medical expense deductions (7.5% of $109,487, or $8,211.53). They can deduct the amount by which all their unreimbursed medical expenses, including $5,720 (Donald's $3,000 plus Jennifer's $2,720) for LTCI premiums, exceeds $8,211.53.

Because LTCI premiums for qualified policies are deemed to be health insurance premiums, self-employed persons qualify for a more generous rule. For 2002 and later tax years, 100% of the premium is deductible.[63] Amounts that exceed the percentage limitation can be aggregated with other medical expenses and deducted to the extent that they exceed 7.5% of adjusted gross income.

Although federal income taxes are larger, and therefore have more of a planning impact, state income taxes are also a factor in the individual's financial picture. As of mid-2000, the following states allowed deductions or credits for LCTI premiums: Alabama, California, Colorado, Hawaii, Illinois, Indiana, Iowa, Kentucky, Maine, Maryland, Minnesota, Missouri, Montana, New York, North Carolina, North Dakota, Ohio, Oregon, Utah, Virginia, West Virginia, and Wisconsin. Bills to create or extend a deduction have also been introduced into several state legislatures.[64]

The AARP's research shows that almost all LTCI policies sold—close to 90%—satisfy the requirements for tax-qualified policies.[65]

MARKETING ISSUES

Thanks to a major study performed by LifePlans, Inc. on behalf of HIAA, published in October 2000 we now have a much clearer baseline for understanding what motivates LTCI sales among persons age 55 and over, and how this has changed as of three measuring points (1990, 1995, and 2000).[66] When the first survey was done in 1990, 1.9 million LTCI policies had been sold to persons over 55, as compared with 4.5 million in 1995, and more than 6 million in 2000.

The persons surveyed showed a willingness to use their personal savings to pay premiums as well as to pay premiums out of current income. In 1995, buyers spent an average of 6% of their income on LTCI premiums, which declined to 4.8% in 2000. Almost none of the respondents received help from their children in paying LTCI premiums. However, 52% used some of their savings for this purpose, a percentage increasing with age and declining with increasing income. For instance, 40% of buyers with income over $50,000 tapped their savings to pay premiums, versus 66% of those with income under $25,000. (Note, however, that many insurers set their suitability standards to exclude applicants with income under $20,000.)

The survey shows that buyers in 2000 were slightly younger, noticeably wealthier, and somewhat more likely to continue to be employed, than comparable persons in the sample who did not buy LTCI. The average income and asset level of LTCI buyers went up significantly between 1990 and 2000.

In 1990, only 37% of LTCI policies covered both nursing homes and home care, whereas in 2000 the vast majority (77%) did so. Comprehensive policies cost an average of 15% more than policies limited to institutional coverage. In 2000, 85% of LTCI buyers were first-time buyers; 11% replaced their policy, and only 4% added to an existing policy.

Between 1995 and 2000, the average daily benefit in LTCI policies increased 28%–more than inflation. The HIAA/LifePlans study shows that the value for the buyers' premium dollar has increased over time. In 2000, the average premium was $1,677 (up 11% from $1,505 in 1995)–but, because the policies tended to be more comprehensive, the premium would have been expected to increase 20% rather than 11%.

Johnson and Uccello's 2005 study, cited above, says that in 2002, the average annual premium for a 40-year old purchaser of a 4-year benefit, $150/day subject to a 90-day waiting period, without inflation protection, was $422. At age 50, the same policy would cost an average of $564; at 65, $1,337; and at 70, $5,330. For coverage purchased at ages 40 or 50, adding 5% inflation protection would more than double the premium, but at age 79 (as a result of the much shorter time horizon), inflation protection would add less than 50% to the premium.[67]

A recent survey by MetLife's Mature Market Institute reminds us of another factor that should influence purchase decisions and benefit selections: long-term care for persons suffering from dementia is even more expensive than long-term care in general, and it can be difficult to find a suitable facility. According to this study, only half of the nursing homes in the United States have separate dementia care units, and less than two-thirds of Assisted Living Facilities can accommodate residents with dementia. Even if a suitable placement can be found, the patient and family can expect to pay extra: perhaps $10-$25 a day more for nursing home residents in dementia units, or as much as $3,000 extra over and above an ALF's regular charges.[68]

Purchase Motivations

There are multiple motivations behind most LTCI purchases. LTCI buyers usually believe that the risk of needing long-term care is greater than non-buyers do. About twice as many buyers as non-buyers strongly agree that it is important to plan now to handle LTCI risks. Non-buyers, on the other hand, are twice as likely as buyers to believe that the government will pay for whatever long-term care they require. About one-third of LTCI buyers say their primary motivation is protecting their assets and estate. Another 45% say they are motivated by tax benefits–but 62% could not say whether or not their policy was tax-qualified! Other reasons cited for purchasing LTCI are guaranteeing the affordability of long-term care that is needed, and protecting the buyer's living standards.

Purchasers are usually influenced by several people in the purchase decision: financial planners and insurance professionals as well as family members (especially spouses, because children usually have little input into the purchasing process). A large majority of both buyers and non-buyers have a positive opinion of insurance agents, agreeing with the statements that they are knowledgeable, understand coverage options, recommend the best policy for each client's needs, and are good listeners.

At the 2004 NAIC fall meeting, AARP's survey about consumer need for LTCI information was on the agenda to help NAIC update its LTCI Model Regulation (which has been adopted in some form by 36 states; 25 states have adopted the amendments dealing with rating practices and enhanced disclosure). Most (79%) of the 836 survey recipients owned LTCI. Sixty-four percent knew how long their insurer had been in business, and 57% knew the company's financial rating—but only 24% knew the ratio of claims filed to claims paid. About half (49% and 47% respectively) knew the size and frequency of premium increases on their policies. But more than half (54%) said that they were not informed of the number of complaints against the insurer. Of sample participants who believed they were informed buyers, 70% said the information available to them made them more confident about choosing an insurer, 73% said they felt more confident choosing a policy.

As for survey recipients who did not own LTCI, 83% said the speed at which the premium increases is an important factor in making an informed decision, and 82% said the number of complaints against the insurer is.[69]

Opinions of Non-Buyers

In all three surveys (1990, 1995, and 2000), non-buyers cited the cost of LTCI as the main barrier to purchase. However, in 1990, 87% of non buyers said that the LTCI product was too confusing to purchase; only 46% agreed with this statement in 2000. In 1990, close to three-quarters (71%) of non-buyers did not believe that, if they ever were in a position to make a claim, the insurer would not pay benefits as stated. Only 44% of non-buyer respondents agreed with this statement in 2000.

Non-buyers said they might be willing to buy LTCI if they could deduct the entire premium; if the government offered a stop-loss program once insurance benefits were exhausted; or if they trusted policy premiums to remain stable. About one out of seven to one out of eight non-buyers expressed willingness to purchase LTCI, paying the premium appropriate for their age, under the right circumstances. However, non-buyers said that they were willing to pay an average of $924 a year for LTCI protection–only about half of what it would actually cost.

One depressing effect on LTCI purchases is that many people overestimate the cost of long-term care insurance while simultaneously underestimating the cost of long-term care itself. According to General Electric's Genworth Financial unit, in 2004 the average cost of all kinds of long-term care (including home care and Assisted Living Facilities as well as nursing homes) was $72,240 a year.[70]

LIMRA's 2002 survey of retirees (the first number in each pair) and pre-retirees gave their reasons for not purchasing LTCI. 67% and 54% respectively said that the insurance was too expensive. 28%/25% said they don't need it. 21%/17% expected Medicare to pay for their long-term care needs, 14% of retirees but no pre-retirees expected Medicaid to pay; 19%/17% said they had enough assets to pay for care; 9% and 14% found the topic too depressing to think about, 9/11% found it too complicated; 6/5% said that LTCI was not recommended for their situation; and 9/5% said they would not qualify if they applied for a policy.[71]

Effective Marketing

Unquestionably, LTCI marketing is difficult. The agent must learn a lot of difficult technical information and communicate it intelligibly to potential customers who may be psychologically unwilling to make meaningful plans or who may be hampered by misconceptions about long-term care and insurance coverage.

A 2004 study by MetLife showed that most American mid-life and older adults (ages 40-70) lack the information they need to make informed long-term care planning decisions. Close to 40% think that long-term care is covered by Medicare, and people over 70 often expect that their children will meet their care needs. According to LTC specialist Kathy Halverson, educational efforts are most likely to succeed if they target people in their forties and fifties (especially because this group often has responsibility for aging parents). She suggests that once a contact is established, it's a good idea to follow up by sending trustworthy objective information (for example, the NAIC Shopper's Guide to LTCI or relevant articles) to keep your name in front of the prospect's eyes.[72]

Management consultants Milliman Inc. suggest that agents are losing sales because they are stressing multi-year benefits, when most claims are for relatively short periods. Milliman's figures show that only 1.4% of LTCI claims are for five years or longer. However, that could change as sales are made to younger people, because there is the potential for claims based on disability caused by accidents or disease other than aging-related ailments. When they analyzed 2003 data for unlimited-claims policies, 4.3% of the claims lasted five years or more and, because some of the claims were ongoing, the final figure could be higher. Close to 10% of policies with two years of benefits were terminated for exhaustion; this was also true of 8% of three-year policies and only 5% of five-year policies. However, the three-year policies were about 39% less expensive than unlimited-period policies, and two-year policies cost up to 53% less than unlimited ones, so some buyers will opt for some protection if they cannot afford full-spectrum protection.

Bob Miller (LTC Financial Partners, Washington state) says that affordability options can be a smokescreen: customers are often receptive to a personally tailored plan, such as a "short, fat" plan (high reimbursement over a limited claims period). For couples, he suggests a shared-policy rider (which adds 10-15% of the cost) but gives each spouse four years of benefits with carry-over of unused benefits to the surviving spouse.[73]

Wilma G. Anderson suggests marketing to seasonal populations (like "snowbirds" who flock to warm states in the winter) via seminars, and doing direct mail to full-year residents in the off-season. She suggests that it takes an average of nine contacts (e.g., three letters, three seminar invitations, and three advertisements) to get a potential client to respond. The initial sale is not only important in itself, but as a source of referrals and sales of additional products. Anderson suggests annuities as a comparatively easy first sale because they carry less emotional baggage than life insurance or LTCI.[74]

ASSESSING THE CLIENT'S OBJECTIVE

Not all middle-aged and older persons purchase LTCI for the same reasons. There are several ways that LTCI can fit into an elder care plan. Selection of one objective over another is a matter of personal taste and style, rather than choosing a valid over an invalid objective.

Some purchasers are extremely interested in securing coverage of most or all LTCI costs. Clients having this "front-end" objective will want to select a policy with no waiting period or a short waiting period; a broad spectrum of benefits; and a high daily benefit (probably with the home care benefit close to or at 100% of the institutional benefit). Such purchasers may prefer a qualified policy because of its broader range of coverage triggers, especially if they qualify for tax benefits.

Clients with a "back-end" objective see the possibility of a prolonged nursing home stay or a need for extensive home care as a catastrophic financial event but believe that there is less than a 50% chance of it happening to them. Therefore, they are interested in limiting their LTCI premium by accepting a higher degree of risk but want to be prepared if their worst-case scenario comes true. They will therefore accept a longer waiting period (during which they will use savings to pay the full cost of care out-of-pocket) but will want a four-year or lifetime duration of coverage. They may also be willing to accept a smaller daily benefit on the theory that they can manage copayments but not the full cost of care. In many instances, the back-end objective will appeal to an individual who has significant assets (and perhaps a fairly low income for the level of assets) and is extremely interested in protecting those assets and in estate planning.

In 2004, the *Wall Street Journal* noted increasing availability of policies with longer elimination periods—six months, one year, or even four years. True, such policies mean that the insured person will have to make a substantial up-front payment at the beginning of the stay, but he or she will be covered against catastrophic costs of a nursing home stay that continues for a number of years.

Increasing the deductible is one way to make the policy more affordable. The article cited a policy issued to a healthy 40-year-old man, with three years of coverage and a $150 daily maximum. John Hancock would charge $1,398 a year, and UnumProvident would charge $794 a year (highlighting the company-to-company variation in premiums) for a policy with a 30-day deductible. By raising the deductible to 90 days, the John Hancock premium would fall to $1,165; with a full one-year deductible, John Hancock would charge the 40-year-old purchaser $932 a year, and UnumProvident would charge $529/year. However, state laws in many states restrict deductibles to, e.g., 90 days.

PLANNING TIP: See http://ltcq.net/index.php?action=needs (no www) for a calculator for LTCI policy needs. The federal Department of Health and Human Services' long-term care planning kit (covering financial planning and home modifications as well as LTCI) can be obtained by calling 1-866-PLAN-LTC (752-6482); the TTY number is 877-486-2048.[75]

Mark Gebhart (President, Commercial Markets Insurance Cos. Inc.) emphasizes the importance of buying early—perhaps even when the customer is in his or her forties—to avoid the risk that older prospects will not be able to qualify. Younger buyers can also lock in good-health discounts. Gebhart suggests using Health Savings Accounts in conjunction with limited-pay (e.g., 20-pay) LTCI policies.

Chuck Eberle of American Insurnet Agency says that older boomers can use some income from their retirement savings to purchase LTCI. It they can't buy a lifetime benefit, a 2-4 year policy still provides meaningful protection, and if they can't afford a policy with compound inflation protection, they can opt for a higher daily benefit initially (e.g., $130 rather than $100). If there is more life insurance in the portfolio than the plan requires, perhaps entering into a life settlement will provide funds that can be used to pay LTCI premiums. (The yield of selling the policy should be compared to what could be obtained by surrendering the policy for its cash value.) However, taking a 180-day rather than a 90-day waiting period doesn't reduce the premium much, and there is a real risk that any stay that lasts 90 days will extend to 180 days and further, so it is likely that significant out of pocket payment would be required.[76]

TO "Q" OR NOT TO "Q"?

Some prospective purchasers will find themselves faced with a choice between qualified and non-qualified policies in selecting their desired benefit package. The question then becomes whether to select the qualified or non-qualified plan. Qualified plans must furnish extensive disclosures to potential buyers and must offer certain forms of consumer protection. However, it is quite likely that issuers of non-qualified plans will furnish at least as much disclosure and a good insurance professional will respond to clients' questions and will provide them whatever information they need for an informed purchase even if it is not mandated by federal law.

The purchaser should try to forecast how and when the policy will be used, although admittedly this is difficult. The point is to determine how likely it is that a particular kind of care or service will be needed that is covered by the qualified policy but not by the non-qualified one, or vice versa. The next question is whether the individual client will obtain any tax benefit from purchasing a qualified policy and, if so, how large the benefit will be. The tax benefit (the potential deduction available in the client's income tax bracket) should be subtracted from the qualified policy's premium to compare the real cost of the two plans.

COORDINATING LTCI AND MEDICAID

Before the passage of Medicaid provisions in DRA '05 (see Chapter 6), individuals who wanted to make large-scale transfers of assets could easily use LTCI as a component in an overall Medicaid plan. By making sure that they had enough private insurance coverage to provide benefits during the penalty period, they could be reasonably sure that either the transfers would be made before the three-year look-back period; that the penalty period would expire before they made a Medicaid application; or that if the Medicaid application.

As Chapter 6 now shows, Medicaid planning is much more difficult, with a five-year look-back instead of three years, and with the penalty period starting when the application is made rather than when the transfer was made, making it much harder to "wait out" transfers. These are both strong arguments in favor of underwriteable clients who have assets to protect purchasing LTCI.

ROBERT WOOD JOHNSON PROGRAMS

The Robert Wood Johnson Foundation created a program of public-private partnership for the funding of long-term care. Under the partnership plan, individuals agree to purchase and maintain at least a minimum of LTCI coverage of specified types. The state agrees that, once this coverage is used up, the individual will automatically be Medicaid-eligible, whatever his or her asset level may be.

These plans were quite popular with state governments because they offered a chance to cut the Medicaid rolls and provide an incentive for individuals to pre-fund their own long-term care. As of 1993, five states (California, Connecticut, Indiana, Iowa, and New York) had partnership plans in existence and had secured federal approval. Several other states had passed their own laws authorizing partnership plans.

Unfortunately, Congress cut off development of partnership programs by enacting legislation, effective May 14, 1993, basically forbidding creation of new partnership programs. Five "grandfathered-in" states were able to keep their programs and are not required to seek estate recovery from the estates of decedents who had used the partnership. The other states would be required to apply ordinary Medicaid rules for eligibility and estate recovery to people who owned partnership policies. Obviously, then, there would be little incentive to buy these policies.

Since 1993, Iowa terminated its Partnership program. In the four remaining Partnership states (California, Connecticut, Indiana, New York), 180,000 LTCI policies were sold between 1993 and 2005, and LTCI sales grew 23% faster in those states than in the other states. Benefits have been exhausted under only 89 of those policies.[77]

Partnership programs were given another chance at wider availability under DRA '05. The Social Security Act has been amended to allow all of the states to adopt Partnership programs. Owners of Partnership policies will be exempt from Medicaid estate recovery up to the amount of Partnership coverage purchased after the effective date of the state's amendment of its Medicaid plan to authorize Partnership coverage. Congress intended to allow owners of non-Partnership policies to exchange them for Partnership policies if and when their state adopts a Partnership amendment to the Medicaid plan.[78]

DRA '05 defines a qualified Partnership policy as one that:

- Is a tax-qualified policy as defined by Code § 7702B(b);

- Satisfies NAIC standards with regard to issues such as minimum standards, suitability, policy replacements, post-claims underwriting, and disclosure by insurers; and

- Offers an amount of inflation protection inversely proportional to the purchaser's age. That is, if the insured person is younger than 61 at the time of purchase, the policy must provide compound inflation protection. If the purchaser is 61-76, the policy must provide "some level" of inflation protection, although compounding is not mandatory. Purchasers over 76 can be offered inflation protection, but it is acceptable to sell policies without it.

THE FUTURE OF LTCI

It's very hard to predict if the shutting down of Medicaid planning options will create an incentive for more LTCI purchases. Some potential purchasers will refuse to think about such depressing matters; some will continue to misunderstand the relative provisions of the Medicare and Medicaid programs and the changes in Medicaid. Some will seek coverage, but will be turned down.

One clear trend is the development of a greater range of policies, including "shared care" features that allow transfer of benefits between spouses who are both insured in case one of them exhausts benefits. Insurers are also rolling out combination products that have investment features, or that add LTCI protection to other forms of insurance. Not only can combination policies serve as an incentive to purchase for some people who would be reluctant to buy an LTCI-only policy, they can make certain applicants more attractive to insurers who might turn down marginal or bad risks.[79]

New York State—a highly populous state that has an immense and very expensive Medicaid program—enacted a tax credit (20% of the premium) as an incentive for LTCI purchases. The state's Insurance Department published a major study in 2005 exploring the LTCI market and making suggestions for increasing the number of policy owners and improving the insurance products available to them.[80] Although usually producers of products are urged to offer more comprehensive products, the New York State report suggested the greater availability of more **limited** products, including Nursing Home Only and Home Care Only policies, so that customers could satisfy their planning objectives with a less expensive and easier-to-understand policy. The report also suggests development of limited policies for those who wish to be insured but have pre-existing conditions, and policies with longer (e.g., one year) elimination periods so insurers will be more willing to insure marginal risks. The report also favored promotion of combination products, on the grounds that they could be more flexible and more affordable than LTCI-only policies. The combination products the department analyzed are LTCI and disability income and combinations of LTCI with life or annuity products.

In terms of public policy changes, the report favors creation of a federal tax deduction for LTCI premiums (current law makes them subject to the requirement that medical expenses are deductible only if they exceed 7.5% of AGI); permitting penalty-free IRA withdrawals to pay LTCI premiums; and allowing cafeteria plans and Flexible Spending Accounts to include LTCI.

CHAPTER ENDNOTES

1. Stephen A. Moses, "LTC Insurance Could Play Role in Solving Medicaid Woes," *National Underwriter*, Life and Health/Financial Services edition, January 11, 1999, p. 13.

2. Ralph D. Leisle, "LTC Policies Are Critical in Estate Planning," *National Underwriter* Life and Health/Financial Services edition, October 23, 2000, p. 25.

3. See "Long-Term Care Product Survey," *National Underwriter* Life and Health/Financial Services edition, November 13, 2000, p. 45; this survey contains information on the policy structure, benefits, and options of LTCI products issued by approximately 30 insurers.

4. Peter M. Goldstein, "Disability-Model LTCs Can Be an Option for Some Clients," *National Underwriter* Life and Health/Financial Services edition, September 11, 2000, p. 31. Also see Vicki

Lankarge, "Unum's New Disability Insurance Allows Conversion to Long Term Care Insurance," www.insure.com/health/unumdisability1000.html, describing a disability insurance product that allows conversion from disability to LTC coverage between the ages of 60 and 70; the daily benefit can be used to pay for LTC instead of replacing income.

5. News Brief, "UNUM Adds 'To Age 65' and '10-Year' LTC Payment Options," *National Underwriter*, Life and Health/Financial Services edition, August 24, 1998, p. 13. For product developments, also see Linda Koco, "LTCs For the Late '90s Hit the Streets," *National Underwriter*, Life and Health/Financial Services edition, August 3, 1998, p. 25 and "Companies Bring Out LTCs for Varied Reasons," *National Underwriter*, Life and Health/Financial Services edition, February 1, 1999, p. 27.

6. Allison Bell, "Agents Keep Wary Eye on Long Term Care Inflation," *National Underwriter*, Life and Health/Financial Services edition, August 3, 1998, p. 7.

7. Trevor Thomas, "Producers Reluctant to Switch Clients to Newer LTC Policies," National Underwriter LTC e-Wire 2004 Issue #33 (August 16, 2004).

8. (no by-line), "New Features May Help Group LTC Insureds Stay Home," National Underwriter Online News Service, November 30, 2004.

9. Trevor Thomas, "LTC Carriers Upgrade Products," NU Online News Service (December 15, 2004).

10. No by-line, "N.Y. Life to Pay LTC Policy Dividends," National Underwriter Online News Service (February 16, 2005).

11. NAIC Long-Term Care Insurance Model Act, Section 4A.

12. NAIC Long-Term Care Insurance Model Act, Section 4E.

13. NAIC Long-Term Care Insurance Model Act, Section 6A.

14. Stephanie Lewis, John Wilkin, and Mark Merlis, "Regulation of Private Long-Term Care Insurance: Implementation, Experience, and Key Issues," (2003), http://www.kff.org/insurance/loader. cfm?url=/commonspot/security/getfile_cfm&PageID=14371.

15. NAIC Long-Term Care Insurance Model Act, Section 6B.

16. NAIC Long-Term Care Insurance Model Act, Section 6C.

17. NAIC Long-Term Care Insurance Model Act, Section 6D(1).

18. NAIC Long-Term Care Insurance Model Act, Section 6D(2).

19. NAIC Long-Term Care Insurance Model Regulation, Section 27.

20. NAIC Long-Term Care Insurance Model Act, Section 6F.

21. NAIC Long-Term Care Insurance Model Act, Section 6G.

22. See NAIC Long-Term Care Insurance Model Act, Section 6H.

23. NAIC Long-Term Care Insurance Model Act, Section 6I.

24. NAIC Long-Term Care Insurance Model Act, Section 6J.

25. The June, 2005 draft of NAIC's Long-Term Care Insurance Model Act (Model 640) is available online at http://www.naic.org/committees_models0506_ltcact6.pdf.

26. See NAIC Long-Term Care Insurance Model Regulation, Section 24.

27. See NAIC Long-Term Care Insurance Model Act, Section 7.

28. NAIC Long-Term Care Insurance Model Act, Section 7D.

29. NAIC Long-Term Care Insurance Model Regulation, Section 26E.

30. See NAIC Long-Term Care Insurance Model Regulation, Section 26D.

31. NAIC Long-Term Care Insurance Model Regulation § 26.

32. The case is *Hanson v. Acceleration Life Insurance Co.*; see litigator and law professor Allan Kanner's testimony before the Senate Subcommittee on Aging, www.senate.gov/7Eaging/hr58ak.htm. The

Senate hearing was held on September 13, 2000, with testimony from Iowa Senator Chuck Grassley, Kathleen Sebelius of the NAIC, William Scanlon of the Government Accounting Office, HIAA's Charles N. Kahn, and David Martin of John Hancock Life Insurance.

33. Bill Hogan and Trish Nicholson, "Big Premium Hikes Jolt Owners of Long-Term Care Insurance," (April 2004), http://www.aarp.org/bulletin/longterm/Articles/a2004-03-24-bigpremi…

34. Trevor Thomas, "Delaware Watchdog Turns Down Some LTC Hikes," National Underwriter Life & Health Week in Life & Health, October 7, 2005.

35. AARP Research Center, "Long-Term Care Insurance," http://research.aarp.org/health/fs7r_ltc.html.

36. In their fall, 1998 survey, Ted Pass and Beverly Brenner asked 35 major LTCI insurers about their underwriting policies. Twenty refused to provide any numbers at all, so their results reflect only 15 insurers. See "LTC Survey Pinpoints Underwriting Issues," *National Underwriter*, Life and Health/Financial Services edition, November 16, 1998, p. 7.

37. Ted Pass and Beverly Brenner, "LTC Survey Pinpoints Underwriting Issues," *National Underwriter*, Life and Health/Financial Services edition, November 16, 1998, p. 7.

38. Andrea Coombes, "Insurers Struggle With Long-Term Care," *Wall Street Journal*, June 15, 2005, p. B2B.

39. See, e.g., Breaking News, "Hancock Eases LTC Screening Rules," *National Underwriter* Online News Service December 5, 2005 referring to Hancock's decision to sell policies to applicants who have 14 conditions that were previously grounds for rejection of an application or for postponement of coverage, including hypertension that is being actively treated, and applicants who rank in the lowest positive range of a test for susceptibility to Alzheimer's.

40. Stephen K. Holland, "Less-Than-Standard LTC Risks Can be Insured," *National Underwriter* Life and Health/Financial Services edition, November 6, 2000, p. 10.

41. Allison Bell, "'Tight' LTC Writers Have Lower Claim Rates," *National Underwriter* Life and Health/Financial Services edition, October 9, 2000, p. 3.

42. NAIC Long-Term Care Insurance Model Act, Section 6K.

43. Glenn Ruffenach, "The Best of Both Worlds?" *Wall Street Journal*, December 20, 2004, p. R6.

44. Treas. Regs. §§1.7702B-1, 1.7702B-2; Notice 97-31, 1997-1 CB 417.

45. IRC Secs. 7702B(b), 7702B(e).

46. It has been argued that this requirement gives non-qualified policies an extra measure of flexibility and therefore they are better choices for some potential buyers.

47. IRC Sec. 7702B(c).

48. IRC Sec. 7702B(c).

49. IRC Sec. 7702B(c).

50. IRC Sec. 7702B(c).

51. NAIC Long-Term Care Insurance Model Regulation, Section 27.

52. NAIC Long-Term Care Insurance Model Regulation, Section 28.

53. NAIC Long-Term Care Insurance Model Regulation, Section 28.

54. Terri Cullen, "As Fee Increases Hit Holders of Insurance for Long-Term Care, Is It Safe to Buy?" *Wall Street Journal*, March 2, 2005, p. D1.

55. Richard E. Johnson and Cori E. Uccello, "Is Private Long-Term Care Insurance the Answer?" CRR Issue in Brief #29 (March 2005), http://www.bc.edu/centers/crr/issues-ib_29.pdf.

56. Karen Lee, "Ignorance is Risk," Employee Benefit News (January 2005), http://benefitslink.com (no www); Cindy Waxer, "The Mixed Message of Long-Term Care Coverage," *Workforce Management* (May 2004), http://www.workforce.com/s ection/02/feature-23/70/96/index_printer.html.

57. Glenn Ruffenach, "Shopping for Security," *Wall Street Journal* June 27, 2005, p. R6.

58. These somewhat startling figures come from Rick Pullen, "Lighting a Fire Under Long-Term Care," *Best's Review*, Life/Health Edition, June, 1998, p. 12.

59. "LAN's Twelfth Annual Long-Term Care Insurance Survey," *Life Association News*, October, 1998, pp. 70-88.

60. IRC Secs. 7702B(a), 7702B(d).

61. IRC Sec. 213(d)(10)(A); see Rev. Proc. 2001-13, 2001-3 IRB 337.

62. IRC Sec. 213(a).

63. IRC Sec. 162(l).

64. This information comes Larson Long Term Care Group's May 1, 2000 report, "State Income Tax Deductions and Credits for Long Term Care Insurance Premiums," available for $10 from the Larson Long Term Care Group, Subscription Department, 3303 Monte Villa Parkway Suite 300 Bothell, WA 98021.

65. AARP Research Center, "Long-Term Care Insurance," http://research.aarp.org/health/fs7r_ltc.html.

66. "Who Buys Long-Term Care Insurance in 2000? A Decade of Study of Buyers and Non-Buyers," available for purchase from the HIAA.

67. Richard E. Johnson and Cori E. Uccello, "Is Private Long-Term Care Insurance the Answer?" CRR Issue in Brief #29 (March 2005), http://www.bc.edu/centers/crr/issues-ib_29.pdf.

68. News item, "MetLife: Dementia Adds to LTC Burden," NU Online News Service, February 6, 2006.

69. Jim Connolly, "AARP to NAIC: Consumers Want LTC Information," NU Online News Service, September 22, 2004.

70. Kelly Greene, "Be Prepared: Government Funding for Nursing-Home Care May Be Cut," *Wall Street Journal*, September 7, 2005, p. D1.

71. Eric T. Sondergeld, Mathew Greenwald, "Public Misperceptions About Retirement Security," (LIMRA International 2005), http://www.soa.org/ccm/cms-service/stream/asset?asset_id=.

72. Trevor Thomas, "Educating Clients on LTCI: Still An Uphill Battle," National Underwriter LTC e-Wire Issue #43 (October 18, 2004).

73. Trevor Thomas, National Underwriter Life & Health, "How Many Clients Really Need Long-Duration LTC Protection?" LTC e-Wire (August 2005).

74. Wilma G. Anderson, "Reaching Seniors on LTC," National Underwriter The Week In Life & Health 2005 Issue #15 (April 15, 2005).

75. Christopher Oster, "Is Long-Term Care Worth the Price?" *Wall Street Journal*, September 16, 2004, p. D4.

76. Trevor Thomas, "Advising Boomers: Helping the Non-Wealthy Boomer Pay for LTC Insurance," National Underwriter Life & Health The Week In Life & Health, October 4, 2004.

77. Kelly Greene, "Be Prepared: Government Funding for Nursing-Home Care May Be Cut," *Wall Street Journal*, September 7, 2005, p. D1.

78. Deficit Reduction Act of 2005, P.L. 109-171, Conference agreement § 6021, amending Social Security Act § 1917(b)(1)(C)(ii).

79. See also Jeff D. Opdyke, "Insurers Push Policies for Long-Term Care," *Wall Street Journal* December 27, 2005 p. D1; David Wessel, "Insurance Helps Balance Risk in Retirement," *Wall Street Journal*, November 17, 2005, p. A2.

80. "Long Term Care Insurance Options In New York State: A Report to the Governor and Legislature," (2005), http://www.ins.state.ny.us/lntmcare.htm.

Chapter 5

Medicare

In 1965, the Medicare program was launched to address two problems: senior citizens had very poor access to health insurance, and they were spending more than 20 percent of their income on out-of-pocket payments for health care. Since it was launched over three decades ago, the Medicare program has become immense. It is one of the most significant factors in health care reimbursement. However, many senior citizens are still spending more than 20 percent of their income on out-of-pocket payments, by paying deductibles and coinsurance, and supplementing Medicare's coverage.[1]

Unfortunately, when it designed the Medicare program, Congress failed to understand the age-related differences in the way people use the nation's health system. Although senior citizens sometimes suffer accidents or acute illnesses (which Medicare and the supplemental private "Medigap" insurance do a pretty good job of covering), they also often suffer chronic conditions that cannot be cured. Medicare has very limited nursing home coverage (only 100 days, in a skilled nursing facility, when recuperating from an episode of acute illness) and no custodial nursing home coverage, although millions of older people need custodial care. Although Medicare has home care provisions, the amount of home care available is not enough for the needs of many impaired elders even though the cost of providing this benefit grew tremendously in the 1990s.

Tremendous changes were made in the Medicare program by the Medicare Prescription Drug, Improvement and Modernization Act of 2004 (MPDIMA; Public Law 108-173). MPDIMA modified the Medicare managed care program, changing the name of Medicare Part C from Medicare + Choice to Medicare Advantage (MA). Even more revolutionary was the addition of a prescription drug benefit, Part D.

As Chapter 6 shows, many older people turn to Medicaid as a way to deal with the limitations of the Medicare program. Medicaid, also created in 1965, was intended as a way to provide health care for the "indigent:" people without a meaningful amount of resources. Medicaid does include custodial nursing home coverage, and in many states includes a level of home care far greater than Medicare provides.

The Medicare program is administered by private companies (insurers) acting under contract with the Centers for Medicare & Medicaid Services (CMS) to process medical claims. Part A contracting companies are called "fiscal intermediaries;" those that administer Part B are called "Medicare carriers."

The financial problems of the Social Security system are well-known (see Chapter 9); Medicare's financial problems may be even worse. The cost of the Medicare program increases every year much more than the general rate of inflation. Premiums rise each year, and several other tactics have been suggested to preserve the long-term financial health of the system. For example, it is possible that the age of basic Medicare eligibility will be raised from its current level of 65 (a step that the Social Security system has already taken).

Another suggestion is that ways should be found to make the care of the chronically ill less costly, because a small percentage of high-cost beneficiaries account for a majority of the system's spending. In 2001, for example, the 5% of beneficiaries who had the largest medical bills accounted for 43% of Medicare spending, and the costliest 25% of the Medicare population accounted for 85% of the spending.[2]

Or, the Medicare system might add some degree of means testing, or impose higher financial responsibilities on higher-income beneficiaries. Some steps in this direction have already been taken. Starting January 1, 2007, and phasing in over five years, high-income seniors will pay much higher Part B premiums than their lower-income counterparts.

In 2005, the trustees of the Medicare system projected that the Part A (hospital insurance) trust fund would run out in 2020. Furthermore, they expected Medicare costs as a percentage of Gross Domestic Product to soar from about 3% now to close to 15% in 2080. The trustees expected Social Security costs to stay fairly level at about 6% of GDP from 2020 on, while Medicare costs would continue their stratospheric rise. Social Security's problems were far more predictable, because the current size of the senior population is already known; but the number of medical services seniors will use in the future and the cost of those services, is much harder to predict.[3]

The system is set up to trigger Congressional action if the trustees of the Medicare system predict that general revenues (rather than Medicare revenues such as premiums) will cover more than 45% of total Medicare spending for two consecutive years in the first seven years of the system's long-range financial projection. In 2005, the trustees projected that the 45% threshold would be reached in 2012, which would require Congress to give urgent consideration to Medicare cost control measures.[4]

MEDICARE ELIGIBILITY

Eligibility for Medicare depends on age (having reached one's 65th birthday) or disability (being totally disabled for two years or more). It is not related to whether the person is currently working, and has nothing to do with the person's level of income or assets. However, at least 40 credited calendar quarters of work experience are required. Those who do not qualify for automatic Part A coverage can buy this coverage. People with at least 30, but less than 40, quarters of work experience can get Part A coverage for a premium of $216 a month (2006 figure). Otherwise, the 2006 Part A premium is $393 a month.[5]

Therefore, people who retire before age 65, and are not disabled, are not entitled to Medicare coverage, so they need COBRA continuation coverage (see Chapter 8) or private insurance to fill this gap. Nor does Medicare have spousal coverage, so a person who retires at age 65 but whose spouse is age 61 is eligible for Medicare, but the spouse (unless disabled for two years) is not.

In 1967, shortly after the Medicare program began, it covered only 19.5 million people. By 1996, the Medicare population had nearly doubled, to 38.1 million people. In 1995, there were close to six million "dual eligibles": people entitled to both Medicare and Medicaid.

In 2005, Medicare covered 35.4 million seniors and 6.3 million people with permanent disabilities. According to the Kaiser Family Foundation, 18% of Medicare beneficiaries are "dual eligibles." Seventy-one percent of Medicare beneficiaries have two or more chronic health conditions; 29% are in either fair or poor health; and 23% suffer from cognitive impairment.

About half of Medicare beneficiaries (51%) have income at or below 200% of the federal poverty line. For 2005, that means their income is less than $19,140 for a single person or $25,660 for a couple—a percentage that implies that many of them will be unable to pay for long-term care, and many of them will be unable to afford long-term care insurance. Forty-eight percent of beneficiaries had savings and stock portfolios below $10,000.

AARP's estimate is that in 2003, Medicare beneficiaries spent 22% of their income on Medicare premiums and out of pocket spending to fill in the gaps in the Medicare system (which covered only about 45% of total health expenses of seniors and disabled beneficiaries)—ironically, higher than the level that triggered the creation of the Medicare program.[6]

In 2004, Medicare spent $265 billion, which was 12% of all federal spending and 17% of all U.S. spending on health care.[7]

Low-income persons with limited resources may also qualify under federal programs such as Qualified Medicare Beneficiary (QMB) and Specified Low-Income Medicare Beneficiary (SLMB). Under these programs, persons who do not qualify for the full package of Medicaid benefits can have the state Medicaid program pay some of their Medicare cost-sharing obligations. The QMB program is the most comprehensive: it covers the Parts A and B premiums, deductibles, and coinsurance.

About a quarter of Medicare beneficiaries are entitled to subsidies for the Part B, Part D premium, or both, because they meet income and asset tests. About a third of beneficiaries are entitled to Part D subsidies because of their income level.[8]

MEDICARE SERVICES

The Medicare program is divided into four main Parts. Part A helps pay for care in hospitals and skilled nursing facilities, and for home health and hospice care. Part B (also known as Supplementary Medical Insurance or SMI, not to be confused with private "Medigap" Medicare Supplement Insurance) helps to pay for physician services. Part C is Medicare managed care, which deals with the way services, will be reimbursed, not with which services are covered. Part D is the prescription drug program, which reached full operation January 1, 2006 (after a trial run under which drug discount cards were made available to Medicare beneficiaries).

Medicare's coverage of its services is calculated on the basis of "benefit periods." A benefit period begins on the first day of inpatient treatment in a hospital, and ends 60 days after the patient's discharge from the hospital or from a skilled nursing or rehabilitation facility. There is no limit on the number of benefit periods a Medicare patient can have. The same deductible applies to repeated hospitalizations during the same benefit period; but the patient must pay a new deductible if another hospitalization occurs more than 60 days after a discharge from a hospital or a skilled nursing or rehabilitation facility.

Part A coverage is limited to 90 days inpatient hospitalization per benefit period, but if a longer duration is required, each person has 60 "lifetime reserve days" which can be applied to any hospitalization. However, once a lifetime reserve day is used, it cannot be renewed.

Medicare does not cover private nursing, telephone or television rental in hospital rooms, or care (other than emergency care) provided in a hospital that does not have a Medicare participation contract. With limited exceptions for urgent care rendered in Canada, Medicare does not cover care rendered outside the United States.

Medicare Part A coverage includes

- Up to 90 days inpatient hospitalization per benefit period (in a semi-private room, unless a private room is medically necessary);

- Up to 100 days recuperation in a Skilled Nursing Facility (SNF);

- Part-time or intermittent home care services rendered by skilled professionals or home health aides;

- Hospice services elected by terminally ill persons to replace all other Medicare services;

- Blood, after the first three pints;

- An initial comprehensive physical examination for first-time Medicare enrollees (e.g., screening for cancer and glaucoma; flu and hepatitis vaccine; assessment of ability to perform ADLs; an EKG; vision and hearing tests) within their first six months of enrollment;

- Certain preventive services such as mammograms and diabetes screening for people already in Medicare. These provisions mark a change from earlier rules that specifically excluded routine physical examinations;[9] and

- Positron Emission Tomography (PET) scans to diagnose Alzheimer's Disease and other dementias.[10]

Part B coverage includes

- Medically necessary services rendered by a physician;

- Outpatient hospital services;

- X-rays and laboratory tests;

- Certain Durable Medical Equipment (e.g., wheelchairs, hospital beds used at home);

- Home health care for people who are enrolled in Part B but not in Part A; and

- Blood, after the first three pints.

Skilled Nursing Facility Coverage

A Skilled Nursing Facility (SNF) is a facility, either free-standing or a separate part of a hospital, that provides skilled nursing and other professional services (such as physical or speech therapy) to persons who do not need a hospital level of care, but who do require skilled care every day and, as a practical matter, must get the care at an SNF rather than at home or in another setting. In this context (and with respect to Medicare home health services) skilled services are services that inherently require professional training for their proper performance. Caring for a surgical incision, giving an injection, or setting medication dosages are skilled services. Feeding patients, helping them to the bathroom, or helping them dress are not skilled services.

An SNF must have a state license, have at least one physician on call at all times, and have enough staff to offer 24-hour-a-day nursing services, with at least one full-time registered nurse on staff.

Medicare covers up to 100 days of care in an SNF per benefit period, but the SNF care must be closely related to a hospitalization during that same benefit period. The patient must have spent at least three consecutive days in the hospital (not counting the day of discharge) before being discharged to the SNF. The basic rule is that the patient must enter the SNF within 30 days of the hospital discharge. Furthermore, a physician must formally certify the need for the care. In practical terms, then, SNF care is available when a person is recovering from an acute illness (e.g., a stroke) or injury (typically, a hip fracture caused by a fall), but not when a person experiences a deterioration in condition.

After the 100th day, no Medicare coverage is available. There is no deductible, and there is no co-payment responsibility for the first 20 days of SNF treatment during a benefit period, but coinsurance of $119. per day (in 2006) is required for days 21-100. (All Medigap policies, other than Plans A and B, cover this coinsurance amount.)

Home Health Care

In order for a Home Health Agency (HHA) to be reimbursed for care of a person under Medicare, the agency must have a state license and a contract with the

CMS. Medicare will not reimburse care provided by individuals hired privately by a Medicare beneficiary, or care provided through an agency that has a state license if it does not have a contract with the CMS.

HHAs provide services such as in-home nursing, physical therapy, occupational therapy, and home health aide services in the homes (or other community settings) of their patients. Medicare covers HHA services, with no deductibles or coinsurance. Medicare managed care beneficiaries face an additional requirement in that they must obtain their home care from an HHA that also has a contract with their own managed care plan.

However, the Medicare home health care benefit is strictly limited. The services must be part-time or intermittent (although full-time intermittent services, or continuing part-time, services are possible). Intermittent skilled care means care provided less than seven days a week, or less than eight hours a day for a period of up to 21 days. The 21-day period can be extended if the patient can prove that more care is needed, but on a finite and predictable basis. Part-time care means a combination of skilled nursing and home health aide services adding up to less than 8 hours a day and less than 28 hours a week, even if care is provided seven days a week. The local CMS office can authorize 35 rather than 28 hours of care a week on a showing that the patient needs the extra care.

Someone who needs a nursing home level of care on a permanent basis does not qualify (but see Chapter 6 for a discussion of Medicaid programs that provide nursing home-level care in the patient's home). Medicare home health services must be rendered in accordance with a care plan drawn up and supervised by a physician.

Under the basic Medicare home health care plan, people who have only Part A receive their home health services under Part A, while those who have Part B but not Part A (a very small group of people) receive their home health services under Part B.

The Balanced Budget Act of 1997 (BBA '97) introduced a new category of Medicare home health care called "post-institutional home health services" for Medicare beneficiaries enrolled in both Part A and Part B. Under this program, home health services must be prescribed by a medical professional and must start within 14 days of being discharged from a hospital where the patient spent at least 3 days, or within 14 days of leaving a Medicare SNF. Furthermore, only 100 home health visits are covered under this program.

Another requirement is that the recipient of Medicare home health services must be "homebound," meaning not necessarily bedridden, but definitely spending most of the time at home.

If the patient needs and requires skilled services, the care plan can legitimately include part-time or intermittent home health aide services consisting of personal care such as assistance with getting dressed, bathing, or using the toilet. However, the personal care services must be adjuncts to professional services. Someone who needs only personal care and not skilled services does not qualify for Medicare home care even if home-bound.

BBA '97 had to cut back on Medicare home health growth, because the cost of this part of the Medicare program grew explosively. Between 1988 and 1997, there was an annual growth rate of 30% in Medicare home health care spending, because the number of people and the amount of home health services they received both expanded.

In 1997, Medicare spent $18.3 billion on home health care–but this figure was cut almost in half, to $9.5 billion in 1999, in large part because of the changes implemented by BBA '97. As of 1999, about 9 out of every 100 Medicare beneficiaries received home health care, with an average of 41 visits per beneficiary. Under the prospective payment system set up by BBA '97, Medicare pays the home health agency a single amount for every 60-day "episode" of home care that a Medicare beneficiary receives, no matter how many services are received.[11]

PRACTICE TIP: A federal district court case provides that Medicare home health care beneficiaries are entitled to a written notice of denial of termination of benefits. Before benefits are reduced or terminated, CMS must give them notice explaining why Medicare will not cover (or will no longer cover) home care for this patient. They must also be informed of their appeal rights. In this analysis, home health agencies are acting on behalf of the state (because Medicare pays them) so their patients have due process rights.[12]

Hospice Services

Terminally ill Medicare beneficiaries (diagnosed as having six months or less to live) have the option of substituting hospice services, provided under Part A by a Medicare-certified hospice program, for all other Medicare services. If the beneficiary recovers, he can return to the regular Medicare program and Medicare will cover other illnesses or injuries that occur but are not related to the terminal illness (e.g., a cancer patient's heart problems).

Hospice services are primarily home care services. The hospice benefit includes: (1) care from doctors and nurses, (2) medical equipment and supplies, (3) pain medication, (4) medical social services, (5) physical, occupational, and speech therapy, and (6) home health aide and homemaker services. Although most services are rendered in the home, the patient can be hospitalized if medically required (e.g., a flare-up of pneumonia) or for up to five days to provide respite for a spouse or other family member who is significantly involved in the terminally ill person's care. Hospice benefits are not subject to a deductible, but small copayments are required for respite care and outpatient drugs.

Most hospice beneficiaries use Medicare hospice services for only a very short time, whereas many terminally ill people could benefit from longer hospice care. There is a misconception that dying people can be deprived of coverage or even penalized financially if they live longer than six months; Medicare policy has been changed to provide that services can be provided without penalty if a person who has been diagnosed as terminally ill survives for more than six months but continues to need the services.

PRACTICE TIP: About one-quarter of Medicare beneficiaries in the hospice program enrolled so late that they received a week or less of hospice care. This program can be helpful to the terminally ill and their families if elected earlier, so discuss this option with your clients as part of estate and especially end-of-life planning.[13]

Prescription Drug Coverage Under Part D

Medicare Part D is a voluntary program. Beneficiaries decide whether or not to enroll. Reasons for not enrolling could include having low prescription drug expenses (although that could change in the future); having coverage under an employee group health plan or retiree health benefit plan; and not being able to afford the premiums. However, MPDIMA includes provisions for subsidies for low-income seniors that cover 75% of the cost of Part D premiums and provide additional assistance with copayments. Official notices were sent out to inform Medicare beneficiaries of this possibility (although advocates say that the application process is so confusing and cumbersome that many people will avoid applying).

Those who enroll in Part D pay a monthly premium. At first, it was announced that the initial premium would be about $35 a month, but the estimate was scaled down in August, 2005, when it was projected to average $32.20 a month, based on bids submitted by insurers wishing to serve as plan administrators. (Premiums will differ somewhat by region.) Part D is financed in the same way as Part B: the premium is supposed to provide 25% of the cost of the program. The other 75% comes from general federal revenues.[14]

Part D plans have been marketed to satisfy a number of different market niches. When the plans went on sale in 2005, there were at least 40 options available in most states—and the number of plans, and the variations of coverage offered—were expected to expand greatly in 2006. Some plans compete on price: premiums can be as low as $1.87 (some Humana plans in the West). Others appeal to convenience shoppers, by offering convenient mail-order service or a large number of in-network pharmacies so there will be one close by. Some plans offer coverage for the "doughnut hole" (the range of expenses between $2,250 and $3,600 where Part D drops out), so these plans would be especially attractive for chronically ill seniors who anticipate high prescription drug costs. Some Part D plans have low deductibles; others pare the monthly premium by including a significant deductible. Some plans structure copayments as a percentage, others as a dollar amount per prescription.

PRACTICE TIP: The Medicare site, http://www.cms.hhs.gov/map/map.asp, gives state-by-state information about the various plans available, including details such as which drugs are covered by the plan's formulary—useful information for someone who wants to make sure his or her current prescriptions will be covered. Look for the "Prescription Drug Plan Finder" Web tool, which focuses on drug coverage of Medicare Advantage plans. An additional wrinkle is that some plans will not cover certain expensive medications unless the plan itself gives prior authorization, or unless the patient tries a less expensive alternative drug first.[15]

Before Part D coverage kicks in, the beneficiary must satisfy a $250 deductible each year. Then, for drug costs between $250 and $2,250 each year, the beneficiary pays a 25% copayment and Part D covers the other 75%. For drug costs falling between $2,250 and $5,100 a year, there is no Part D coverage, and the beneficiary is responsible for the full costs. But if drug costs reach a catastrophic level, Part D pays 100% of the cost, unless the beneficiary's income is above 150% of the federal poverty line, In that case, the beneficiary pays 5% and Part D pays the other 95%. There is no maximum amount of coverage.

CMS estimates that beneficiaries who are not eligible for low-income subsidies will save about half of their current drug costs by signing up for Part D. Their examples assume that about half of Medicare beneficiaries will spend more than $2,400 for prescription drugs in 2006 and half will spend less. A senior who does not qualify for the low-income subsidy and who uses the average $2,400 worth of prescription drugs will have to spend $697.50 on Part D, and will save 53%, or $1,262.50 as a result of the program. Someone who is a Medicare/Medicaid dual eligible nursing home resident will not have to spend anything to get Part D benefits, so he or she will save the full $2,400. For a person with extremely high drug bills ($10,000 a year) who does not qualify for subsidies, savings will be 58% because out of pocket cost will be $3,770, resulting in savings of $5,790.

Part D is an alternative to other coverage, so a person who has retiree health coverage that covers prescription drugs has to choose between them. In May, 2005,

CMS issued guidance about the disclosure notices that employers have to give their employees who are eligible for Part D. The guidance includes two model forms: one where the employer's coverage is "creditable" (at least as generous as Part D) and the other where it is not. Coverage is creditable if its actuarial value is at least as great as Part D.

Medicare Advantage plans must offer at least one option under which enrollees receive prescription drug coverage. The MA plan can either offer a basic plan or, to attract subscribers, can offer a plan that costs no more than the standard premium but provides additional prescription drug coverage. MA plans are also allowed to offer different levels of prescription drug coverage, some of which cost more than the basic Part D premium.

The U.S. Pharmacopeia, an influential scientific organization, acted as an advisory panel for HHS in developing the list of covered drugs, and suggested that Part D plans should cover at least two drugs of each type. There is no standard drug formulary imposed by the federal government; each Part D plan develops its own list. Creating the formulary is controversial because the drug companies want as many of their products as possible to be included in the formulary. Doctors and consumers usually want to increase the choices available. But insurers and Pharmacy Benefit Manufacturers want to cut down the list so they can negotiate with manufacturers for big orders and larger discounts.

PLANNING TIP: Therefore, one of the most important factors for your clients in choosing whether to enroll in Part D, or which plan to choose if more than one is available, is whether the prescriptions they already take are covered under the plan. Of course, the calculation could be thrown off if the formulary and/or your clients' prescription drug needs change in the future![16] Another thing to be aware of is that a number of drug companies decided to terminate programs under which they donated drugs to low-income patients, or stopped offering charity drugs to persons who enrolled in Part D.[17]

Also, advise your clients to be wary of drug plan scams. The Medicare Rights Center warns that it is illegal for plans to send spam e-mails; to take enrollments over the phone; or to make home visits unless the Medicare beneficiary invites them. Anyone who says that seniors have to enroll in a particular Part D plan (or to enroll in Part D at all) to maintain other Medicare benefits is misinformed—or trying to manipulate vulnerable seniors. Furthermore, plans are not permitted to ask for Social Security numbers until a person is enrolling in the plan, and asking for credit card or bank account information is allowed only if the senior citizen wishes to authorize automatic payments.[18]

Final Regulations published January 28, 2005 flesh out some of the details of the program. A person who enrolls in Part D after the initial enrollment period can be subjected to a late enrollment penalty if there was a period of 63 days or more when that person did not have creditable prescription drug coverage. To determine creditable coverage status, therefore, plan sponsors that offer prescription coverage have to notify their employees who are eligible for Part D whether or not coverage under the employer's plan is creditable. If the coverage is not creditable, the recipient of the notice must be informed that there are limitations on enrollment periods, and that late enrollment carries a penalty. Notices are required at several times: before the person's initial enrollment period for Part D; before the effective date of that person's enrollment in the employer's prescription drug plan; when coverage becomes or stops being creditable; before November 15 of each year (because this is the start of the Part D open enrollment period); and also at any time that the individual asks for a notice (for example, a person who is making an elder care plan discovers that he or she can't find notices that were issued in the past).

By February, 2006, 20 million Medicare beneficiaries had been automatically enrolled in a Part D plan because they were already covered by Medicaid or by another government program or employer plan. Another 22 million Medicare beneficiaries had the option of enrolling voluntarily; about 5.4 million of them chose to do so. Many senior citizens avoided enrolling in a plan simply because they could not master its complexities. Others decided that, bearing in mind the recurring premiums and the potential for deductibles and coinsurance (including the sizeable "doughnut hole," the plan would not really save any money for them, especially if they normally took generic drugs, if their doctors gave them drug samples, or if they bought drugs from Canada or Mexico to save money.[19]

Claims Administration and Hearings

Senior citizens are entitled to a notice whenever a benefit claim is denied. In most instances, they are also entitled to a hearing to appeal the denial.

On a day-to-day level, Medicare is administered by insurance companies known as "fiscal intermediaries" (intermediaries) for Part A and "Medicare carriers" (carriers) for Part B.

Health care providers send the claim form to the intermediary. The Medicare beneficiary is responsible for deductibles and coinsurance (or has Medigap insurance to cover it), but the provider cannot bill more than the rate schedule for the health care services.

Part B claims can be either assigned or unassigned. An assigned claim is handled in the same way as a Part A claim. The beneficiary or Medigap policy pays the deductible and coinsurance, and Medicare pays the rest. For unassigned Part B claims, the doctor is still responsible for submitting the paperwork, but the patient pays the doctor's fee and is then reimbursed by the CMS (at the rate of 80 percent of the CMS' schedule amount), and perhaps by Medigap insurance.

Once the health care provider submits a bill to the intermediary or carrier, the insurance company will review the claim and determine whether to approve the claim, deny it entirely, or approve it at a lower level than requested. If it approves the claim, the beneficiary will receive an "Explanation of Medicare Benefits" or "EOMB."

PRACTICE TIP: Your clients should keep their EOMBs, because they are helpful for tracing deductibles and coinsurance that may be entitled to Medigap reimbursement. They also are useful for determining whether the expenses might be tax deductible as medical expenses. They may also be used to ascertain whether a caregiver child has the ability to claim the parent as a dependent.

A 2000 federal statute known as the Medicare, Medicaid and SCHIP Benefits Improvement and Protection Act of 2000 (Public Law 106-554; BIPA for short) revised the appeals process for Medicare. Responsibility for handling appeals has been transferred from the Social Security Administration to the Department of Health and Human Services. The transition began on July 1, 2005, and federal law required it to be completed by October 1, 2005.

Under the new procedure, the first level of appeal is a review of the file (that is, there is no in-person hearing) by HHS's CMS contractor. HHS will enter into contracts with at least four Quality Independent Contractors (QICs,) who will handle the second level of appeals. The QICs began by handling Part A appeals starting May 1, 2005; Part B appeals were phased in starting January 1, 2006.

The third level of appeal goes to HHS's Administrative Law Judge unit, and the final level of appeal is HHS' MAC. If the beneficiary or provider is still dissatisfied, at that point administrative remedies have been exhausted and suit can be filed in federal court. If a request is made for expedited review, the review entity must make a written reply within 60 days; if the review entity fails to do this, the Medicare applicant can go to federal court.

Before the transfer, hearings were held at more than 140 Social Security offices nationwide. After the changeover, however, all the judges work at only four sites (Cleveland, Miami, Irvine, California and Arlington, Virginia). Under the new procedure, hearings are normally held over the telephone or by videoconferencing.

A beneficiary who wants an in-person hearing has to show special or extraordinary circumstances to justify it.[20]

If the claim is denied on the grounds that the services were custodial, that they were not "reasonable and necessary," or that home care was not warranted because the individual was not "homebound" (see above), it is possible to obtain a "waiver of liability." That is, as long as the patient did not know that Medicare would not cover the services, the patient will not be required to pay for them out-of-pocket. (However, if a similar claim has already been denied in the past, the patient will know that the claim was invalid, and a waiver of liability will not be granted.) If the service provider knew the services were not covered by Medicare, the provider will be stuck with the bill. The CMS will be stuck if neither the patient nor the provider knew the services were not covered.[21]

MEDICARE COPAYMENTS

Most Medicare enrollees receive Part A services without a premium, but those without the necessary quarters of Social Security coverage pay monthly premiums. Technically speaking, Parts A and B are independent, and it is possible for a Part A enrollee to turn down Part B coverage. Signing up for Part B requires paying a monthly premium of $88.50 (in 2006), although usually payment is made by a deduction from the Social Security check, so the enrollee does not pay anything out-of-pocket. There is a single annual $124 (in 2006) deductible requirement for Part B. The fee-for-service Medicare system is essentially an indemnity system. Medicare generally pays 80 percent of its schedule amount for the particular medical service rendered. If the claim is assigned (see below), the doctor cannot charge more than the schedule amount.

Theoretically the patient would be responsible for the full balance of an unassigned claim, but Medicare forbids "balance billing" (making the patient responsible for more than 15 percent over and above the Medicare amount). The permitted 15 percent surcharge is known as the "limiting charge." Some states (such as New York and Massachusetts) impose even stricter limits on balance billing. See below for a discussion of physicians who opt out of the Medicare system and bill their patients privately.

For 2006, the Part A hospital deductible (the amount the patient must pay before any Medicare payment is available) is $952 for each benefit period. If there is more than one hospitalization during a benefit period (which begins with initial hospitalization and ends 60 days after the person has been in the community without being an inpatient at a hospital or SNF), only one deductible is required. Once the patient has satisfied the deductible (whether out-of-pocket or by using Medigap insurance), the Medicare system pays the full costs of up to 60 days of inpatient hospitalization in each benefit period. Medicare covers up to 90 days hospitalization in each benefit period, not just 60, but for days 61 through 90, the patient becomes responsible for coinsurance of $238 per day. A person using lifetime reserve days is responsible for $476 per day coinsurance.

There is no deductible for Medicare SNF coverage (i.e., this is "first-day coverage," unlike many long-term care insurance policies, which have a waiting period; see Chapter 4). There is no co-payment responsibility for days 1-20 of the stay. For days 21-100, the patient's co-payment liability is $119.00 per day (in 2006). Medicare home health care is rendered without any deductible or coinsurance, except for a 20 percent coinsurance requirement imposed on most items of Durable Medical Equipment.

The beneficiary is responsible for paying for the first three pints of blood used each year, although a few Medigap plans cover this "blood deductible."

The Part B beneficiary is responsible for a copayment of the first $124 in expenses. This is the 2006 level; before 2005, it had been stable at $100 for many years. Now it will be indexed each year for inflation.

The Part B premium has risen from $58.70/month (2003) to $66.60 (2004), $78.20 (2005), and $88.50 (2006). The general rule is that the Part B premium is set to generate 25% of the cost of the program. The cost increases were attributed to higher billing by doctors for longer office visits, more tests, and more sophisticated medical imaging.

Starting January 1, 2005 and extending over five years, a new system will be phased in under which high-income beneficiaries (individuals with income over $80,000 a year; couples with income over $160,000 a year) pay a Part B premium higher than the standard 25% of costs.[22]

Persons who receive outpatient hospital services under Part B are responsible for 20% of the actual hospital charge, for which there is no limit set by Medicare fee schedules. For outpatient mental health services, the patient is responsible for 50% of the Medicare schedule amount, rather than the 20% charged in other contexts.

Assigned and Unassigned Claims

Most doctors who take Medicare patients "accept assignment." They agree to bill Medicare directly for 80 percent of the schedule amount, and also agree not to charge more than the schedule amount. The patient must satisfy the $110 annual deductible, and must pay the physician directly for the 20 percent coinsurance. For an unassigned claim, the patient pays the doctor directly, and then seeks reimbursement from Medicare for 80 percent of the schedule amount. The patient is responsible for (1) the annual deductible, and (2) the difference between the actual charge or the greatest amount the doctor is allowed to charge (typically, 115 percent of the schedule amount) and 80 percent of the schedule amount.

In many instances, senior citizens will want to select a doctor who accepts assignment, so that they can benefit from the greater convenience and lower cost of assigned claims. The CMS assists them in finding a doctor by publishing "The Medicare Directory of Participating Physicians and Suppliers," available from Social Security offices and State Offices on Aging. Part B carriers are obligated to send free copies on request.

MEDICARE ENROLLMENT

People who start receiving Social Security benefits before age 65 are automatically enrolled in Medicare Part A. The CMS mails a Medicare card to arrive approximately three months before the beneficiary's 65th birthday. The Medicare card is also mailed automatically to persons who have satisfied the official definition of disability for two years. People who remain in the labor force, or otherwise are not receiving Social Security benefits, must take steps to apply for Medicare. The optimum time to apply is three months before the 65th birthday, so the transition to Medicare coverage will be made smoothly.

All Part A enrollees automatically qualify for Part B unless they opt out. The initial enrollment period for Part B (or for buying into Part A) starts on the first day of the third month before the month of the enrollee's 65th birthday and ends seven months later. A person who fails to enroll during this period not only must pay extra for late enrollment, but will not be able to enroll until the next "general enrollment period" (January 1-March 31 of the following year), and coverage will not begin until July 1 of that year.

The Part A buy-in premium is 10 percent higher for late enrollment. The Part B premium increases 10 percent for every 12 months of late enrollment. However, there is no penalty for late Part B enrollment if the individual deferred enrollment because he was covered by an employer's group health plan (EGHP). (See immediately below for a discussion of the relationship between Medicare and EGHPs.)

Secondary Payor

For EGHPs maintained by employers with 20 or more employees, the EGHP is required to be the primary payor. If the EGHP pays the full bill, Medicare has no theoretical responsibility for payment. (Theoretical, because Medicare often ends up paying bills that should have been covered by an EGHP.) Medicare is supposed to be a secondary payor for services that fall within Medicare coverage and which are not fully covered by the EGHP.

Employers are not allowed to draft their plans to exclude older employees from coverage, or even to make Medicare the primary payor and the EGHP merely a secondary payor. However, employees do have the option of rejecting the EGHP and electing to make Medicare their primary payor. Individuals who make this election, and who enroll in Part B, also start their six-month open enrollment period for Medigap insurance. If they do not also purchase Medigap insurance within this six-month time frame, they may find that coverage is denied or unaffordable.

MEDICARE MANAGED CARE: MEDICARE ADVANTAGE

Since the 1970s (that is, fairly early in the history of Medicare) there have been attempts to use managed care to keep down the high cost of medical care for seniors and the disabled. At first, Medicare managed care was limited to HMOs. Then the program was renamed "Medicare + Choice" and the types of plans were expanded to include Preferred Provider Organizations, provider-sponsored organizations, private fee for service plans and Medical Savings Accounts. MPDIMA renamed the program Medicare Advantage and set up special needs plans for institutionalized persons and those with severe disabling conditions.

Before MPDIMA, the managed care program had both successes and failures. It was fairly popular with patients, especially those who valued special benefits such as prescription drug coverage. (Of course, now that MPDIMA has added prescription drug coverage, this advantage no longer applies.) But many insurers started plans that achieved popularity, then suddenly withdrew from the managed care market, leaving their customers stranded. The providers' side of the story is that they did not receive enough reimbursement to make the plans worthwhile, especially if they had many chronically ill enrollees.

In some cases, the increased reimbursement rates for managed care plans enacted in 2003 (an estimated $46 billion in Medicare managed care reimbursement over a ten-year period) led managed care companies to return and seek new enrollees in areas where they had shut down their previous plans. (Over 2.4 million enrollees were dropped by their Medicare managed care plans in the early 2000s, when over 400 local plans were terminated.) According to a 2004 study by Mathematica Policy Research, the increased HMO reimbursement meant that HMOs would be reimbursed an average of 7% more than the average per capita spending for a fee-for-service Medicare beneficiary.

Patient advocates charged managed care plans with "cherry picking" (seeking to ensure only the healthiest seniors). Congress responded by increasing reimbursement rates for managed care plans—but that defeats the entire managed care objective of requiring patients to accept reduced choice of providers in order to cut costs so the system will remain financially viable. Medicare Advantage is a "capitated" plan: CMS pays the managed care plans a "per head" figure for every enrollee.

Medicare Advantage plans are required to provide their enrollees with all Part A and Part B services. They must also offer at least one plan that includes prescription drug coverage. There are 26 Medicare Advantage coverage areas throughout the country, and an insurer that wants to offer Medicare Advantage must offer it throughout the entire region.[23]

In 1990, there were only 96 Medicare managed care plans. The number of plans rose steadily until 1997, reaching a peak of 346 and declining after that. There were only 179 managed care plans in 2001, 155 in 2002 and 151 in 2003. The number began to rise again, reaching 154 in 2003 and almost equaling the previous peak: in June 2005 there were 340 plans. In 2000, 16% of Medicare enrollees were in managed care plans—the highest percentage enrollment ever reached. In mid-2005, In 2005, there were 5.74 million Medicare beneficiaries in managed care plans, or 13.2% of the total.

Over three-quarters of Medicare beneficiaries had access to a managed care plan if they wanted to sign up, but managed care is popular in only a few states. More than one-quarter of all Medicare Advantage clients live in California. In California, Arizona, Colorado, Oregon, Pennsylvania, and Rhode Island, more than 20% of the Medicare population have enrolled in managed care plans, but there are 16 states where less than 1% of the Medicare beneficiaries are in managed care.[24]

Managed care plans received an average of 10% increase in reimbursement in 2004. Certain members of Congress expressed anger that Medicare Advantage plans would receive more than traditional fee-for-service plans (anywhere from 107% to 123% of the cost of covering the same patients; the highest reimbursement went to rural plans, because traditionally the insurance industry avoided rural areas). Overall, Medicare's chief actuary estimated that paying Medicare Advantage more than fee-for-service rates would cost Medicare about $50 million over ten years (not counting $10 billion in incentive payments authorized by Congress to bring new plans into the managed care system).[25]

To the health care industry, however, this was a positive development, making it likely that Medicare patients would have access to a greater variety of financially strong managed care plans. According to the management consulting firm Towers

Perrin, 40 major MA plans (covering well over half of all Medicare Advantage enrollees in the U.S.) said that they were likely to use some or all of the extra reimbursement amounts to cut their premiums; a quarter of the plans intended to increase benefits. Almost one-quarter of the plans said they would improve their provider networks (e.g., by paying more to participating doctors; recruiting additional physicians); and the same proportion said they would set up a reserve fund to help keep premiums on an even keel.[26]

THE PRIVATE-PAY OPTION

The Balanced Budget Act of 1997 (BBA '97) clarified the status of private contracts between doctors and their senior citizen patients. Before BBA '97, it was uncertain whether it was legal for doctors to go outside the Medicare system and arrange to treat over-65 persons on a fee-for-service basis without reference to Medicare reimbursement provisions (including Medicare fee schedules), and with no necessity to complete the cumbersome Medicare paperwork.

Under the BBA '97, a doctor may opt out of the Medicare system entirely, and charge patients whatever amount the doctor sees fit. However, Medicare will not make any reimbursement at all to opted-out physicians. Medigap insurers have no obligation to cover any part of the bills of such physicians. The patient must pay purely out of pocket (or use acute health insurance). Furthermore, the exit from Medicare must be complete. It is not permissible to treat Mr. Bigbucks as a private-pay patient and Mrs. Everyday as a Medicare patient.

A doctor who chooses to opt out of Medicare may not return to the Medicare system for two years. In a 1999 lawsuit, a senior citizen advocacy organization and four senior citizens claimed that this statutory requirement is unconstitutional because it limits their freedom to contract.[27] However, the D.C. Circuit upheld the statute, agreeing with government's argument that the statute applies only to services that Medicare would otherwise pay for. Patients can make any arrangements they like with respect to cosmetic surgery, hearing aids, and other products and services that are excluded from Medicare or services that Medicare does not consider reasonable and necessary.

Very few doctors have chosen to opt out: according to one study, only 300 doctors nationwide had chosen to withdraw from Medicare in favor of the private-pay option.

LEARNING MORE ABOUT MEDICARE

The Center for Medicare and Medicaid Services (CMS; formerly known as the Health Care Financing Administration, or HCFA) has plenty of resources—for consumers, professionals, and health care providers— on its Web site, http://www.cms.hhs.gov, including the Medicare Compare databases that give information about hospitals and nursing homes.

The Kaiser Family Foundation, http://www.kff.org is a leader in studying the health care system, especially issues affecting the elderly, disabled, and uninsured. The site includes a Medicare Health Plan Tracker that provides data about the various Medicare Advantage plans: http://www.kff.org/medicare/healthplantracker/index.jsp.

PRACTICE TIP: Although there is a toll-free telephone help line, (800) MEDICARE, and official publications encourage beneficiaries to use it to learn about the new benefits and resolve questions about the system as a whole, its advice probably should be taken with a grain of salt. In late 2004, the Government Accountability Office (GAO) found that when its employees called for information, 29% got incorrect information about the prescription drug benefit, and 10% didn't get answers at all. The volume of calls rose from 5.6 million in 2003 to 16.5 million in 2004, a fact that CMS blamed for its inability to handle the traffic.[28]

The National Consumers League has information about preventing Medicare fraud: http://www.fraud.org/tips/internet.medicare.htm. State health insurance programs can be reached through http://www.medicare.gov/contacts/Static/SHIPs.asp. To find out if an entity that represents itself as a "drug plan" is actually state-licensed, check with your state insurance department—contact information for insurance regulators is available at http://www.naic.org/state_web_map.htm.[29]

SUMMARY

Although it does not cover the kind of custodial care that is necessary for many senior citizens, Medicare does play a vital role in covering the acute health needs of the elderly and disabled. Older people should always be aware of the Medicare benefits available to them (especially the less known skilled nursing facility, home health, and hospice benefits), and should use their hearing and appeal rights to challenge rejection of meritorious benefit claims.

The Medicare Advantage system has the potential to shift a large proportion of beneficiaries into managed care plans, if enough plans are created, and if enough older people opt to get their care in this manner. Meanwhile, clients should only sign up with a managed care plan if it offers an adequate number of skillful, compassionate doctors in the right specialties and sub-specialties, if its gatekeeper policies are not unduly restrictive, and if there are assurances that the plan will remain in the managed care marketplace and not terminate its CMS contract.

CHAPTER ENDNOTES

1. The conventional wisdom, cited by AARP and other organizations and persons interested in Medicare reform, is that the average elderly person spends 19% of income on out-of-pocket medical expenses, and low-income elderly people devote 35% of their income for this purpose. However, a study by RAND, a nonprofit policy analysis organization, suggests that the real figures are about 12% for the average senior citizen and 20% for poor senior citizens, because the often-cited Medicare Current Beneficiary Survey actually understates the income of individual citizens by 20% and of senior citizen households by 41%, thus producing an inaccurate impression of health care spending. See RAND'S press release, "Health Expenses Are Less Burden on Elderly Than Thought," www.rand.org/hot/Press/elderly.html (February 9, 2001).

2. Julie Lee and Todd Anderson, "High-Cost Medicare Beneficiaries," Congressional Budget Organization (May 2005).

3. David E. Rosenbaum, "Medicare Outlook Called Direr Than Social Security's," *New York Times*, March 24, 2005, p. A18.

4. Sarah Lueck, "Medicare Is Set to Lift Premiums For Doctor Visits, Other Services," *Wall Street Journal*, March 28, 2005, p. A4.

5. See 66 FR 54264 (October 26, 2001).

6. KFF Fact Sheet, "Medicare At a Glance" (April 2005) http://www.kff.org/medicare/loader.cfm?url=commonspot/security/getfile.cfm&PageID=52974.

7. KFF Fact Sheet, "Medicare Spending and Financing," (April 2005) http://www.kff.org/medicare/loader.cfm?yrk=commonspot/security/getfile.cfm&PageID=52969.

8. CMS press release, http://www.cms.hhs.gov/media/press/release.asp?Counter=1557.

9. Robert Pear, "Medicare Will Foot the Bill For an Initial Exam at 65," *New York Times*, July 28, 2004, p. A12.

10. News item, "Medicare to Cover Scans for Alzheimer's," *Wall Street Journal*, September 17, 2004, p. B6.

11. GAO/HEHS-00-176, "Medicare Home Health Care: Prospective Payment System Could Reverse Recent Declines in Spending," September 2000.

12. *Healey v. Shalala*, 2000 WL 303439 (DC Conn. February 11, 2000).

13. Robert Pear, "More Patients in Hospice Care, but for Far Fewer Final Days," *New York Times*, September 18, 2000, p. A23; Laurie McGinley, "Terminal Patients Stay at Hospices for Shorter Period," *Wall Street Journal*, September 18, 2000, p. B2; Lucette Lagnado, "Medicare Head Tackles Criticism on Hospice Care," *Wall Street Journal*, September 15, 2000, p. B1.

14. Anna Wilde Mathews, "Medicare Drug Benefit to Cost Less," *Wall Street Journal*, August 10, 2005, p. D3; Robert Pear, "Lower Costs Are Seen for Premium in New Medicare Drug Benefit Program," *New York Times*, August 10, 2005, p. A18.

15. Barbara Martinez and Sarah Lueck, "How To Choose a Medicare Drug Plan," *Wall Street Journal* October 4, 2005 p. D1; Sarah Lueck, "Details of Medicare Drug Plan Are Released," *Wall Street Journal* October 1, 2005, p. A4; Robert Pear, "Drug Plans in Medicare Start Effort on Marketing," *New York Times*, October 1, 2005, p. A9.

16. Robert Pear, "Advisory Panel Lists Drugs It Wants New Law to Cover," *New York Times*, January 4, 2005 p. A12. There were also a lot of problems when seniors were automatically enrolled in one plan; chose to enroll in a different plan; and were charged two sets of copayments, or had problems getting the correct drugs because the two plans had different formularies: Robert Pear, "In Medicare Maze, Some Find They're Tangled Up in 2 Drug Plans," *New York Times,* March 1, 2006, p. A1. Many of the plans required pre-authorization before prescriptions for expensive drugs could be filled, and it was often difficult to secure the correct form to apply, much less to

get drugs on a timely basis to the patients who needed them: Robert Pear, "Rules of Medicare Drug Plans Slow Access to Benefits," *New York Times*, February 14, 2006, p. A17.

17. Stephanie Saul, "Another Choice for Elderly: Charity or Medicare?" *New York Times*, November 7, 2005, p. C1.

18. Kelly Greene, "Watchdogs Warn of Scams Arising Alongside Modified Drug Benefit," *Wall Street Journal*, October 18, 2005, p. D2.

19. Associated Press, "Medicare Enrolls 5.4 Million People for Drug Benefit," *Wall Street Journal* February 23, 2006 p. D2; Vanessa Fuhrmans, "Many Seniors Do the Math and Decide Not to Sign up for the Drug-Benefit Plan," *Wall Street Journal*, February 21, 2006, p. D1.

20. "Plan for the Transfer of Responsibility for Medicare Appeals," http://www.hhs.gov/medicare/appealsrpt.html (March 2004); see also the Government Accountability Office's report MEDICARE: Incomplete Plan to Transfer Appeals Workload from SSA to HHS Threatens Service to Appellants (October 2004). The appeals regulations are found at 70 FR 20224 (April 18, 2005); Robert Pear, "Medicare Change Will Limit Access to Claim Hearing," *New York Times*, April 24, 2005, p. A1; (no by-line), "CMS Restructures Medicare Claims Appeals Process," CCH Medicare & Medicaid Guide, Issue No. 1349, p. 1 (March 8, 2005).

21. See 42 USC 1395pp and 42 CFR §411.400(a).

22. Robert Pear, "Premium for Basic Medicare Increasing 13% Next Year," *New York Times*, September 17, 2005, p. A8; Sarah Lueck, "Physician Visits Under Medicare to Cost More Than First Disclosed," *Wall Street Journal*, April 1, 2005, p. A4.

23. Sarah Lueck, "Medicare Creates Structure to Spur Private Insurance," *Wall Street Journal*, December 7, 2004, p. A6.

24. Kaiser Family Foundation Fact Sheet, "Medicare Advantage" (April 2005), http://www.kff.org/medicare/loader?cfm?url=/commonspot/security/getfile/cfm&PageID=52979; "H.M.O.'s Return for a Piece of Medicare Pie," *New York Times*, March 9, 2004, p. C1.

25. Robert Pear, "Private Plans Costing More for Medicare," *New York Times*, September 17, 2004, p. A16.

26. Towers Perrin Monitor, "Boost in Medicare Payment Rates Means Good News for Employers and Retirees," (April 2004).

27. *United Seniors Ass'n v. Shalala*, 182 F.3d 965 (D.C. Cir. 1999).

28. Robert Pear, "A Help Line for Medicare Doesn't Help 39% in Study," *New York Times*, December 12, 2004, p. A37.

29. Kelly Greene, "Watchdogs Warn of Scams Arising Alongside Modified Drug Benefit," *Wall Street Journal*, October 18, 2005, p. D2.

Chapter 6

Medicaid Planning

Originally, Medicaid was designed as a program for the indigent, whereas Medicare was designed as a program to cover all senior citizens. But Medicare is limited to coverage of acute and rehabilitative care and excludes coverage of custodial long-term care. Medicaid planning developed as a response to this exclusion, so that people who needed nursing home care or equivalent levels of home care would be able to satisfy the Medicaid eligibility rules—for example, by giving away money, establishing trusts, or purchasing annuities. Medicaid is such a large, expensive, and fast-growing part of federal and state budgets that government agencies tried hard to control Medicaid planning.

These efforts culminated in the Deficit Reduction Act of 2005, P.L. 109-171, (DRA '05) which made it much harder to qualify for Medicaid, because many planning techniques were made more difficult or were ruled out entirely. (Congress adopted many of the suggestions made by state governors and legislators.) This Chapter covers both the rules that were in effect pre-DRA '05 and the new rules, because it's easier to understand the changes in light of the older rules they replace. It also takes many years for court cases to be resolved. Your clients may have created trusts, or be beneficiaries of trusts, that date back before DRA '05. Congress or the courts might reinstate the old rules, or otherwise alter the new DRA '05 scheme of things. DRA '05 was signed into law on February 8, 2006, which is now a crucial date, because many of the statute's provisions took effect on that date.[1]

Why does Medicaid matter so much? Because paying privately for long-term care is so costly, and because Medicaid is such an important factor in financing long-term care. In 2003, Medicaid covered six million senior citizens, eight million people with disabilities, 13 million other adults (mostly low-income working parents), and 25 million children—more than one-fourth of all children in the U.S. In 2002, there were about seven million Medicare/Medicaid dual eligibles. Six million received all Medicaid services; the other million were only helped with Medicare premiums and/or cost sharing. Although dual eligibles were only one-seventh of all enrollees in Medicaid, services for them consumed 42% of Medicaid spending. The overall bill for nursing home care (also in 2003) was $111 billion: 46% was paid by Medicaid, 12% by Medicare, 28% out of pocket, 8% by private insurance, and 6% by other sources.

Looking at it from the other side of the market, in 2003, Medicaid spent $83.8 billion on long-term care (36% of all Medicaid spending). About half of that amount (53%) was spent on nursing homes, 22% on home care and other services provided under waivers (programs that have permission to bypass some of the federal Medicaid requirements in order to provide services like personal care, transportation for the elderly and disabled, homemaker and chore services, and respite care), 13.5% on facilities for the developmentally disabled, 8% on personal care, and 3.5% on other home health services. In 2003, Medicaid spent an average of $1,700 for child enrollees, $1,900 for adult enrollees, $12,300 for the disabled, and $12,800 for elderly enrollees.[2]

Senior citizens and their families often find themselves between a rock and a hard place if they suffer a catastrophic medical event (such as a stroke or hip fracture) or a gradual decline in physical and mental capacity. The rock is the high cost of custodial care ($70,000 a year is a typical average figure; $175,000 a year is possible in an area where real estate prices and health care costs are especially high). The hard place is Medicare's exclusion of custodial care. A small but growing number of senior citizens have provided for these risks by buying long-term care insurance (see Chapter 4), but coverage will certainly be unavailable once an older person's health has deteriorated.

The Medicaid program, however, does cover custodial nursing home services. States are required to provide some Medicaid home care, although in most states the amount and level of care will not be adequate to meet the needs of a seriously impaired person.

Medicaid rules are complex, confusing, and change frequently. Furthermore, there are really several overlapping sets of rules. There are rules that determine how states must set up their Medicaid programs, rules that govern the eligibility of people who apply for Medicaid, and rules that govern financial transactions of Medicaid recipients and their spouses after the applicant has become eligible for Medicaid.

Before the effective date of DRA '05, Medicaid applicants had to provide information about all their financial transactions going back for three years (or five years for certain transactions involving trusts). After DRA '05, the "look-back period" for all kinds of transactions has been extended to five years. Furthermore, if the applicant is married, all of the spouse's financial transactions are also scrutinized under the same standards. It does not matter that there were sound reasons for the transactions such as re-balancing the portfolio, profit-taking on appreciated securities, saving income taxes, planning the estate, or helping a family member in financial distress. It does not even matter that the person did not know anything about Medicaid or had no intention of making a Medicaid plan until catastrophe struck.

It follows, therefore, that potential earnings from a transaction, or possible tax savings or beneficial estate tax consequences, must be balanced against potential loss of future Medicaid benefits. What makes this decision process so difficult is that current financial and tax consequences can be determined absolutely, but it is impossible to tell if a client will ever need nursing home care or extensive home care. If such care is needed it will not be known when this care will be needed, what the client's financial situation will be at that time, and what rules the Medicaid program will follow.

One important caution is that eligibility for benefits depends on following the Medicaid rules, not rules for other legal systems. The fact that something is tax-deductible, or has been removed from the potentially taxable estate, does not apply for Medicaid purposes. There is no Medicaid charitable deduction or annual exclusion, for instance, and although there is a kind of marital deduction, it does not work in the same way as it does for the estate tax. Similarly, the fact that a transaction is permitted by Medicaid rules does not exempt it from income taxation or negative estate tax consequences. There is no substitute for careful planning based on all the alternatives, by considering what will be the income tax consequences of a proposed transaction, how it will affect a possible future Medicaid application, and how it will affect the administration and taxation of the estate.

A Medicaid applicant who is denied eligibility for coverage or services has the right to an administrative hearing. All state Medicaid plans must provide for hearings when a claim is denied or not acted on with reasonable promptness. Once somebody is found eligible for Medicaid, written notice must be given when eligibility or services are reduced, suspended, or terminated. If an administrative hearing is requested, it must be carried out by an impartial hearing official at a reasonable time, date, and place. The Medicaid applicant or recipient (the term "A/R" is used to refer to both) must be allowed to present witnesses, cross-examine opposing witnesses, present arguments, and establish facts to support his or her case.

The burden of proof (that is, what the A/R has to prove to win the case) depends on what kind of case it is. Generally, whoever wants to change a situation must provide proof, so in case of denials, that would be the applicant, who has to prove eligibility in all respects. In case of reduction or stopping benefits, the burden of proof would fall on the agency. So, for example, if home care is going to be terminated, and the recipient appeals, the agency has to show that termination is justified—for example, because they are no longer medically necessary.[3]

But those rules apply to situations in which someone applies for benefits that are part of the Medicaid program and gets turned down. What about the situation where someone needs care and says that the Medicaid system should pay for it? In 2005, some federal judges limited the kinds of lawsuits that could be brought to seek broader Medicaid benefits (for example, home health and nursing home services). In 2002, the Supreme Court ruled that private suits are only allowed if Congress shows a clear intent to provide rights to individuals and not just create obligations that can be enforced by federal agencies, and judges are using this approach to say that Congress did not make provisions for private suits.[4]

Not everyone who can get to court wins. The federal District Court for the District of Connecticut held that a dementia sufferer living in an Assisted Living Facility has legal standing (acting through her guardian) to challenge Medicaid's refusal to cover ALFs. After spending down all her funds to pay for ALF care, she would be eligible for Medicaid. But, although the court held that she had standing to bring the case, she still lost, because the Medicaid statute covers room and board only in hospitals and SNFs, not in ALFs. The court rejected the guardian's arguments that the Americans With Disabilities Act, equal protection, and/or due process require adding new Medicaid services. The ADA requires even-handed treatment of all people, whether or not they have disabilities—but does not require addition of new benefits. Even if an ALF was the least restrictive alternative and the plaintiff's condition would deteriorate if she were placed in an SNF, she still would not have a legal right to require Medicaid to provide services in the setting she prefers.[5]

To make sense of the tangled thicket of Medicaid rules,[6] it helps to divide the rules into four major categories:

- Treatment of income;

- Treatment of assets;

- Rules about transfers; and

- Protection for the community spouse.

THE MEDICAID GAMBLE

Most clients do not even think about Medicaid until they are in a crisis situation. Long-term care is needed and there is little or no insurance available. Medicare benefits are used up or close to exhaustion, and the cost of care is much more than can be afforded out of current income. Paying for the care out-of-pocket therefore requires digging into assets, and perhaps depleting them and leaving the spouse short of money or even destitute. The Medicaid system includes some built-in protection for healthy spouses, and does not require the sale of a homestead as long as a spouse or minor, blind or disabled children continue to live there. These protections are not available in the private-pay system.

However, as you will see in the balance of this chapter, Medicaid eligibility can be delayed or precluded by either spouse's transactions that occurred over a period of three or five years before the application. People who wait until the last minute often discover that they are Medicaid-ineligible because of harmless, or even intelligent, activities undertaken to increase investment returns, invest in a valuable home whose value only increases over time, save taxes, or plan the estate. That is, they need care right away but their penalty period (see below) lasts for many years, or even past their predictable life expectancy.

Does that mean that the problem can be solved by engaging in Medicaid planning well before long-term care is needed? Well, yes and no. Yes, because transactions can be tailored to safeguard eligibility under current rules. But a Medicaid plan may turn out to be a bad choice for a person who does not require long-term care, such as someone who dies in an accident, suffers a catastrophic heart attack or stroke, or dies after a serious illness that is acute enough to be covered by Medicare and Medigap insurance. It is impossible to predict what Medicaid law will look like in the future. We have seen some, dramatic changes in estate tax law, and estate taxation is a subject that generally moves at the stately, slow pace of a glacier. Medicaid law is notoriously unstable.

Furthermore, tax and estate planning and Medicaid planning do not work well together. The interests of the Medicaid plan may require sales, transfers of assets, or creation of trusts at times or in ways that raise rather than lower the tax bill. Sound estate-planning moves (such as adding ascertainable standards powers to trusts) can have bad Medicaid consequences. We know for a fact that all our clients will die eventually, so some kind of estate plan is needed. We do not know if our clients will ever apply for Medicaid, when they might apply, or what the rules will be at the time of application.

It is easy to be short-sighted, and make a plan that covers only one spouse's needs. In the short run, it may make sense for the sicker spouse to make large transfers to the healthier spouse, and for the healthier spouse then to make further transfers of those amounts. But if the comparatively healthy spouse falls ill or is injured during the five years after the re-transfer, he may lose, or suffer a delay in, Medicaid eligibility because of those re-transfers.

The tax consequences to the recipient are different depending on whether a lifetime gift or an inheritance is received. The parent's Medicaid plan may call for transferring excess assets to a child or other person who would actually prefer, and have a better tax outcome, from an inheritance.

Why don't people just make better plans, and use long-term care insurance to fill the gap? The Kaiser Family Foundation, using data from the 2001 Survey of Income and Program Participation, used the Medicaid asset eligibility rules and did not count housing assets (which are exempt for most Medicaid purposes). The data can be sorted and interpreted in many ways.

The foundation assumed that $70,000 a year is the average cost of going to a nursing home. In 2005, 65% of elderly people living in the community (that is, not already residing in a nursing home) did not have enough assets to cover a year of nursing home care. Sixteen percent had enough assets to cover one to three years of care, and only 19% could cover a stay lasting three years or more. Among the low-asset group, 57% had non-housing assets of $5,000 or less. Looking at the sub-group of residents who had been in a nursing home for 90 days or more, two-thirds had been there for at least a year, and one-third for three years or more.

The people at highest risk of going to a nursing home also tended to have low assets. About a quarter (28%) of married senior citizens had enough assets to pay for three years of nursing home care, but only 8% of those with no spouse. Ability to pay declined with age: 22% of "young-old" seniors aged 65-74, 17% of those 75-84, and 12% of those 85 and over. This is predictable, because the longer a person stays retired, the more assets he or she is likely to use up even before health care needs kick in, but the more likely the person is to suffer age-related cognitive impairments or frailty that require nursing home care. One-fifth (21%) of cognitively intact seniors could afford an extended stay, but only 11% of the cognitively impaired, and while only 14% of "young-old" seniors suffered from cognitive impairment, this was true of 34% of those over 85.

Men were more likely to be able to afford prolonged nursing home care than women: 23% of men, 16% of women—but women far outnumber men as nursing home residents. If you concentrate on the one million senior citizens at high risk of nursing home use (single people over 85 impaired cognitively or with respect to ADLs), only 7% have enough assets to pay for three years of nursing home care, and 84% cannot even afford one year of care. On a more optimistic note, only 1% of the elders with enough assets to pay for three years of care are at high risk of needing an extended nursing home stay.

This calculation does not include housing equity, so adding it back into the equation could make the situation seem more promising. But for married seniors who need nursing home care, selling the home or even getting a reverse mortgage creates problems for the surviving spouse. Economists are worried that current housing prices are a bubble, which will collapse and lead to much lower values—and thus much less home equity available to pay for care. In any case, there is no simple solution to the problem of paying for care.[7]

ETHICAL AND PRACTICAL ISSUES

If you add in the ethical quandaries, you can see why many people (not all of them inside the insurance industry) consider long-term care insurance a superior alternative to Medicaid planning or want to integrate private insurance and Medicaid planning.

There is no question that Medicaid was designed, and has always been operated, as a program for the indigent (i.e., persons with very limited assets). At first blush, that is not the description of the average financial planning client. The baseline ethical issue, then, is whether it is morally appropriate to undertake steps that are permitted by law, but that take advantage of loopholes within the law. The lawyers who do Medicaid planning take the position that it is no different from tax planning or estate planning, which often require some very elaborate measures that would never be undertaken without a tax motivation.

However, other people find this exploitation of loopholes morally questionable, or simply a bad gamble. For instance, DRA '05 ruled out Medicaid eligibility for many people who engaged in elaborate planning mechanisms, even if a significant amount of time passed between the planning step and the Medicaid application. Today's elaborate planning steps could generate a big tax bill, without ever making Medicaid benefits available. Furthermore, the Medicaid system limits its recipients' freedom of choice.

Instead of being able to enter what is believed to be the best nursing home that has an available bed, the Medicaid recipient must accept the first available placement in a nursing home that has a Medicaid contract, even if the nursing home has quality problems, or is inconvenient for family visits. The simple solution to this problem is to retain enough funds to enter the preferred nursing home as a private-pay patient, then make a Medicaid application after those funds are exhausted. However, this will not work if the preferred nursing home does not participate in Medicaid.

MEDICAID HISTORY

Medicaid, like Medicare, was part of President Lyndon Johnson's Great Society program of social innovations. The two programs were supposed to take care of the medical needs of two groups of people who could not be accommodated by conventional health insurance: senior citizens (for Medicare) and the indigent (for Medicaid).

Medicare is a completely federal program. The federal government funds the program, using Medicare taxes paid as part of the Social Security tax on wages, as well as Part B and Part D premiums (and Part A premiums paid by a small group of people who would otherwise be ineligible for Medicare). Although the Medicare rules laid out in Chapter 5 may seem complex, at least there is only one set of rules for the whole country.

Medicaid works differently. The federal and the state governments collaborate. Medicaid programs are run by the states, and the individual states can customize their Medicaid programs (and set many of their own rules). The federal government subsidizes Medicaid by providing a Federal Medicaid Assistance Percentage (FMAP) to the states.

The poorer the state, the higher the level of FMAP. FMAP levels range from 50 to 83% of the cost of Medicaid. The state itself makes up the difference between the FMAP level and the actual cost of the program. In order to qualify for FMAP, state Medicaid programs must satisfy minimum standards set by the federal government. At the other end of the scale, certain programs are too generous for federal standards, and do not qualify for FMAP. If the state wants to provide such programs and services, it must pay 100% of the cost. The result is that each state has its own Medicaid rules and its own mix of Medicaid services.

Federal law provides for "waivers": situations in which a state obtains federal permission to create programs that receive FMAP even though they fail to satisfy the basic federal requirements. Waiver programs are especially important for provision of Medicaid home care.

The Medicaid program is Title XIX of the federal Social Security Act. Medicaid law is found at Title 42, United States Code Section 1396 *et seq.* Complete understanding of Medicaid also requires understanding of a state's policies. Unfortunately, in many states, important Medicaid rules are not enacted in the state's code of laws, where anyone can read them. Important issues are often settled by hard-to-find state and local regulations and the internal rules of the Medicaid agency of a particular state.

Although it is not an official regulation, and therefore neither the CMS nor state Medicaid agencies are obligated to follow it, the CMS' State Medicaid Manual (SMM) is an excellent, clearly-expressed resource for understanding Medicaid rules and their practical application. You may be able to obtain a printed copy from your local Medicaid office or from an elder law attorney with whom you work. The SMM can also be downloaded from Web sites such as the Kansas Elder Law Network or the CMS' website.

When this edition went to press in the spring of 2006, there were many pressures on the Medicaid system, including an increasing caseload (swollen by unemployed and uninsured persons as well as by the growing number of senior citizens) and increasing health care costs. These problems motivated the big changes in the Medicaid program imposed by DRA '05.

A study published in 2005 for the National Governors Association showed that Medicaid is the largest health program in the United States—even larger than Medicare—offering health care, including long-term care, for 53 million people.

Total federal and state Medicaid spending for 2005 is estimated to be about $329 billion, more than 2.5% of the Gross Domestic Product. In 2003, 46% of nursing home bills were paid by Medicaid, and more than two-thirds of nursing home residents were on Medicaid. (The difference is due to the fact that Medicaid pays lower rates than the private-pay rates).

In 1990, Medicaid represented 12% of total expenditures by state government, and education for kindergarten through high school was 23%. In 2003, Medicaid was 21% of the state budget and education was 22%. In most states, the problem is even worse because actual spending is much higher than the budgeted amount. The *New York Times* reported that in 2004, 21 states passed cost control measures that reduced or restricted their Medicaid programs, and 14 states planned to do that in 2005.[8]

In 2005, Utah adopted an experimental plan providing partial Medicaid coverage. Recipients can get doctor or emergency room visits for a small fee, but are not covered for extended hospitalization or visits to medical specialists. The assumption is that if Medicaid beneficiaries need these services, they will find charity care. Utah took this step reasoning that it's better to increase the number of people covered under the Medicaid program even though some of them will not be fully covered.[9]

MEDICAID VOCABULARY

A married person who needs long-term care is usually referred to as the "sick spouse" or "Medicaid spouse." Some Medicaid provisions affect both people who have already qualified for Medicaid and those who have applied (or might apply in the future), so the term "Medicaid A/R" (standing for "applicant or recipient") is often encountered. The date of institutionalization is the date on which the sick spouse enters a nursing home or begins to receive a comparable level of Medicaid home care.

One of the most important choices that state Medicaid programs can make is whether the state will be a "medically needy" state or a "cap" state. In a "medically needy" state, Medicaid services can be provided to a person who is "medically needy": whose assets are within the state eligibility limits, and who agrees to "spend down." "Spend down" means to pay all excess income to the nursing home or other long-term care provider, before Medicaid payments to the provider begin.

In a "cap" state, however, most Medicaid services (including nursing home care) will be denied to a person whose income exceeds the "income cap," even if that person has no assets and cannot afford to pay privately for nursing home care. A state's income cap may not exceed three times the benefit that the individual would receive if he were poor enough to receive Supplemental Security Income (SSI) benefits, which are a federal welfare program for the aged, blind, and disabled. The 2005 cap amount is $1,737.00[10]

Medicaid planning is very difficult in cap states, because for many, their Social Security benefit plus their private pension will exceed the cap, and there is no way to anticipate these amounts or transfer them to someone else. Therefore, in a cap state, it is often advisable for people who have access to lump-sum pension payments to elect the lump sum (which can be transferred or placed into a trust) instead of a continuing stream of pension payments. Another possibility is to put the extra income into a trust. In some states or some circumstances, a court must approve the creation of the trust, and supervise trust administration.

In January, 2001, CMS published a Final Rule making technical changes in the way states determine eligibility for medically needy applicants and to certain other Medicaid applicants, including Qualified Medicare Beneficiaries (QMBs, those who get help with their Medicare co-payment responsibilities, but not other health care services, from the Medicaid system). The result of these changes is that more Medicaid applicants will be able to "spend down" their excess income and therefore qualify for Medicaid, including Medicaid home care–so fewer people will be institutionalized inappropriately.[11]

Income Issues

The Medicaid definition of "income" generally includes anything, such as Social Security benefits or pension payments, that is paid on a one-time or continuing basis. "Assets" are financial assets such as bank accounts, securities, and real estate other than the homestead. Medicaid law has been revised to make it clear that barriers between income and assets are not absolute. For example, if income is received in a particular month, anything that is not spent in that month becomes an asset. Also, many kinds of income received by senior citizens cannot be "anticipated," meaning that it is not permitted to assign rights to future Social Security or pension benefits. For income that can be anticipated, transfers of income follow the same rules as transfers of assets (see below).

A New York court has held that although a nursing home resident and Medicaid recipient cannot literally be forced to turn over Social Security benefits to the nursing home, because federal law prevents garnishment of Social Security benefits, the resident still has a legal obligation to contribute the "spend-down" amount toward the cost of care. In practical terms, this will usually require using part or all of the Social Security benefits.[12]

Protecting the Spouse at Home

Assets can be "available" for Medicaid purposes even if they are entitled to protection in other contexts. The Supreme Court of New Jersey held that one spouse's IRA is available to the other spouse for Medicaid purposes, even though IRA accounts have favorable tax treatment and are protected against the claims of creditors.[13] A few months later, an Ohio appeals court made a similar decision.[14] However, at the end of 1999, a Wisconsin appeals court disagreed with the New Jersey decision, finding that community spouses should not be required to tap into pension funds or IRAs to make the sick spouse eligible for Medicaid. In this analysis, pension funds and IRAs are not easy to transfer between spouses when one spouse needs to be institutionalized, so there is little potential for abuse of the system.[15]

The Medicaid system makes provisions for the needs of the "community spouse" (also called the "healthy" or "well" spouse). The community spouse is the spouse of an institutionalized Medicaid recipient. Without these provisions, the financial condition of the community spouse would often be desperate, because of the need to pay the mortgage or rent and meet other personal financial needs while the couple's entire financial resources were devoted to the care of the sick spouse. Because over three-quarters of nursing home residents are not married, these provisions are not available to many needy nursing home residents.

To protect the community spouse, the community spouse is allowed to have an amount of assets that will not cause the sick spouse to be ineligible for Medicaid. This amount is known as the Community Spouse Resource Allowance (CSRA). When the obligation of the sick spouse to "spend down" is computed, there is allowed a monthly payment to the community spouse, which reduces the amount that must be spent down. This monthly payment is referred to as the Community Spouse Income Allowance (CSIA).

States are allowed to set their own CSIA and CSRA levels, as long as they stay within federal guidelines. The CSIA must be at least $1,604 a month (through June 2006) and may not be higher than $2,378 (for 2006). Although there are some technical differences, the CSIA is similar to the concept of the "minimum monthly maintenance needs allowance" (MMMNA) for the community spouse. The MMMNA has two components: basic needs and housing needs.

The CSRA can be anywhere from $19,908 to $99,540 (2006 figures), and states may use many different techniques for calculating the CSRA. Federal law provides that a state must allow at least the minimum CSRA, and may allow up to the maximum. Or, it can let the healthy spouse get either the "snapshot" spousal amount (see below) or the maximum, whichever is less. In addition to the generally applicable CSRA, if the healthy spouse can convince a Medicaid hearing officer to allow a larger amount, or can obtain a court order for a larger amount, that must be permitted as the CSRA.

Some of the states simply look at the personal assets of the community spouse, and if his assets are below this level, a transfer can be made. A more complex methodology compares half of the couple's joint resources to the CSRA level, and also compares the healthy spouse's personal assets. The community spouse can retain half of the combined assets, but can retain the minimum CSRA (even if it is more than half), but cannot retain more than the maximum (even if it is less than half).

See below for a more detailed discussion of "post-eligibility" financial issues.

Assets and the "Snapshot"

A Medicaid application triggers a one-time calculation of the "snapshot" amount. The applicant discloses all assets he owns (and his spouse owns, if the applicant is married). The assets are aggregated, and half the assets are considered to belong to each spouse. The spouses are entitled to require that an assessment be done as soon as one spouse enters a nursing home, even if the Medicaid application will not be made immediately. Having the assessment done in advance speeds up the application if and when it is made.

The snapshot is not very significant if the person enters the nursing home as a Medicaid recipient, or applies immediately after entry. Nor is it significant in states (such as New York and Pennsylvania) which have adopted the maximum CSRA. But it can make a big difference if the person enters the nursing home as a private-pay patient and does not apply for Medicaid until later, at a time when marital assets have declined significantly (probably as a result of paying privately for care.)

The State Medicaid Manual's (SMM) Section 3262.2 adds the concept of the "spousal share" to the determination. The spousal share is half of the couple's combined non-exempt resources at the time the sick spouse enters a nursing home. The spousal share does not change, even if the actual amount of marital assets changes.

When the actual Medicaid application is made, the community spouse is entitled to the "protected amount," which is the highest of these four figures:

- The spousal share, but not more than the maximum CSRA (2006 figure: $99,540);

- The CSRA level actually adopted by the state;

- The enhanced CSRA allowed by a court support order (see below); or

- The enhanced CSRA permitted after a Medicaid fair hearing.

The sick spouse is eligible for Medicaid if his resources, after the community spouse receives the protected amount, are below the state's Medicaid resource level (usually set at $1,500 to $2,000).

The SMM gives the example of a couple whose non-exempt resources at the time the sick spouse enters the nursing home are $120,000. That makes the spousal share $60,000 (half the resources). The application for Medicaid does not occur until their resources have been reduced to $90,000.

Assume that the couple does not have a court order or fair hearing to enhance the CSRA. Also assume that the state has adopted a CSRA of $35,000. The state's Medicaid resource level is $2,000. From the $90,000 in combined resources, $60,000 is subtracted (the larger of the spousal share ($60,000) or the state's CSRA ($35,000)). This remaining $30,000 is the amount used to determine the institutionalized spouse's eligibility. The sick spouse is not yet eligible for Medicaid because the remaining resources exceed $2,000. But as soon as the couple's combined resources fall below $62,000 (the spousal share plus the $2,000 limit), the sick spouse will become eligible.

What if the couple had started out with more resources? The spousal share could never be more than the maximum CSRA. If they had started out with less, then in all probability, all of the assets would be able to go to the community spouse. The SMM gives another example of a couple with combined resources of $20,000 when the sick spouse entered the nursing home, and resources of $10,000 at the time of the Medicaid application. The spousal share is $10,000 (half the resources upon entry into the nursing home). The community spouse would be entitled to the state's CSRA level of $30,000. The sick spouse would be entitled to retain the state's Medicaid resource level (the example assumes that it is $3,000). If his personal resources are $8,000 out of the couple's $10,000, he is immediately eligible and can transfer $5,000 of the $8,000 to the community spouse. Because the spousal share is lower than the CSRA, the CSRA rather than the spousal share is used in the calculation.

SPOUSAL REFUSAL

Theoretically, husbands and wives have an equal duty to support one another. In many instances, the spouse with more income and assets gets sick and enters a nursing home first. The CSRA and CSIA recognize this duty of support. However, it is perfectly possible that the sick spouse will have very limited personal income and resources. What is the obligation of the healthy, more affluent, community spouse?

Perhaps surprisingly, federal Medicaid law contains a "just say no" provision. That is, state Medicaid agencies are not allowed to deny Medicaid benefits to patients on the grounds that their wealthier spouses refuse to support them or let any of their own income or resources be used. However, part of the Medicaid application process is an agreement to assign support rights to the Medicaid agency. The Medicaid agency then has a legal right to sue the community spouse for non-support. Whether this is a meaningful threat to individual community spouses depends on the local policy. Some Medicaid agencies are very active in this matter, but most bring few or no non-support suits.

Community spouses who want to preserve their own financial position, but who do not want to engage in outright "spousal refusal" can enter into an agreement with the state Medicaid agency. Usually, offering 25% of the difference between the community spouse's actual income and the MMMNA will be acceptable. For instance, a person with $3,000 a month income as compared to a $2,000 MMMNA will probably not be sued if he offers, and actually pays, $250 a month to the Medicaid agency for the care of the sick spouse.

PRACTICE TIP: Medicaid benefits can be denied to the spouse of a healthy person who refuses to provide information about his financial situation, so make sure that potential community spouses provide disclosure, even if they want to make a spousal refusal.

A New York case held that, to recoup its Medicaid expenditures from a community spouse who made a spousal refusal, the state must show that the spouse had enough income and resources to pay for the care at the time the right of refusal was exercised. In the case, $221,000 in Medicaid benefits were expended on behalf of a sick spouse between 1993 and 1997. New York's Medicaid law creates an implied contract for reimbursement, as long as, at the time of the initial assessment, the refusing spouse can afford to contribute to care. The initial assessment date is chosen to relieve the agency of the burden of having to make constant re-calculations.[16]

In July of 2005, the Second Circuit upheld the principle of spousal refusal—the first Court of Appeals to tackle the issue. After the husband entered a nursing home, he applied for Medicaid and made the required assignment of his spousal rights to the state. The wife (the community spouse) submitted a spousal refusal form. At that point, her assets were about $150,000 greater than the Community Spouse Resource Allowance. The Second Circuit noted that the statute permits spousal refusals; the proper action for the state agency is to grant Medicaid and then sue the spouse for non-support.[17]

TRANSFER PENALTIES

The planner must never forget that Medicaid is a program for the indigent, so the level of non-exempt assets is crucial in determining eligibility. If it were possible simply to give away the excess assets, then everybody could qualify for Medicaid. To protect the financial stability of the system, Medicaid law imposes transfer penalties on people who give away assets and then apply for Medicaid nursing home care, or Medicaid home care provided under a waiver program.[18]

A transfer is either an outright gift, or selling an asset for less than its fair market value (in this instance, only the uncompensated part of the transaction is a transfer). The transfer-of-asset rules are found in 42 USC Section 1396p(c). Before 1993, the transfer rules applied only to transfers of resources, but since then, transfers of income have also been subject to penalties.

Transfers that are exempt (they do not affect Medicaid eligibility) include the following:

- A transfer by one spouse to the other spouse;

- A transfer by one spouse to someone else, for the sole benefit of the other spouse;

- A transfer to the Medicaid applicant's blind or disabled child, or to a trust that benefits only blind or disabled children of the transferor;

- A transfer to a trust whose sole beneficiaries are one or more disabled persons under age 65;

- A transfer that was made only for a purpose other than qualifying for Medicaid;[19]

- A transfer by someone who intended to dispose of the assets at their fair market value;

- A transfer that is reversed, in that the property is given back to the transferor (even though there is no transfer penalty, the person may become ineligible because of possessing the additional property); and

- A hardship case, where denying Medicaid would be life-threatening (applicants who claim hardship must be given an administrative hearing to prove their case).

The exempt transfer of homestead is discussed below.

Some transfers are so remote in time from the Medicaid application that they will not be taken into consideration. The "look-back" period is the amount of time during which a Medicaid agency can scrutinize financial transactions. Under DRA '05, the look-back period for all transfers is 60 months. That is, when a person applies for Medicaid, he must disclose information about all financial transactions, including gifts and charitable contributions that occurred in the 60 months before the application. Of course, the applicant who has to disclose all of his or her assets and financial transactions may find this loss of privacy infuriating or humiliating, but it is part of the "cost of doing business" with the Medicaid system.

Apart from emotional factors, many older people lack the detailed financial records that the Medicaid application requires. This is especially true of people with poor eyesight, or some degree of mental confusion. In such cases, the planning team may have to hire a "daily money manager," accountant, or even a private investigator to straighten out the transaction history and present it in an acceptable form.

Once Medicaid eligibility is established, it runs three months retroactively. Therefore, if the applicant can prove that he paid out-of-pocket for health costs, or that a family member or friend paid these expenses, then the Medicaid agency has an obligation to reimburse the applicant. If the applicant reimburses someone who advanced funds for health expenses, this constitutes repayment of a loan, not a transfer. However, there must be contemporary (not after-the-fact) financial records to substantiate the reimbursement argument.

In September of 2005, the Government Accountability Office reported to Congress about the transfer practices of senior citizen households. In 2003, GAO found that nationwide expenditures for all kinds of long-term care (not just nursing homes) were $183 billion. Medicaid paid almost half of the total: $93 billion. Obviously, keeping these costs in control is an important problem for federal and state budgeters. Congress asked GAO to study whether there is a widespread practice of potentially abusive transfers to qualify for Medicaid, or whether this is a small-scale phenomenon that doesn't have much effect on the Medicaid system. The budget for FY 2006 proposed by the Bush Administration looks for $1.5 billion savings over a five-year period by tightening up asset transfer rules.

Because figures are not available right away, the GAO used data from the 2002 Health and Retirement Study (HRS). Their findings have some important implications for Medicaid policy. In 2002, HRS found that there were 28 million "elderly households" (i.e., households where at least one member was a senior citizen). Just under half (46%) of elderly households consisted of elderly couples; 41% of elderly households were single women, and 13% single men. Single women had the lowest level of income and assets.

Only 20% of those households had annual incomes of $50,000 or more. The median income (i.e., the point at which half the households had more income and half had less) for senior citizen households was $24,200. About half the households had non-housing assets over $50,000; the other half had lower assets. (Therefore, even if a person devotes all assets to paying for long-term care, it takes only half a year of $70,000 care to run through life savings of $35,000!) However, a meaningful percentage of elderly households (20%) had non-housing resources over $300,000 (one person studied had more than $40 million), so this is a group where the Medicaid system might be able to make some savings in terms of greater payments responsibilities or enhanced estate recovery. For all of the elderly households in the study, the median value of the primary residence (net of mortgage and other debts) was $70,000, although the range was from below zero (because of heavy indebtedness) to $20 million!

More than one-fifth of elderly households (22%) reported that they made cash transfers in the two years before the study. Of course there are many reasons other than Medicaid planning why someone would make financial transfers: estate planning; generosity to family members; assisting family members with their own financial problems; charitable contributions. In general, a Medicaid applicant who has made transfers during the look-back period will be given a chance to prove that gifts were made for other reasons (e.g., a son or daughter needed an operation and didn't have insurance) and not so the senior transferor could qualify for Medicaid.

The higher the level of disability in a household, the less income and assets it was likely to have (because disability often limits earning capacity, and because of the need to pay for medical care). More disability also means a higher risk of requiring long-term care. Senior citizens with limitations in three or more ADLs had a median income of $13,200 and median non-housing assets of $3,200. About a fifth of these households made transfers in the two years before the study; the median transferred amount was $3,000—a small amount that, even if recaptured, would have little impact on Medicaid's financial problems.

Nearly all of the states (38 of them) require Medicaid applicants to provide detailed information about their assets. Seven more states required submission of general information about assets. The other six states raised the question of assets at the application interview but didn't require paperwork. (Thirty states use either a face-to-face application interview or a phone interview with the applicant or the applicant's personal representative.)

An even larger number of states (44) require disclosure of asset transfers. In 11 states, applicants have to state whether they have transferred assets in the previous 36 months (the general look-back period), 13 ask about transfers over 60 months (the look-back period for trusts), and 17 ask about both.[20]

Georgetown University's Health Policy Institute concluded that the Medicaid system is not suffering from the inappropriate efforts of "Medicaid Millionaires"; the author of the report, Ellen O'Brien, concluded that the average gift by Medicaid applicants was $5,000, and these gifts had minimal impact on the program. Dr. O'Brien said that the "poor widow" scenario is much more common: a healthy senior citizen woman is involved in her husband's long-term care, which depletes the family's assets. Then she's widowed, and has to get by on surviving-spouse benefits. Close to a third of her income has to be devoted to paying medical expenses that Medicare doesn't cover (as well as premiums to Medicare itself). Although she assumes she'll never end up in a nursing home, that's just what happens. "That's the heart of the Medicaid story [...] and it's just horrible."[21]

The Penalty Period

If non-exempt transfers did occur during the look-back period, Medicaid law requires the imposition of a "penalty period:" a number of months during which Medicaid services will be denied. The calculation involves dividing the non-exempt transfers made during the look-back period by an official figure used to represent the cost of private-pay nursing home care in the relevant geographic area of the state. Before DRA '05, in most cases, the penalty period would begin when the transfer was made, giving applicants some opportunity to control the situation by deferring their Medicaid applications until all transfers were safely before the look-back period, until the penalty period for all transfers had elapsed, or both.

EXAMPLE [using pre-DRA '05 rules]: Gail Lespinasse made two transfers: a gift of $25,000 to her daughter, made 40 months before her Medicaid application, and a gift of $50,000 to her son, made 20 months before her Medicaid application. Because these are outright gifts, the look-back period is 36 months (not 60 months). The gift to her daughter occurred outside the look-back period, so it does not count. The gift to her son occurred during the look-back period, so it does count. If the official cost-of-care figure is $5,000 a month, then Mrs. Lespinasse's penalty period is 10 months. If there were no other factors involved, Mrs. Lespinasse would be eligible for Medicaid as soon as she applied, because her penalty period began 20 months ago (when the transfer was made) and ended 10 months later.

Under the current rules, however, both transfers fall within the 60 month look-back period.

Until 1993, there was a maximum penalty period of 36 months. No matter how large the transfer, the penalty period would never be longer than 36 months. (It is just a coincidence that this is the same as the look-back period.) So anyone who had three years of long-term care insurance coverage could be certain of qualifying for Medicaid once the coverage was used up. However, a 1993 federal law removed the maximum, so that the theoretical penalty period is unlimited in length.

Under the old rules the penalty period runs from the date of the transfer, which is simple enough to apply if there is only one transfer. If there is only one transfer, but it is less than one month's official cost of care, the state can choose between imposing a penalty for part of a month, or not imposing a penalty at all. If the penalty is not an even number of months, most states round down. A transfer of $40,000 and an official amount of $3,000 a month will generally give rise to a 13-month penalty (13⅓, rounded down).

If there are several transfers, the penalty periods must run consecutively. In the past, some states allowed "stacking" of transfers, so that the penalty for one transfer would expire in March, and the penalty for a second, smaller transfer would expire in February. Congress put a stop to that in 1993. Individuals cannot gain any advantage by splitting up transfers into an overlapping series, and a second penalty period does not begin until the first has been exhausted.

According to the State Medicaid Manual Section 3258.5H, if assets are transferred in a way that the penalty periods would overlap, the A/R will be subject to a single penalty period that begins on the first day of the first month of the first transfer. For example, in a state where the official cost of care is $2,500, transfers of $10,000 each in January, February, and March would be treated as a single transfer on January 1, giving rise to a 12-month penalty ($30,000/$2,500). This is so because there would be a four-month penalty period for each individual transfer, so the periods would overlap. If there are multiple transfers but the penalty periods would not overlap, then each penalty period starts and ends, then the next one starts and ends. If the official cost-of-care figure is $4,000, and transfers of $8,000 each are made in January, August, and November, there will be three separate penalty periods: January and February (because of the two-month penalty generated by transferring $8,000 in January), August and September, and November and December.

The new law changes the situation by starting the penalty period on the later of two dates:

1. the first day of the first month during or after which there has been a non-exempt transfer of assets, and which does not occur in any other period of ineligibility (this refers to the new rules for handling multiple transfers); or

2. on the date on which the applicant is already getting long-term care, and would otherwise be eligible for Medicaid.

That is to say, in the common situation that a senior citizen is sick enough to be placed in a nursing home and makes a Medicaid application, if there were any transfers during the five-year look-back period, the penalty period does not begin until the person applies for Medicaid.

Typically, a senior citizen will make donations of money or property for a variety of reasons: charity, reducing future estate tax, cutting income tax obligations, helping family members, and, yes, Medicaid planning.

EXAMPLE: Celia Kroeger enters a nursing home and applies for Medicaid on June 8, 2006. During the five years before the application, she made gifts and transfers of $42,000. Her state uses an official cost figure of $7,000 a month. Therefore, her penalty period is six months. Under prior law, she would probably be eligible immediately (depending on when the transfers were made). But under post-DRA '05 law, the penalty period does not start until June 8, 2006, so she is not eligible until December 8, 2006.

The problem is that merely because a penalty period is incurred, it does not mean that the transferred assets can be taken back and used to pay for care—or that the elder has other assets or insurance to pay privately during the penalty period. It is certain that this provision will be challenged in court, and Congress may move to amend it, because it creates very serious problems for the health care industry. Hospitals are not allowed to discharge patients unless there is a safe and appropriate place to send them; nursing homes are generally not allowed to discharge patients for non-payment. So the new rules create a risk that either patients will be discharged inappropriately, hospitals will bill Medicare for the patients they can't discharge, or nursing homes will go out of business because of the amount of uncompensated care they are forced to provide.

Before DRA '05, states had options about how to treat small transfers, or transfers resulting in fractional months of ineligibility. For example, if the state's official cost of care figure was $6,000, a transfer of $5,000 would create a penalty period of less than one month; a transfer of $32,000 would create a penalty period of 5.4 months. Under prior law, states, could disregard the less-than-one-month penalty period, or could round down the 5.4 month period to an even 5 months. DRA '05 tightens up the rule: states must impose partial month penalties, and are no longer allowed to round down.

The DRA '05 rules for calculating penalty periods when there are multiple transfers allow the state to add up all the non-exempt transfers during the penalty period and treat them as a single transfer, with the penalty period beginning on the earliest date that would apply to all of the transfers.

Because a transfer by one spouse will affect the other spouse's eligibility, and if a penalty is assessed against the first spouse to enter a nursing home, the penalty period is divided between the spouses if the one-time community spouse makes a Medicaid application (i.e., the same transfer does not create two separate penalty periods).

However, once one spouse qualifies for Medicaid, the community spouse will be able to transfer his or her own assets–transfers by the community spouse will no longer affect the sick spouse's Medicaid eligibility.[22]

Although the DRA '05 rules are harsh, they do require states to waive (forgive; not apply) the penalty period in cases of "undue hardship." As amended, Social Security Act § 1917(c)(2)(D) defines undue hardship as deprivation of the necessities of life (food, clothing, shelter), or deprivation of medical care to the point that health or life is endangered. All of the state Medicaid agencies have an obligation to notify Medicaid applicants and recipients of the possibility of applying for a hardship waiver. The states are required to have application procedures and appeals procedures for those who protest denials. If a nursing home resident or the resident's guardian agrees, nursing homes have legal authority to file a hardship waiver on the resident's behalf.

TREATMENT OF THE HOMESTEAD

The Medicaid rules about family homes have also been changed drastically by DRA '05. Under earlier law, the value of one principal residence was disregarded in determining Medicaid eligibility. This was true no matter how luxurious or costly the home was, and how recently it was purchased before the Medicaid application. Therefore, a bedrock Medicaid planning technique was to use excess cash, or to sell stock or other excess assets, and use the money to buy a home (if the person did not already own one); to fix up the existing home (either by making repairs or making it handicap-accessible); or to sell the existing home and use both the sales proceeds and the excess assets to purchase a more valuable home. Purchases made at market price have never been considered transfers. The net result, under the old rules, was that eligibility was created or preserved by transforming excess assets into exempt housing equity.

The family home remains exempt for Medicaid eligibility purposes as long as it is a "homestead," meaning as long as the Medicaid beneficiary lives there and receives home care. It also remains exempt after the Medicaid beneficiary enters a nursing home, as long as a community spouse or a minor, blind, or disabled child continues to live there. But note that if the Medicaid beneficiary is a single, childless person (or has adult children who live elsewhere) and is permanently confined to an institution,[23] the home is no longer a homestead, and its value will be treated as an excess asset. Therefore, the single nursing home resident may have to sell the home and go off Medicaid until the excess amount has been spent down. Another possibility is to do a "half a loaf" plan (see below) and transfer some of the excess value and spend down the rest.

DRA '05 denies Medicaid eligibility to persons who have excess homestead equity. The general rule is that a person with equity over $500,000 will be ineligible for Medicaid (even if he or she has not made any transfers during the look-back period) unless the homestead is also the home of the applicant's spouse or his or her minor, blind or disabled child. States have the option of increasing this figure to $750,000, but no further. In many areas of the country, even a modest house (especially one that has sheltered the family for a long time, especially if it has been passed down between generations) will cost more than $500,000, and senior homeowners typically are mortgage-free so they have a great deal of equity. The intent of the statute is to require elders to enter into reverse mortgages or get home equity loans, and then use the proceeds to buy long-term care insurance or pay privately for care.

Homestead Transfers

Medicaid law contains some special, permissive provisions for transfers of homesteads. At this point, you may be shaking your head in disbelief. If the homestead is favored for Medicaid purposes, why transfer it? Because, unless it is transferred, the state Medicaid agency may be entitled to place a claim against the estate after the recipient dies (see below).

Certain transfers of the homestead to close family members can be made without penalty. No matter how large the value of the transfer, it does not give rise to a penalty period. The permitted transferees are

- a spouse;

- a minor, blind, or disabled child;

- one or more siblings who already have partial ownership of the home, and who lived there for at least a year before the transferor entered the institution (this provision copes with the common situation of parents leaving the family home to a group of siblings); or

- a "caregiver child;" a son or daughter who, for a period of at least two years provided hands-on care to a parent that was able to delay the need for nursing home institutionalization. Caregiver child status is not available to a child who lives elsewhere, even if he provides significant financial support.[24]

Reverse Mortgages

In an ordinary mortgage, the lender advances a lump sum for purchase of the home and the homeowner then repays the lender in a series of monthly payments. The mortgage usually requires immediate repayment of the balance if the home is sold, unless the purchaser wants to and is allowed to assume the mortgage. However, the majority of senior citizens own homes that are fully or nearly mortgage-free.

A reverse mortgage, like a home equity loan, is a means of achieving liquidity in the home equity without selling the home. The lender agrees either to provide a lump sum or to make a stream of continuing payments (this is known as a reverse annuity mortgage, or RAM) to the homeowner. The lender is entitled to repayment at a stated rate of interest, but repayment is not required as long as the mortgagor or mortgagor's spouse continues to live there. Once the spouses are both deceased, in nursing homes, or have moved out of the house, repayment is required. Some reverse mortgages also give the lender a share in the appreciation in value of the home.

The Medicaid planning significance of reverse mortgages is that federal rules consider the mortgage to be a transaction for value in which the Medicaid beneficiary assumes a debt obligation. Therefore, there is no transfer and no transfer penalty, and the money paid by the mortgagee-lender to the mortgagor-homeowner does not constitute income for Medicaid purposes.

The downside is that, sooner or later, the mortgage must be repaid, and this is usually done by selling the home and turning the proceeds over to the lender. So if the family intends for children to inherit and live in the house, or for them to receive the entire sale proceeds (not just whatever is left after the reverse mortgage is paid off), the reverse mortgage will conflict with this plan. But if there are no children to inherit or the children have homes of their own or have no intention of living in the area, or if it seems likely that a Medicaid application will be made in the near future (so transfers would create an unwieldy penalty period), the reverse mortgage can be a worthwhile device.

ESTATE RECOVERIES

Before 1993, Medicaid planning fit in well with conventional planning, because most transfers were made to spouses or family members, who would normally be the beneficiaries of the estate plan. Furthermore, if assets could be made unavailable (for instance, by placing them into trusts), in many cases they could be transmitted free of claims from the state Medicaid agency, because at that time, the only asset that could be claimed after the Medicaid recipient's death was an interest in the homestead.

When a Medicaid recipient dies, the state Medicaid agency is still entitled to place a claim against the homestead. However, if the recipient's surviving spouse or minor, blind, or disabled child lives in the homestead, the enforcement of the claim must be delayed until they die or move away. (This is similar, but not identical, to the list of people to whom the home can be transferred without penalty.) This provision protects vulnerable people who want to remain in their homes. But if they decide to sell the home, an estate recovery claim can be placed on the sales proceeds.

The estate recovery claim against a homestead is theoretically the amount that the Medicaid agency spent to provide nursing home care to the recipient, but it is limited by the deceased recipient's interest in the home.

EXAMPLE: Crystal Davis spent three years in a nursing home. The state Medicaid agency paid $40,000 a year for her care, or a total of $120,000. Before moving to the nursing home, she lived in a home that she inherited from her parents and owned with her sister Evelyn. After Crystal's death, Evelyn sold the home for $200,000. The state Medicaid agency could place a claim of $100,000 against the sale proceeds. Crystal was a one-half owner, so her share of the home (no longer a homestead, because Evelyn was not a spouse or minor, blind, or disabled child) was worth $100,000, which is less than the $120,000 expended on her behalf by the Medicaid agency. If Crystal had transferred the home to Evelyn before moving to the nursing home, the state Medicaid agency would not have been able to recover against Crystal's estate.

Since 1993, the state agency's recovery power has been extended, and now covers all of the deceased recipient's interests in financial assets. Under most circumstances, the Medicaid beneficiary would have transferred all financial assets in order to qualify. However, there may be interests in items like income-only trusts.

Federal Medicaid law defines the "estate" to include the decedent's entire interest in all kinds of assets. However, some state statutes limit the state's recovery power to the probate estate, with the result that jointly owned property and revocable trusts are not subject to estate recovery, because they do not enter the probate estate.

If the state decides to pursue estate recovery, it must wait not only until the Medicaid recipient has died, but, if there is a surviving spouse, until the surviving spouse has died, too.

Although the Medicaid rules require that applicants be informed of the possible consequences of the application, including estate recovery, there is no provision for warning potential heirs that they will not receive the inheritance they expected because of Medicaid paybacks. The estate recovery provisions are more than a decade old, but in practice for many years states did little to go after estates. That is beginning to change as the financial impact of Medicaid on state budgets increases.

AARP's Public Policy Institute says that in the 46 states that provided survey information, total collections more than tripled between 1995 and 2005, reaching $350 million a year in the later year.

California announced plans to seek estate recovery based on Medicaid expenditures of as little as $500. Ohio passed a law allowing recovery of non-probate assets as well as assets included in the probate estate—including homes jointly held with a child. Massachusetts passed a similar law in 2003 but repealed it in 2004 because it was so controversial.

West Virginia made a dramatic turn-around. The state sued the federal government twice to protest the Medicaid rule requiring estate recovery, a rule that West Virginia denounced as "abhorrent." But by May 2005, the state, facing a severe budget shortfall, announced that it would seek recovery against all estates greater than $5,000, rather than the previous policy of seeking recovery only when the estate exceeded $50,000. Texas found estate recovery politically unpopular in 1989, when the state was criticized for going after widows and orphans—but reinstated it in 2005.

California recovered more than $54 million from the estates of persons who received benefits under Medi-Cal (the state's Medicaid system), but it's also the state with the largest Medicaid population. In the 2003 fiscal year, Oregon recovered $10 million from estates, representing about 2% of the state's long-term care budget. In contrast, Louisiana recovered only $85,907 that year. Most of the states turn the recovered funds over to the state Medicaid agency, but about a dozen states put some or all of the recovery into general funds.

According to AARP, more than half of the states waive making recovery if that would deprive the Medicaid recipient's survivors of the necessities of life—but the states have different definitions of what this means. When it comes to recovering what used to be the family home, most states defer the recovery effort at least until the surviving spouse dies, but about a dozen states will begin recovery proceedings if the surviving spouse does not live there (for instance, is in an assisted living facility or nursing home).[25]

The general rule is that estate recovery applies only to the estate of the Medicaid recipient, not the estate of a surviving spouse. However, some recent cases permit states to apply their own statutes, calling for recovery against the estate of the surviving spouse despite arguments from attorneys that these state laws contradict the Social Security Act. North Dakota allowed recovery from the community spouse's estate if that estate includes only assets acquired from the Medicaid recipient by joint tenancy, tenancy in common, life estate, living trust, or other arrangement. A Minnesota court allowed the state Medicaid agency to receive reimbursement from the surviving spouse's estate up to the amount of assets that were jointly owned or marital property at any time during the marriage.[26] The moral? Make sure that you understand the local Medicaid rules.

The state of New Hampshire had aggressive estate recovery policies, including filing liens against the surviving spouses of Medicaid recipients, against property in which the surviving spouse had an interest; demanding payment from the community spouse as a condition of releasing the Medicaid lien; and trying to recover against the entire value of joint property, not just the institutionalized spouse's share. A class action by six widows against New Hampshire was settled in September, 1999.

The state agreed not to impose liens on homesteads in which a surviving spouse or other protected person resides; not to demand payment from the surviving spouse as a condition of releasing the Medicaid lien; and to limit recovery to the Medicaid recipient's share of joint property, not the entire jointly held property. New Hampshire also agreed to adopt hardship rules as required by federal law.[27]

HALF A LOAF: A BASIC STRATEGY

Although a full understanding of all the complexities of Medicaid is a matter for specialists, there are a few basic tools that any financial planner can understand and use or keep in mind when significant financial steps are undertaken.

Wise homestead planning is critical. Depending on the circumstances, it may make sense to buy or improve a homestead, thus reducing the amount of excess assets, but depending on local housing values and whether the house is above or below average, that could easily result in. However, if there is a risk of estate recovery, transferring the homestead could be worthwhile, especially if an exempt transfer is possible.

The "half a loaf" theory is based on the old proverb that "half a loaf is better than no bread." As discussed above, making non-exempt transfers gives rise to a theoretical penalty period. The penalty period is only theoretical if the Medicaid application is delayed until after the penalty period has expired. But what if, instead of transferring enough resources to create a 20-month penalty period, a person transfers only enough resources to create a 10-month penalty period, and retains the rest of the assets? True, the person would be ineligible during those 10 months. On the other hand, there would be enough funds to pay privately for nursing home care during the period of ineligibility. When the funds ran out, so would the penalty period, and he would then be eligible for Medicaid.

EXAMPLE [pre-DRA '05 rules]: Hiram Wiswell is a widower. He lives in a state where the officially published cost of care is $4,000 a month. A non-exempt transfer of $50,000 in March, 2004 would create a 12-month period of ineligibility (most states disregard fractional months): $50,000/$4,000 = 12, so he would be ineligible until April 1, 2005. But if he transferred only $25,000 and kept the rest, his period of ineligibility would be only six months, and he would have $25,000 available to pay privately for treatment during that time. It might make sense for him to transfer only $20,000 and keep $30,000 in case the actual cost of private payment was higher than the official figure used in calculating penalty periods.

EXAMPLE [DRA '05 rules]: Michael Rizzo is also a widower. In his state, the official monthly cost figure is $7,000. He enters a nursing home in June, 2006. His $70,000 in non-exempt transfers give rise to a penalty period of 10 months, so he would not be eligible until April, 2007. However, the nursing home where he resides actually charges $8,000 a month for private-pay patients. So he will need to have LTCI benefits, other funds, or gifts from his family to cover the $80,000 he will need for private payment.

Medicaid beneficiaries have a duty to collect any funds they are entitled to, even if this has the result of terminating their Medicaid eligibility. See below for a discussion of the exercise of a waiver of the right of election in the estate of the beneficiary's spouse.

As discussed below, there are some complex planning strategies that can be undertaken involving trusts. The basic strategy is to make assets unavailable by placing them into an "income-only" trust, that is, a trust from which the Medicaid beneficiary can never receive any distributions of principal, under any circumstances. Under Medicaid rules, that principal is fully insulated from the beneficiary, and therefore does not affect eligibility. However, the look-back period for such a transfer to trust is 60 months, not 36, and the beneficiary's interest in the trust corpus is subject to estate recovery after death.

MEDICAID AND INSURANCE

A small (not over $1,500) burial fund is considered an exempt asset. A life insurance policy with cash value of up to $1,500 is exempt, but a policy with a higher cash value is not exempt. Because of cash-value life insurance, many Medicaid applicants will have significant assets they are not aware of. It stands to reason that buying additional cash-value insurance should be approached with caution if the potential purchaser is likely to make a Medicaid application.

However, term insurance does not have cash value. One strategy that might work in emergency Medicaid planning would be to shed excess non-exempt assets by purchasing term insurance benefiting the spouse. There is no transfer, because the insurance has been purchased for value in an arm's length transaction. Of course, the insurance will probably be quite expensive, if obtainable at all, because of the insured's age and deteriorated health. The advantage of this strategy over simply giving the funds to the community spouse is that, although there is no penalty period on an inter-spousal transfer, the assets will still be reflected in the snapshot.

MEDICAID PLANNING WITH TRUSTS

Trusts are an important elder planning vehicle, because they create an income stream and relieve the senior citizen of financial planning responsibility for the trust corpus. Trusts can save taxes, and can make it easier to carry out a complex estate plan after the trust grantor's death. Also, revocable trusts can serve as will substitutes. You cannot escape application of Medicaid rules by calling the arrangement something other than a "trust." Any legal arrangement with trust-like consequences will be treated as a trust. If the trust contains assets of several persons, only the part traceable to the Medicaid beneficiary will affect eligibility.

PLANNING TIP: These Medicaid rules apply only to inter vivos trusts. Testamentary trusts under which a Medicaid applicant or recipient is a beneficiary are not covered. See 42 USC Section 1396p(d) for trust rules.

Trusts that are already in force will naturally have Medicaid consequences, and individuals making a long-range Medicaid plan may create new trusts as part of the plan. There are several Medicaid questions to be considered in reviewing any trust: how its income will be treated; whether part or all of the trust corpus is an "available" asset for Medicaid purposes; whether creating the trust is a transfer and, if so, how long the penalty period will be; and whether the remaining corpus, at the time of the Medicaid recipient's death, is subject to estate recovery. An important point to remember is that a trust set up by either spouse will affect the eligibility of the other spouse, even if the applicant spouse is not a trust beneficiary or remainderman.

Trust Income

The basic Medicaid rule is that income actually received from a trust, or that the beneficiary has a right to receive but rejects, is available for Medicaid purposes, whether the beneficiary is the grantor of the trust or not. In a medically needy state, the income will increase the spend-down obligation. In a cap state, it may render the person ineligible for Medicaid.

If income could be paid to the beneficiary, but instead is paid to someone else, those funds are considered transfers by the beneficiary to the recipient. However, if the trust is drafted to allow the trustee to invest in unproductive assets, and the trustee does so, thus reducing the income, this will not have negative Medicaid consequences.

This must be contrasted with a "trigger trust," a trust whose terms change (such as to terminate the beneficiary's status) when a beneficiary applies for Medicaid or enters a nursing home. Trigger trusts are considered contrary to public policy, and are void for Medicaid purposes. If the Medicaid recipient is a beneficiary under a testamentary trust created under the will of someone else, the testamentary trust is not considered an improper trigger trust even if it contains provisions that would be invalid in an inter vivos trust created by the recipient.

Availability of Corpus

The next question is availability of the trust corpus. For Medicaid purposes, trust principal is available if the terms of the trust say it is available, as well as to the extent that a person is a trustee or can otherwise determine how the principal will be disposed of.

A revocable trust's corpus is always fully available, because the grantor can amend or terminate the trust at any time, or can withdraw funds from it. When it comes to irrevocable trusts, even if there is an independent, neutral trustee, or even a trustee with an adverse interest, any amount of principal that the trustee could remove from the trust for a patient's benefit, using the maximum powers of discretion, is available to the patient. This is true even if, in fact, the trustee never does invade the principal. Remember that tax rules do not apply to Medicaid, so the trustee's neutrality or adverse interest is irrelevant.

In many situations, attorneys who are oriented toward estate planning but unfamiliar with Medicaid rules will draft trusts containing a "HEWS" power. A HEWS power (it stands for Health, Education, Welfare, and Support, also called an "ascertainable standards" power) limits invasion of the trust to instances that satisfy an objective, ascertainable standard such as the health or support needs of the trust beneficiary, to prevent trust amounts from being included in the grantor or beneficiary's taxable estate.

Of course, an excellent argument could be made that anyone sick enough to need nursing home care needs invasion of trust principal to pay for the care. Therefore, HEWS powers are a problem in Medicaid planning. It does not mean they should never be used, only that the potential estate tax saving should be balanced against potential loss of Medicaid benefits, bearing in mind that most estates can be free of estate tax for other reasons such as the marital deduction and credit shelter trusts. See Chapter 13.

The CMS itself has agreed to the acceptability of "income-only" trusts in Medicaid planning. If the patient is entitled to receive income from the trust, but there is no circumstance under which the patient can require the trustee to invade the principal on his behalf, and if the trustee has no discretion to invade corpus on the patient's behalf, then trust income is available, but trust corpus is not.[28]

Transfer Issues

The next Medicaid question is whether there has been a transfer that will give rise to a penalty period. The pre-DRA '05 rule is that if the trust was created more than 36 months before the Medicaid application (or more than 60 months, for an irrevocable trust from which the patient cannot receive invasions of principal under any circumstances), then the transaction was too remote in time, and will not affect Medicaid eligibility. But if the trust was created or added to during the look-back period, then a transfer occurred to the extent that funds were removed from the patient's control. The transfer is exempt to the extent that it was made to or for the benefit of the patient's spouse, or to or for a minor, blind, or disabled child. Otherwise, a penalty period will be created, calculated as discussed above.

The CMS' position is that the look-back period for income-only trusts should be 60 months, even though the language of the statute refers to trusts from which the patient cannot receive funds of any kind. CMS also uses a 60-month look-back in situations where funds are transferred out of a revocable trust and to someone other than the patient (such as a son or daughter). There is no additional penalty when assets are transferred out of an irrevocable trust that are not available to the patient to a third party, because the penalty period was imposed when the trust was created. However, if a transfer is made to a third party from a revocable trust whose principal could be invaded for the patient's behalf, the look-back period for the transfer is 60 months.

Trusts established before the enactment date of DRA '05 are treated under the old rules, not the new ones.

Other Trust Planning Issues

A 1999 New York case held that an irrevocable trust created three years before the grantor's wife made a Medicaid application was available to pay for the wife's care, and was also subject to estate recovery.[29] The applicant's husband created the trust in 1987, naming two of the children as trustees. The trustees (who were also trust remaindermen) were given the discretion to distribute income and principal to maintain their parents' standard of living (measured as of the time the trust was set up). In 1990, the grantor applied for Medicaid home care for his wife. In 1991, he executed a spousal refusal (see above for a discussion of spousal refusal). The wife eventually entered a nursing home, and received Medicaid benefits from late 1993 to 1996, when she died.

After her death, the New York Medicaid agency sought estate recovery for the cost of the home care and nursing home care it provided. The New York court treated the entire corpus of the trust as available to the grantor for the support of his wife. The "standard of living" criterion for invasion would have permitted invasion of the entire corpus. Therefore, in the court's view, the availability of these assets to the grantor created an implied contract to reimburse the Medicaid agency for the services it provided when he made the spousal refusal.

Although federal law imposes limitations on estate recovery when Medicaid benefits were "correctly" paid, agencies have broader recovery powers when benefits were "incorrectly" paid. A 1999 New York case allowed estate recovery in a case where the state agency itself made a mistake, providing benefits to someone who should have been deemed ineligible because of the existence of a self-settled discretionary trust (i.e., a trust whose corpus was available, thus resulting in excess resources). The broader recovery was allowed even though there was no fraud or misrepresentation on the part of the Medicaid recipient, and it was the agency itself that made the mistake.[30]

SNTs

In some areas, SNT stands for "special needs trust;" other areas use the phrase "supplemental needs trust." In either case, the meaning is the same: a trust that can be used to provide comforts of life for a person who receives Medicaid or other public benefits, but whose corpus is not available for Medicaid purposes and therefore does not impair eligibility for public benefits. SNTs are a very significant part of the planning process for accident victims (who are critically injured enough to need long-term care), and for the process under which adults plan for the future of their disabled children.

They are much less significant in elder care planning, because it is difficult or impossible to set up an SNT to benefit oneself or one's spouse. One exception is a testamentary trust created under the will of one spouse, to take care of the supplemental needs of the other spouse after the testator's death. Medicaid law does allow one special kind of self-settled SNT (a trust set up for a person's own benefit). This is called a "pooled fund" or a "d(4)" trust; "d(4)" is shorthand for the section of the statute that makes these trusts possible.[31]

In one type of d(4) trust arrangement, the elderly person contributes to a fund administered by a charitable organization and benefiting a large number of persons. The individual's share of income from the fund can be used to provide the same small comforts that an SNT would provide, but the contribution to the fund is not available for Medicaid purposes. When the person who contributed to the fund dies, first the charity receives an agreed-upon amount for managing the fund. Next, the state Medicaid agency is entitled to estate recovery until it has recovered the full amount it expended for the Medicaid recipient's care. If anything is left over, it becomes part of the decedent's estate and can be distributed according to the estate plan.

Late in 2004, the Connecticut Supreme Court found that it was proper for the Medicaid agency to deny Medicaid eligibility because the assets of a trust were greater than the asset eligibility limit. The court held that a probate court finding that the trust was not available to the Medicaid agency as a creditor did not prevent this result, because the issue was the trust's availability to the Medicaid applicant as a beneficiary of the trust. It was treated as a "general support trust," not a Supplemental Needs Trust that gets favorable Medicaid treatment, because the trustee had broad discretion to use the income and principal of the trust to assist the beneficiary. When the disabled person died, the corpus went to the trustees of the trust and not the Medicaid agency. Therefore, the trust was an available asset that ruled out Medicaid eligibility.[32]

MEDICAID PLANNING WITH ANNUITIES

As discussed above, having too many non-exempt assets will prevent Medicaid eligibility. Sometimes transferring the assets to someone else will work, but often (especially in an emergency situation), the transferor will fall afoul of the transfer-of-asset rules and will be ineligible for Medicaid benefits when they are needed. Sometimes, placing the assets into an income-only trust will work. Yet, in many Medicaid plans, it is necessary to find a way to convert assets into income without making a transfer.

The definition of "transfer" depends on a change in ownership that is partially or totally uncompensated. Buying products, services, or financial goods at their fair market value is not a transfer, because there is no uncompensated element. Therefore, some interesting planning techniques involve annuities, either commercial annuities purchased from an insurance company (see Chapter 12) or private annuities (non-commercial arrangements, such as with a family member).[33]

Some annuity transactions do have a transfer element, because the annuity is not "actuarially sound:" it does not represent a reasonable estimate of the annuitant's life expectancy. If, based on tables issued by the CMS (not the IRS tables used in other annuity contexts), the annuitant's life expectancy is 10 years, a 12-year annuity would represent a transfer of two years worth of payments to the remainderman.

Actuarially sound annuities must satisfy another requirement. The amount that the annuitant would receive under an immediate annuity, over the course of the predicted remaining life expectancy, must be at least as great as the purchase price of the annuity. If there is a shortfall, that represents a transfer to the insurance company or the person providing the private annuity.

One important pre-DRA '05 Medicaid annuity planning technique is for the community spouse to take assets over and above the CSRA and use them to purchase an actuarially sound immediate annuity.[34] That way, the couple's resources will be reduced, there will not have been any transfer, and the income that the healthy spouse receives from the annuity will not be considered available to the sick spouse. However, if the community spouse later needs institutional care, the income from the annuity will need to be spent down (in a medically-needy state), or could even block eligibility (in a cap state). Another problem is that the more income the healthy spouse has, the less income the sick spouse can transfer as part of the CSIA, and the more that the local Medicaid agency is likely to demand as an income contribution from the healthy spouse.

Buying an annuity is one of the few Medicaid planning options available to a single person. Once again, excess resources are turned into income, which can be used as long as the individual making the plan can remain in the community. After institutionalization in a medically-needy state, the annuity income is spent down.

If the single person has children or other heirs he wants to benefit, a limited amount of estate planning can be done as part of the Medicaid plan. The individual buys an actuarially sound term-certain annuity, naming the potential heirs as beneficiaries. If he dies before the term ends, the balance goes to the beneficiaries. But, of course, the beneficiaries will not receive anything if the individual lives at least as long as the term certain. If the main objective is transmitting assets to heirs, not enhancing current income, it makes more sense to do a half-a-loaf transfer. The annuity plan works better if estate planning is only a subsidiary objective to extra income.

Two expert elder law attorneys have some useful tips for planning with annuities.[35] They remind us that the annuity must be immediate (a deferred annuity is an available resource unless it is converted to an immediate one), irrevocable, non-assignable, and must make its payments over a term certain that is not longer than the purchaser's actuarial life expectancy. Most annuities are designed to be assignable, so it may be necessary to obtain a special endorsement from the insurer to make the annuity non-assignable. Insurers typically use IRS rather than CMS tables, so the elder care planner should inform the insurer of the correct number of years of payments for a Medicaid-oriented annuity purchase.

These attorneys also say that, although the Medicaid rules do not specifically require it, it is good planning to make an irrevocable designation of the payee, to prevent the Medicaid agency from making a later demand that the nursing home or the Medicaid agency itself be named as payee.

Begley and Jeffreys point out that if the annuity is purchased in the name of the community spouse, there will probably be no estate recovery when the institutionalized spouse dies, because the annuity will not be included in the institutionalized spouse's estate. In general, Medicaid agencies are not entitled to estate recovery against the estate of the community spouse (see above for exceptions).

Although CMS' Transmittal 64 says in so many words that assets in excess of the CSRA can be used to buy an actuarially sound commercial annuity without creating a penalty period, CMS representative Robert Streimer issued a letter to an elder law attorney in 1998 saying that the corpus of a trust set up for the community spouse, funded with an annuity is a countable resource. However, a subsequent letter, from a CMS Associate Regional Administrator to the National Senior Citizens Law Center says that CMS does not require estate recovery as long as there is a surviving spouse or dependent child of the deceased Medicaid beneficiary, even if the remainderman of the annuity is someone other than the survivor or dependent. The value of the decedent's interest in the annuity is the remainder balance that the Medicaid recipient owned at the time of death.[36]

Since then, several cases have ruled that a Community Spouse Annuity Trust (CSAT) is countable. A CSAT is an actuarially sound trust created for the sole benefit of a community spouse; all the corpus and income are supposed to be distributed to the community spouse over the course of his or her life. In fact, Pennsylvania even treats commercial annuities as available resources.[37]

In an Ohio case, a Medicaid applicant's husband transferred $221,000 of marital assets into an irrevocable CSAT, with all the corpus and income to be paid out to him over a five-year period (which is much shorter than his life expectancy under the CMS tables).[38] However, the state Medicaid agency deemed the transfer to be for inadequate consideration, and therefore rejected the sick spouse's Medicaid application, and the court agreed with the agency instead of the applicant.

The court said that the trust was not for the "sole benefit" of the community spouse, because the couple's two children were remaindermen. The court held that CSATs and commercial annuities should be treated differently, but that transfers to the community spouse in excess of the CSRA will lead to ineligibility.

Some 2004 cases suggest that the tide of judicial opinion may be turning against Medicaid annuities. In one case, at about the time he made a Medicaid application, the applicant transferred a $50,000 annuity payable to him to his wife. When his wife (who at that point was the community spouse) was told she could be held financially responsible for his care, she made gifts to her children out of the account where the annuity money was deposited, and she signed a Durable Power of Attorney allowing them to make withdrawals from the account.

In 2003, it was ruled that the North Dakota Medicaid agency's claim for his nursing home care could not be enforced against the estate of the surviving spouse, and the surviving spouse's transfers to her children could not be recovered. The trial court found that the applicant lawfully transferred the annuity, making it her property to dispose of as she wished.

But in 2004, the North Dakota Supreme Court reversed this decision, holding instead that the Medicaid agency's claim could be recovered from any assets traceable to the beneficiary's estate, whether or not they were included in the probate estate. The state Supreme Court ruled that the surviving spouse's gifts in contemplation of death made to avoid estate recovery were fraudulent conveyances because she made herself insolvent to avoid paying a debt. Although the wife did not receive Medicaid, the state agency was able to trace funds from her Medicaid-recipient husband to her and then to her donees—and the agency was allowed to recover those funds.[39]

A 2004 North Dakota case holds that Medicaid benefits were properly denied to a nursing home resident because the owner of a non-assignable annuity (the community spouse) only offered to sell the annuity itself, and this was not an adequate effort. Instead, she had an obligation to use the "factors market" to sell the contractual rights to receive the income stream from the annuity to receive at least 75% of the fair market value of the annuity. Because she failed to do so, the annuity was properly counted as an asset, so the applicant had too many assets to qualify.[40]

This trend was continued in DRA '05. Annuity purchases on or after February 8, 2006 are considered transfers subject to a penalty period unless the state is named as remainder beneficiary for at least the total amount of Medicaid expenditures on behalf of the annuitant. If the annuitant has a community spouse or minor, blind or disabled child, it is acceptable to name such a person as primary remainder beneficiary, with the state Medicaid agency taking second place. Transfer penalties are also imposed on annuity purchases made by or on behalf of a person who has already applied for Medicaid long term care services.

Retirement annuities, or annuities purchased with funds from a conventional or Roth IRA, are not considered to involve transfers. DRA '05 also provides that transfer penalties will not be imposed if the annuity

- is irrevocable,

- is non-assignable,

- is actuarially sound, as measured by the standards promulgated by the Social Security Administration's Chief Actuary,

- provides for equal payments throughout the term, and

- does not have "balloon payments"—i.e., small payments for most of the term, ending with a disproportionately large payment.

Private Annuities and SCINs

In most families, the Medicaid applicant will be receptive to the idea of transferring excess assets to a spouse or children, because those are the people he wants to benefit, and the people who would figure in his estate plan. Unfortunately, the Medicaid consequences of such a transfer can be negative.

A private annuity can come to the rescue. Instead of giving the surplus funds to the children, the applicant can enter into an arrangement under which the excess funds are exchanged for the child's promise to make regular annuity payments which represent an appropriate actuarial return on the investment, in light of the parent's life expectancy.

The child must continue making the payments even if the parent outlives the predicted life expectancy. In this case, the child has made a poor financial bargain, but let us hope that he is glad that the parent's lifespan is long. If, on the contrary, the parent dies before the entire investment in the annuity contract is recovered from the annuity payments, IRC Section 72(b)(3) allows the decedent's final income tax return to include a corresponding loss deduction. In most family private annuity situations, a life annuity will be desirable, because the older person is critically interested in securing income. However, if the individual is unusually healthy, the child may prefer an annuity for a term of years, because this limits the exposure if a life annuity would require payments much in excess of the original consideration paid for the annuity.

An important feature that distinguishes the private annuity from the commercial annuity is that an insurance company insists on being paid in cash for the annuity. Family members may very well be willing to accept property (such as a homestead or other real estate, shares in the family business, or art works) that would otherwise become the subject of transfer or inheritance.[41] In many cases, the private annuity will be purchased with appreciated property. The purchaser will not have to pay capital gains taxes when the annuity is purchased, provided that the annuity is unsecured, meaning that the parent must accept the risk that the child will fail to make the scheduled payments.

Before DRA '05, some plans used the self-canceling installment note (SCIN) or death terminating installment note, as another intra-family planning device. A SCIN might be preferred to a private annuity by the child, because the tax consequences for the child are better. The parent makes an installment sale of property to the child, receiving back an installment note. Unlike an ordinary commercial transaction, however, the note's terms provide that the obligation to pay the remaining installments will be canceled when the parent dies. The term of the note must be shorter than the parent's life expectancy. Also, the SCIN must provide benefits to the parent, either by paying an above-market interest rate or by paying more than fair market value for the purchased property. The self-canceling feature was used so that there would be nothing relating to the note in the parent's estate after his or her death, and therefore nothing subject to Medicaid estate recovery.

DRA '05 provides that any transfer for less than fair market value is subject to a transfer penalty, unless the arrangement is actuarially sound, makes equal payments during the loan term without deferrals and without disproportionate balloon payments—and does NOT terminate with the lender's death.

MEDICAID IMPLICATIONS OF JOINT PROPERTY

Older people often have joint bank or brokerage accounts, but these accounts can be classified either as "true" joint accounts or "convenience" accounts. In a true joint account, each joint owner has an equal right to the money in the account and, when one joint owner dies, the other automatically inherits the balance. Such accounts often, but not always, involve spouses or cohabitants, and in many cases both parties have deposited funds into the account.

A convenience account adds the name of a child, friend, or employee to the account, so that a more mobile person can perform banking transactions on the older person's behalf. People sometimes try to dispose of these convenience accounts by will. Whether the will provision can take effect depends on state law, and whether it was made clear that the account was not a true joint account, only one for convenience.

The Medicaid implications of joint accounts begin with the presumption that all the money in the account belongs to the patient and is available to him. But if the other joint tenant deposited funds into the account, the patient is entitled to a hearing to prove this point. Part of the process of getting ready to make a Medicaid application is compiling bank records to prove how funds entered and left the joint account during the look-back period.

The tricky part about joint accounts is that anything that has the effect of reducing the patient's share of the joint account is treated as a transfer made by the patient. That is, if the other joint tenant withdraws money from the account, this is considered a transfer by the patient, even if the patient did not authorize or even know about the withdrawal, and even if it was part of a pattern of financial elder abuse victimizing the patient.[42]

PLANNING IN SPECIAL SITUATIONS

The rules and strategies described above work best for married couples, only one of whom requires Medicaid benefits, living in a "medically needy" state where excess income can always be spent down. This discussion also assumes that the need for Medicaid is caused by an age-related illness or frailty. The rules are somewhat different when the care is required because of injuries due to an accident, medical malpractice, or other cause for which someone can be held financially liable. In this situation, it is likely that a tort settlement will be reached. An important part of structuring the settlement is to make sure that the Medicaid agency that has provided benefits in the interim will be repaid. States differ in their approach to how high a priority the repayment takes. Some states are more generous than others in allowing the injured person and family to benefit from the settlement.

A person who has never married, a divorced person, or a widow or widower will not be able to make use of the spousal protection provisions. For them, placing assets into an income-only trust or purchasing an actuarially sound annuity (commercial or private) is likely to be the best route to take.

In the "cap" states, planning advantages can be achieved by using a Miller trust, named after the case of *Miller v. Ibarra*, 746 F. Supp. 19 (D. Colo. 1990), and also referred to as a Qualified Income Trust. See 42 USC Sections 1396p(d)(4)(A) and (B), and HCFA (now CMS) Transmittal 64. To make use of such a trust, the Medicaid patient must receive the income, then deposit it into a special trust. Funds from the trust can only be used to pay the patient's personal needs allowance, allowances to the spouse and dependents, medical expenses that are not covered by Medicaid, or (if the state has rules allowing this use), maintenance of the homestead. The terms of the trust must provide specifically that, when the patient dies, the Medicaid agency will have the right to recover from the estate, up to the full amount of benefits paid. Of course, in many cases the estate will be smaller than the benefits, so the agency will not be able to get a full recovery, but there will also be no assets available to be inherited by the decedent's family.

A later case about income trusts in Colorado upholds Colorado regulations that allow income trusts if, and only if, the person's monthly income is below the average cost of care in the region.[43] In this case the cost of care was defined as $3,034, and the person who sought to create an income trust had pension income and veterans' benefits of approximately $3,900 a month. The Tenth Circuit's position is that federal law requires states to count various kinds of trusts in determining Medicaid eligibility, and gives them the option either to count or not to count income trusts, and therefore states can restrict the types of income trusts that can be excluded.

In many families, financial planning revolves around planning for the needs of a disabled child. The child may no longer be able to work, because of physical or mental illness or injury, or the child may never have been able to work because of life-long disability. Until the disabled child reaches the age of majority, his parents have a duty to support him. But once the child reaches majority, financial efforts by parents and grandparents are deemed voluntary.

Attempts to benefit a disabled child should be structured carefully to avoid limiting the individual's access to Supplemental Security Income and Medicaid benefits. This can often be done by

- making the disabled person just one of a class of potential beneficiaries under a "sprinkle" trust and tailoring the amount actually paid to that person to his needs and public-benefit eligibility;

- by setting up a Supplemental Needs Trust as the limitations on self-settled trusts do not apply if the trust is created by a parent or grandparent who has no duty to support the disabled person; or

- by creating a trust for the benefit of the child that is a "discretionary" trust (one where the trustee has complete discretion to distribute income and principal) rather than a "support" trust which is obligated to satisfy the beneficiary's support needs, even if the result is loss of valuable public benefits.

Once the disabled person dies, the state Medicaid agency is entitled to seek estate recovery, but only for benefits paid after age 55. Part of the estate (or all of it, for a person who died before reaching age 55) will thus be exempt from estate recovery.

In some families, there are two generations of benefit eligibility to think about: an elderly parent and a disabled child. From the parent's perspective, remember that the homestead can be transferred to or for the sole benefit of a minor, blind, or disabled child without penalty.

HOME CARE

Most of this chapter has revolved around nursing home care, which is the service that people usually think of when they engage in Medicaid planning. However, institutionalization is usually a last resort. Clearly, most impaired elderly people prefer to remain at home and most caregivers and other family members also prefer that care be available there.

All of the states have at least one "waiver" program for providing home care. State Medicaid agencies are allowed to offer home care services without the need to conform to all of the federal requirements that would otherwise apply. Most importantly, a waiver program can be made available only to certain Medicaid beneficiaries, such as sufferers from a specific disease, or elderly people who need a nursing home level of care, without being made available to all Medicaid beneficiaries. Waiver programs can also be limited to only part of a state. The financial eligibility rules for waiver programs, including transfer penalties, are the same as for Medicaid nursing home care.

Everyone benefits from waiver programs. Sick people can stay at home instead of being placed in institutions. The Medicaid agency benefits, because it costs less to provide care under a waiver program than to place the patient in a nursing home.

Although in general DRA '05 cuts back on the Medicaid program, this legislation gives states more flexibility in administering and expanding the Medicaid home care service package known as Home and Community-Based Services (HCBS), starting January 1, 2007. (Most other provisions took effect when DRA '05 was signed.) Before DRA '05, states had to get permission from federal regulators to set up an HCBS program; now states can create these programs and cover persons whose income does not exceed 150% of the federal poverty line. Prior law required the state to limit HCBS services to those who were sick enough to require a nursing home level of care; DRA '05 allows HCBS to be provided to people who are in better condition, and perhaps can retain this higher level of functioning if they receive appropriate home care. State plans can also offer "Cash and Counseling" as an option. That is, Medicaid recipients who receive personal care (such as help with getting dressed, bathing, transferring in and out of a wheelchair etc.) can be given a budget by the state and allowed to select, hire, fire, and pay the personal care workers of their choice.

PACE Programs

In the mid-1980s, On Lok Senior Health Services of San Francisco developed a model for providing high-level, intensive home care to the frail elderly. In 1997, Congress authorized the Program of All-Inclusive Care for the Elderly (PACE), a demonstration program that pays providers a capitated rate for delivering home care to people who would otherwise have to be institutionalized. In 1998, there were 12 PACE demonstration programs, with 36 more sites considering joining the program.

PACE is based on an interdisciplinary team that assesses the needs of the frail elderly, develops a care plan for them, then furnishes the necessary services at adult day health centers and home care. PACE patients who are Medicare-eligible pay a monthly premium with the state Medicaid agency paying for the care of Medicaid-eligible patients. See www.hcfa.gov/medicaid/pace/pacegen.htm for more information.

MEDICAID AND DIVORCE

There are plenty of legitimate criticisms that can be raised against Medicaid as a whole, and against Medicaid planning, but the Medicaid system is sometimes unjustly accused of forcing harmonious senior citizen couples to divorce. In fact, Medicaid rules favor married couples. Medicaid-motivated divorce (as distinct from couples who are genuinely unhappy, or where one partner wants to remarry) is usually a bad idea.

When a couple divorces, either their property is community property, which is equally divided between them, or it is marital property which must be "equitably" divided. There are many factors in equitable distribution, but the needs of the parties are considered more important than who owned the property originally, or who contributed the funds used to purchase it. Therefore, it is possible that a large percentage of the couple's property will be distributed to the sick spouse, with resulting negative consequences for Medicaid planning.

Similarly, divorce courts have the power to order spousal support, depending on the relative needs of the parties. Clearly, a person who needs extensive long-term care is incapable of self-support, so it is possible that the divorce court will order the healthy spouse to provide income to the sick spouse.

What if the person who needs medical care is in a stronger financial position that the healthy spouse? While the Medicaid system provides for protection of the community spouse, an ex-spouse is not a community spouse. Not only can the Medicaid patient not transfer the CSRA or CSIA to the ex-spouse, but many states take the position that court-ordered alimony does not reduce the spend-down obligation. So the divorced person residing in a nursing home would in effect have to spend down all income other than the personal needs allowance (because no CSIA could be transferred), but would still have to make payments under the separation agreement or court-ordered alimony payments.

There are also technical legal problems that can complicate or prevent senior citizens' divorces. If the state allows no-fault divorce, it is not necessary to prove any marital wrongdoing, but it is usually necessary for a period of time to elapse between separation and the grant of a divorce.

If the state does not allow no-fault divorce, or if the waiting period is inconveniently long, the spouse seeking the divorce has to be able to prove some kind of marital fault by the other spouse. It is possible that illness-related behavior will count as "insanity" or "mental cruelty" entitling the healthy spouse to a divorce, but also possible that such matters will be treated as beyond the control of the sick person and therefore not "fault."

Capacity is also a problem. Legal capacity is required to sue or be sued, and a person suffering from Alzheimer's Disease or other dementing illness may lack such capacity. If a guardian has already been appointed, the guardian may be able to handle the divorce case (or a special "guardian ad litem" might be appointed just for the suit). On the other hand, some states have taken the position that divorce litigation is so inherently personal that a guardian cannot take part in it. In those states, a demented person's marriage is effectively permanent, because there's no way to dissolve it by divorce.

GUARDIANS' PLANNING POWERS

There is a high correlation between the need for the kind of lengthy custodial care that Medicaid provides, and mental incapacity. Some people apply for Medicaid because they are physically frail although cognitively intact, but in many cases, the real need for institutionalization comes from loss of mental capacity. If the elderly person has a well-drafted contingency plan that copes with possible loss of capacity as well as Medicaid eligibility, it is likely that the plan can be brought into operation and will be effective. Unfortunately, the vast majority of the elderly do not have such a plan.

As discussed in Chapter 13, the legal system's response to capacity loss is either guardianship or guardianship alternatives. When a guardian is appointed, one of the basic tasks is to figure out what the ward (impaired person) owns, and take steps to collect any amounts owed to the ward. Some courts interpret this to mean that the guardian must be proactive, even if gathering additional resources would impair the ward's Medicaid eligibility. Other courts are more permissive, recognizing that in the long run the ward is better off qualifying for Medicaid than receiving a sum that is less valuable than the health care.

Some courts are very hostile to Medicaid planning in general, and see their role as protecting the public treasury. In these courts, guardians who ask permission to make Medicaid-oriented transfers, create trusts, or do half-a-loaf planning are likely to be turned down.

Other courts, however, conceptualize the guardian as taking the ward's place. Under this theory, the guardian can do anything that the ward would have been able to do personally if he still had capacity, including creating a Medicaid plan. These courts see Medicaid planning as the equivalent of income tax or estate planning, in that a person can undertake any lawful measures, however complex they are, to take advantage of the system's loopholes to save money or obtain other financial benefits. Under a June, 2000 New York case, for instance, the wife/guardian of a comatose New Jersey man who resided in a New York nursing home was allowed to transfer all his assets to her for her own support, and to engage in a spousal refusal under New York law. New York law applied because he resided in a facility in New York.[44]

An intermediate position is also possible, under which the guardian is allowed to carry out the intentions already shown by the ward during capacity (including gifts to charities and family members), but cannot implement new tactics on the ward's behalf. Thus, a sound incapacity plan either includes Medicaid planning as well, or establishes a pattern during capacity that can be followed if and when incapacity occurs.

CONTRACTS FOR SERVICES

Medicaid law explicitly recognizes one kind of payment for care provided by family members: the gift of a homestead to a "caregiver child" (see above). Such a gift is not penalized as a transfer, because in effect the child has assisted the Medicaid system by deferring the parent's need for nursing home care.

Otherwise, the CMS' position is that it will be presumed that family caregivers perform their services without expecting to get paid. However, the presumption can be rebutted if, at the time the care was provided (but not after the fact), the elderly person and the caregiver entered into a written contract under which reasonable payment would be made for services.[45]

The elder law attorney in the planning team should be able to draw up a simple contract, spelling out what the caregiver will do, the cash or property that the caregiver will receive, and that the compensation is fair based on market rates for similar services, or is based on the financial sacrifice that the caregiver made to provide the services.

Note that the compensation does constitute taxable income to the caregiver. The caregiver may be covered by the "Nanny tax" rules (i.e., the simplified procedure for remitting FICA taxes). Under the Nanny tax rules, the employer of a household employee reports the FICA tax on his own tax return. The employer has a choice to either withhold the employee's share of Social Security tax from the employee's wages, or to assume responsibility for paying the entire FICA tax (15.3% of the household worker's wages). Household employers do not need to withhold federal income tax on household worker's wages, unless the employee asks the employer to withhold, and the employer agrees to do so.

POST-ELIGIBILITY ISSUES

Before 1988, Medicaid had a policy of "deeming," meaning that all of a couple's income and resources were considered available to pay for the sick spouse's nursing home care, with no provision for the needs of the community spouse. Given the high cost of nursing home care, this policy often caused both a sick spouse's Medicaid application to be denied (on the basis of excess funds), and required most, if not all, of a couple's combined funds to be applied to the sick spouse's care needs. In 1988, the Medicare Catastrophic Coverage Act (MCCA) added provisions for safeguarding at least some assets and income for the healthy spouse, so that he can continue to maintain a home and pay his own living expenses.

The Medicaid system recognizes that it takes a long time to process an application, so there is a provision for making a retroactive reimbursement of expenses that the applicant paid during the three months before the application was granted. In a 2005 Sixth Circuit case, the plaintiff's Medicaid application was initially denied. She paid expenses out of pocket, and appealed the denial. She was successful, and was awarded three months' retroactive payment. In calculating the size of reimbursement, the Sixth Circuit said she was entitled to reimbursement at the rate she actually paid, not the (much lower) Medicaid rate. However, the retroactive payment must be reduced to account for the extent to which her out of pocket payments reduced her assets and allowed her to qualify for Medicaid. Family members who paid expenses for her were also entitled to reimbursement, even though they were not legally responsible for paying for her medical care.[46]

The Spend-Down Process

Once Medicaid eligibility has been established, and the sick person has been placed in a nursing home or begins to receive Medicaid home care, he has an obligation to "spend down" each month. First the individual's income is calculated.[47] The patient must be allowed to retain a "personal needs allowance" set by the state. Federal rules require the state to set the allowance (used, for example, to buy shampoo and toothpaste) at a level of at least $30 a month.

If the Medicaid recipient continues to pay health insurance premiums or pays or makes co-payments for health care, funds used for this purpose are excluded from income. (However, once an individual enters a nursing home, LTCI premiums will probably be suspended, and once a person qualifies for Medicaid, LTCI benefits will probably also be suspended.) Finally, the CSIA, and any allowance for dependent children, is subtracted. The result (known as the "share of cost" or "patient pay amount") is the amount that must be spent down. The Medicaid system pays the nursing home the difference between the Medicaid payment rate and the amount spent down by the nursing home resident.

EXAMPLE: Claire Finneran is a 76-year-old nursing home resident. Her income, from pensions and Social Security, is $1,700 a month. Her husband Frank's income is $1,200 a month, and the CSIA for their state is $1,500. Because Frank's income is $300 short of the CSIA, Claire can transfer $300 a month to him for his own needs. After this $300 transfer and her personal needs allowance of $50 a month, Claire's patient pay amount is $1,350 ($1,700-$300-$50). If the Medicaid nursing home rate is $3,000 a month, the state Medicaid agency pays the nursing home $1,650 a month ($3,000 - the $1,350 paid by Claire).

As this example shows, the spend-down obligation can be quite substantial. Is it worth for a person who can satisfy the DRA '05 rules it to apply for Medicaid? The answer could be yes, if the significant transfers can be made before the look-back period begins, or if any transfers are small enough to generate only a short penalty period, and the individual will have funds to pay privately for care during the penalty period, thus preventing the need to liquidate the assets to pay privately for care. Furthermore, as this example shows, Mrs. Finneran pays about half the Medicaid rate each month for her care. It is very likely that the private-pay rate for the same nursing home bed is $4,500 or more. Without Medicaid, Ms. Finneran would need to pay $4,500 a month, with income of only $1,700, requiring her to liquidate $2,800 of assets a month.

Enhancing the CSRA and CSIA

An important legal principle is that even if a basic rule is fair, a system may provide a "relief valve" for cases where application of the rules would be unfair. Accordingly, the Medicaid system includes provisions for adjustments, which may be based on court orders, such as family court orders directing the institutionalized spouse to increase the level of support provided to the healthy, as well as for administrative hearings (called "fair hearings") within the Medicaid system itself.[48]

A fair hearing can also grant a higher than normal CSIA level, especially in states where housing costs are high and a special housing allowance can be provided.[49] However the concept of fairness merely requires that the community spouse be protected from dire poverty. It is not necessary to preserve the lifestyle the community spouse enjoyed before the nursing home spouse became sick.[50]

According to recent cases from Connecticut, the community spouse's high prescription drug costs can be exceptional factors that justify increasing the community spouse income allowance–but normal factors in the community spouse's aging process, such as increasing frailty and confusion, are not.[51]

The CSRA can also be adjusted if a Medicaid fair hearing, or a court order, allows a higher level to be transferred to the healthy spouse. The adjustments are to be made only in exceptional circumstances, and to prevent unusual financial duress. If the judge or hearing officer accepts the argument and orders a higher CSRA level, then the institutionalized spouse may transfer this additional amount without penalty.

PRACTICE TIP: If there is evidence to support a higher level, going through a hearing can be very worthwhile. Any person who has knowledge of the facts (the person need not be a lawyer) can represent a Medicaid claimant. Because the ordinary CSIA and CSRA levels are guaranteed by federal law, the community spouse will not lose by requesting a hearing, because the provisions for the community spouse may not be cut back because of the hearing.

Before DRA '05, states took two different approaches to what to do if the community spouse's income was below the CSIA. Some of them allowed the institutionalized spouse to use a "resources first" approach—that is, to transfer enough additional resources so that the income earned by these resources would lift the community spouse's income to the necessary level. Most of the states took the "income first" approach—that is, the sick spouse would have to transfer income, not resources, for this purpose. DRA '05 enacts the "income first" approach, so that, for transfers and allocations made on or after February 8, 2006, all states must use "income first" calculations.

In a case from New York, a nursing home resident's wife made a Medicaid application on behalf of her husband. The community spouse's income was below the MMMNA (which was $2019; her monthly income was $487 from Social Security and $396 from investments) but her assets of $169,000 were well over the applicable CSRA of $80,760.

The state Medicaid agency said that she had to use her excess assets, because her sick husband's income of about $3,000 a month was attributed to her. The Second Circuit said that attributing this income does not violate ERISA, the federal pension statute, which has anti-alienation provisions but which apply only while benefits are in the hands of pension plan administrators and have not yet been paid out to retirees. However, the Second Circuit also held that the state's policy does violate the Social Security Act's anti-alienation provision.[52]

Right of Election

A general estate planning rule (see Chapter 13) is that spouses cannot be disinherited against their will. In most circumstances, if a married person dies without a will, the surviving spouse is entitled to a share (typically, one-third to one-half) of the decedent's estate. If the decedent did leave a valid will, but that will provides less than the statutory "elective share," the surviving spouse has the right to "elect against the will" by filing an election to receive the statutory share. This share will be granted at the expense of the bequests in the will.

What if a Medicaid recipient's spouse dies, leaving less than the statutory share? Part of the process of applying for Medicaid is a promise to garner all funds to which the applicant is entitled, so the spouse must elect against the deceased spouse's will, even though the likely result is the loss of Medicaid eligibility after receiving the funds. What usually happens with a post-eligibility inheritance is that the Medicaid recipient takes the funds, makes arrangements to go off Medicaid and re-apply, and either spends down the funds or does a half-a-loaf transfer. Refusing to elect against the will is treated as a transfer of assets. See *Tannler v. Wis. Dep't of Health and Social Servs.*, 564 N.W.2d 735 (Wis. 1997).

A strategy that usually works is, while a Medicaid plan is being made but before the application, the spouses waive their rights of inheritance and election. Waivers of the right of election are often made as part of a pre-nuptial agreement, but they can also be made after marriage. Usually the best move is for each spouse to renounce rights in the other's estate. This is legally sufficient, even though in practice one spouse may have much more money than the other. Then, by the time one spouse is a Medicaid recipient and the other one dies, the existing waiver of the right of election will control.

This strategy "usually" works, but not always. The New York case of *Estate of Dionisio v. Westchester DSS*, 665 N.Y.S.2d 904 (N.Y. App. Div. 1997), involved a couple who signed mutual waivers of the right of election two weeks before Mrs. Dionisio went into a nursing home, but 20 months before she applied for Medicaid. After she had been in the nursing home for only four months, Mr. Dionisio died, leaving an estate of close to half a million dollars with none of it left to Mrs. Dionisio.

Mrs. Dionisio's Medicaid application was denied, on the grounds that she had transferred $156,500, which was the one-third share of the estate she would have received by electing against the will. Although her lawyer claimed that the waivers of the right of election were made to save estate tax, and not for Medicaid purposes, the court rejected this argument. The *Dionisio* case highlights the kind of problems that often arise after hurried, last-minute plans. Perhaps the result would have been different if the waiver had occurred not only long before the Medicaid application, but long before nursing home admission.[53]

Income Issues Post-Eligibility

If income is payable in the name of just one spouse, it is considered to belong to that person. If income is paid jointly to both spouses, the income is considered to belong in equal shares to each of them. Income paid to a spouse and someone else is assigned proportionately to the spouse. For example, if 50% goes to Joseph (the spouse) and 50% to his sister Kathleen, only Joseph's 50% affects his eligibility. If there is no written document establishing ownership of income, it is considered to belong equally to both spouses. If the income derives from a trust, then the terms of the trust govern assignment of income. If the trust is not specific, then the rules above apply.[54]

Post-Eligibility Assets: Head 'em Off At the Pass?

In some circumstances, a Medicaid recipient will become entitled to new assets after eligibility. The most common case is an inheritance or insurance benefits on the life of someone who has died after the person became Medicaid-eligible. The usual result is that the person will lose Medicaid eligibility, and will not be eligible again until the funds have been spent, or until they have been transferred and the penalty period has ended.

PRACTICE TIP: Most states have a fairly simple procedure for going off Medicaid, paying privately for a while, and going back on Medicaid. It is not necessary to go through a full-scale application process each time, or to move out of the nursing home and into another nursing home as a private-pay patient.

It is not enough for the Medicaid recipient simply to turn down the assets, because part of the Medicaid application is an ongoing promise to collect all funds to which the recipient is entitled. The problem is that accepting the assets leads to termination of Medicaid eligibility, but rejecting them is a transfer subject to a penalty period. Therefore, wherever possible, a person contemplating a Medicaid application should limit the amount of assets that will come into his possession after eligibility.

See above for a discussion of electing against the will of a deceased spouse. Potential Medicaid recipients can discuss this issue with family members, other than the spouse, who might make bequests, and ask them to leave the money to someone else. There is no obligation to leave money to a non-spouse, and no right of election against a non-spouse's will. But this will not work where a relative dies intestate, and the Medicaid recipient becomes a distributee (a person who receives an inheritance from a person who died without a will). Medicaid patients can also ask family members to remove them as insurance beneficiaries, and substitute someone who is not likely to be a Medicaid recipient.

CRIMINAL PENALTIES FOR PLANNERS?

Not only did the Health Insurance Portability and Accessibility Act of 1996 (HIPAA) revolutionize the tax treatment of long-term care insurance (see Chapter 4), it had dramatic but short-lived impact on Medicaid planning. A HIPAA provision, nicknamed the "Send Granny to Jail Bill," made it a federal misdemeanor for an individual to transfer assets in order to become eligible for Medicaid, followed by an application for Medicaid made during the penalty period. This was not a politically popular provision. There are lots of senior citizens, they vote, and their relatives are very interested in their well-being.

The Balanced Budget Act of 1997 amended this HIPAA provision, this time affecting a much less popular group of Americans. It was no longer a crime for individuals to transfer assets and then apply during a penalty period. Instead, the federal misdemeanor (punishable by up to a year's imprisonment and/or a $10,000 fine) was re-defined as advising someone else to make transfers (if the advisor was paid to render advice), if that person later applied for Medicaid during a penalty period. Potentially, criminal liability could have been applied to lawyers, accountants, financial planners, insurance professionals selling annuities, or anybody else who gave professional advice about Medicaid planning. This provision was nicknamed the "Send Granny's Lawyer to Jail Bill."

As you can imagine, lawyers soon rallied to get rid of this provision, and suits were brought in federal courts in New York and Rhode Island. In the spring of 1998, the New York court issued a permanent injunction to prevent the Department of Justice from ever enforcing the provision. In a letter to Congress, Attorney General Janet Reno informed Congress that the Department of Justice would not prosecute any paid advisors on the basis of their clients' Medicaid applications. This letter sets policy nationwide, not just in New York, so there is no real risk of prosecution for giving your clients advice about Medicaid planning.

Although DRA '05 is harsh on the process of Medicaid planning, this time around, there was no attempt to penalize the planners! The policy turn-around also gives hope for potential amendments to DRA '05, once Congress realizes that it not only penalizes neutral or even valuable behavior (such as donating to charity and home ownership) on the part of senior citizens, it also puts the long-term care and financial services industries at a disadvantage.

BUY-IN PROGRAMS

Many individuals are "dual eligibles." Dual eligibles are senior citizens or disabled persons who qualify for both Medicare and Medicaid. The Balanced Budget Act of 1997 changed previous law by making it clear that states are not required to pay Medicare deductibles or co-payments to the extent that the total payment to a health care provider would exceed the Medicaid rate. This has practical as well as philosophical consequences. In nearly all circumstances, Medicare pays more for services than Medicaid does, so health care providers often receive less for treating dual eligibles than they would for treating the same people if they were only Medicare beneficiaries.

Another group of senior citizens do not qualify for full-scale Medicaid benefits, but they need some financial assistance with health care costs. There are three federal programs to assist persons in this category: Qualified Medicare Beneficiary (QMB), Specified Low-Income Medicare Beneficiary (SLMB), and Qualifying Individuals (QI).

The Qualified Medicare Beneficiary (QMB) program pays part or all of the Medicare cost-sharing (deductibles, coinsurance, and Part B premiums) for elderly persons who are enrolled in Medicare Part A.

The Specified Low-Income Medicare Beneficiary (SLMB) program covers the Part B premium ($88.50 a month in 2006), but otherwise the enrollee is responsible for other Medicare cost-sharing.

Qualifying Individuals (QIs) are eligible for partial or full payment of their Part B premium, depending upon income.

Note that the income figures for buy-in programs change once a year, based on changes in the official federal poverty line. Usually the new poverty line is announced in February, unlike Social Security and Medicare changes, which are usually announced in late October. Figures can found in the publication "Medicare and You," which is available on the Medicare Web site at www.medicare.gov.

WHAT IS THE FUTURE OF MEDICAID?

Before DRA '05 was enacted, the Senate Committee on Aging held hearings in July of 2005 to look for ways to trim the ever-growing Medicaid budget. Douglas Holtz-Eakin of the CBO testified about Medicaid's pharmaceutical purchasing policies. Medicaid spending on drugs has gone up an average of 15% per year even after adjustment for inflation; with Medicare Part D on line, it will reduce

Medicaid prescription spending for dual eligibles, but then spending will climb again. He reported that Medicaid often overpays for generic drugs, especially ones that were recently prescription-only, because the price schedules are not adjusted frequently enough, and CMS is lax about collecting rebates it is owed by manufacturers.

Gordon H. Smith, who chaired the hearing, stated that the Medicaid spend-down process must be monitored to "block intentional fraud while protecting people who truly qualify for care."

Julie Stone-Axelrad, a Congressional Research Service policy analyst, testified that it was impossible to determine how many people do Medicaid financial planning to qualify for benefits. She raised the question of who will pay for the care of persons debarred from collecting Medicaid benefits if look-back periods are extended, pointing out that it is unlikely that there would still be traceable funds that could be recouped and used to pay privately for care. Not all transferees could or would return the funds. It would be bad policy to discourage senior citizens from making charitable contributions or helping their families with financial needs.

Elder law attorney Vincent J. Russo (a past president of the National Academy of Elder Law Attorneys) spoke about the way that the health care system "penalizes people who have pursued the American dream, saved for retirement, and then get the wrong disease" because Medicare covers acute illnesses but not the effects of dementing diseases that require custodial care. He made the point that tougher look-back periods don't necessarily generate a pool of funds that can be used to pay for care; in many instances, either nursing homes would go uncompensated after private payment funds ran out, or the senior citizen would do without necessary care. There are already bad situations where an elderly patient is ready for discharge from a hospital, and is too sick to return home—but no nursing home placement can be found because there are payment problems.

Russo also pointed out that it's inaccurate to say that Medicaid recipients get a free ride. Even if they are able to use financial planning to shelter assets, they are still required to spend down all of their excess income, which can be hundreds or even thousands of dollars a month. His position was that really rich people don't engage in Medicaid planning, because the tax and cash flow consequences would be so onerous. He also pointed out that in many older couples, the husband is solely responsible for financial planning, so a community spouse or surviving spouse may not even have been aware of a transaction, much less have initiated it. Long look-back periods can also be unfair to cognitively impaired seniors who have little insight into the reasons for past decisions.

Russo criticized the extension of the lookback period for both home and institutional care to 60 months, stating that it would require record-keeping far greater than most senior citizens practice. He recommended that annuities should be considered available assets for Medicaid purposes unless they are either part of a qualified plan or IRA, or are irrevocable, non-assignable, actuarially sound, and make equal payments during the annuity term without deferrals or balloon payments.[55]

The Congressional Budget Office (CBO's) estimate was that over a 10-year period, DRA '05 would cut federal Medicaid spending by $26.5 billion—not just because of the tougher transfer rules, but because more Medicaid recipients would have to pay premiums and would have to pay for each prescription and medical visit. The CBO estimated that 45,000 people would be dropped from the Medicaid rolls in 2010, because of non-payment of premiums, and 65,000 people, the majority of them children, would be in the same situation in 2015. The CBO estimates that 13 million low-income people would be required to make copayments for the first time because of DRA '05, or their copayments would increase. About 1.6 million people would lose benefits, including dental, vision, and mental health care. Looking specifically at long-term care Medicaid, the CBO expected that 15% of the new Medicaid nursing home applications each year—120,000 applications—would experience additional penalty periods as a result of DRA '05, and about 2,000 people a year would be ineligible for nursing home benefits because of excess housing equity.[56]

Clearly, DRA '05 has created a revolution in the Medicaid system, and has made the planning process much harder. However, there have been previous attempts at various kinds of Medicaid reform, and, like various efforts at tax reform, has resulted in the development of ever newer and more ingenious planning mechanisms.

Congress responded to calls for greater involvement of the private sector, and greater personal responsibility in the form of long-term care insurance coverage. However, no limitations have been placed on insurers' ability to reject applications on underwriting grounds, and there are no limitations on premium increases for those who own LTCI policies. Nor are there any limitations on the cost of long-term care, so the insurance industry could get caught in a financial "death spiral."

CHAPTER ENDNOTES

1. The Conference report for DRA '05 "Deficit Reduction Act of 2005," House Report 109-36.
2. AARP Public Policy Institute Fact Sheet #1020, "The Medicaid Program: A Brief Overview," http://assets.aarp.org/rgcenter/post-import-fs102_medicaid.pdf and Fact Sheet #18R, "Medicaid and Long-Term Services and Supports for Older People," http://assets.aarp.org/rgcenter/post-import/fs18r_medicaid_05.pdf.

3. The statute is 42 USC Sec. 1396a(a)(3); the Regulations are found in 42 CFR Secs. 431.201, 431.206(b), 435.912 and 435.919; see Sarah Somers and Jane Perkins, "Fact Sheet: The Burden of Proof in Medicaid Cases," http://www.healthlaw.org/library.cfm?fa=download&amp.

4. Robert Pear, "Rulings Trim Legal Leeway Given Medicaid Recipients," *New York Times*, August 15, 2005, p. A12.

5. *Leocata v. Wilson-Coker*, CCH Medicare/Medicaid Guide ¶301,568 (D. Conn. November 3, 2004).

6. The Kaiser Family Foundation's site, http://www.kff.org includes both basic Medicaid information and coverage of news developments.

7. Kaiser Family Foundation Issue Paper, "The Distribution of Assets in the Elderly Population Living in the Community," http://www.kff.org/medicaid/loader.cfm?url=commonspot/security/getfile-cfm&PageID=53591.

8. Rick Lyman, "Florida Offers a Bold Stroke to Fight Medicaid Cost," *New York Times*, January 23, 2005, p. A25.

9. Kirk Johnson and Reed Abelson, "Model in Utah May be Future for Medicaid," *New York Times*, February 24, 2005, p. A1.

10. See Social Security Administration Notices at 66 FR 54047 (October 25, 2001); and (October 24, 2000).

11. See 66 FR 2316 (January 11, 2001).

12. *Park Hope Nursing Home v. Eckelberger*, 713 N.Y.S.2d 918 (N.Y. Sup. Ct. 2000); see *The ElderLaw Report*, December 2000, p. 6.

13. *Mistrick v. Division of Medical Assistance & Health Servs.*, 712 A.2d 188 (N.J. 1998).

14. *Martin v. Ohio Dep't of Human Servs.*, 720 N.E.2d 576 (Ohio Ct. App. 1998). For discussion of these issues, see "Community Spouse's IRA Is a Countable Resource," *The Elder Law Report*, February, 1999, p. 6.

15. *Keip v. Wisconsin Dep't of Health & Family Servs.*, 606 N.W.2d 543 (Wisc. App. 1999).

16. *Comm'r of DSS v. Fishman*, 720 N.Y.S.2d 493 (N.Y. App. Div. 2001).

17. *Morenz v. Wilson-Coker*, No. 04-4107-cv (2nd Cir. July 14, 2005).

18. Theoretically, states have the option of providing non-waivered Medicaid home care, although few states have decided to do so. In order to receive FMAP, states must impose the same transfer penalties on waivered home care as on nursing home care. States can, but are not required to, impose transfer penalties on non-waivered home care. In fact, in New York State, it is possible to qualify for non-waivered home care immediately after transferring all non-exempt assets, but the CSRA and CSIA are transfer-related rules, and are not available to a recipient of non-waivered home care.

19. This is a tricky one. It is not good enough that Medicaid was not the only motivation. Usually, financial planning clients have several motivations, including helping family members, saving income taxes, and estate planning.

20. GAO Report, "Medicaid: Transfers of Assets by Elderly Individuals To Obtain Long-Term Care Coverage," GAO-05-968 (September 2005), http://www.gao.gov/cgi-bin/getrpt?GAO-05-968.

21. "In Effort to Pare Medicaid, Focus is On Long-Term Care" *New York Times*, p. A1.

22. CMS' Roy Trudel cleared up this potentially confusing point in an e-mail to Massachusetts elder law attorney Brian E. Barreiera. See *The ElderLaw Report*, March, 2000, p. 4.

23. Some states use a subjective test: whether the nursing home resident wants to return home. Others use an objective standard: whether it is reasonable to believe that a return home is possible.

24. See 42 USC 1396p(c)(2)(A) for details.

25. Sarah Lueck, "Some Heirs Find a Costly Surprise: Bill From Medicaid," *Wall Street Journal*, June 24, 2005, p. A1.

26. *In re Estate of Thompson*, 586 N.W.2d 847 (N.D. 1998); *In re Estate of Wirtz*, 607 N.W.2d 882 (N.D. 2000); *In re Estate of Jobe*, 590 N.W.2d 162 (Minn. Ct. App. 1999) (up to the extent of assets that were jointly owned or were marital property at any time during the marriage).

27. *DesFosses v. Shumway*, discussed in "New Hampshire Forced to Change Its Medicaid Recovery Policies," *The ElderLaw Report*, February 2000, p.1.

28. CMS' Robert A. Streimer, Director of Disabled and Elderly Health Programs, made this point in a letter dated February 25, 1998 and addressed to Dana E. Rozansky, Esq. See Thomas D. Begley, Jr., "Income Only Trusts: Having Your Cake and Eating It Too," *The ElderLaw Report*, October 1998, p.1.

29. *Case v. Fargnoli*, 702 N.Y.S.2d 764 (N.Y. Sup. 1999); discussed in David Goldfarb, "Trusts impact Medicaid in Complicated Ways," *New York Law Journal*, July 17, 2000, p. 7.

30. *Oxenhorn v. Fleet Trust Co.*, 722 N.E.2d 492 (N.Y. 1999).

31. The full citation is 42 USC 1396p(d)(4)(C). Details are in the State Medicaid Manual Section 3259.7B.

32. *Corcoran v. DSS*, CCH Medicare/Medicaid Guide ¶301,565 (Conn. Sup. November 9, 2004).

33. See Harry S. Margolis and Eric R. Oalican, "The Use of Annuities in Long-Term Care Planning," *The ElderLaw Report*, November 1998, p. 1, for an excellent review of these strategies.

34. A deferred annuity could be purchased as part of a long-range plan, but there may be heavy penalties on premature withdrawals from such an annuity, and these funds may be required to pay long-term care expenses. *Id.*

35. Thomas Begley, Jr. and Jo-Anne Herina Jeffreys, "The Use of Annuities in Medicaid Planning: An Update," *The ElderLaw Report*, July-August 2000) p.1. *The ElderLaw Report*, has excellent coverage of this issue, also including Cynthia L. Barrett's "Recent Attacks on Medicaid Annuities," (December 2000) p. 1 and Michael J. Millonig, "Effective Arguments in Medicaid Annuity Litigation," February 2001, p. 1.

36. See "HCFA Further Clarifies Treatment of Annuities," *The ElderLaw Report*, September 2000, p. 3.

37. See *Johnson v. Guhl*, 91 F.Supp.2d 754 (D.N.J. 2000); *Dempsey v. Dep't of Public Welfare*, 756 A.2d 90 (Pa. Commw. Ct. 2000); *Bird v. Pennsylvania Dep't of Public Welfare*, 731 A.2d 660 (Pa. Commw. Ct. 1999).

38. *McNamara v. Ohio DHS*, 744 N.W.2d 1216 (Ohio Ct. App. 2000).

39. *State of North Dakota v. Bergman*, CCH Medicare/Medicaid Guide ¶301,563(D.N.D. November 25, 2003), *reversed* 2004 ND 196, 688 N.W.2d 187, CCH Medicare/Medicaid Guide ¶301,564 (N.D. October 20, 2004).

40. *Gross v. North Dakota DHS*, 2004 North Dakota 190 (http://www.court/state.nd.us/court/opinions/20040071.htm), CCH Medicare/Medicaid Guide ¶301,527 (N.D. October 12, 2004).

41. These strategies are discussed in Alexander A. Bove, Jr., "Making Resources Disappear: The Magic of PANs and SCINs," *The ElderLaw Report*, October 1997, p. 1.

42. See the State Medicaid Manual Section 3258.7 for more guidance.

43. *Keith v. Rizzuto*, 212 F.3d 1190 (10th Cir. 2000).

44. *In re Shah*, 733 N.E.2d 1093 (N.Y. 2000).

45. For tax implications of contracts for care, see *Estate of Stern v. Treasury*, 98-1 USTC ¶60,299 (S.D. Ind. 1998), in which an estate was allowed to deduct $182,500 from the $1 million estate inherited by a caregiver, on the theory that this money was reasonable payment for her protracted services as caregiver. The court accepted an "implied contract" theory, under which a person who agrees to pay for care but does not clarify the amount is deemed to be liable for paying a reasonable amount comparable to the market rate. (In this case, reducing the taxable estate also reduced the estate tax and thus increased the net amount inherited by the caregiver.)

46. *Schott v. Olszewski*, Nos. 03-2490, 03-2536 (6ᵗʰ Cir 3/15/05).

47. If the Medicaid recipient receives World War II reparations, the reparation money is not considered income.

48. See Ron M. Landsman, "Going to Court to Improve Spousal Benefits," Parts 1 and 2, *The ElderLaw Report*, September and December 1998.

49. Fair hearing provisions are in 42 USC 1396r-5(e).

50. Cases such as *Schachner v. Perales*, 648 N.E.2d 1321 (N.Y. 1995), *Gomprecht v. Sabol*, 652 N.E.2d 936 (N.Y. 1995) and *Jenkins v. Fields*, 1996 U.S. Dist. Lexis 5852 (S.D.N.Y. 1996) make this point.

51. *Fortier v. Thomas*, 1999 Westlaw 1081350 (Conn. Super. Ct. November 10, 1999) (prescription drugs); *Genser v. Thomas*, 2000 Westlaw 38474 (Conn. Super. Ct. June 10, 2000) (aging process).

52. *Robbins v. DeBuono*, 218 F.3d 197 (2d Cir. 2000), *cert. denied*, 531 U.S. 1071 (2001).

53. Also see *Matter of Mattei*, 647 N.Y.S.2d 415 (N.Y. Sup. Ct. 1996), in which a Medicaid recipient's daughter was appointed as guardian for her mother specifically in order to satisfy the mother's obligation as a Medicaid recipient to elect against her deceased husband's will, and to use the funds to pay for her mother's care while she was rendered ineligible for Medicaid by the inheritance.

54. State Medicaid Manual Section 3261.

55. For the hearing testimony, see http://www.aging.senate.gov/public/_files/hr146gs.pdf; http://www.aging.senate.gov/public/_files/hr146dh.pdf; http://www.aging.senate.gov/public/_files/hr146ja.pdf; http://www.aging.senate.gov/public/_files/hr146vr.pdf.

56. Jay Romano, New Medicaid Rules on Home Ownership, *New York Times*, February 12 2006, Real Estate p. 12; Robert Pear, "Budget Measure Would Hurt the Poor on Medicaid Report Says," *New York Times*, January 30, 2006, p. A14 and "Budget Accord Could Mean Payments by Medicaid Recipients," *New York Times*, December 20, 2005, p. A26.

Chapter 7

The Family Home: A Special Resource

The family home has undoubted sentimental value. Owning a home is an important part of most financial plans, and most senior citizens prefer to receive their long term care at home instead of moving to specialized housing or a health care facility.

Most senior citizens are homeowners, and most of their homes are mortgage-free. Furthermore, except for very wealthy people, the home is one of the largest (if not the single largest) financial assets in the financial plan. For all these reasons, planning for the home and its financial value looms large in the elderplan, and home equity is a major asset that must be handled wisely.

Sometimes remaining in the same home is the right strategy. Sometimes it makes sense to choose a different, more suitable home. The existing home may:

- Need too much maintenance;

- Be too hard to take care of;

- Cost too much to heat and cool;

- Be too far away from recreational and medical resources (especially for senior citizens who can no longer drive safely, and have little access to public transportation);

- Be located in a neighborhood that has deteriorated and become dangerous;

- Not be handicap accessible; or

- Be too large for "empty nesters."

It may make sense to stay in the larger home if grown children are likely to move back in, or if space is needed for a home sharer or live-in home health care worker.

A traditional strategy is for older people to sell their home, take advantage of the tax exclusion for certain home sale gains (see below), and move to (1) rented accommodations, (2) a smaller, more convenient home, or (3) a retirement community or health care facility. Investing the home sale proceeds actively, or using them to purchase an annuity, can generate a gratifying stream of additional income for post-retirement needs. Whether this is the best strategy depends on emotional as well as practical (e.g., cash-flow, Medicaid, tax) factors.

Senior homeowners can face additional challenges if the rising value of their homes means higher real estate taxes: they must pay higher taxes out of fixed incomes if property tax relief programs for senior citizens have been eliminated or cut back. For a long time, these programs were very popular, and interfering with them would have been political suicide, but state and local governments are now severely short of cash and need to find revenue sources.[1]

As described below, one of the important changes the Deficit Reduction Act of 2005, P.L. 109-171 made to Medicaid law is a limit on the amount of home equity that a person can have and still qualify for Medicaid—a change which is likely to trigger added interest in reverse mortgages and home equity loans.

OLDER CLIENT HOME STRATEGIES

- Stay in the home and plan to leave it to a child or grandchild. One problem with this is that the heirs may already be homeowners, or otherwise not interested in living in the older client's home. This also is not very practical if the intent is to divide the ownership among a large group of heirs. The simple alternative might be to direct the executor to sell the property and divide the proceeds. This brings up the problem of hurried "estate sales" that do not always generate optimum prices, especially if the death happens to occur shortly before a slump in the real estate market.

- Stay in the home and fix it up to make it more suitable for the needs of an older person, such as by replacing loose rugs with bare floors or carpeting, enhancing the lighting, adding security features including a response system for health emergencies, adding a lift on the staircase, widening doorways, and retrofitting bathrooms and kitchens for a wheelchair user.

- Stay in the home but transfer ownership of the home to a trust (see below) or transfer ownership as part of a Medicaid plan (see Chapter 6). It is also possible to do a sale-leaseback or gift-leaseback within the family, but these "split-interest" transactions are difficult, sophisticated, and mandate current advice from a top-flight tax advisor.

- Share living quarters with the parent moving in with a son or daughter, or vice versa. Also a possibility is an informal "home sharing" arrangement, which can provide companionship and perhaps some household services in return for rent-free or low-rent accommodations.

- Obtain a home equity loan or reverse mortgage. The funds can be used to pay for home care, nursing home care of a spouse who remains at home, or for travel or ordinary living expenses.

- Sell the home and use the proceeds of the sale to buy admission to a retirement community or a continuing care retirement community that does not offer equity ownership. The advantage of this strategy is that a person with a small taxable estate may be able to move enough funds out of the estate to avoid federal estate taxation, while making sure that he will have a comfortable, appropriate living environment, or access to quality health and custodial care, or both. This can work especially well for a single or widowed person who is unable to use the estate tax marital deduction.

According to recent research, 90% of married couples and 62% of single persons go into retirement owning their own homes, and life-cycle events seldom trigger home sales. Only 4% of households sell the home when a spouse dies, and only 11% when a homeowner enters a nursing home. AARP's 2000 survey has not been repeated, but the conclusions would probably be the same today: 80% of respondents aged 45 and over, and more than 90% of seniors, want to remain in their own homes as long as possible. Nearly all (82%) prefer not to move even if they need help with self-care.[2]

Many of the projections for increasing the role of the family home in providing funds for care (and reducing the burden on Medicaid) are based on the assumption that the home will be mortgage-free, reflecting the conventional wisdom that seniors went into retirement as debt-free homeowners. That's still true in many cases, but the percentage of those still burdened by mortgage debt has climbed. In 1989, 20%

of the households headed by a senior citizen had mortgage debt. This was true of one-third of senior households in 2001, with an average mortgage of $39,000. Mortgage debt in the United States as a whole has grown 12% a year, so the current figure is probably much higher. Not surprisingly then, the number of senior households with mortgages—and the size of the mortgages—continues to grow. Seniors are the group with the fastest-growing home debt, and the fastest-growing share of personal bankruptcy filings. In 1992, 24,000 senior citizens filed for bankruptcy protection; the number rose to 82,000 in 2001. (That last factor could change once the 2005 bankruptcy reform act takes effect.)

According to the Federal Reserve's 2001 survey of consumer finances, one out of every seven senior citizen households was heavily indebted—that is, had to devote 40% or more of its income to debt payments. Many senior citizens ran into debt problems not because of their own financial decisions but because of the need to help children and grandchildren cope with divorce, unemployment, drug addiction, or the younger generation's medical bills.[3]

One potential planning technique is to refinance the balance of the loan with a 30-year fixed-rate mortgage just before retiring, which would mean lower payments (because they're stretched out over so long). Much of each payment in the early years would be deductible interest—which can offset taxable IRA withdrawals. Mortgage debt is usually cheaper than other debt, so it might be worthwhile to borrow more and pay off high-interest credit card debt. Increasing the mortgage to get funds to invest is risky, because a poor investment return could lead to loss of the family home. A fixed-rate mortgage is probably safest, unless the client intends to move within five years, in which case a hybrid mortgage with an initial five-year fixed rate could work well.[4]

PRACTICE TIP: Financial consultant Charles Farrell suggests that a 50-year-old planning client should have savings equal to at least 4.5 years' income, and debt, including mortgage debt, should be less than three quarters of a year's income. At 60, he suggests savings should total at least 8.9 years income and debt should be under 20% of annual income. At 65, his benchmark is that the client should be debt-free and have accumulated 12 years' income.[5]

CAPITAL GAINS EXCLUSION

The Taxpayer Relief Act of 1997 (TRA '97) liberalized the capital gains exclusion available for the sale of a homestead. As part of TRA '97, Congress enacted a single Code provision to replace two earlier provisions. These earlier provisions dealt with the "rollover" of gain when a home seller purchased a more expensive home within two years of the sale transaction and with sales by individuals over the age of 55. The current provision, which is effective for sales taking place on or after May 7, 1997, can be used by taxpayers of any age.[6]

If both the "use test" and the "ownership test" are met, up to $250,000 in capital gains (i.e., gross home sale proceeds minus the basis of the property) on home sales can be excluded from income. Furthermore, gains of up to $500,000 can be excluded by a married person who files a joint return for the year of the sale, where both spouses satisfy the "use test" and at least one spouse satisfies the "ownership test," provided that neither of them has excluded home-sale gain in the previous two years, not taking into account sales before May 7, 1997.

The ownership test requires owning the property for at least two of the five years prior to the sale. The use test requires having used that property as the taxpayer's principal residence for at least two of the five years prior to the sale. The use test is modified to generally allow the exclusion if absence from the home was caused by living in a nursing home and the taxpayer used the residence for one year as a principal residence. The ownership and use tests can be satisfied in different years, and ownership and use need not be continuous.

A widow or widower is deemed to satisfy the ownership or use test if the deceased spouse satisfied the test prior to the home sale. If an individual marries in a year in which he has already sold a home, that individual can exclude up to $250,000 if the use and ownership requirements are met by that spouse. If each spouse satisfies the tests as to a different home, each can exclude up to $250,000. See IRS Publication 523, "Selling Your Home," (www.irs.gov/pub/irs-pdf/p523.pdf) for more details. This publication contains many detailed examples and worksheets.

If the property is jointly owned by persons who are not spouses, then each owner figures gain or loss separately on the basis of his or her percentage of ownership.

The IRS Restructuring and Reform Act of 1998 (IRSRRA '98) clarified the availability of a partial exclusion to taxpayers who could not satisfy the full-scale ownership and use tests. In other words, someone who owned or used the property for only one year out of the five can exclude up to $125,000 (single person) or up to $250,000 (married person filing jointly) if they satisfy other conditions required by the Code.

For example, a partial exclusion can be claimed by someone who failed to meet the ownership and use tests because he or she had to sell the home for health reasons, because of a work-related move, or because of unforeseen circumstances. A sale is considered health-related if the primary motivation for the sale was to obtain treatment for a "qualified person's" health problems. The qualified person is not just the homeowner, but a member (including step- and half-relatives and in-laws) of the homeowner's immediate family.

The capital gain calculation begins by deducting selling expenses (commissions, legal fees, advertising, and points paid by the seller) from the selling price. In many cases, it will be necessary to adjust the basis (tax value) of the home to account for factors such as depreciation already claimed and improvements made to the property. Special rules apply if the property was inherited, was a gift, was transferred as part of a divorce settlement, or if the property is located within a community property state. A further set of rules applies to properties that were partially used as residences and partially as income-producing rental property and/or for a home business.

PRACTICE TIP: Some plans, including Medicaid plans, involve transferring a remainder interest in the home. A remainder interest is a legal structure under which the original owner is allowed to remain in the house for his or her lifetime, at which point ownership passes to the person who has received the remainder interest. However, IRS Publication 523 says that a homeowner cannot exclude gain from the sale of a remainder interest to a close family member.

ACCESSING HOME EQUITY WITH REVERSE MORTGAGES

In many instances, home equity can be a promising source of funds by either obtaining a conventional home equity loan or line of credit, or through a "reverse mortgage," which is a special type of financial instrument usually used by senior citizens. However, it should be noted that using home equity reduces the value of the home that is available for inheritance, thus altering or defeating the estate plan.

PRACTICE TIP: All of the people named on the deed must be at least age 62, so reverse mortgage strategies will not work if the client's children have been added to the deed, or if the house has been given to the children subject to the parents' right to live in it for the balance of their lives.[7]

Under a reverse mortgage, the elderly homeowner enters into an agreement with a lender. Usually the lender will be a financial institution such as a bank, but sometimes an insurance company. Some states have guarantee programs to provide incentives for banks to make such loans, and a few state agencies write the mortgages directly, without bank involvement. As part of the reverse mortgage, the senior citizen receives regular payments. If these payments take the form of an annuity, the arrangement is known as a Reverse Annuity Mortgage (RAM). In return, the lender receives an equity interest in the home. Usually, the interest is limited to the amount advanced, plus interest. However, if the deal includes an "equity kicker," the lender will be entitled to a share of the appreciation in value of the property.

Loans with such "shared equity" or "shared appreciation" features are no longer being written, and they were never permitted for FHA-insured reverse mortgages, but you may encounter a client who has an older mortgage of this type.[8]

The National Council on Aging, using statistics about home ownership in 2000, estimates that about 13.2 million senior citizen households could qualify for reverse mortgages of at least $20,000. The average reverse mortgage they could tap would be $72,128. The aggregate home equity available would be $953 billion (a sum that could relieve some of the financial burdens on the Medicaid system). The organization estimates that of the 9.8 million senior households that could get substantial reverse mortgages, six million included a person with functional limitations and 3.8 million included people who needed assistance with daily tasks.

Although the traditional role for reverse mortgages is to provide funds for up-keep, repairs, and real estate taxes, the National Council estimates that 5.2 million of the reverse-mortgage-eligible households either already are Medicaid beneficiaries or are at risk of applying for Medicaid after exhausting their savings paying for long-term care.

The organization estimates that a $72,000 reverse mortgage could provide four hours a day of home health aide care for close to three years; 6½ years of adult day care every weekday for an Alzheimer's sufferer; or payments of $500 a month to reimburse a family member for care expenses, including one day of respite care per week—for 14 years! Another example they give is a 75-year-old with a federally insured reverse mortgage with an interest rate of 4.35%. Taking a line of credit against a $100,000 home could pay for 2.4 years of four hours a day of care from a home health aide; close to five years of adult day care; or respite care and expense reimbursement to a family member for 11.5 years.

Early in 2006, the New York Times reported on factors promoting the use of reverse mortgages and home equity as key sources of cash within retirement plans.[9] Homeowners often found that trends within the economy raised the value of their home, and even older people with small savings and few investments often own valuable homes. Furthermore, a number of people have lost their pensions because of corporate actions, and many people are concerned about future trends within the stock market and the sustainability of Social Security—leaving the home as the only substantial planning tool for some older couples and singles. This article reports that the number of new FHA-insured reverse mortgages was six times as great in 2004 as in 2000, with over 43,000 such transactions in 2004.

Nevertheless, there are many reasons why reverse mortgages have not gained widespread popularity. A generation that survived the Depression may place a very high premium on remaining debt-free. The National Reverse Mortgage Lenders' Association said that 8,700 reverse mortgage loans were made between October 2003 and January 2004—much higher than the corresponding period for the previous year, when only 4,948 loans were made.

According to the National Reverse Mortgage Lenders' Association, there are 65,000-70,000 reverse mortgages in effect. The National Council on the Aging's survey showed that only one-seventh of elderly householders said that they were likely or very likely to use reverse mortgages. Often, the elderly are leary of losing their homes or depleting the inheritance they intend to leave their children. However, close to two-thirds of the adult children surveyed by the National Council agreed that reverse mortgages are useful for helping the elderly remain at home (only half of the elderly agreed).

Clearly, because these transactions can involve high fees and can frustrate inheritance expectations, they should be used only to meet real needs, not to enhance an older couple's recreation budget. A generation that is used to, and values, being debt-free may find reverse mortgages psychologically uncomfortable. All federally insured reverse mortgages have the same interest rate, but other fees can vary depending on the lender. In some ways, rising interest rates are bad for reverse mortgage borrowers (reducing the size of a new loan that can be taken out), but the borrower under a line of credit reverse mortgage will find the balance still available will continue to grow, and the size of the credit line will rise and fall to reflect interest rate changes.[10]

Payments continue for a term of years, or for the lifetime of the homeowner. If the homeowner decides to sell the home, the loan becomes due and payable immediately. The loan also becomes payable on the death of the survivor of a home-owning couple. One advantage for homeowners who want to make a Medicaid plan is that for Medicaid and Supplemental Security Income (SSI) purposes, the funds paid by the lender to the homeowner are not considered income. The arrangement is considered a loan, not an income-generating investment. The typical reverse mortgage yields payments of under $8,000 a year, which is certainly not enough to pay for nursing home care, but may be enough to assist in paying for home care.

Whether the advantages outweigh the disadvantages depends on the facts of the case. See www.reverse.org, the Website for the National Center for Home Equity Conversion Mortgage (NCHEC), for more information about reverse mortgages, and on-line calculators for determining the amount that a particular person could raise via a reverse mortgage. AARP has a Home Equity Information Center that is also a valuable source of objective information, including a reverse mortgage calculator:

www.rmaarp.com and www.aarp.org/revmort. Other Web resources are available at www.reversemortgage.org, and www.financialfreedom.com.

When the interest rate is 9%, the 65-year-old owner of a $100,000 home could borrow up to $22,000; a 75 year-old could borrow $41,000; and an 85-year-old could borrow as much as $58,000 (in all cases, closing costs would be extra). There is no limit on the value of a home that can get a reverse mortgage, but the maximum amount that can be borrowed is determined by the FHA's mortgage limit for the area where the home is located. For most areas, that falls somewhere between $172,632 and $312,895, although amounts are higher in Alaska, Hawaii, Guam and the Virgin Islands.

In mid-2004, the *Wall Street Journal*'s Jonathan Clements provided some examples. A 75-year-old unmarried person who owned a $250,000 home could be able to borrow up to $169,750. Out of this amount, closing costs and servicing fees of close to $19,000 would be set aside, yielding about $150,000 that could be taken as a lump sum, credit line, or monthly income of $1,026, all of them tax free.

In comparison, a conventional mortgage would have much lower costs, and a home equity line could be created at very low cost—but would require repayment during the homeowner's lifetime. His example is 30-year fixed-rate mortgage for $200,000 on the same $250,000 home, yielding $197,000 net of closing costs of $3,000. Investing that sum in corporate bonds paying 5.5% provides $903 a month in income—but if the interest rate on the mortgage is 6.3%, the monthly mortgage payment would be $1,238. Or, if the entire $197,000 were invested in an immediate fixed annuity, a 75 year-old woman would receive $1,643 a month, a 75 year-old man would get $1,809. That would more than cover the mortgage, but at least part of the annuity payment would be taxable.[11]

Federal Rules for Reverse Mortgages

According to federal statutes (specifically 15 USC Section 1602(b)), a reverse mortgage is a nonrecourse transaction that secures one or more advances of credit from the lender to the homeowner. ("Nonrecourse" means that repayment can be taken only from the property, not against the homeowner's other assets or his or her estate.)[12] Repayment must wait until the consumer dies, vacates the home, or transfers ownership of the dwelling. Truth in Lending disclosures for adjustable-rate mortgages must be made to the homeowner.

If the lender offers an annuity as part of the deal, or arranges an annuity transaction or helps the borrower set up the annuity transaction, 12 CFR Section 226.33

requires the lender to include the cost of the annuity in its disclosure of the cost of the transaction.

Under the Home Equity Conversion Mortgage (HECM) program, the FHA insures five types of mortgages for homeowners aged 62 or over. HECMs are not limited to single-family houses: duplexes, triplexes, and four-family homes, as well as certain condominium units, can qualify. The National Reverse Mortgage Lenders Association (NRMLA) reported in late 2005 that about 90% of all reverse mortgages are HECMs, and the FHA insured 43,131 HECMs in fiscal 2004, 14% higher than in FY 2003.[13]

PRACTICE TIP: A counseling sessions with an approved HECM counselor is a prerequisite for obtaining a federally insured reverse mortgage. There is a list of qualified counselors at www.hud.gov/offices/hsg/sfh/hecm/hecmlist.cfm, or call (800) 569-4287.

"Tenure plan" FHA-insured mortgages provide a fixed annuity for the life of the homeowner, as long as the purchaser remains in the home; the annuity ends if he moves away. "Term plan" mortgages offer a fixed annuity for a term of years. Funds are not made available immediately under the "line of credit plan," but funds will be made available on request, once eligibility has been established. The other two plans combine various features of these three plans.

The percentage of the value of the home that can be borrowed under a FHA-approved plan depends on the homeowner's age. The older he is, the larger the percentage that can be borrowed. The percentage increases rather than decreases with age because the older the person, the shorter the life expectancy and the shorter the time horizon over which the lender extends credit. The maximum size of the loan is set regionally, and ranges from $115,200 to $208,800 for single family homes.

The Federal National Mortgage Association ("Fannie Mae") also has a reverse mortgage program; the Home Keeper Mortgage is generally limited to one-third to one-half of the amount of equity. Fannie Mae maintains a toll-free number, (800) 572-4562, for information on reverse mortgages and a directory of participating lenders.

A HUD rule issued in the spring of 2004 was expected to cut reverse mortgage costs by lowering the premiums for refinancing reverse mortgages (see 26 CFR § 206.53). The previous rule required homeowners to pay a premium to the Federal Housing Administration (a subsidiary of HUD) equal to the lesser of 2% of the home's value, or 2% of the federal limit for home values in the area for that type of mortgage, and another premium of 2% the new (and probably higher) appraised value was usually charged for refinancing. Almost 90% of reverse mortgages are federally insured, so federal regulations make a big difference.

Under the 2004 Regulation, however, the FHA premium cannot be higher than 2% of the difference between the maximum amount of the original reverse mortgage and the refinanced one. For example, refinancing of a reverse mortgage on a home once valued at $100,000, but whose value had risen to $200,000 at the time of refinancing, would cost only $2,000 in FHA premiums, not $4,000. But the regulation does not eliminate the other fees, such as appraisal costs and servicing charges, that can make reverse mortgages expensive. Costs can absorb up to 9% of the value of the home (although 5-6% is more typical).[14]

A suit was filed in California in July, 1998 against Transamerica Corporation and Metropolitan Life Insurance, alleging that their "House Money Lifetime" reverse annuity mortgage product was unconscionably unfair, involving onerous terms and multiple fees, to the extent of constituting financial elder abuse.[15] The suit alleges that this product was sometimes sold to mentally impaired, very aged persons who were unable to understand the disclosures and who ended up owing two to six times the amount of proceeds that they received from the insurer. This particular product required customers to purchase a deferred annuity that would make payments to especially long-lived customers who outlive the equivalent of the value of their housing equity. It also gave the mortgagees a 50% interest in the appreciation of the value of the home after the arrangement was entered into, and required a "maturity fee," payable at the termination of the arrangement, equal to 2% of the appreciated value of the property. (The House Money product is no longer sold, although the issuers say that the discontinuance was due to market factors, not the lawsuit.) When this edition went to press, the suit had not been resolved.

HOUSE TRUSTS: PRTs AND QPRTs

In some circumstances, transferring ownership of a personal residence to a trust can be beneficial. The Code includes provisions for two related types of house trusts: the Personal Residence Trust (PRT) and the Qualified Personal Residence Trust (QPRT). The main difference between them is that a PRT contains nothing but the house, while a QPRT can contain a limited amount of other assets that can throw off enough income to pay taxes and other expenses of the house. Any home (whether principal residence or vacation home, and whether free-standing or condominium or co-op unit) can be placed into trust. The advantage is that ownership of the home can be transferred to the couple's children for far less than fair market value, thus removing the house and its potential appreciation from the parents' estate.

The parents can keep using the property for a term of years. The downside? If the parents are still alive at the end of the term (and the optimum term should be shorter than the parents' predictable life expectancy), the children get full ownership, and if the parents want to keep living there, they have to rent the house at a fair market rental. If they use the house and pay less than fair market value, the value of the house goes back into the estate, because the transaction then becomes a transfer with a retained life estate, which is part of the estate. Both a PRT or QPRT must be drafted to forbid the trust grantor and/or his spouse to re-purchase the home when the term ends.

If both parents die during the term of a PRT or QPRT, then the value of the home will be included in their estates. If one dies during the trust term but the other survives, then only the half interest of the deceased parent will be included in his estate, so the trust will achieve only half of its objectives. Just as second-to-die insurance is often used to shore up estate plans, life insurance can be used to make sure that a PRT or QPRT will achieve its objectives even if one or both of the former-owner spouses dies during the term.

An early 2006 *New York Times* article gives some examples of QPRT planning.[16] The article points out that even though the estate tax exemption has increased a great deal, it is easy to accumulate a seven-figure estate in an area where even houses that are far from mansion quality sell for $1 million. According to Virginia trust lawyer Farhad Aghdami, putting a $1 million home into a QPRT with a three-year duration can yield tax savings of close to $150,000; an 18-year trust term could save close to $850,000. The savings that can be achieved depend on the homeowner's actuarially predictable life expectancy and prevailing interest rates. If the parents outlive the term and must start paying rent, at least the rent is a way to transmit money to the younger generation without making a transfer for tax or Medicaid purposes. (There is no transfer element because the rent is paid in the equivalent of an arm's-length transaction.)

INTRAFAMILY TRANSACTIONS

The higher the tax bracket of the senior citizen client, the more important tax planning becomes, and the more likelihood that there might be a federally taxable estate. Intrafamily transactions involving the family home may come to the rescue.

One possibility is for the older generation to sell (not give) their home to the younger generation. In a sale-leaseback transaction, the elders continue to live in the home and pay rent to the new owners. The home is removed from the potentially taxable estate. Although the older generation must pay rent, they receive a large sum of money for the sale (or continuing income payments if they grant a purchase-money mortgage).

But for the transaction to achieve the desired tax consequences, it must have real economic consequences. Structuring it as a "wash" (where each generation's financial obligation offsets that of the other), or failure to actually make or demand payments as required, will result in disregard for tax purposes.[17] Do not forget that capital gain on a home sale within the family must be recognized (although it will probably escape taxation because of the capital gains exclusion for home-sale profits), but loss on the sale of a home (whether to a family member or third party) is considered personal and thus is not tax-deductible.

A gift-leaseback involves the gift of a residence, while the donor continues to live there and pay rent. Probably, this will use up part of the unified credit against gift and estate taxes (see Chapter 13) or even, in extreme cases, lead to the need to pay gift tax. Internal Revenue Code Chapter 14 should also be consulted for large gifts. See above for a discussion of residence trusts.

Sometimes a home will be transferred to a family member, friend, or other unpaid caregiver based on past provision of care, or an agreement to provide care in the future. If the recipient is the child of the homeowner, and the child lives in the house for at least two years before the transfer, providing care that defers institutionalization, then the transfer to the "caregiver child" will not carry a Medicaid penalty (see Chapter 6). The transfer will also escape penalties if it is made more than 36 months before the Medicaid application, or if it can be proved that the value of the care was at least equal to the value of the home, so there was no gratuitous element in the transaction. For this purpose, the contract should be in writing, and must have existed before the care was rendered, not afterwards.

Another inter-generational housing option is for the parents to provide mortgage financing for their children's purchase of their own home. The National Association of Realtors reported that in 2005, about a quarter of all first-time home purchasers received financial help from family members. Usually, the more affluent members of the family make gifts or informal loans to help the less affluent members buy homes, but the transaction can also be structured formally, and can provide a sound investment return to the parent or other older-generation lender. Private bankers for wealthy families say that intra-family mortgages can be a good addition to the older generation's portfolio. From the tax point of view, however, intra-family loans that do not charge a market rate of interest will be deemed to include a gift component, reducing the estate tax exemption or even creating gift tax liability, depending on the facts. The older generation can also provide "gap" financing (for construction of a new home) or a second mortgage if the home purchase costs more than bank financing will provide.[18]

MEDICAID TREATMENT OF HOMESTEADS

As Chapter 6 explains in more detail, the Medicaid system treats the homestead as an asset entitled to favorable treatment. Funds used to fix up the property (for medical purposes or otherwise) are not transfers, because there is no "give-away" element.

A property remains a homestead as long as a nursing home resident's spouse or dependent relative continues to live there. Property ceases to be a homestead if it is owned by a single person who is in a nursing home and is too sick to return home.

In 2004, the New York State Department of Health allowed an elderly person to put part of his income into a Special Needs Trust (See Chapter 5) and still qualify for Medicaid home care. Before the trust was created, the Medicaid recipient, "M.O." had income of $1,078.70 a month, whereas home-care Medicaid was available only to persons with income of $642 per month or less. If he spent down the $358.01, he would not be able to pay his rent. The state Health Department decided that it would be wiser to allow M.O. to put the excess income into a trust administered by NYSARC, an advocacy group for the disabled, and continue to receive home care, than for him to lose his apartment and enter a nursing home—at much greater cost to Medicaid.[19]

The 2005 federal budget bill, the Deficit Reduction Act of 2005 (DRA '05) made major changes in Medicaid treatment of homesteads. Under prior law, there was no limit on the amount of housing equity that would be treated as exempt for Medicaid purposes. For Medicaid applications filed on or after January 1, 2006, however, an applicant can be found ineligible on the basis of excess housing equity. "Excess" equity means more than $500,000, although states have the option of increasing this amount to $750,000 (e.g., if it is a high-cost area with high housing prices). The $500,000 and $750,000 figures will not be indexed for inflation until 2011. The excess-equity rule will not be applied if the applicant's spouse, minor, blind, or disabled child lives in the homestead. DRA '05 states specifically that reverse mortgages and home equity loans are not considered transfers, and can be used to reduce home equity. The intention is that the home equity will be used to pay privately for care, either deferring or preventing a Medicaid application.

CHAPTER ENDNOTES

1.   Ray A. Smith, "Dark Side of the Boom," *Wall Street Journal,* March 30, 2005, p. B1.

2.   Alicia H. Munnell and Mauricio Soto (Center for Retirement Research, Boston College), "What Replacement Rates Do Households Actually Experience in Retirement?" (August 2005), www.bc.edu/crr/papers/wp_2005-10.pdf.

3.   Jennifer Bayot, "As Bills Mount, Debts On Homes Rise for Elderly," *New York Times*, July 4, 2004, p. A1.

4.   Jonathan Clements, "How to Keep Rising Mortgage Debt from Derailing Your Retirement Plans," *Wall Street Journal*, August 24, 2005, p. D1.

5.   Jonathan Clements, "Ugly Math: Soaring Housing Costs Are Jeopardizing Retirement Savings," *Wall Street Journal*, March 23, 2005, p. D1.

6.   IRC Sec. 121.

7.   Lisa Nachmias Davis, "Paying for Staying Home: Reverse Mortgages" (revised June 8, 2005), www. sharinglaw.net/elder/paying_for_staying_at_home.htm.

8.   Jay Romano, "For Lenders, A Cut of Profits," *New York Times*, April 18, 2004, Real Estate p. 7.

9.   Motoko Rich and Eduardo Porter, "Increasingly, the Home Is Paying for Retirement," *New York Times*, February 24, 2006, p. C6.

10. Kelly Greene, "Elderly Remain Skeptical About Reverse Mortgages," *Wall Street Journal*, January 27, 2005, and "Reverse Mortgages Are Viewed As Way to Fund Care of Elderly," *Wall Street Journal*, April 14, 2004, p. D4; Ruth Simon, "Tapping the Piggy Bank," *Wall Street Journal*, June 14, 2004, p. R7; Jim Connolly, "What Boomers Should Know About Reverse Mortgages for Mom and Dad," National Underwriter Life & Health The Week in Life & Health 2004, Issue #20.

11. Jonathan Clements, "Tapping Your House to Fund Retirement: Alternatives to Costly Reverse Mortgages," *Wall Street Journal*, July 7, 2004, p. D1.

12. The basic federal rules about reverse mortgages are found in 24 CFR Part 206, although there are also banking rules about reverse mortgages: see 12 CFR Part 226 Appendix K and 226.31, 226.33.

13. Breaking News, "Reverse Mortgage Volume Rises," NU Online News Service, November 2, 2005.

14. Kathy Chu, "Seniors Get Break on Mortgage Fees," *Wall Street Journal*, April 20, 2004, p. D2.

15. Ralph T. King Jr., "Insurers Face 'Elder Abuse' Charge in Mortgage Suit," *Wall Street Journal*, October 15, 1998, p. B1; Amanda Levin, "Insurers Sued Over Reverse Mortgages," *National Underwriter*, Life and Health/Financial Services Edition, September 14, 1998, p. 28.

16. Damon Darlin, "With a Little Estate Planning, Your House Can Stay in the Family," *New York Times*, January 21, 2006, p. C1.

17. See *Estate of Maxwell v. Comm.*, 3 F.3d 591 (2nd Cir. 1993).

18. Diya Gullapalli, "When Mom & Dad Are the Bank," *Wall Street Journal*, January 21-22, 2006, p. B1.

19. Motoko Rich, "Helping the Elderly Stay Put," *New York Times*, March 4, 2004, p. F10.

Chapter 8

Retirement Planning

An older client base will probably consist of three groups: persons in their 50s and 60s who are contemplating retirement (the largest group), those who have already retired, and a small group of those who have retired and want to return to the workforce. Therefore, the planner's task includes giving advice about the best timing for retirement, the tax- and Medicaid-wise ways to handle retirement benefits (whether to be selected or already in pay status) and how the estate plan should deal with these funds.

There are some factors that work in favor of older people remaining in the workforce. The Age Discrimination in Employment Act makes it illegal to force any person over age 40, who is still qualified to perform the job, to retire when he prefers to keep working. (There is an exception for "bona fide policymakers," who can be required to retire at 70, if their job functions during working life included significant management responsibility, and if they are entitled to a pension of $44,000 or more per year when they retire. There is also an exception for tenured university faculty.) So theoretically, almost anyone who can still tackle the job can keep working. Congress has changed the tax laws several times (see below) to make them more favorable to continued employment. Many employers not only tolerate but actively recruit older workers, because of their skills and a work ethic that can be hard to find in younger employees.

With or without these incentives, most people prefer to retire before age 70, and many prefer to retire before the traditional retirement age of 65.

Until about the mid-1990s, there was a trend toward earlier and earlier retirement, cutting the labor force participation of seniors and near-seniors. In 1994, about two-thirds of men over 55 were in the labor force, a percentage that rose to over 69% in 2002. The Bureau of Labor Statistics expects it to be close to 70% in 2012. For men 65 and older, labor force participation is now about 19% and expected to be close to 21% by 2012. For women aged 55-64, more than 56% were working in 2004, and 60% are expected to be employed in 2012. But this trend is turning around, in response to economic as well as personal factors.

In 2002, 14% of the U.S. workforce consisted of workers 55 and over, a percentage that is expected to grow to 19% by 2012, so the wishes of workers near retirement age will become more significant to employment planning. In fact, between 2002 and 2012, the number of workers over 55 will grow by 49%—while the number of workers under 55 will grow only 5%. So personal decisions about when to retire also have a "ripple effect" if widespread retirement makes it hard for employers to get enough workers with the skills and work ethic that the employers need.

A 2004 study by John Hancock Financial Services showed a steady increase in the expected retirement age: the average expected age was 64.4, more than three years older than the 2002 study and five years older than the 1995 study. Eighteen percent said they didn't think they'd be able to retire until they were 70 or even older—twice the 2002 figure and triple the 1995 figure. Among defined contribution plan participants surveyed, 70% are very concerned or somewhat concerned that they won't have enough retirement income.[1]

When the financial services company UBS AG carried out its 2004 survey (the third since 1998), 57% of respondents planned to retire after age 62, versus 47% in 2002 and 36% in 1998. Over half (51%) of pre-retirees, and 35% of those already retired, were very or somewhat concerned about outliving their assets.[2]

In 2003, the average male worker spent 18 years in retirement, versus less than 12 years in 1950. So the challenge is providing for 50% more retirement years in a time of rising prices. In 1970, a man's life expectancy at age 65 was about 13 years; it was about 16 years in 2005, and is projected to reach 17 years in 2020. For women, it was 17 years in 1970, more than 19 years in 2005, and is projected to reach more than 20 in 2020.

In 1950, the "dependency ratio" (the number of senior citizens compared to the working-age population aged 15-64) was less than 15%, rising to close to 20 in 2000, and is projected to be over 30 between 2030 and 2050.

Early in 2006, the Employee Benefit Research Institute published figures showing that between 1987 and 2004, the proportion of income that people aged 65-79 derived from earnings on their assets was cut in half, falling from 30% to 15% of overall income. But the percentage of income attributable to employment increased, rising from 26% to 37% between 1987 and 2004 for persons aged 65-69, doubling from 7% to 14% for those aged 75-79, and even going from 2.4% to 3.4% for those over 85.[3]

Barbara Bovbjerg of the General Accounting Office has pointed out that whether someone will be financially better off by delaying retirement depends on individual factors. For some people, for example, retiring at 65 rather than 55 would mean that their real income at age 75 would be twice was high. But other people are better off by retiring early.

When the Normal Retirement Age (NRA) for Social Security was 65, benefits were cut by 20% for retirement at 62; in 2002, 56.1% of people elected to retired at 62 despite the benefit cut. The NRA is being phased up toward 67, and benefits will be cut by 30% rather than 20% for early retirement. According to Bovbjerg's testimony, most workers 62-67 do not have health problems that would prevent them from staying in the labor force, although some of them face age discrimination. So, if employers need to react to the aging of the workforce by retaining older workers for longer time periods, in most cases, the older employee's health will not prevent continued employment.

The Employee Benefit Research Institute's 2004 Retirement Confidence Study showed that two-thirds of retirees who also worked for pay said they liked to be active and stay involved, but at least 81% of those still working identified financial motivations for remaining employed.[4] In some instances, continued work is beneficial for both employers (who retain skilled, literate employees with loyalty and other good work habits) and for employees (who have an interest and direction in life).

The optimistic part of the story is that many older people stay in the workforce longer or return to work because it makes them feel valued and useful, and companies are glad to retain their skills. The downside is that other older people want to retire but cannot afford to, especially with retiree health benefits hard to find. Some older workers face age discrimination, or find that employers prefer to hire less experienced—and less expensive—younger workers. If we look at men aged 55-64 (i.e., presumably at their peak earning years, and making serious plans for retirement), 87% of men in that group were in the workforce in 1950; workforce participation dropped below 65% in 1994, then started to climb again, reaching 69% in 2004. In the mid-1980s, only 26% of women over 55 were in the paid workforce in the late 1960s, and only 21% were in the mid-1980s.[5]

Social Security laws have been changed (see Chapter 9) so most older workers can earn without impairing their Social Security benefits. However, delayed retirement can also stem from negative causes, such as lost or disappointing pensions and inadequate health benefits.

On a personal level, the retiree must find interesting and satisfying activities for this time period, including activities that can be pursued if health deteriorates. On the financial planning level, they must have an adequate level of income that will not be outlived. Furthermore, since the retirement plan can be expected to continue for decades, the planner might want to adjust the portfolio to maintain or add at least some growth investments, instead of having a pure income orientation.

The planning challenge is to make sure that adequate income is available, and is not outlived. However, there may be circumstances in which *less* income is better than *more*. Income that is not needed may accumulate, making the potentially taxable estate larger. And, as Chapter 6 indicates, additional income is a negative rather than desirable factor for a person who receives Medicaid or is going to make a Medicaid application.

There's a debate among economists about the effect that retirement of Baby Boomers will have on the stock market. One theory is that massive sales pressure (from retirees who want to liquidate their assets for everyday expenses) will push down prices unless foreign investors step in to buy up the stocks and other assets. Finance professor Jeremy Siegel says that retirees won't be able to sustain the 90% of preretirement standard of living that they desire, and the gap between their target withdrawals and actual return on investments adds up to $123 trillion between now and 2050—but that gap could be eliminated by workers staying in the workforce until age 75. Another theory holds that most stocks are owned by people who are affluent enough to be able to live on their other assets as they slowly liquidate their portfolios.

The ratio of working-age people to retirees is currently about 5:1, but will fall to 2.6:1 in 30 years. As a recent article points out, in 1935, the average worker stayed in the workforce until age 69, and was dead by age 77. Today, the average worker retires at 62—and lives for two more decades. Clearly, the rules of retirement saving have changed.[6]

This chapter deals with qualified and nonqualified retirement plans provided by employers; see Chapter 10 for a discussion of Individual Retirement Accounts (IRAs). A plan is "qualified" if the employer that furnishes the plan follows an elaborate set of tax and labor law rules. In return, generally the employer can deduct the cost of sponsoring the plan, and the employees do not have to pay taxes on the funds in the accounts until they retire and start to draw the benefits.

Qualified plans are not allowed to discriminate in favor of highly compensated employees. Some companies that don't want to offer a qualified plan, or that want to provide extra benefits for top management, sponsor nonqualified deferred compensation plans. The tax consequences of these plans, as discussed below, are less favorable to both employer and employee than qualified plans.

Baby Boomers seem likely to receive more income in later life than earlier cohorts did, but rising health costs and other consumption expenses could take away this advantage. The Employee Benefit Research Institute's 2004 Health Confidence Survey showed how hard rising health costs have hit retirement planning. Almost half (48%) of respondents said they saved less because of health care costs; 30% had trouble paying their other bills for this reason; 26% have used up all or most of their savings; 25% have reduced their retirement plan contributions; 18% found it difficult to pay for the necessities of life, and 15% had to borrow money. Four-fifths of them substitute generic for brand-name drugs to save money. Three-quarters say they are taking better care of themselves because they cannot afford to go to the doctor, and close to half have delayed doctor visits for financial reasons.[7]

Researchers from the Boston College's Center for Retirement Research project that the typical older married couple will have the same income after taxes and health care spending in 2030 as in 2000, despite three decades of productivity growth.

It should also be noted that even older people who have Medicare and retiree health coverage are likely to face significant expenses for health care premiums and co-payments. Part B and Part D premiums will probably grow each year, because they are set to cover 25% of program costs. The trustees of the Medicare program estimate that by 2030, the Part B premium will be about $150 a month in 2004 dollars.

The study projects that the before-tax median income for married couples in 2000 was $36,800, and predicts that it will rise to $50,690 by 2030, but health spending as a percentage of after-tax income will more than double, from 16.0% to 35.1% For single people the corresponding projection is income growth from $15,380 a year to $$23,130, and 17.3% to 30.3%.

Those worst off will be low-income people who do not qualify for Medicaid. In 2000, the median married couple in the lowest income quintile (that is, those with income in the lowest 20% of the income distribution) were still ineligible for Medicaid.[8]

A study released by Fidelity Investments in 2006 concluded that a married couple aged 65 (if they are among the majority of retirees who do not have employment-related retiree health benefits) would need $200,000 to cover predictable health expenses other than long-term care. This sum includes Medicare premiums, acute health care expenses incurred but excluded by Medicare Part A, and payments for medications not covered by Part D, but not dental care or over-the-counter drugs—and this does not take into account the recent rules that raise Part B premiums for high-income Medicare beneficiaries. Fidelity estimates that these costs have increased by an average of 5.8% annually since 2002. Fidelity estimated that less than half of retirees have health coverage related to their past employment, and that this number would drop even further. The Employee Benefit Research Institute's estimate was even higher: $216,000 if they reached 80, $444,000 if they lived to be 90 and $778,000 if they managed to become centenarians. EBRI pointed out that in 2006, life expectancy for men was 82 years, 85 years for women.[9]

In 2001, the last time the Federal Reserve Board did a wide-ranging study of consumer finances, the typical pre-retirement age worker (age 55-64) had $42,000 saved in 401(k)s and IRAs—enough to generate an annuity payment of about $200 a month. EBRI found that for all employees, their reported savings and investments other than the family home were under $25,000 for more than half the households (52%); $25-$49,000 in 13%, $50-$99,000 in 11%, $100-$249,000 in 12%, and $250,000 or more in 11%. Looking just at people over 55, 39% of households had saved under $25,000, 12% $25-$49,000, 23% $50-$99,000, 23% $100-$249,000, and 19% $250,000 or more.[10]

In 1998, the Federal Reserve Survey of Consumer Finances found that in 1998, only 26% of senior households had mortgage debt, a percentage that rose to 32% in 2001. The *Wall Street Journal's* Jonathan Clements made some persuasive arguments about why mortgage debt is a bad idea for senior households.

His first example is a couple with $24,000 in pension and $16,000 in Social Security income. Because they fall below the income limit (see Chapter 9), their Social Security benefits are not taxable. They own their home free and clear and therefore have neither a mortgage interest deduction nor the cash flow impact of having to pay a mortgage. They owe $600 income tax on their IRA withdrawals, leaving them with $39,400 after tax.

The second hypothetical couple have a 30-year fixed-rate (6%) mortgage. They have to pay $1,200 a month until they reach 80. Therefore, to match the first couple's after-tax income, they have to make $14,400 in mortgage payments plus $39,400 ($58,000 in pre-tax income, requiring $42,000 in IRA withdrawals). They receive tax advantages from their mortgage interest deduction, but as they amortize the mortgage, the deduction decreases because more of each payment goes toward principal. This couple will probably have to make large (taxable) withdrawals from their IRA to pay the mortgage—which would probably raise their income to the point that Social Security benefits are taxable, generating $4,300 more federal tax liability. If they are unsophisticated or do not have good advice, they might not realize that the Social Security benefits would be taxable, so they might omit estimated tax payments, leading to penalties.[11]

SOURCES OF POST-RETIREMENT INCOME

After retirement, income typically derives from several sources:

- Qualified plan benefits provided by the employer;

- Nonqualified plan benefits provided by the employer;

- Individual Retirement Accounts (IRAs);

- Social Security benefits;

- Employment income—either from post-retirement employment (see below) or earned by one spouse who has not yet retired;

- Investment income, including annuity income and income from mutual funds, stock dividends, bond interest, rental from investment real estate, etc.; and

- Income from trusts set up by the retiree or by others for the retiree's behalf.

In some instances, the retiree will also inherit funds or become the beneficiary of life insurance on the life of a spouse or relative. Some of these income sources are regular, others intermittent. Some are predictable, some fluctuate. Some continue for life, others for a period of years. Income may become available at various times in the post-retirement period; for instance, a deferred annuity may begin payments several years after Social Security benefits and qualified plan distributions become available.

PRACTICE TIP: There are many online retirement income calculators, such as T. Rowe Price's (http://www3.troweprice.com/ric/RIC; http://www.early-retirement.org). In mid-2005, Ira Carnahan reported on the best planning tools: see http://www.forbes.com/forbes/2005/0606/092.html. Financial supermarkets such as Fidelity, Vanguard, and Morningstar have a lot of planning tools on their sites. Specialized computer financial management software such as Quicken also includes retirement planning tools. Many financial services companies are developing internet and other tools to take the next step (beyond accumulating investments for eventual retirement). Some of the web tools send e-mails to warn users if they are spending more than their goals permit.[12]

PATTERNS AND PERSONALITIES

In its 1998 Retirement Confidence Survey, the Employee Benefits Research Institute (EBRI)[13] grouped workers into six categories, reflecting differing views of how to fund retirement. This survey is useful to planners because, by characterizing their clients, they can highlight clients' real vulnerabilities and help them shift from financially self-destructive behaviors to more productive behaviors.

The "Deniers" group, say that there is no point in saving for retirement because it's too far away, they can't estimate their future needs, and retirement planning is too difficult. The "Strugglers" group (9% of the population) constantly encounter financial setbacks that sabotage their financial plans.

One-fifth of the population are described as "Impulsives," and 60% of these are under 45. Impulsives usually hope to retire early, but few of them have started a savings program, and those who have usually have under $10,000 accumulated. They count on qualified plan distributions, perhaps in conjunction with late-life employment, to take care of them.

The "Cautious Savers," most of them 35 to 44 years old, are quite likely to have begun retirement saving. The "Planners" group believe that anyone can have a comfortable retirement as long as adequate provisions are made in advance. The highest point of the pyramid, the "Retiring Savers," have a demonstrated history of accumulation for retirement.

A planner who can analyze where clients fit with respect to these groups can help them steer between the extremes of inappropriate lack of confidence ("Why bother—it's hopeless anyway") and excessive confidence ("I don't need a retirement savings program—something will turn up"). Furthermore, the planner can help clients develop better saving habits and can recommend investment alternatives that are prudent but not so stodgy as to deprive them of needed returns.

According to Prudential Financial Incorporated, although about two-thirds of older workers (ages 55-64) have made a projection of their income after they retire, only 10% have made an accurate estimate. Only 7% of full-time workers in this group have a formal financial plan covering their post-retirement income and projected spending. Only 10% can make an accurate estimate of how much income they can expect when they retire. Almost one-fifth (17%) admitted they need help to understand Social Security. Many of them are confused about even basic planning concepts like systematic withdrawals, long-term care insurance and estate planning.[14]

Bain & Company found that 84% of persons aged 55 to 70 with incomes over $100,000 (a group that controls about half of all rollover assets) employ financial advisers, but only about 30% consult an adviser about rolling over assets at retirement. The survey group had an average of $450,000 in retirement assets (such as qualified plans and IRAs) and $300,000 in other assets—clearly, a group worth targeting for marketing efforts, because of their need for asset planning and tax advice.[15]

The number of "micro-businesses" (self-employed persons with no employees) has grown a lot: in 2003 the Census Bureau says there were 18.6 million one-person businesses, 5.7% more than in 2002. But the National Association of the Self-Employed found that 56.6% of those surveyed did not feel confident about retirement, and only 7.5% felt very confident. Close to 30% of those answering the survey had no retirement savings at all, and another 25% had some savings, but under $15,000. Self-employed people often prefer to keep their funds in current accounts instead of tying them up in retirement savings, because of the frequent need to respond to business problems. So the financial advisor can play an important role not only in informing the self-employed about the savings options available to them, but in acting as "coaches" to encourage better savings habits.[16]

CHALLENGES TO RETIREMENT SECURITY

Traditionally, under conventional defined benefit pension plans, the retiree was assured of a predictable, fixed pension. In times of high inflation, this could create severe problems, as the fixed income failed to adapt to inflationary conditions. Current trends have shown a move away from the defined benefit plan to more market-responsive, defined contribution plans, including the extremely popular 401(k) plan. However, one problem with such plans is that they shift market risk to the retiree; in other words, if retirement occurs at a time when stock market conditions are unfavorable, the value of the retirement account may decline, and an annuity purchased with that account may consequently be smaller than anticipated. If the retiree has also made below-average investment decisions in managing the account, poor returns could further depress the size of the account.

For instance, although there was a very long bull market, fueled by technology stocks and especially by internet stocks, when the prices of internet stocks collapsed in March, 2000, the stock market as a whole suffered a significant decline, affecting workers whose compensation depended heavily on stock options, but also affecting retirees and potential retirees.

Since the beginning of the twenty-first century, there have been many large-firm bankruptcies, including bankruptcies in major industrial and transportation corporations. The reorganization plan often includes pension cutbacks. Many other companies, although not bankrupt, have frozen their pension plans, so that they do not make any new contributions—or have amended their plans so that newly hired employees will not participate in the plan.

Many companies have converted traditional defined benefit pension plans to a hybrid plan known as the "cash balance" plan.[17] It is anticipated that by the first decade of the twenty-first century, the cash balance plan will become the dominant form for large corporate plans. Unfortunately, however, the cash balance form favors younger workers and can seriously reduce the benefits available to older workers (those closest to retirement). The pension might be reduced 20%, or even cut in half, as compared to a traditional defined benefit plan.

It is common for a defined benefit plan to be designed so that the pension is based on years of service times a set percentage (e.g., 1.5%). This amount is then multiplied by the employee's average salary in either the last few years of employment or the highest-paid years of employment, to determine a dollar benefit amount. The result is that a large part of the pension–perhaps as much as half–accrues during the last five years of service. Some plans offer especially generous late-year accruals to motivate early retirement.

In contrast, the cash balance plan is a defined benefit plan that creates a portable pension account for each employee. (The account is merely hypothetical; unlike a defined contribution plan, there is no separate account for each employee.) A percentage of the employee's salary is contributed to the plan (4% is common). A cash balance plan is a "career-average" plan; in other words, the pension depends on earnings over the whole career. The accrual percentage does not change over time to increase the accrual rate in later years.

The actual pension amount is determined by the annuity that can be purchased with the account at the time of retirement, taking into account the interest rate (typically, 5%) promised by the plan. Unlike a 401(k) plan, where the employee often has some control over investment of the account, the employer controls investment of the cash balance pension account.

In practice, this means that younger employees receive a larger pension accrual each year than they would in a traditional defined benefit plan, but those who are close to retirement receive much less. The younger employees are motivated by the change, but the older workers no longer have the incentive of remaining in the workforce in the hope that a few extra years of service will significantly enhance their pension entitlement. (If it wishes to, the employer can cushion the effect of the change by allowing older workers to retain their benefits under the former plan, or can increase their accruals.) Some employers that switch to a cash balance plan at least increase their 401(k) match, so the employee has the potential of a larger 401(k) plan to help offset the smaller pension.

The employer is entitled to keep any earnings on the account balances over and above the plan's promised interest rate, and can use these earnings to make contributions to the plan in future years, so the net cost of the plan can be quite low if the employer can earn significantly more than the interest rate it promises. In effect, the plan can become a profit center for the company.

Another benefit to the company–but a risk to the employee–is that the cash balance plan may use different actuarial assumptions from those used in the old plan. At the time of conversion, the employer calculates the present value of the pension credits earned by each employee prior to conversion, but may adjust the value downward if the assumptions change.

Interest rates are also a potent factor. At the time of conversion, the employer calculates the accrued benefit already earned. Although this amount is a constant, its present value will change depending on interest rates. As interest rates fall, the accrued benefit is worth *more* because its present value is discounted less. Correspondingly, as interest rates rise, the accrued benefit must be discounted more heavily and thus decreases in value. Of course, with a lower balance and lower accruals each year (or no accruals, if the employer believes that it has already satisfied its obligations, based on its own calculations), the eventual pension will be much lower. This phenomenon is known as "wearaway" or "plateauing"; in other words, it can take several years for the older employee's pension account under the new assumptions to reach its level under the old assumptions. A number of employee lawsuits have been filed to challenge conversions to cash balance plans.

It might seem surprising that, given the minutely detailed regulation of pensions under the Internal Revenue Code and ERISA, employers would be permitted to do this. However, so long as the workers are entitled to receive their full vested balances if they change jobs (which is required under ERISA and the Code); the employer is given wide discretion to value the opening balances in a cash balance plan. It is possible that federal courts will find that these plans satisfy ERISA requirements, but violate the Age Discrimination in Employment Act; this is one of several theories that have been pursued by attorneys for some disgruntled participants.

The U.S. Government Accountability Office (GAO) reported in November, 2005 that employees (even the more mobile younger employees who are supposed to do best with cash balance conversions) usually lose benefits when a defined benefit plan is converted to cash balance form. The agency's conclusion was that the average 40-year-old worker would have a monthly pension of $188 less from a cash balance than from a defined benefit pension plan; the average 50-year-old worker would see a pension diminution of $238 a month. Some employers do make special efforts to protect workers, or at least long-tenure older workers, when there is a conversion.[18]

Federal law requires employers to issue a "204(h) notice" (i.e., a notice of reduction of benefits, as set forth in ERISA Section 204(h)) to workers whose benefits will be reduced. If the client has received such a notice, it is important that the planner try to determine the level of his future pension. Participants in a cash balance plan should automatically be issued quarterly balance statements, which can be used to predict the amount of the pension. Any plan participant is entitled to receive a statement of his "vested accrued benefit" once a year, by making a written request to the plan, and the employer is required to disclose the amount of a single-life annuity payment the employee would receive for retirement at age 65. Most cash balance plans (but less than half of traditional defined benefit plans) permit lump sum payouts, so an analysis should be made of the desirability of taking the plan payout as a lump sum.

By 2005, half of the workforce entitled to pensions could take them in lump-sum form, and 95% of those given the lump-sum option take it. Unfortunately, few of them are able to achieve consistent returns that beat the market, and many of them spend the money fairly quickly. In addition, lump sums paid to early retirees are often discounted by as much as 20% to take the early retirement incentives into account. (Regulations finalized in 2004 require employers to disclose the disparity between the value of the lump sum and the predicted value of taking an annuity payout.)[19]

In January of 1999, the Supreme Court decided a case involving GM's Hughes Electronics subsidiary.[20] The plan in that case was funded in approximately equal shares by contributions from employees and from the employer. In 1986, the plan's investments were so successful that the plan was operating at a surplus. At that point, the company stopped making contributions; workers continued making contributions until 1991. The suit arose when a group of retirees sued, claiming that the changes in the plan's operations were drastic enough to constitute termination of the plan. (When a plan terminates, participants gain full, immediate rights to their account balances.)

The Supreme Court accepted the employer's argument that its sole obligation was to make the pension payments called for by the plan. As long as it did that, it was entitled to use the pension surplus to reduce the employer's contributions on behalf of other workers. In other words, the plan surpluses did not belong to the employees and retirees, even though their contributions created some of the surplus.

In practical terms, however, this case won't affect very many people, because most defined benefit plans (i.e., plans that promise a specific pension check instead of whatever annuity can be purchased with the value of the employee's account at the time of retirement) do not require employee contributions. Employers that want employees to contribute usually use 401(k) plans, not defined benefit plans.

Traditionally, employers would terminate a pension plan only in case of the company's complete financial failure. In the middle of the first decade of the 21st century, however, several very large corporations terminated their pension plans, and many more "froze" their pension plans (i.e., stopped making new contributions for existing employees, and did not provide new hires with pension benefits). The Employee Benefits Research Institute published a report in March, 2006 estimating the amount that an employee would need to save in a 401(k) plan to replace the benefits that would have accrued under a defined benefit, defined contribution, or cash balance plan. Pension freezes have the worst effect on younger employees, because they lose more years of accruals, but older workers have only a few years to repair their retirement plans if they discover that the pension from the employer will be lower or much lower than anticipated.[21]

BAD LUCK OR BAD JUDGMENT?

The next part of this chapter looks at outside forces that could reduce or even eliminate the pensions and other retirement income your clients expect to receive. But it would be unfair to blame everything on employers, the government, or the stock market. Some older workers and retirees have contributed to or even caused their financial problems because they didn't plan ahead, they didn't save enough, or they didn't manage their portfolios well.

LIMRA International's Eric T. Sondergeld and Mathew Greenwald identified ten ways in which Americans fail in their quest for realistic and workable retirement planning:

- Not saving enough;

- Retiring earlier than they planned, when they're not financially ready (for example, when they were caught in corporate downsizing, or because of unexpected health problems);

- Outliving their income;

- Not making plans to pay for long-term care;

- Taking a lump-sum payout instead of an annuity, putting themselves at risk of outliving their money;

- Having poor investment skills;

- Getting bad advice;

- Having to live on less than they planned because of lack of understanding of their sources of income;

- Not protecting their funds against inflation; and

- Not making provisions for the surviving spouse after the first spouse dies.

The researchers say that 57% of households have not even tried to estimate how much they need to save for retirement. Even those who have started to plan haven't used all of the sensible planning tools. Almost a quarter of those Sondergeld and Greenwald looked at in their research had received an estimate from a financial advisor or used forms or worksheets. About a third used "back of an envelope" calculations, and 20% just guessed.

About 41% of people with current income below $35,000—and even 8% of those earning $75,000 or more a year—think they will need to save less than $250,000 for retirement. Only a third estimate that they will need savings that will replace even half their current income, even though the traditional assumption among financial planners is that 70-80% of pre-retirement income must be replaced for a comfortable retirement (and some planners suggest that women replace 100% of their pre-retirement income to take care of their longer life expectancy and greater health care costs).

Nor do conventional planning tools necessarily reflect post-retirement realities. They often assume that the retiree will only spend assets and will not continue to save, so they may be overly pessimistic—but, by assuming that work-related expenses, Social Security taxes, and health care expenses will cease, they may also be overly optimistic.

Calculations based on certain kinds of average longevity have the obvious flaw that half of the people in the sample will live longer than the average. The chances of a 65-year-old male living to be 70 are 88%; to age 80, 55%; to 90, 16%, and even 1% to age 100. For women, the corresponding figures are 93%, 68%, 28%, and 2%.

Although many people say they want guaranteed income, annuity sales remain low. Of retirees who were entitled to a lump sum under their defined benefit or defined contribution retirement plan, only 9% took an annuity; 23% took installment payments of income (not guaranteed for life), 37% rolled over their balance to an IRA, and 14% took a lump sum. Looking at defined benefit retirees, 49% of those who knew an annuity was available took it, but overall only 16% got their benefits in annuity form. (It's possible that survey recipients who said they got installment payments actually did get an annuity but didn't know how to describe it.)[22]

One problem with stock-market-oriented retirement plans, including 401(k) plans is that many people—including those lower down on the income scale—do not do a good job of managing investments. The Employee Benefits Research Institute surveyed a group of current retirees (people born between 1931 and 1941). For more than half of this group, their wealth increased more than 50% between 1992 and 2002. But 15%, mostly lower-income retirees, lost more than half of their total wealth, which the research attributed to effects of the bear market during the latter years of this decade. Economist Edward Wolff found that between 1983 and 2001, the average pension wealth of workers aged 47-64 rose by two-thirds (to $171,000 in constant dollars)—but most of the gains went to people who were already wealthy.

People who earn a good income and make smart investment choices can do very well. Economists Annika Sunden and Alicia Munnell calculated that workers who contributed 6% a year to a 401(k) plan each year, with a 3% company match, and earned 4.6% over inflation would save over $350,000 in the course of a career, and could retire at 62, if they had a final salary of $52,650 a year, and get a life annuity of about $31,000 a year.

Figures from EBRI show that less than 10% of eligible workers make the maximum contribution to their 401(k) plans, and 25% don't contribute at all. Many younger workers access (and spend) their 401(k) funds when they change jobs.[23]

EBRI research shows a lot of wishful thinking. Although two-thirds of employees think they will reach their retirement savings goal by the time they retire, less than half claim to be on schedule now. The ones who fail to meet their goals blame the shortfall on medical and child care costs and everyday bills. Another study by EBRI shows that almost half of those whose employers raised employees' obligations to pay health care costs had to cut back on saving or making 401(k) contributions to find money for this purpose. Although half of workers expect to retire at 65 or later, only 27% of the retirees in the sample actually did work that long; the other two-thirds retired even before reaching 65. Many of them (41%) retired earlier than they planned because of disability or health problems; about a third were affected by layoffs or plant closings.

Even high-income individuals (who might be expected to have the most disposable income and the best access to professional advice) often get within five years of retirement without having a formal plan. Phoenix Affluent Marketing Service looked at pre-retirees (aged 50-59 in 2006) who had non-housing net worth with an average of $1.7 million. Of this group, 36% planned to retire within six to ten years; 28% planned to retire in less than five years, yet 62% of those who intended to retire did not have a written financial plan, and 27% had never discussed retirement planning with an advisor.[24]

Furthermore, sometimes bad things happen to good planners. The Center for Retirement Research at Boston College tracked the incidence of adverse financial effects at older ages. For example, more than a quarter of pre-retirement adults (aged 51-61) had at least one major health problem, and about one-fifth had a health problem that limited their ability to work. By age 70, over half had at least one serious medical problem, and 4.2% were severely disabled. During the decade between 51 and 61, almost a fifth were laid off from their jobs, close to 10% lost a spouse, and 41.3% suffered a new major medical problem. Nine-tenths of married couples experienced a financial shock during the 51-61 decade. If they had a job layoff, married men lost over a quarter of their wealth, and single men lost almost half their wealth. The need for nursing home care for women over 70 usually led to a loss of one-third of their wealth for married women, and more than half of wealth for single women.[25]

RETIREMENT TIMING

When is the best time for older working clients to retire? There are many factors to consider:

- Pension formulas;

- Early retirement Incentives;

- Stock market conditions;

- Tax effects;

- Career opportunities;

- Payment for health care; and

- Personal, family factors.

Social Security reduces benefits below the full amount by 6⅔% per year for the first three years of payments beginning before the normal retirement age (NRA), then by 5% for each additional year when benefits are first received before NRA. For people who reach 62 in 2005, benefits go up by 8% for every year that benefits are delayed past NRA, but the increase stops at age 70, so waiting longer will not enhance the benefit. (Note that required minimum distributions from IRAs and qualified plans must also be made starting shortly after age 70½.)

Some retirement plans define the benefit as an unchanging percentage of each year's compensation, but others include "stairsteps," so that working slightly longer may qualify the individual for a more favorable pension formula. If the benefit is based on the highest-paid three or five years, or on average compensation for a certain number of years, it may make sense to retire soon after an especially successful year—or to keep working after an especially unsuccessful year in the hope of a turnaround!

The *maximum* benefit available under a defined benefit plan is $175,000 for plan years *ending* in 2006. The Economic Growth and Tax Relief Reconciliation Act of 2001 (EGTRRA) not only increased the maximum benefit that could be provided under a defined benefit plan, it eliminated the required reduction for retirement between ages 62 and 65.

Changes by EGTRRA 2001 also increased the annual addition limits for defined contribution plans (plans in which the funding is determined by the employer's promised contributions, not by the employer's promise to provide a certain level of benefits at retirement). Just before EGTRRA 2001 was enacted, the employer was allowed to contribute up to 25% of the employee's compensation to the plan, subject to a limit of $35,000 in contributions a year no matter how much the employee earned. EGTRRA 2001 changed the rules so that for years beginning in 2006, the employer can contribute up to *the lesser of* $44,000, or 100% of compensation, rather than just 25%. (Employers are not required to contribute more than 25%, they're just allowed to.)

Employers who want to reduce their workforce often prefer to induce early retirement instead of laying off workers who want to keep their jobs. For instance, a person who accepts early retirement after 17 years at the company may be offered a pension as if he had worked for 20 years, or other more favorable formulas might be applied.

The traditional, defined benefit pension is paid based on the plan's formulas. Unfavorable stock market conditions may affect the amount the employer must pay to fund the plan, but they do not affect the pensions received by retirees. Today, however, the majority of plans are defined contribution plans, where the investment risk is shifted to the employee. The size of the employee's pension depends on the size of the annuity that can be purchased with the account proceeds at the time of retirement. Naturally, it's better to retire with a defined contribution plan when the stock market is at a high point rather than a low point.

Retirement timing incentives work differently in defined benefit and defined contribution plans. In effect, workers who have defined benefit plans may sacrifice a year of pension benefits for each year that they stay at work once they have reached NRA. Depending on the plan, the benefit might or might not be tailored to make up for that loss. Workers with defined contribution plans do not lose any benefits by working longer.[26]

As this book has often emphasized, senior citizens must plan for their medical care needs, and this is an important factor in the retirement calculation. Medicare benefits are not available until age 65 (unless the person has been disabled for two years), so a person who retires early cannot necessarily apply for Medicare right away.

A number of employers offer retiree health benefits; that is, the employer continues to insure retirees as well as active workers. This is especially true if the employer wants to create incentives for early retirement. However, if the employer has drafted its health insurance plan so that it retains the right to modify the plan (almost all employers adopt such provisions), it is perfectly legal for the employer to terminate its retiree health plan, to require retirees to pay part of the premium, to make them pay for coverage of their dependents, or to make them pay higher deductibles and coinsurance. (In technical terms, this is possible because health insurance is a "welfare benefit," not a pension. Consequently, it doesn't vest and the employer can lawfully alter the plan.) Therefore, retiree health benefits can't be relied on as a complete solution to the problem of paying for senior citizens' health care.

One personal factor that is often ignored is that spouses may be at different stages in their careers. A common scenario is that the husband is somewhat older than his wife, and has been employed continuously. The wife has often interrupted her career to accommodate childrearing needs. The upshot is that when he's ready to retire, she may just be hitting her stride. That tends to work against a plan that calls for an immediate move to a retirement community. Even if there is no planned move, there can be tensions between a retiree spouse who wants to travel or wants company on the golf course or tennis court, and a workaholic spouse who puts in long hours.

Retirement Planning Issues for Women

Although it is not inevitable, it is very common for married women to survive their husbands. The period of widowhood can be prolonged, because not only do women have a longer life expectancy than men, but women tend to marry men who are older than they are. If, for instance, a couple marries when he is 28 and she is 23, and he lives to be 75, she will be widowed at age 70. If she lives to be 81 and does not remarry, she will be a widow for 11 years.

During those 11 years, her financial security will depend on her own pension and Social Security benefits, as well as provisions the couple has made for the surviving spouse.

The basic form of pension payment is the qualified joint and survivor annuity (QJSA, see below), and the payment from a QJSA is often cut in half when the first spouse dies. Many women do not qualify for pensions in their own right. Maybe they were full-time homemakers who never held paid jobs, or they might have worked for companies that didn't sponsor a pension plan. Perhaps they worked only part-time. The Retirement Equity Act of 1984 made it easier for workers to accumulate vested pension benefits despite interrupted work histories (such as years spent raising children), but many of today's senior citizen women spent a significant part of their working life employed before 1984.

Even women who put many years in the work force usually accumulate smaller pensions than their male counterparts, because:

- They often hold lower-paid jobs,

- They are less likely to have access to nonqualified deferred compensation, and

- In plans that let employees control investment of their accounts, women often lose out because of extreme conservatism in investing; many pick safer but low-yielding options.[27]

As economist Alicia H. Munnell points out, unmarried women are the senior citizens most likely to be poor. In 2000, 18% of single senior women were poor, and another 10% were "near-poor" (their income was under 125% of the federal poverty line). Widowed, divorced, and never-married women represent a large part of the total senior population, increasing with age. In 2002, for example, single women constituted 30% of the senior households aged 65-69, 40% of senior households aged 70-74, close to half of those 75-79, more than half of those 80-84 and over 60% of households 85 and older.

There are many reasons for senior women to be at risk of poverty. The retirement system is based on employment earnings, and women tend to spend fewer years in the workforce than men because of their child-care and elder-care obligations, and to earn less when they do work. The typical man spends 44 years in the labor force, versus 32 years for the typical woman. MetLife's 1999 survey says that one-third of women had cut their work hours to take care of a child or parent; 22% took a leave of absence; 20% moved from full-time to part-time work because of family responsibilities; 16% quit their jobs for this reason, and 13% took early retirement. When women with defined contribution plans retire, if they choose to buy an annuity with their plan balances, they'll have to pay more than men, because of their longer life expectancy. (Federal law requires employers, not employees, to absorb the impact of this demographic fact if the plan is a defined-benefit rather than a defined-contribution plan.)

Among married women 65-69, only 7% are living in poverty or are near-poor—but this is true of 27% of single women in this age group. Poverty among single women increases with age: 29% of those 70-74, 30% age 75-79, 27% age 80-84, and 33% of single women 85 and over are near or below the poverty line. Because life expectancy at age 65 is 16.6 years for men and 19.6 years for women, and many husbands are older than their wives, widowhood is an event that can be expected. And, for couples with joint and survivor retirement annuities, the survivor annuity is usually lower than the income received while both spouses were alive. Furthermore, baby boomer women are much more likely than older age cohorts to be divorced or never to have married.

The Social Security Administration's figures show that the number of women receiving a benefit based at least in part on their own earnings (not just on their husbands' earnings) has increased, but in 2001, only 38% of women received benefits solely based on their own earnings. According to the Department of Labor, in 1996 55% of retired men had pensions, averaging $44,764 a year. Only 32% of retired women had pensions, and furthermore their pensions were much smaller—an average of $5,230.[28]

Alicia Munnell, writing with Steven A. Sass, says that the shift away from conventional pension plans and to 401(k) plans actually has some benefits for women. It's good for them because, while they are still in the workforce, they are more likely to change jobs, so portability is beneficial for them. However, when they finally retire, the 401(k) balance has to support a longer anticipated retirement lifespan. Furthermore, for women whose husbands have 401(k) plans, the husband has the legal right to control the account; the requirement of the wife's consent to change the form of distribution applies to defined benefit plans, but not to 401(k) plans.

The example they use to illustrate this is a defined benefit plan that pays 1% of final earnings per year of service. A participant in that plan who leaves at age 45 with 15 years of service and a $50,000 salary would be eligible for an annual benefit at age 60 of $7,500 a year (15 x (1% x $50,000)). If the same worker had stayed at the same company until age 60 and retired with a final salary of $90,000, the annual benefit for the same 15 years' service would be $13,500, because the calculation would reflect the higher annual salary.

Because women live longer than men, a 65-year-old woman would get $616 a month when purchasing a $100,000 lifetime annuity contract, while a man the same age would get $654/month, according to a December, 2004 calculation. Women at 65 are expected to live about three years longer than men: 31% of women at 65 can be expected to live at least to 90.[29]

Ellen E. Schultz, writing in the *Wall Street Journal*, looked at the financial problems faced by many widows. If their late husbands had pensions in the form of qualified joint and survivor annuities, the pension check could have been cut in half at the husband's death. Or the couple could have made a long-ago choice to take a single-life annuity to get a larger monthly benefit—in which case, the pension ends completely when the first spouse dies. The single-life annuity could also have been elected more recently, when the stock market was more robust or the employer's stock was doing especially well. Women who were stay-at-home moms who didn't have paid jobs are especially hard-hit, often ending up with no income except for Social Security, and unable to afford health insurance or COBRA continuation coverage until they reach Medicare eligibility age. Many companies used to provide a death benefit (of up to one years' salary)—but few companies now do so.[30]

The Center for Retirement Research published a paper by Richard W. Johnson, examining whether married couples coordinate their retirement decisions. In the past, this was not much of an issue, when few married women worked for pay; the husband's retirement needs would govern. However, many women are now eligible for substantial retirement benefits of their own. The percentage of women entitled to a pension is almost the same as the percentage of men, although the average benefits for women are lower.

Many couples want to retire together and, since many married men are older than their wives, this could mean deferred retirement for the men. (In the average couple in which the husband is close to retirement age, the husband is four years older than the wife; in 10% of marriages, the husband is a decade or more older than the wife.) Men who were five years or more older than their wives tended to stay at work longer than men who were the same age or younger than their wives. However, when one spouse was laid off or had to retire because of disability, the other spouse's retirement plans usually weren't affected.

Johnson found that in almost 20% of couples, both spouses retired in the same year, and in another 30%, the husband's retirement occurred within a year or two before or after the wife's. Among 9% of couples, the husband retired more than ten years before the wife did, and in 3%, the wife retired a decade or more before her husband.[31]

PAYMENT FORMS

All defined benefit plans have to make benefits available to married plan participants in "qualified joint and survivor annuity" (QJSA) form. This requirement does *not* apply to all defined contribution plans; target and money purchase plans, for example, must provide a QJSA benefit, but 401(k) plans are not required to do so. Under a QJSA, benefits are paid (usually each month) for the lifetime of the employee and spouse, whoever lives longer. See IRC Sec. 401(a)(11). The basic form is a 50% survivor annuity; in other words, the benefit is cut in half when one spouse dies. However, employers are allowed to subsidize the survivor annuity at any level from 51% to 100% of the initial payment. If a married employee wants to elect payments for 10 years or 20 years, or a lump sum, or any form other than the qualified joint and survivor annuity (QJSA), the consent of the other spouse is required. For unmarried employees, the basic pension form is the single life annuity.

The "pension max" strategy calls for increasing income for the period just after retirement by electing a 10- or 20-year (or single life) annuity rather than a QJSA, and using some of the additional income to purchase life insurance that will benefit the surviving spouse.

Plans that are required to provide the QJSA benefit must also provide a qualified preretirement survivor annuity (QPSA) for the surviving spouse of any employee who dies before becoming entitled to retirement benefits.

Although plans have no obligation to permit lump sum withdrawals, many plans do so. For one thing, it's a convenience for the plan: it just has to make one payment and close the file. (However, the option primarily belongs to the employee; a plan is not allowed to "cash out" a participant involuntarily, unless the account balance is under $5,000, in which case it is deemed too small to administer.) If a client receives a notice that a small balance will be cashed out, the client should be informed that the cashed out amount can be rolled over into an IRA without a tax penalty, as long as the rollover takes place within 60 days of receipt of the cashout. (If a direct rollover is not elected, the employer must withhold 20% of the cashed-out sum, because the Internal Revenue Code requires income tax withholding from such distributions.)

In addition, lump sum withdrawals are desired by many plan participants. As fiduciaries, plan managers must be quite conservative in their investment strategies. Many participants believe that they can achieve higher returns on their own, or with good professional advice. That doesn't mean that they're right–or that their ability to administer money will continue forever.

Lump sums can be especially useful in elder planning because, in addition to traditional financial planning objectives, the older person can use a lump sum to:

- Create a trust that will be used in incapacity planning;

- Create an income-only trust (possibly useful in Medicaid planning);

- Set up a giving program to divest assets that are excessive, from the standpoint of Medicaid planning and/or estate planning. This is especially important in "cap" states (see Chapter 6), where the income from a pension in ordinary annuity form is likely to be high enough to preclude Medicaid eligibility;

- Purchase a home that can become a Medicaid "homestead,"[32] or elder-proof an existing home; or

- Pay the admission fee to a continuing care retirement community.

401(k) PLANS

The 401(k) plan (its rules are found in IRC Section 401(k)[33]) is also known as a CODA (cash or deferred arrangement) because it is funded through an employee's choice to have a portion of compensation paid into the 401(k) account rather than paid currently. Many 401(k) plans offer employer matches (e.g., for every $2 or $3 deferred by the employee, the employer contributes an additional $1) as an incentive.

EGTRRA 2001 made major changes in the rules for 401(k) plans, significantly increasing the amount that can be contributed to such plans, and offering more freedom to transfer amounts to and from 401(k) plans from other types of retirement plans.

PLANNING TIP: Congress seems to be sending the message that employees should take more responsibility for planning their own retirement security, by saving more. Make sure that your clients who are still in the workforce and planning for retirement understand that their employers may concentrate on 401(k) plans rather than the conventional plans involving employer contributions–and that their investment strategy should reflect this fact. Funds placed into a 401(k) plans do not have to be subject to current income tax, whereas ordinary investments are made with after-tax income, so for many (if not most) clients, it is more cost effective to maximize use of 401(k) plans as a major part of the retirement plan.

In 2006, the elective deferral amount for 401(k) plans is $15,000. For plan years beginning after 2006, the limit will be indexed to keep pace with inflation. It should be noted that in the absence of further action by Congress, all provisions of EGTRRA 2001 are scheduled to sunset (expire) for years beginning after December 31, 2010. In addition to elective deferrals, employees who are at least 50 years old may be allowed to make extra "catch-up" contributions. Catch-up contributions are purely voluntary; employees decide whether to make them or not, based on their anticipated post-retirement needs and whether they can afford to defer additional sums instead of receiving them in current paychecks. The maximum catch-up contribution is $5,000 for 2006; after 2006 and through 2010, the amount will be subject to indexing for inflation.

Taxpayers with adjusted gross income below $25,000 (single person) or $50,000 (joint return) may be eligible for a tax credit of up to $1,000 for their 401(k) deferrals, which may provide some incentive to help lower-income employees participate in 401(k) plans or step up their level of deferrals. This credit, known as the "saver's credit" is scheduled to expire December 31, 2006.

Beginning January 1, 2006, employers may offer a Roth 401(k) feature. This will allow employees the option of making after-tax elective deferrals to a Roth 401(k) account. The deferred amounts (unlike pre-tax 401(k) contributions) will be taxable income, subject to withholding, for the year of the deferral–but distributions from the account will be tax-free when they are withdrawn from the 401(k) account, provided they remained in the account for at least five years, and the participant is at least 59½ or disabled at the time of the withdrawal (or the estate withdraws the funds after his or her death). For 2006, the maximum deferral in all of a person's 401(k) accounts, whether Roth or traditional, is $15,000. Persons over 50 can make catch-up contributions of up to $5,000. Although people whose adjusted gross income exceeds certain amounts are not allowed to make Roth IRA contributions, this income limitation does not apply to Roth 401(k) contributions.[34]

The *Wall Street Journal* points out that contributing to a Roth 401(k) could create cash flow problems—the example given is a person who earns $100,000 a year, is in the 28% tax bracket, and puts $10,000 into the 401(k) plan. If he or she has a pretax 401(k) account, after-tax income would be $64,800; if it's a Roth, after-tax income would be only $62,000. Because the Roth contributions are not deductible, the account holder would have more taxable income, which could have the unintended result of making certain deductions phase down or become unavailable, or triggering or increasing the alternative minimum tax (AMT).

PRACTICE TIP: One easy coping mechanism is to maintain both Roth and conventional 401(k)s, and consult a tax professional each year about the best allocation between the two. After retirement, the best strategy is probably to withdraw from the conventional 401(k) in the early years of retirement, then switch to taking tax-free income after age 70½ (when it is necessary to take required minimum distributions –i.e., taxable income--from the IRA to avoid tax penalties).[35]

The employee always has the option of taking the money currently instead of adding it to the account. It is understandable–though unfortunate–that the rate of 401(k) participation and the amounts deferred tend to vary in direct proportion to the employee's income. Although low-income workers are in the most serious need of additional savings for retirement, they are the least likely to defer much if they have a 401(k) account at all.

In 2006, the maximum 401(k) basic contribution is $15,000, and the catch-up contribution is limited to $5,000. According to the Vanguard Center for Retirement Research, in 2004, only 13% of persons over 50 made catch-up contributions to their 401(k) plans. The maximum catch-up contribution permitted in that year was $3,000; the average catch-up contribution made by eligible people was $2,207. Only 5% of 401(k) owners with income under $50,000 made catch-up contributions, whereas almost one-third of households with income of $150,000 or more did. Making these contributions makes a dramatic difference in the size of the fund available at retirement: those who did make catch-up contributions had an average account balance of $253,244; those who did not, averaged a balance of $89,060. In contrast, the Profit Sharing/401(k) Council's research shows that 24% of workers over 50 made catch-up contributions.[36]

401(k) plans were introduced in 1978. They took off slowly, with 7 million participants in 1985, growing to about 34 million participants in 340,000 plans in 1999. In 1985, 401(k) plan assets were less than one-tenth of a trillion, growing to about 1.7 trillion in 1999.

It takes about 13 years of contributions for a 401(k) account to grow large enough to provide a meaningful supplement to Social Security benefits, although fewer than 20% of 401(k) owners have reached that level. Looking at workers aged 21-64, in 1996, 23.3% participated in 401(k) plans and 27.9% in 2001. In constant 2001 dollars, the mean contribution was about $3,330 to $3,350 a year in this time period. Older workers were more likely to participate and to make maximum contributions, which makes sense because they can be expected to have higher earnings and also to be more conscious of the need to save.

At the end of 1996, 18.2% of workers 21-64 who had only a 401(k) plan and no other form of retirement savings, a percentage that rose to 21.7% at the end of 2002. In the same time period, the percentage of workers with both a 401(k) plan and an IRA rose from 5.9% to 9.2%, and the percentage with only an IRA was constant at about 10% throughout the period.[37]

Boston College's Center for Retirement Research says that the most important factor in determining 401(k) participation is the employee's planning horizon. Those that look only two years into the future, for instance, are not very likely to sign up for salary deferrals.

In some situations, especially in small companies, lack of participation by low-income workers limits the ability of more affluent clients to defer the full 401(k) amount. This happens because 401(k) plans are required to be nondiscriminatory, and the Internal Revenue Code generally mandates nondiscrimination testing of them on the basis of comparing contribution rates for highly compensated to those of rank-and-file employees. If the plan fails the test, deferrals by high-income employees must be cut back (and usually returned to them as taxable compensation). However, design-based safe harbors are available that exempt a 401(k) plan from nondiscrimination testing.

The last two decades have shown a steady shift from traditional defined benefit plans toward defined contribution plans, particularly 401(k) plans. Employers like 401(k) plans because they are funded at least in part by the employee's own salary. The employer's administrative and contribution burdens are much lower under a 401(k) plan than under a pension plan. Close to 90% of employers who have 401(k) plans make matching contributions to the plan; the average "match" rate is about 60 cents for every dollar deferred by the employee.

Although employee deferrals are always 100% vested (i.e., the employee is always entitled to 100% of the balance), the employer match is considered a qualified plan contribution, so the vesting of the match amount can generally be subject to a vesting schedule as set forth in the plan document. For plan years beginning before 2002, it was common for the employer to require five years of service for 100% vesting in the employer contribution. For years beginning after December 31, 2001, faster vesting is required for employer matching contributions. Such amounts must be 100% vested after three years, or subject to a gradual vesting schedule of 20% after two years, followed by 20% per year until 100% is reached after six years. Employees who leave (or are laid off or fired) before they have vested in any portion of the matching contributions are entitled only to that portion of the funds attributable to the employee deferrals, and earnings on them. Furthermore, the employer may provide higher match levels where the employee invests in the employer's stock, or may offer higher match levels as a bonus or employee incentive.

The typical 401(k) plan offers several different investment alternatives from which the employee can choose, such as various equity and income-oriented mutual funds. Some plans, especially those of large corporations, include investment in the employer corporation's stock as one of the choices. In many cases, those clients who are contemplating retirement should be warned about the risk of concentrating too much of the 401(k) account in employer stock; more diversification could yield better post-retirement results.

Probably only 15-20% should be invested in the employer's stock; however, employer stock often makes up one-third or more of the 401(k) portfolio. The closer the employee is to retirement, the greater the risk from failure to diversify; the employee might retire at a time when the employer stock, or other dominant investment, is at low tide. Of course, sometimes the employee is simply lucky, or is able to time retirement based on investment factors, and leaves the workforce when the value of the retirement fund is at a peak.

Even after extensive publicity about the risks of piling up employer stock, many retirement plan participants still keep most or all of their nest egg in the employer's stock. According to Greenwich Associates, employee in large defined contribution plans (plans with over $100 million in assets) are almost 23% in company stock, whereas the average defined benefit plan is less than 2% invested in its own stock, thus providing much greater diversification. At least employers are paying attention: in 2003, 30% of large companies made their matching contributions in the form of their own stock, whereas the percentage declined to less than 20% in 2004. Experts suggest that 401(k) investors avoid having more than 10% of their account invested in any one security, including stock in the company they work for. 401(k) plan participants shouldn't just make an allocation and walk away; the portfolio should be reviewed often to re-balance it.[38]

Plan loans are permitted by many 401(k) plans—that is, the account holder is allowed to borrow up to one-half of the account balance (usually subject to a dollar limit), and to repay the loan over a period of at least five years, with longer repayment terms available for those who use the funds to buy a home. The interest paid by the borrower (at rates close to prime) is redeposited into the account. Account holders should be careful not to abuse plan loans. Failure to repay can result in the borrowed amounts being treated as withdrawals from the plan. Also, if they occur before age 59½, the 10% penalty on premature withdrawals will apply. And, of course, outstanding loans will decrease the size of the account that will be available at retirement.

A plan loan can be very worthwhile if there is a health emergency that is not covered by Medicare or private insurance, but the real cash flow and tax impact of the loan should be compared with the outcome of using other sources of money for the care needs (such as taking out a home equity loan, liquidating investments and profit-taking, or borrowing against life insurance cash value).

PRACTICE TIP: Although the conventional wisdom is that retirement is the cue for rolling over the 401(k) balance into an IRA, there can be good reasons for leaving the balance in the employer's plan after retirement; for example, if the plan provides a good menu of investment choices and low fees and expenses. Especially if the sponsor is a large company, the 401(k) plan may receive discounted rates because so much money is under management.[39]

SUCCESSION PLANNING FOR THE FAMILY BUSINESS

One of the greatest causes of failure, or of involuntary takeover, of family businesses is the lack of succession planning. Individuals in top management, unwilling to consider the possibility of their own death, incapacity, or even retirement, sometimes refuse to name a successor, provide appropriate training for potential successors, or develop a plan to gradually turn over the reins. As a neutral outsider, the financial planner can play an important part in stressing the value of a practical succession plan to the business and the post-retirement financial well-being of the top management.

The financial planner can also point out the common situation in which the business owner's estate is much too concentrated in shares of the business, and indicate the need for diversification, as well as for life insurance and other means of providing liquidity.

Often, disaster occurs because of the praiseworthy desire to be fair. A parent who owns a majority interest in a close corporation, or a large plurality interest, may divide that interest among his or her children in equal shares. The result is that each heir owns a block of stock that is difficult to sell and may not pay dividends. (This is especially true if the board of directors is controlled by other family members who work in the business and want to cut back on dividends and reinvest earnings in corporate needs–including higher salaries for top management!) This is a recipe for corporate deadlock.

An effective planner can help the entire management team and board of directors develop a plan (possibly including recapitalization) for an orderly increase in the responsibilities of heirs, or a buyout of some family interests by nonfamily managers. A buy-sell agreement serves many purposes; not only does it set terms for the transition, but, if properly drafted to reflect meaningful values, can establish the value of otherwise hard-to-value stock for estate tax purposes. In a stock redemption agreement, the corporation itself redeems stock belonging to a major stockholder. In a cross-purchase transaction, the other major stockholders buy out the retiring stockholder or the estate of a deceased stockholder.

Retirement planning for the founder can also be a good time to evaluate the corporation's life insurance portfolio. Key-person insurance can compensate the corporation for the loss it sustains when a leader dies. Life insurance purchased by the corporation (entity purchase) or by the designated successor (cross-purchase) can be used to fund payments to the decedent's family under the buy-sell agreement. Disability insurance can be used to fund buyouts premised on the founder's inability to continue leading, rather than upon his death; however, such insurance would not cover payouts resulting from the voluntary retirement by the founder, since this is not an insurable event.

Sometimes the greatest planning challenge is convincing business owners to retire at all! According to the National Federation of Independent Business (NFIB), 46% of business owners don't intend to ever withdraw completely from working in their businesses. About a quarter plan to retire early—9% before 60, 13% at 60-64, 12% at ages 65-69, 11% when they are at least 70, and 8% didn't have a retirement schedule. Even those who plan to retire from the business they own now are likely to want to work somewhere else.

The NFIB says that more than two-thirds of those surveyed have given a lot of thought to retirement. Less than a third of respondents have a work-based pension plan (for one thing, surplus funds tend to go toward health care and health insurance), but 90% of those who have a plan for their company as a whole participate in it. Most of those who plan to retire are somewhat confident about being able to afford retirement (79% said this), but 16% were dubious about whether they could afford to retire. Six-tenths of respondents said they were on track, or even ahead, of their plans for retirement savings, but 38% said they were behind as to meeting those goals.[40]

See Chapter 13 for a discussion of the estate tax laws governing succession issues in the family business.

"UN-RETIREMENT": RE-EMPLOYMENT

The decision to retire is not always irreversible. Sometimes a job will open up with the former employer; the retiree already understands the corporate culture, and has a highly relevant track record with the same company. Part-time or full-time employment with another company, or signing on with a temporary agency, are other possibilities. An increasing number of older people take advantage of early retirement incentives or lump sum pension payouts to turn long-cherished entrepreneurial dreams into reality.

Going back to the workforce is a necessity for those who can't maintain a comfortable lifestyle on their retirement income, and is desirable for those who feel stultified without the challenges of work. However, the financial consequences of re-employment are not simple, and retirees should consider all the implications before getting a new job.

As Chapter 9 explains, Social Security benefits are no longer reduced for persons who retire at or after the normal retirement age, but continue to have employment earnings. So, there is one less disincentive to continued workforce participation. However, the earnings will be subject to income and FICA taxes.

If the employment is short-term, the senior employee may not even qualify for participation in the pension plan, because employers can impose a requirement of one year's tenure (three years if the plan provides immediate vesting) before a new hire can participate in the plan. Even after participation, the plan often requires either 7-year graded vesting (i.e., the employee's final entitlement to the pension account phases in over time) or 5-year cliff vesting (no vesting for five years, then immediate 100% vesting).

A plan can set its normal retirement age as the later of 65 or the fifth year of plan participation (see IRC Sec. 411(a)(8)), so a late hire might have a personal normal retirement age of, for instance, 68 or 73. Thus, the older employee will probably not earn a pension, or at least will not become fully vested in it, on the basis of the new position. (However, it is unlawful for a qualified plan to impose a maximum age for participation in the plan (IRC Sec. 410(a)(2)) or to cease accruals to the plan because of age (IRC Sec. 411(b)(1)(G)).)

It should also be noted that an employer may defer the initial pension payment until 10 years after the date of initial participation, so even an earned and vested pension may not come into pay status until the older individual is quite aged–or deceased. See IRC Sec. 401(a)(14)(B).

PHASED RETIREMENT

Traditional thinking says that a person is either in the workforce or retired, but more and more, that is too inflexible a way to look at it. Many people formally retire, but then go back into the workforce to some extent. This could be because they need more income, or because they want to be more active and feel useful.

AARP's 1998 Health and Retirement Study showed that 73% of workers between the ages of 51 and 61 said they wanted to do paid work after retiring from their main job. More than 70% of the baby boomers expected to work at least part-time after nominal retirement. But when AARP checked back in March, 2003, only about a third of men who received pension or retirement plan income in 2002 were actually working, and this was true of only one-eighth of male senior citizens who received retirement income.[41]

The basic rule under current tax law is that a qualified retirement plan must be operated primarily to provide benefits after retirement, although ancillary benefits (such as insurance and health care) can be provided—within limits. This rule has been a stumbling block, preventing development of plans under which employees could reduce their hours as they move closer to retirement.

Then, in late 2004, the Treasury Department published Proposed Regulations giving a possible framework for phased retirement. (The proposal deals only with tax issues of plan qualification—not age discrimination or health insurance questions.) Under this proposal, an employee who makes a significant cut in his or her work schedule under a phased retirement scheme can take part of his or her retirement benefits while still getting paid for the reduced work schedule.

Under the proposal, a phased retirement plan has to satisfy various requirements:

- Phased retirement distributions are made before the plan's normal retirement age, but after age 59½;

- There is a bona fide written program;

- Phased retirement must be voluntary—employers cannot force employees to take phased retirement when they would prefer to keep up a normal work schedule;

- The employee electing phased retirement must be permitted to continue to participate in the employer's qualified plan;

- Early retirement benefits, subsidies, and optional benefit forms that would have been available at full retirement must be made available at phased retirement, but lump sum distributions are not allowed;

• The employer and employee must expect that the employee's working hours will be reduced by at least 20% under the phased retirement plan. The pension that is distributed will reflect the ratio between reduced hours and normal hours; and

• The employer must check each year (until the employee is within three months of normal retirement age) to make sure that the actual hours worked were not more than 90% of a regular schedule, or more than one-third greater than the reduced schedule agreed to by the employer and the employee.[42]

Research published by AARP in March, 2005 shows that before the survey, only 19% of the sample of persons aged 50 and over had heard of phased retirement. But once they heard a description, 38% were interested in phased retirement as an option. Of those who were interested, 78% said that being able to retire in stages would extend their work life past their projected retirement date. The average age at which they wanted to begin phased retirement was 61. More than half (53%) wanted to reduce their schedule by at least 12 hours a week, whereas 39% wanted to reduce their hours by 10 hours a week or less. Almost half agreed that phased retirement would be less attractive if it involved a different job with the same employer, but nearly the same percentage would be willing to do that, and 8% would actually prefer that.

Almost all respondents said that it was important to them to be able to continue accruing pension benefits in the course of phased retirement, and 63% were concerned that phased retirement would reduce their final pension benefits.[43]

As an example of phased retirement opportunities already available, Procter & Gamble has a program matching up retirees with hard-to-find skills with short-range, part-time assignments. Procter & Gamble has partnered with Eli Lilly to start a company called YourEncore; some of the problems of phased retirement are solved by retirees' becoming employees of YourEncore and then taking temporary assignments with other companies.[44]

TAXATION OF RETIREMENT BENEFITS

Pension plans are a form of deferred compensation; that is, instead of the employee receiving all compensation currently in the year it is earned, part of the compensation is placed into a pension plan. When the employee retires, he will presumably be in a lower tax bracket than during working life, and so will be able to save taxes by receiving the money post-retirement instead of earlier. The enactment of the Small Business Job Protection Act of 1996 (SBJPA '96) made 1996 a watershed year in the taxation of pensions. The rules of SBJPA '96 are, by and large, quite favorable to taxpayers, and make it easier to fund a financially comfortable retirement. For example, before 1996, a tax penalty was imposed on those who continued working beyond age 70½ and neglected to take their first plan distribution by April 1 of the year after the year in which they reached age 70½ (i.e., the required beginning date for qualified plans). A 50% penalty is imposed on individuals who take less than the required minimum distribution (basically, a distribution sufficient to liquidate the entire fund over the lifetime of the retiree, or the joint lifetimes of the retiree and a chosen beneficiary).

One of the changes made by SBJPA '96 was to change the required beginning date for most qualified plan participants to April 1 following *the later of* (1) the year in which the participant reaches age 70½, or (2) the year in which the participant retires. See IRC Sec. 401(a)(9)(C)(i). This change does not apply to more-than-5% owners of the employer sponsoring the plan, nor to distributions from IRAs. However, rank-and-file employees who remain employed after age 70½ can generally defer the first plan distribution until they actually retire.[45]

The majority of pension payments (i.e., those made in the form of a continuing stream of monthly payments) are annuities. The taxation of annuities requires a distinction between the tax-free return of the taxpayer's capital and taxable sums that represent investment appreciation or contributions made by the employer. Therefore, an exclusion ratio must be calculated for the annuity.

Before SBJPA '96, this was somewhat complex, involving actuarial calculations. For annuity starting dates after November 18, 1996, a simplified schedule is available for life annuities. (If the annuity is provided for a term of years, the actual number of payments, e.g., 120 payments for a 10-year annuity, is used to calculate the exclusion ratio.) See IRC Sec. 72(d)(1)(B). The annuity is taxed as if the following number of payments will be made, based on the age at retirement:

Age	Number of Payments
55 or less	360
56-60	310
61-65	260
66-70	210
71 or over	160

For individuals who defer retirement for many years, note that in the case of an annuitant whose annuity starting date occurs after age 75, this table can be used only if there are fewer than five years of payments guaranteed under the annuity.

The Taxpayer Relief Act of 1997 extended this concept by enacting another schedule, this time for the number of payments that can be expected under a joint and survivor annuity. This schedule is available for annuity starting dates beginning after December 31, 1997.

Combined Age for Both Annuitants	Number of Payments
110 or less	410
111–120	360
121–130	310
131–140	260
141 or over	210

With either table, the calculation is performed by dividing the employee's basis in the retirement annuity, measured as of the retirement date, by the applicable number of payments. The result is the excludable portion of each monthly payment.

Lump Sum Distributions

Without special relief provisions, taking a lump sum distribution would not be feasible for most retirees because the entire amount of the lump sum, typically in five or six figures, would be taxable income for the year of receipt. Before SBJPA '96, two forms of income averaging were permitted. The taxpayer would still have to pay the tax in the year of receipt of the lump sum, but the amount of tax would be calculated as if the lump sum were received in five or ten installments.

Although in general, SBJPA '96 was helpful to taxpayers, it repealed five-year averaging, effective for distributions occurring after December 31, 1999. Ten-year averaging continued to be permitted, but only for individuals born before 1936; thus, the large baby boom cohort was excluded from using 10-year averaging.

These limitations were not onerous, however, because an IRA rollover can be used to defer taxation of all or part of a lump sum distribution. Any portion of a lump sum that is not desired for immediate use (and immediate taxation) can be placed in an IRA. Qualifying individuals may be able to convert a traditional IRA to a Roth IRA; however, such a conversion will result in immediate tax consequences (see Chapter 10). Once rolled over, the funds become part of the IRA, and are subject to the minimum distribution requirements applicable to traditional IRAs. Roth IRAs are not subject to the lifetime minimum distribution requirements.

EGTRRA 2001 and other 2001 legal developments allowed employers to discontinue certain forms of distributions, but if the plan ever allowed lump-sum distributions, retirees must retain the right to receive their distribution in this form.

PRACTICAL AND TAX CONSEQUENCES OF NONQUALIFIED PLANS

For a corporation to receive a current tax deduction for sums contributed to its qualified plans, the corporation generally must make benefits available on a nondiscriminatory basis to those employees who have worked long enough to be eligible for plan participation. Employees do not recognize taxable income as a result of contributions made to the plan on their behalf, nor are they taxed on the appreciation in the value of the account as it grows during their working life.

Qualified plans are subject to detailed and often onerous requirements imposed by the Internal Revenue Code and ERISA. Some businesses (especially small businesses) may find it impossible to fund and manage qualified plans. For others, it may be possible to maintain a plan, but the benefit level that top management would receive is not high enough to have a motivating effect. In these situations, it makes sense to have a nonqualified plan instead of, or as a supplement to, the qualified plan.

The hallmark of nonqualified plans is that they are permitted to discriminate. Instead of covering all employees who have stayed with the company for a few years, the plan can be limited to only one executive, or a small group of executives. Or, the plan can have broader coverage, but provide unequal benefits. The tradeoff for this additional flexibility is that tax consequences are less favorable.

The employee is taxed as soon as he has "constructively received" benefits under the nonqualified plan. In general, income is constructively received when it is available, regardless of whether the employee actually receives it. However, income is not constructively received as long as the employee's rights are forfeitable, such as where the employee's control of its receipt is subject to substantial limitations or restrictions, or a contingency which might result in forfeiture of the employee's rights to the future payments. However, the IRS has ruled that there is no constructive receipt where the employee's rights are nonforfeitable, provided that (1) the agreement to defer compensation is entered into before the compensation is earned, and (2) the employer's promise to pay is not secured in any way.

The American Jobs Creation Act of 2004 (AJCA; P.L. 108-357) added Sec. 409A to the Internal Revenue Code. Deferred compensation amounts provided in years after 2004 (including compensation paid to independent contractors, or to a corporation's outside directors) are subject to new restrictions on elections, distributions, and funding mechanisms. Amounts that were deferred before December 31, 2004, and earnings on those deferrals, are not subject to Sec. 409A.

Compliance with Sec. 409A is very important, because noncompliance carries a huge tax burden. If the taxpayer does not comply with Sec. 409A, all of the compensation deferred under the plan in earlier years is included in the taxpayer's gross income retroactive to the original year of deferral. In addition, the taxpayer incurs a 20% penalty tax and owes interest at 1% higher than the usual underpayment rate.

Sec. 409A applies to all nonqualified deferred compensation plans, but does not apply to welfare benefit plans such as health and vacation plans. This statute generally requires employees to make elections to defer compensation in a nonqualified plan no later than the end of the taxable year before the year in which the compensation will be earned.

AJCA only permits deferred compensation to be paid to a person under limited circumstances. Distributions can be made when the person leaves, retires, dies, becomes disabled, or suffers an unforeseeable emergency. Distributions are also allowed on a schedule set in advance, but the employee can't just use the deferred compensation plan as a bank account and make withdrawals whenever he or she wishes.

A common strategy is for the corporation to avoid funding the nonqualified deferred compensation plan in advance. (This is not permitted for qualified plans; contributions must be made on a regular basis.) The executive is therefore subject to the risk that the corporation's creditors will be entitled to funds that would otherwise have been used to pay the nonqualified plan benefits.

The employer's tax deduction is deferred until the employee becomes taxable on the contributions. Of course, the employee will prefer not to have constructive receipt until after retirement, when presumably he will be in a lower tax bracket. The worst-case scenario occurs when the employee is deemed to have constructively received the income, but has not received any cash with which to pay the tax liability.

Even if the plan allows gifts of the benefits (most plans forbid such gifts), this is bad tax planning. The employee is still considered the recipient of the income, and therefore still has to pay income tax on it, despite also having made a taxable gift of a future interest that doesn't even qualify for the annual exclusion.

Generally, any unpaid balance of nonqualified compensation remaining at the executive's death will become part of the taxable estate. Furthermore, benefits remaining unpaid at the time of the executive's death will be subject to income tax, as income in respect of a decedent; however, the recipient of the income is then allowed to take a corresponding deduction for estate and generation-skipping tax paid on the income. See IRC Sec. 691.

Types of Nonqualified Plans

Employers have developed various ways to structure nonqualified plans:

- A Salary Continuation Formula plan provides a specified deferred amount, payable in the future, in addition to benefits provided under other plans and requires no reduction in the covered employee's salary. It generally uses a defined benefit type of formula. Such a plan for a selected group of executives is one type of "SERP" (for "supplemental executive retirement plan").

- A Salary Reduction Formula plan involves an election to defer a specified amount of the employee's compensation, similar to a 401(k) plan. Actual reduction of salary is not required; the contribution can be in the form of a "bonus."

- An Excess Benefit plan provides benefits for executives whose qualified plan benefits are limited under the Internal Revenue Code, making up the difference between the amounts payable under their qualified plan and the amount they would have received if there were no benefit limitations.

- Stock appreciation rights (SARs) and phantom stock formulas use a benefit formula determined on the basis of the value of a specified number of shares of employer stock, or stated in terms of shares of employer stock rather than cash.

- A Rabbi trust is an irrevocable trust set up by an employer for advance funding of nonqualified deferred compensation. The employer is not allowed to recoup assets from the trust until all deferred compensation obligations are satisfied. However, the employees covered by the nonqualified plan are subject to the risk that the corporation's general creditors will be able to place claims against the Rabbi trust assets. (This risk yields tax benefits, because executives covered by the plan do not recognize income at the time funds are placed into the Rabbi trust.) Rabbi trusts are so named because the first one was created to benefit the clergyman of a synagogue. Under new IRC Sec. 409A, assets in a Rabbi trust may not be located outside the U.S. or include triggers that provide additional protection if the employer experiences financial difficulties.

- Secular trust: A variation on a Rabbi trust that protects trust assets from the claims of the corporation's general and bankruptcy creditors.

However, the executive covered by a secular trust must recognize current income (which is taxed under the Internal Revenue Code's Section 72 annuity rules) from the contributions to the trust and perhaps the income earned by those contributions.

For unfunded plans, the following methods may be used:

- An Employer Reserve Account is an actual investment account where funds remain available to the employer and its creditors.

- An Employer Reserve Account with employee investment direction gives the employee the right to "direct" the investment of his account among broad types of investments, such as a family of mutual funds. However, a choice of specific investments may result in constructive receipt, as will direction that is binding and not merely advisory.

- Corporate-owned life insurance policies on the employee's life, owned by and payable to the employer corporation, provide a substantial death benefit even in the early years of the plan, which can be quite valuable to younger employees.

RETIREE HEALTH BENEFITS

Before 1990, many companies, especially large corporations, provided health benefits to their retirees throughout their lifetimes. In many cases, the employer paid the full cost of the benefits and often covered the retiree's spouse as well. However, federal law makes it much harder for employers to change their pension plans than their welfare benefit plans, because pension benefits become vested (legally guaranteed). In most cases, welfare benefits (benefits dealing with health and related non-pension issues) do not vest. Especially if they drafted the documents for the benefit plan to offer flexibility, employers usually have the right to amend their retiree health plans or even eliminate them entirely.

In the last 15 years or so, even companies that have not eliminated their retiree health benefit plans have terminated spousal coverage, required the retirees to assume an ever-increasing share of the premiums for coverage, put restrictions on prescription drug coverage, or adopted "caps" (maximum amounts that the employer will pay; if the premiums rise above that level, retirees will be responsible for 100% of the excess).

It is not illegal for employers to put active workers and retirees in different "pools" for benefit structuring purposes, or to create more than one "pool" of retirees for health benefit purposes. One group can be charged higher premiums, in effect subsidizing the other group(s). Retirees can suffer a "double whammy" when they are assigned to a separate pool. Retirees usually use more health care than active workers, so costs are higher. If the employer caps its payment responsibilities, the retirees have to absorb all cost increases over the cap level. And, if some of them decide they can't afford the coverage and drop out, the employer can put a gain on its books because its recorded liability for retiree health benefits is reduced. Companies that employ both union and non-union workers may be stuck with collective bargaining agreements that they can't alter, so they make up for it by reducing non-union retiree benefits.[46]

In 2004, a typical person retiring before age 65 (that is, prior to the age of Medicare eligibility) would pay $2,244 a year for single coverage and $4,644 for spousal coverage—27% more than the 2003 average figures for the same situation. An over-65 retiree would pay an average of $1,212 for single and $2,508 for spousal coverage, up 24% from 2003 levels.

Before MPDIMA was passed, about a third of all retired Medicare beneficiaries had prescription drug coverage through the company they retired from, although most of them still had out-of-pocket drug expenses. With the Part D drug benefit in operation (see Chapter 5), the federal government will pay a subsidy to every company that maintains a retiree prescription drug benefit plan that is at least the actuarial equivalent of Part D. The subsidy is paid on the basis of the number of retirees who choose the employer's plan instead of enrolling in Part D. Employers also have other choices: they can provide a "wrap around" benefit that supplements Part D (although this will not qualify for the subsidy), and they can enter into contracts with private plans to provide either standard or enhanced Part D benefits.[47] More than half of employers surveyed by the Kaiser Family Foundation (58%) expressed an intention of retaining their prescription drug benefit, generally at its current level, and taking the federal subsidy; 17% said they were likely to offer prescription drug coverage to supplement but not replace Part D, and 8% planned to discontinue drug coverage.[48]

In arranging health coverage for retirees, it is important not to forget that Medicare coverage is determined on the basis of age or disability, not employment status. Although Social Security provides spousal benefits, Medicare does not. A spouse under age 65 of a Medicare beneficiary is not entitled to Medicare coverage merely because the beneficiary is covered, even though he or she may have been covered as a dependent under an employment-related health plan. Therefore, a person who retires early and who does not have retiree health benefits must find some other way of filling the "gap" between employer-provided health coverage during work life, and Medicare benefits.

Fortunately, the Health Insurance Portability and Accountability Act of 1996 (HIPAA) protects early retirees who have pre-existing health conditions from being turned down for individual health coverage. This doesn't mean that the premium will be affordable–only that a pre-existing condition limitation will not be applied.

In 2005, the Seventh Circuit looked at a situation where the employer issued plan documents that said retiree medical and dental benefits continue "as long as you and your surviving spouse are living" and "for lifetime at no cost." Furthermore, the plan did not reserve the right to terminate these benefits. Later on, to cut costs, the employer sent out a new Summary Plan Description reducing the benefits and adding the reservation-of-rights language. When retirees sued, the Seventh Circuit said that even though it is presumed that welfare (i.e., non-pension) benefits do not vest, in this case the employer's incautious language was strong enough to defeat that presumption. So the court sent the case back to the District Court to determine whether any benefits had vested.[49]

Retiree Health Benefits and Medicare

At first, a Third Circuit decision was good news for retirees. The court said that it violated the Age Discrimination in Employment Act for an employer to reduce retiree health benefits because the employee had become eligible for Medicare. Under this decision, then, employers could not cut costs by cutting back only on benefits for Medicare-eligible retirees. Opponents of the decision said that it was bad for retirees as a group, because employers would have a motivation to cancel retiree health benefits.

In 2003, the Senate (but not the House of Representatives) voted to reverse the *Erie County*, stating that the decision contradicted the legislative intent of the ADEA. The Senate version of MPDIMA also included this provision, but the AARP persuaded the conference committee (the one reconciling the Senate and House versions of the legislation) to drop it.

In April 2004, the EEOC adopted a Final Rule to allow Medicare benefits to be coordinated with the employer's plan (as Social Security and pension benefits can be coordinated), with the result that employers could provide smaller benefits to Medicare-eligible retirees. The EEOC took the position that such coordination is not age discrimination, and that the EEOC has the power to make reasonable exceptions to the ADEA where the exception serves the public interest.

In 2005, District Court Judge Anita Brody issued a permanent injunction against enforcement of the EEOC's new rule. Judge Brody found that the EEOC did not have the power to issue the rule, because it violates Congress' intent in passing the ADEA, and creates a blanket exemption for illegal behavior rather than granting relief based on the facts of specific cases. Later that year, however, Brody reversed herself, because in the interim the Supreme Court had decided a case about administrative law that requires judges to grant greater deference to administrative agencies' interpretations of their governing statutes. Therefore, it is now lawful for employers to reduce benefits for Medicare-age retirees as compared with younger retirees.[50]

Retiree Health Benefits and Bankruptcy

Ironically, sometimes employees of a bankrupt corporation have more protection against loss of their retiree health benefits than workers for a corporation that is not bankrupt. §1114 of the Bankruptcy Code provides that bankrupt companies are not allowed to modify or terminate their retiree health benefit programs unless the bankruptcy trustee and representatives of the retirees consent, or unless the court orders the modification because it is necessary to re-organize the bankrupt company. The Third Circuit ruled in mid-2005 that a group of senior executives were "retired employees" as defined by Bankruptcy Code §1114 and therefore entitled to protection. In this case, the court would not let their bankrupt former employer use the part of the Bankruptcy Code that allows debtor companies to get the court's permission to cancel future obligations under their contracts.[51]

The Bankruptcy Abuse Prevention and Consumer Protection Act of 2005 (BAPCA; P.L. 109-8) amends this provision of the Bankruptcy Code. If a corporation modified its retiree health benefits during the six months before a bankruptcy filing, and the corporation was insolvent at that time (i.e., did not have enough funds to pay its debts) then anyone with a financial interest in the company's financial affairs can petition the bankruptcy court for a hearing. The basic legal rule is that the court must order the retiree health benefits restored unless the court decides that it is clearly fair to allow the employer to reduce benefits. In other words, the employer has to prove that the modification is fair; the opponents don't have to prove that it is unfair.

Health Savings Accounts (HSAs)

The 2003 federal statute that created the Part D Medicare prescription drug program also enacted a new type of tax-advantaged health-related account: the Health Savings Account, or HSA.[52] To open a Health Savings Account, a person must be covered only under a high-deductible health plan. The HSA account is tax-advantaged because the person who contributes to the HSA gets a tax deduction for contributions to the account, up to the limit of the deductible. People aged 55-64 can make additional, deductible catch-up contributions to their HSA accounts.

When HSA account owners incur medical expenses, they use the funds in the HSA to pay their deductibles and other expenses. Withdrawals for this purpose are not taxable income. Withdrawals that are not reimbursement for medical expenses are taxable income and are also subject to a tax penalty.

HSAs, by themselves, are not an answer to the problem of paying for senior health care. (Nor are they very popular; only 1 million of these accounts have been opened.) According to EBRI, a person retiring at 65 in 2015 would need $160,000 to $687,000 to pay for post-retirement health care, if health insurance premiums and out of pocket expenses go up 7%. The need to pay for medical care could add 20% to the amount of income needed after retirement. A person who puts $1,000 a year into an HSA for 40 years would have $133,400; the amount would rise to $474,200 if he or she put away $2,650 a year (the 2005 limit for a single person; a couple can save $5,250), but that assumes a rollover of 100% of the account balance each year, and more importantly, assumes that none of the balance was ever needed for health care pre-retirement.

Using the example of someone depositing $2,650 a year, but rolling over only 10% each year for 40 years, only $10,000 would remain in the HSA. Another vulnerability of HSAs is that because they are small accounts, fees and expenses may take a heavy toll.[53]

COBRA Continuation Coverage

COBRA stands for Consolidated Omnibus Budget Reconciliation Act of 1985,[54] a statute that seeks to prevent individuals who encounter certain "qualifying events" from losing access to insurance (at least in the short run). In effect, a person who purchases COBRA continuation coverage takes over the obligation of paying the premium formerly shouldered by the employer. But instead of paying the insurer, the ex-employee pays the employer, who is not allowed to charge more than 102% of the actual premium. (The extra 2% is for administrative costs.) COBRA generally does not apply to companies with fewer than 20 employees. COBRA "qualifying events" include death or divorce of the employee, Medicare entitlement, layoff or termination (whether voluntary or involuntary), or the employer's bankruptcy.

In the retirement context, COBRA is especially important because the spouse and dependents of a former worker may have COBRA rights. Therefore, they can elect continued coverage under the employer-provided plan if the retiree is eligible for Medicare but the spouse and dependents are not. Individuals who are at risk of losing their health care coverage because of divorce from a person who has employer-provided health coverage can also make a COBRA election.

Eligibility for COBRA continuation coverage can last for 18, 29, or 36 months, depending on the reason triggering entitlement to the coverage. Entitlement ends as soon as the person electing the coverage becomes eligible for coverage under another employer-provided plan. Typically, this happens when a younger person gets another job that provides health coverage. A 1998 Supreme Court decision, *Geissal v. Moore Medical Corp.*, 118 S.Ct. 1869 (1998), clarifies that COBRA coverage can be terminated only on the basis of coverage obtained *after* making the COBRA election, not coverage (e.g., spousal benefits) existing at the time of the COBRA election.

COBRA eligibility can also be cut off when the ex-employee has actually enrolled in Medicare (although not merely because he is Medicare-eligible.)

Insurance Availability

Another thicket the financial planner can help the older client steer through is the health insurance maze. Fewer and fewer retirees can claim health benefits through their former employers (see above). Those who did not elect under COBRA, or who have used up their COBRA eligibility but are not yet eligible for Medicare, are likely to face substantial premiums for health coverage. The Commonwealth Fund's figures for 2004 show that for older adults (50-70), 54% spent $3,600 or more on health premiums per year, and 26% spent $6,000 or more. Older adults who still had employment-related coverage were much less likely to spend $3,600 or more a year—only 17% did so. High premiums weren't the only problem; individual coverage for seniors and older adults often provided insufficient access to care and involved significant out of pocket expenses once coverage was triggered.

The study also found that older adults seldom had good prescription drug coverage under individual policies, but Medicare Part D should go far toward alleviating this problem. Adding up all health care costs, 50% of older adults with individual health insurance spent $5,500 or more a year, which was true of only 16% of people with employment-related coverage and only 8% of Medicare beneficiaries. The report concluded that 32% of those with individual coverage are "underinsured" (they must devote an unreasonable portion of their income to health care), which was true of only 17% of Medicare beneficiaries and 5% of those with employment-related coverage. Close to one-third of those with individual coverage had access problems (avoided seeing a doctor when they needed one; didn't go to a specialist; didn't take medical tests; didn't fill prescriptions) caused by financial factors.

The net effect is that older adults typically pay more but get less for their health insurance dollar than younger purchasers of individual policies, and especially than persons covered by employers (who can spread the risk among the workforce) or by the Medicare system, which is noted for its low administrative costs.[55]

The Health Insurance Portability and Accessibility Act of 1996 (HIPAA) serves to protect eligible individuals against insurance coverage denials based on pre-existing conditions. However, HIPAA applies only if the individual has at least 18 months of "creditable coverage" under an employer group health plan or other prior health plan, did not have a coverage gap exceeding 63 days, and has used up all COBRA entitlements. Furthermore, the fact that a person can purchase coverage doesn't mean that he can afford the coverage or can do so without severe financial stress. Even if the insurance premium is currently affordable, future increases may place it out of reach.

SUMMARY

For older clients who have not yet retired, it is important to offer guidance about the best time to retire in order to maximize the size of the pension and obtain optimal tax treatment. The client who has not yet retired may also have the option of taking a lump sum distribution instead of an annuity, and then transferring the lump sum, purchasing an annuity, entering a continuing care retirement community or otherwise using it to further an elder plan.

Early retirees should be sure to consider their COBRA options for continued acute health insurance coverage, because they typically will not be Medicare-eligible until age 65. All retirees should be aware that their former employer probably has the legal right to reduce or terminate retiree health benefits, so plans should be made for alternative coverage.

Once retired, older clients need advice about the best deployment of their pensions, as well as how to use income to secure the appropriate housing and health care.

CHAPTER ENDNOTES

1. BenefitNews Connect, "John Hancock Finds Americans Postponing Retirement Plans," http://www.benefitnews.com/pfv.cfm?id=6043 (5/27/04).

2. Glenn Ruffenach, "Growing Numbers of Americans Push Back Retirement Dates," *Wall Street Journal*, October 20, 2004, p. D10.

3. "The Golden Work Years," National Underwriter Online News Service, February 23, 2006.

4. Testimony of Barbara D. Bovbjerg, director of Education, Workforce and Income Security for the GAO, "Redefining Retirement: Options for Older Americans," GAO-05-620T (April 27, 2005), http://www.gao.gov/cgi-bin/getrpt?GAO-05-620T.

5. Eduardo Porter and Mary Williams Walsh, "Retirement Becomes a Rest Stop as Pensions and Benefits Shrink," *New York Times*, February 9, 2005, p.A1.

6. E.S. Browning "As Boomers Retire, A Debate: Will Stock Prices Get Crushed?" *Wall Street Journal*, May 5, 2005, p. A1.

7. Jane E. Kim, "Rising Health Costs Hinder Retirement Savings," *Wall Street Journal*, November 2, 2004, p. D2.

8.   Richard W. Johnson and Rudolph G. Penner, "Will Health Care Costs Erode Retirement Security?" CRR Issue in Brief #23 (October 2004), http://www.bc.edu/centers/crr/issues/ib_23.pdf.

9.   Jilian Mincer, "Experts Disagree on Retiree Health-Cost Estimate," Wall Street Journal March 11-12, 2006, p. B4; Rebecca Moore, "Fidelity Estimates $200,000 Needed for Health Care in Retirement," http://www.plansponsor.com/pi_type10_print.jsp?RECORD_ID-32620 (March 6, 2006); Jennifer Levitz, "For Retired Couples, Coverage for Health May Mean $200,000," *Wall Street Journal*, March 7, 2006, p. D2.

10. Eduardo Porter, "Step By Step," *New York Times*, April 12, 2005, p. G1.

11. Jonathan Clements, "Forget the Deduction: Why You Should Pay Off Your Mortgage Before You Retire," *Wall Street Journal*, October 6, 2004, p. D1.

12. Tom Lauricella, "New Tools for the Nest Egg," *Wall Street Journal,* October 1, 2005, p. B1. Bruce Shutan, "MetLife Suggests Shift in Educational Focus From Retirement Assets to Income," Benefitnews.com (August 29, 2005), http://www.benefitnews.com/detail.cfm?id=7987.

13. "What is Your Savings Personality?" Issue Brief No. 200 (August, 1998), Employee Benefits Research Institute. See http://www.ebri.org/ibex/ib200.htm.

14. "Many U.S. Workers Face Retirement Woes," *Wall Street Journal*, February 24, 2005, p. D2.

15. "Retirees Go It Alone On 401(k) Rollovers," *Wall Street Journal*, March 1, 2005, p. D5.

16. Jillian Mincer, "Self-Employed Aren't Saving Enough for Retirement," *Wall Street Journal,* October 25, 2005, p. D2.

17. See, e.g., Ellen E. Schultz and Elizabeth MacDonald," Employers Win Big With a Pension Shift; Employees Often Lose," *Wall Street Journal*, December 4, 1998, p. A1; Ellen E. Schultz, "Ins and Outs of 'Cash Balance' Plan," *Wall Street Journal*, December 4, 1998, p. C1; Ellen E. Schultz, "Some Workers Facing Pension Hit," *Wall Street Journal*, December 18, 1998, p. C1; Ellen E. Schultz, "Some Pension Funds Look Like 401(k)'s, But They Sure Don't Behave Like Them," "Cash Balance Plans' Key: Interest Rates," *Wall Street Journal*, December 31, 1998, p. C1 and C19; "'Cash' Pensions Trigger Protest of New Allies," *Wall Street Journal*, January 21, 1999, p. C1; and "Older Workers Fight 'Cash Balance' Plans," *Wall Street Journal*, February 11, 1999, p. C1.

18. The GAO report is available at http://www.gao.gov/new.items/d0642.pdf; see Allison Bell, "Researchers Say Typical Pension Shifts Hit Benefits," NU Online News Service November 7, 2005; Marcy Gordon (AP), "GAO: Pension Plan Switch Hurts Employees," http://kevxml2adsl.verizon/net[…] (November 4, 2005).

19. See T.D. 9099, 2004-2 IRB 255. See also Ellen E. Schultz, "Lump-Sum Pensions Make Retirement Even Riskier," *Wall Street Journal*, June 29, 2005, p. B3.

20. See *Hughes Aircraft Company v. Jacobson*, 119 S.Ct. 755 (1999). See also, David Cay Johnston, "Ruling Favors Employers on Pension Gains," *New York Times*, January 26, 1999, p. C1.

21. Jack VanDerhei, EBRI Issue Brief, http://www.ebri.org/pdf/briefspdf/EBRI_IB_03-20063.pdf (March 2006), discussed in Rebecca Moore, "EBRI Studies What Workers Will Need to Offset Pension Freezes," http://www.plansponsor.com/pi_type10_print.jsp?RECORD_ID=32681 (March 9, 2006).

22. Eric T. Sondergeld, Matthew Greenwald, "Public Misperceptions About Retirement Security," (LIMRA International) (2005), http://www.soa.org/ccm/csm-service/stream/.

23. Kelly Greene, "Workers Lag on Retirement Savings," *Wall Street Journal* April 5, 2005, p. D2; Eduardo Porter, "When It Comes to Managing Retirement, Many People Simply Can't," *New York Times*, March 18, 2005, p.C3. Janette Kawachi, Karen E. Smith and Eric J. Toder's Center for Retirement Research Working Paper, "Making Maximum Use of Tax-Deferred Retirement Accounts," http://www.bc.edu/centers/crr/papers/summary/wp_2005-19.pdf (December 2005) says that in 2003, only 6% of participants made the maximum contribution. In 1990 and 2003, the percentage of workers earnings $75,000 a year or less who "maxed out" stayed about the same, but employees earning $130,000-$150,000 were much more likely to make the maximum contribu-

tion in 2003 than in 1990 (38% and 23% respectively). Older and more educated workers were more likely than others to make the maximum contribution; widowhood and divorced reduced the likelihood that the maximum contribution would be made.

24. Rebecca Moore, "Affluent Boomers Nearing Retirement With No Financial Plan," http://www.plansponsor.com/pi_type10_print.jsp?RECORD_ID=32637 (March 7, 2006).

25. Richard W. Johnson, Gordon B.T. Mermin and Cori E. Uccello, "When the Nest Egg Cracks," Center for Retirement Research Working Paper, http://www.bc.edu/centers/crr/papers/summary/wp_2005-18.pdf (December 2005).

26. Richard W. Johnson, "Do Spouses Coordinate Their Retirement Decisions?" CRR Issue in Brief #19 (July 2004) http://www.bc.edu/centers/crr/issues/ib_19.pdf.

27. See Carole Ann King, "Women Face Financial Crisis in Retirement," *National Underwriter*, Life and Health/Financial Services Edition, November 9, 1998, p. 31.

28. Alicia H. Munnell, "Why Are So Many Older Women Poor?" Just the Facts on Retirement Issues (CRR) Just the Facts 10 (April 2004) http://www.bc.edu/centers/crr/facts/jtf_10.pdf.

29. Alicia H. Munnell and Steven A. Sass, "401(k) Plans and Women: A 'Good News/Bad News' Story," Just the Facts on Retirement Issues (CRR) #13 (1/05) http://www.bc.edu/crr/jtf)13.shtml.

30. Ellen E. Schultz, "Widow's Lament," *Wall Street Journal*, June 29, 2005, p. B1.

31. Richard W. Johnson, "Do Spouses Coordinate Their Retirement Decisions?" CRR Issue in Brief No. 19 (July 2004) http://www.bc.edu/centers/crr/issues/ib_19.pdf.

32. Note however, that as a result of the Deficit Reduction Act of 2005, an individual who has more than $500,000 in housing equity--$750,000 in a state that has elected a higher limit—can become ineligible for Medicaid; see Chapter 6.

33. For discussions of 401(k) issues, see, e.g., Danny Hakim, "Controlling 401(k) Assets," *New York Times*, November 17, 2000, p. C1; Alicia H. Munnell, Annika Sunden and Catherine Taylor, "What Determines 401(k) Participation and Contributions?" WP #2000-12 from the Center for Retirement Research (December 2000); http://www.bc.edu/bc_org/avp/csom/executive/crr/wp_2000-12.shtml; Profit Sharing/401(k) Council of America, "Workers Have Less of a Wait to Save for Retirement," http://www.psca.org/pr40.html (December 6, 2000).

34. See IRC Secs. 402A(c)(2), 402A(d)(1). See also McKay Hochman Co. Inc., "Roth 401(k) FAQs," (September 29, 2005) http://www.mhco.com/Commentary/2005/RothK_FAQs_092905.htm.

35. Karen Hube, "New Kid in Town," *Wall Street Journal*, September 26, 2005, p. R6.

36. Len Boselovic, "Few Workers Make Catch-Up Contributions," *Detroit News Money & Life*, August 21, 2005, (benefitslink.com).

37. Craig Copeland, "401(k)-Type Plan and IRA Ownership," EBRI Notes, Volume 26 No. 1 (January 2005), http://www.ebri.org.

38. Kathy Chu, "Individuals Fail to Diversify Retirement Portfolios," *Wall Street Journal*, March 16, 2005, p. D3.

39. Jeff D. Opdyke, "Why Staying In Your Company's 401(k) After Retirement Can Be a Smart Move," *Wall Street Journal*, December 28, 2005, p. D1.

40. Richard Breeden, "Nearly Half of Owners Plan Never to Stop Working," *Wall Street Journal*, October 25, 2005, p. B8.

41. Katharine G. Abraham and Susan N. Houseman, "Work and Retirement Plans Among Older Americans," Pension Research Council Working Paper, http://prc.wharton.upenn.edu/prc/PRC/wp/WP2004-3.pdf (abstract).

42. REG-114726-04, 69 Fed. Reg. 65108 (November 10, 2004); technical corrections at 69 Fed. Reg. 77679 (December 29, 2004).

43. S. Kathi Brown (AARP), "Attitudes of Individuals 50 and Older Toward Phased Retirement," (March 2005) http://research.aarp.org/research/work/retirement/attitudes_of_individuals_50_and_older_toward_phase.htm).

44. John Leland, "Retirees Return to the Grind, But This Time It's On Their Own Terms," *New York Times*, December 8, 2004, p. A18.

45. Employees who started receiving minimum distributions under the pre-SBJPA '96 rules, but who remain employed, may be able to cease distributions and restart them after they retire. See Notice 97-75, 1997-51 CB 337.

46. Ellen E. Schultz, "Employer Actions Drive Health Costs for Retirees Higher," *Wall Street Journal*, December 30, 2004, p. B1.

47. GAO report, GAO-05-205, "Retiree Health Benefits: Options for Employment-Based Prescription Drug Benefits Under the Medicare Modernization Act," (Feb. 2005), http://www.gao/gov/cgi-bin/getrpt?GAO-05-205.

48. KFF survey by Hewitt, "Survey Finds Businesses and Retirees Hit With Double-Digit Increases in Retiree Health Costs In 2004, With Higher Premiums Likely in Future," (December 12, 2004), http://www.kff.org/medicare/med121404nr.cfm.

49. *Bland v. Fiatallis North America Inc.*, 2005 U.S. App. LEXIS 4264 (7th Cir. 2005).

50. The latest decision is *AARP v EEOC*, No. 2:05-cv-00509 (Eastern District of Pennsylvania 2005), and the one that started the ball rolling was *Erie County Retirees Ass'n v. County of Erie*, 220 F.3d 193 (3d Cir. 2000); see Shannon P. Duffy, "Federal Judge Affirms EEOC Proposed Regulation in Wake of High Court Decision," *The Legal Intelligencer*, September 29, 2005 (law.com); Milt Freudenheim, "Health Coverage Dispute Pits Older Retirees Against Younger," *New York Times*, April 30, 2005, p. Bus1; Robert Pear, "Judge Blocks Rule Allowing Companies to Cut Benefits When Retirees Reach Medicare Age," *New York Times*, March 31, 2005, p. A14; Kaiser Family Foundation, "EEOC Rule Allows Employers to Reduce Benefits for Medicare-Eligible Retirees," (April 23, 2004) http://www.kaisernetwork.org/daily_reports/print_report.cfm?DR_ID=…

51. *General Datacomm Industries Inc. v. Arcara*, No. 04-1710 (3d Cir. 5/16/05).

52. The statute is the Medicare Prescription Drug Improvement and Modernization Act, P.L. 108-173; the HSA rules are found in Division B of this law, known as the Health Savings and Affordability Act of 2003.

53. Robert Powell, "Time to Overhaul HSAs," (8/18/05) http://www.marketwatch.com/news/story.asp; EBRI Issue Brief Executive Summary #271 "Health Care Expenses in Retirement and the Use of Health Savings Accounts," (July 2004) http://www.ebri.org/ibex/ib271.htm.

54. COBRA regulations are published in a Final Rule at 64 Fed. Reg. 5160 (February 3, 1999), and T.D. 8928, 66 Fed. Reg. 1843 (January 10, 2001).

55. Sara R. Collins et. al., "Paying More For Less: Older Adults in the Individual Insurance Market," Commonwealth Fund Issue Brief (June 2005), http://www.cmwf.org/usr_doc/841_collins_olderadults_ib_6-30-2005.pdf.

Chapter 9

Social Security

The Old Age, Survivors, and Disability Insurance (OASDI) program is Title II of the Social Security Act. As its name suggests, it provides benefits for persons who are totally disabled and unable to work, but its major function is providing retirement benefits to retired workers and benefits to survivors of retired workers.

The OASDI system is funded by taxes imposed on self-employed persons, and on employers and employees. For 2006, this FICA (Federal Insurance Contribution Act) tax is imposed on earnings up to $94,200. The tax rate is 7.65%, each, for employer and employee, or 15.3% for the self-employed, made up of a 6.2% FICA tax and an additional Medicare tax of 1.45%. The Medicare tax is imposed on all earnings, without limit. It does not phase-out as the FICA tax does.

The Social Security system has tremendous economic impact, not only on senior citizens, but also on employers when they design their pension plans (many of which are integrated with Social Security).

Social Security was the main source of income for seniors in 2003, providing 41.9% of their income, with 20.6% coming from pensions and retirement plans, 13.9% from assets, and 21.7% from work earnings. The picture was different for elderly women, who received 50.8% of their income from Social Security (elderly men received 35.5% of their income from this program). Social Security was also much more significant for poor people than for rich people: the highest income quintile of elderly people received 19.5% of their income from Social Security, whereas the lowest quintile got 91.2% of their income from Social Security.

In 2003, if we look just at the top 20% of income (because this is the group most likely to do financial planning), seniors with income of $30,000 a year or more looked to Social Security for 20% of their income. Pensions and annuities provided 25% of income, assets 19%, work earnings 34%, and other sources 2%.[1]

In October, 2005, the Social Security Administration (SSA) announced a 4.1% cost of living increase. (This was much larger than the 2.7% increase in 2005.) At that point, there were more than 52 million Americans collecting benefits from the SSA (whether on account of disability, as retirees, or from derivative benefits based on another worker's earnings). The SSA estimated that about 161 million workers would be paying FICA tax, and 11.3 million would pay higher taxes because the maximum amount of income subject to FICA tax rose from $90,000 in 2005 to $94,200 in 2006.[2]

PRACTICE TIP: The following are some of the many sources of Social Security benefits information: www.socialsecurity.gov, (800) 772-1213; the Ask Mary Jane online benefit calculator: www.ncpssm.org/contact/ask (advice from the National Committee to Preserve Social Security and Medicare); and the American Savings Education Counsel's retirement worksheet: asec.org/ballpark.

Applications for replacement Medicare cards can be submitted to www.ssa. gov/medicarecard.

Persons aged at least 61 years and nine months could apply for Social Security benefits on line, as long as they plan to receive their first check within four months. The electronic application form appears at www.ssa.gov/applytoretire. However, the applicant must print out the application form, sign it, and mail or bring it to the local Social Security office along with supporting documents such as a birth certificate.

PRACTICE TIP: Some applications for retirement and survivor's benefits can also be made via a toll-free telephone call to (800) 772-1213, if your clients have the relevant documents (birth certificates, tax forms, W-2 forms, bank account information) on hand when they make the call.

SOCIAL SECURITY RETIREMENT BENEFITS

Traditionally, the Social Security Normal Retirement Age (NRA) was set at 65, which is also the conventional level for pension eligibility. However, one step being taken to preserve the soundness of the Social Security system is a gradual increase in the NRA. By 2027, the NRA will have increased to 67. For most members of the Baby Boom generation, it will be 66.

Under the Social Security system, workers can receive a full benefit if they retire at their NRA. The benefit is actuarially reduced if they retire early (i.e., between the ages of 62 and NRA), and actuarially increased if they retire late. Late retirement is much more of a gamble: it is easier to determine the number of additional checks that will be received between actual retirement and the NRA than to determine how long the person will survive after late retirement.

Social Security reduces benefits below the full amount by 6 2/3% per year for the first three years of payments beginning before the NRA, then by 5% for each additional year of benefits received before NRA. For people who reach 62 in 2005 and after, benefits go up by 8% for every year that benefits are delayed past NRA, but the increase stops at age 70, so waiting longer will not enhance the benefit. (Don't forget that Required Minimum Distributions from IRAs and qualified plans must also be made starting at 70½.)

Retirement timing incentives work differently in defined benefit and defined contribution plans. In effect, workers who have defined benefit plans sacrifice a year of pension benefits for each year that they stay at work once they have reached NRA. Depending on the plan, the benefit might or might not be tailored to make up for that loss. Workers with defined contribution plans do not lose any benefits by working longer.[3]

Americans born in 1940 have an average life expectancy of 83 years—which is 4½ years longer than the average life expectancy in the year of their birth. So early retirement, or above-average longevity, means a retirement period of at last 20 years. One way the Social Security system is coping is the gradual increase in the normal retirement age. However, retiring early with a reduced Social Security benefit has been common for many years. In 1965, for example, 17% of men applied to start Social Security benefits at 62; 17% at 63 or 64, 27% at 65, and 39% at 66 or older. By 1975, 29% had commenced benefits at 62, and only 9% waited until 66. The transition was even more dramatic in 2001, when 54% of men took benefits at 62 and a mere 4% waited until 66 or later.[4]

The average monthly Social Security benefit for all workers in 2006 is estimated to be $1,002 a month, and $1,648 for a senior-citizen couple, both of whom receive Social Security benefits (the 2005 averages were $963 and $1,583 respectively). The maximum Social Security benefit for a worker retiring at age 65 in 2006 is $1,961 a month ($1,874 in 2005). This is much higher than the average because the maximum benefit is received by those individuals who paid the maximum FICA tax each year because they earned significantly more than the average worker.

A particular individual's Social Security benefit, based on his earnings record, equals his Primary Insurance Amount (PIA). (Derivative benefits paid to spouses, ex-spouses, etc., are also set as a percentage of PIA–in this case, the PIA of the worker from whose earnings record the benefits derive.)

Generally, the PIA is calculated by indexing the worker's Social Security earnings (after 1950), determining Average Indexed Monthly Earnings (AIME), and applying the appropriate formula to the AIME to determine the PIA. Broadly speaking, indexing involves a comparison between actual FICA earnings and average national earnings. Because FICA earnings are used, earnings above the FICA maximum do not count for this purpose. The indexing computation also involves using the "indexing averaging wage" for each year after 1950 up to, but not including, the "indexing year" (i.e., the second year before the worker reaches age 62, or dies, or becomes disabled before age 62). Thus, the benefits of persons reaching age 62 in 2006 are calculated using the 2004 indexing average wage, which was $35,648.55.

The actual benefit is calculated with AIME and "bend points"–i.e., for 2006, the PIA equals 90% of the first $656 ($627 in 2005) of the person's AIME, plus 32% of AIME between $656 and $3,955 ($627 - $3,779 in 2005), plus 15% of any AIME in excess of $3,955 ($3,779 in 2005).

Before 1996, excess earnings could reduce the Social Security benefit by $1 for every $2 or $3 in excess earnings (depending on the beneficiary's age). The Senior Citizens' Right to Work Act of 1996, P.L. 104-121, increased the amount that Social Security beneficiaries could earn without penalty.

This legislation was extended by the Senior Citizens' Freedom to Work Act of 2000, P.L. 106-182, effective for tax years ending after 1999, which eliminates the earnings test entirely for persons who reach normal retirement age in or after 2000. Federal government sources estimated that 900,000 people would benefit by the change.

For 2006, persons who reach NRA that year are permitted to earn up to $33,240 without losing benefits, but only earnings before the month the person reaches NRA are counted against the $33,240 limit. For those under NRA in 2006 for the entire year, the earnings limit is $12,480.

The current Social Security formulas give a larger return on payroll taxes paid into the system for those born 1956-1964 than those born between 1931-1940; women get higher percentage replacement than men; and low-income workers do better than high-income workers (low-income workers get 60% income replacement under Social Security's current rules; high-income workers get 30% replacement, but have many other sources of income). The result was that the percentage of senior citizens living in poverty dropped from about 50% in the 1930s (pre-Social Security) to about 10% in 2005.

For example, a 65-year-old man retiring in 2005 after earning an average of $36,500 and living to his predicted lifespan of 81.1 years would receive $164,000 (in constant 2005 dollars) in Social Security benefits. That is less than his payroll taxes would earn if invested, even at a 2% real rate of return. However, a woman would receive $206,000, or $28,000 more than her payroll taxes would earn if invested, because of her longer predictable life span.

A male high school dropout who retired in the 1990s would receive the equivalent of a 2.7% real annual rate of return on payroll taxes, whereas a college graduate is expected to live seven years longer, resulting in a 3.2% rate of return. An attempt to save Social Security by raising the retirement age would be a problem for the poor, who have a lower life expectancy. Even if Social Security personal accounts earned 4.6% a year for the worker's whole career, the lowest 20% of wage earners would receive benefits 4% lower under that system than under the current system.[5]

DERIVATIVE BENEFITS

For unmarried people, benefit eligibility is a fairly simple matter–the calculations are made based on the earnings record. However, the majority of workers are married and, thus, matters become much more complicated. A variety of "derivative benefits" for family members can be paid based on a worker's earnings record. The major ones are:

- Spouse. In a two-earner couple, a husband or wife is entitled to a benefit as a retired worker, or as a spouse, but is not entitled to both benefits. If the spousal retirement benefit is higher than the spouse's own retirement benefit, then the spouse may receive a combination of benefits equalling the higher spousal benefit.

- Divorced spouse

- Surviving spouse

- Surviving divorced spouse

Benefits can also be paid to the children of disabled or deceased workers; the dependent, surviving parents (age 62 or older) of a deceased worker are also eligible for survivor's benefits. Generally, a person receives either a derivative benefit or a benefit based on his or her own earnings record, whichever is higher, but cannot receive the full amount of both benefits.

To qualify for derivative benefits, the spouse of a worker must be married to a retired or disabled worker already receiving benefits, and must be at least 62 years old. The divorced spouse of a retired or disabled worker can receive derivative benefits based on that worker's earnings record as long as he or she is at least 62 years old, the marriage lasted at least 10 years, and the divorced spouse is not married at the time of the benefit application. (If the divorced spouse married and divorced someone else after the divorce from the worker, that marriage will not bar the receipt of benefits based on the first spouse's earnings record.) The benefit to a divorced spouse can be paid even if the worker spouse has not yet begun to receive benefits.

The benefit for a spouse or divorced spouse is 50% of the worker's PIA. These derivative benefits are reduced if the worker's own benefit is reduced because of retirement before the NRA, or if the spouse or divorced spouse chooses to receive benefits before his or her own NRA.

The benefit for a surviving spouse or surviving divorced spouse is 100% of the deceased worker's benefit. It can be paid to a surviving spouse or surviving divorced spouse who has reached age 60 (or has reached age 50 and is disabled), and is not married. However, remarriage after the survivor's benefit begins does not always terminate benefit eligibility.

Derivative benefits are limited by a "maximum family benefit" that applies to all earnings based on a particular person's earnings record. For 2006, the family maximum is 150% of the first $838 of the worker's PIA, plus 272% of PIA between $838 and $1,210, plus 134% of PIA between $1,210 and $1,578, plus 175% of PIA in excess of $1,578.

TAXATION OF SOCIAL SECURITY BENEFITS

Low-income Social Security recipients do not have to pay income tax on their benefits. However, for individuals or married couples whose total income ("modi-fied adjusted gross income") plus one-half of the Social Security benefit exceeds the "base amount," ($32,000 for married couples filing a joint return, $0 for married individuals filing separate returns, and $25,000 for other taxpayers) then between 50% and 85% of the benefit will constitute taxable income. Total income includes certain tax preference items, such as municipal bond interest, that generally escape taxation.

Senior citizens may opt to voluntarily withhold income tax from their Social Security benefits. This can provide convenience to individuals subject to taxation on the benefit, and who would otherwise have to make quarterly estimated tax payments (or would have to increase their current estimated tax payments) to compensate.

LONG-RANGE PROSPECTS FOR THE SYSTEM

The Social Security system does not operate like a private pension system–al-though individuals can receive information about the size of their Social Security "account," the account is purely hypothetical. The Social Security system does not accumulate the FICA taxes paid by each person and his or her employer, investing the funds until the individual begins to collect benefits. Instead, the taxes paid by current employees and employers are used to pay benefits to current retirees and disabled individuals.

The Social Security system faces pressures from many directions. The largest generation in U.S. history, the Baby Boomers, is moving into retirement age. Long periods of prosperity mean that a large percentage of the Boomers earned at the FICA maximum and therefore are entitled to maximum benefits. Thanks to increasing longevity, benefits may need to be paid for two or even three decades for retirees who survive into their 80s or 90s. Furthermore, benefits are expected to increase every year, not remain stable or drop.

The soundness of the system depends on many factors, including the "dependency ratio" (size of the group of active workers paying FICA taxes relative to the size of the group of Social Security beneficiaries) and the amount of unemployment within the economy (unemployed persons do not contribute FICA taxes to the system).

According to economist Alicia Munnell, the number of Social Security beneficiaries per 100 workers will rise from 30 today to 54 in 2017. In 2005, the Social Security system had a cash flow surplus of $70 billion, but the costs of paying benefits will outstrip Social Security tax revenues in 2017. Between 2017 and 2027, benefit payments can be covered by tax revenue plus interest on the assets in the Social Security trust fund, but by 2027, income will fall beneath the annual payments, and if the government uses trust fund assets (instead of general federal funds) that would mean that the trust fund would be used up in 2041. However, that would not necessarily mean the collapse of the system, because even without trust fund assets, tax revenues will continue, and are projected to be large enough to pay about three-quarters of the current level of benefits. Raising payroll taxes by about 1% each for employer and employee would permit payment of benefits at the current level at least through 2079, although certainly neither employers nor employees feel that they pay too little in Social Security taxes already![6]

Another complicating factor is that government analysts could be underestimating future increases in life expectancy. For example, the 2004 report of the Social Security Trustees estimated that life expectancy would increase only six years over the next seven decades. The SSA expects male life expectancy at birth to be 81.2 years in 2075—whereas the Census Bureau thinks this landmark will be reached in 2050.[7]

The balance of the Social Security system could also be affected by the increasing inequality of income. The larger the share of national income that goes to the highest wage earners, the more income escapes Social Security taxation, because there is a maximum amount subject to FICA tax (for 2006, this amount is $94,200).[8]

The AARP, which opposes privatization, notes that the proposals for individual accounts assume that the assets will earn the historical average rate in every year. (If the economy continues to grow enough to produce these results, payroll taxes would also rise, which would lessen the Social Security system's problems.) But two workers with the same lifetime average indexed earnings could have very different career patterns. Under the current system, they would get the same benefit, but their benefits would vary greatly under an individual account system. Two workers with the same size individual account retiring in different years, or even at different times in the same year, could fare very differently as a result of market factors.[9]

In 2001, the Social Security commission appointed by President Bush suggested that workers under 55 should be allowed to place 4% of their payroll taxes, up to a maximum of $1,000, in a private account. The amount diverted would reduce the traditional Social Security benefit, and future benefit increases would be reduced by tying them to price changes rather than real wages. The Congressional Budget Office calculated that taking this approach would mean that workers born in the 1940s would get the same benefits (combining Social Security and private account returns) in the first year of retirement, but those who were born in later years would lose benefits as compared to the current system, and the youngest workers would take the biggest hit.[10]

Critics of the plan pointed out that when administration officials discuss the rationale behind the reform plan, they say that growth within the U.S. economy will slow down to 1.9% when the baby boomers retire—but when the same officials advocate the value of private accounts, they base their calculations on returns of 6.5% per year after inflation. The numbers would not work out as well if investment returns were lower: for example, if the return each year is just one percentage point lower than the projection, after 30 years the investor would have one-third less in the account than projected. Because the plan calls for reductions in Social Security benefits, at least 3% a year after-inflation return would be required just to make up for the cuts.[11]

The Bush Administration plan for Social Security reduces benefits by 9.4% ($3,009 in current dollars) for the family of an average worker who is now 25 years old and who dies at age 45. That happens because the administration's plan uses the Pozen Index devised by Robert Pozen of the Commission to Strengthen Social Security, which increases Social Security benefits on the basis of the consumer price index, not average wages. (Generally, average wages grow faster than prices, so changing the index would mean smaller benefits, especially smaller survivor and disability benefits.)

Progressive indexing was adopted to reduce the impact of the proposal on low-income workers. A worker earning $16,000 a year would get a retirement benefit replacing about 49% of his or her wages—approximately equal to the current level. But those earning more would get much smaller Social Security benefits under the reform proposal. Someone who earned $36,500 would get 36% income replacement under the current system, but only 26% under the proposal; those who earned $90,000 would pay the same amount of tax as under the current system but get only 12% income replacement. The proposal highlights the important political question of whether the Social Security system should be considered a universal retirement system covering everybody, or a poverty program.[12]

The administration plan did not cover the treatment of surviving spouses. About 30% of Social Security beneficiaries, most of them women, collect Social Security benefits based on their spouse's or ex-spouse's earnings. Survivor and disability benefits would not fit smoothly into a system based on private accounts, because disability and premature death tend to occur before the worker had a chance to contribute much to a private account.[13]

As of 2005, about 55% of Social Security recipients are disabled workers or family members of disabled, retired, or deceased workers. In December of 2003, there were 47 million people receiving Social Security benefits, 6.8 million of them (including 1.9 million children) receiving survivor benefits. Men in their 20s have a 30% chance of suffering disability prior to retirement age, and about one-third of the disabled persons will die before normal retirement age. A further 10% of men aged 20-29 will die before retirement for other reasons.

Under current law, the Social Security systems covers all of an insured worker's children; it is not clear whether the entire private account of a deceased worker would go to his or her spouse at the time of death, or whether provision would be made for former spouses or children of earlier relationships.[14]

ISSUES FOR ELDERLY WOMEN

As noted throughout this book, women's greater longevity and the tendency of women to marry men older than themselves combine to make it likely that the average married woman will experience widowhood–perhaps a prolonged period of widowhood. The majority of married women today spend most of their adult lives in the work force, and most of them will be subject to FICA taxes. Unfortunately, the basic structure of Social Security has not changed since its inception (after the

Great Depression) when only a minority of married women were employed outside the home. Consequently, they will be eligible to collect a retirement benefit based on their own earnings record, or based on 50% of their husband's earnings record–but not the full amount of both. The benefit paid to a surviving spouse is calculated on the deceased spouse's earnings record.

Women are also at a disadvantage with respect to private pensions due to: a pattern of working in lower-paid jobs; a higher probability of working at a company that does not provide a pension plan; and time spent out of the work force because of child rearing. Furthermore, on the average, women tend to be more afraid of financial risks than men are. In a pension plan that shifts investment risks to participants, a common pattern among women is that they tend to invest in low-risk–but also low-return–investment alternatives, and often end up with smaller pension entitlements as a result. The combination of little or no private pension entitlement, and lower Social Security benefits, can be extremely dangerous to the financial security of elderly women.

In practice, a low-income, two-earner household will receive less in Social Security benefits than a single-earner household earning the same amount.

The Social Security Administration's figures show that the number of women receiving a benefit based at least in part on their own earnings (not just on their husbands' earnings) has increased, but in 2001, only 38% of women received benefits solely based on their own earnings. According to the Department of Labor, in 1996 55% of retired men had pensions, averaging $44,764 a year. Only 32% of retired women had pensions, and furthermore their pensions were much smaller—an average of $5,230.[15]

CHAPTER ENDNOTES

1. "Income of the Elderly Population: 2003," EBRI Notes volume 26 #1 (Jan 2005) www.ebri.org/publications/notes/index.cfm?fa=notesDisp&content_id=3230.

2. Social Security Administration press release, "Social Security Announces 4.1 Percent Benefit Increase for 2006," (October 14, 2005), www.ssa.gov/pressoffice/pr/2006cola-pr.htm.

3. Richard W. Johnson, "Do Spouses Coordinate Their Retirement Decisions?" CRR Issue in Brief #19 (July 2004) www.bc.edu/centers/crr/issues/ib_19.pdf.

4. Robin Toner and David E. Rosenbaum, "In Overhaul of Social Security, Age Is the Elephant in the Room," *New York Times,* June 12, 2005, p. A1.

5. Eduardo Porter, "Who Wins in a New Social Security?" *New York Times,* March 6, 2005, Business p. 6.

6. Alicia H. Munnell, "Social Security's Financial Outlook: The 2005 Update and a Look Back," Just the Facts #16 (March 2005); www.bc.edu/centers/crr/facts/jtf_16.pdf 2005.

7. Robert Pear, "Social Security Understates Future Life Span, Critics Say," *New York Times,* December 31, 2004.

8.   Greg Ip, "Wage Gap Figures in Social Security's Ills," *Wall Street Journal*, April 11, 2005, p. A2.

9.   AARP Issue Brief, "How Earnings and Financial Risk Affect Private Accounts in Social Security Reform Proposals," assets.aarp.org/rgcenter/post-import/ib73_earnings.pdf.

10. Edmund L. Andrews, "Most G.O.P. Plans to Remake Social Security Involve Deep Cuts to Tomorrow's Retirees," *New York Times*, December 14, 2004, p. A22.

11. Edmund L. Andrews, "Social Security, Growth and Stock Returns" *New York Times*, March 31, 2005, p. A23.

12. Edmund L. Andrews and Eduardo Porter, "Social Security: Help for the Poor or Help For All?" *New York Times*, May 1, 2005, p. A1.

13. Karen Damato, "Spouses May Lose With Social Security Overhaul," *Wall Street Journal*, March 3, 2005, p. D2; Alan B. Krueger, "Economic Scene," *New York Times*, March 3, 2005, p. C2.

14. William Spriggs & David Ratner, "Social Security's Cruelest Cut: Bush's Proposal Slashes Benefits For Family Members of Workers Who Die Before Retirement," EPI Issue Brief #211 (June 28, 2005, www.epinet.org/issuebriefs/211/ib211.pdf).

15. Alicia H. Munnell, "Why Are So Many Older Women Poor?" Just the Facts on Retirement Issues (CRR) Just the Facts 10 (April 2004) www.bc.edu/centers/crr/facts/jtf_10.pdf.

Chapter 10

Individual Retirement Accounts (IRAs)

As Chapter 8 shows, there has been a revolution in the labor law and tax rules affecting qualified plans. Equally major changes have occurred in the rules governing Individual Retirement Accounts (IRAs).

Individual Retirement Accounts (IRAs) were originally created by Congress so self-employed people, and people whose employers didn't have a pension plan, could save for retirement. Today, eligibility is much broader.

Thanks to the Economic Growth and Tax Reform Reconciliation Act of 2001 (EGTRRA 2001; P.L. 107-16), taxpayers can get far more financial benefit out of conventional and Roth IRAs than under prior law. EGTRRA 2001 liberalizes IRA requirements in three major areas:

- Much larger contributions;

- The right of persons over 50 to make extra, "catch-up" contributions to their IRAs; and

- A tax credit for low-income persons who contribute to IRAs.

The maximum contribution to either a conventional or Roth IRA for 2005-2007 is $4,000 a year and $5,000 a year in 2008. In 2009 and 2010, the $5,000 limit will be indexed for inflation. (Don't forget, the entire EGTRRA 2001 legislative package expires on December 31, 2010, unless Congress acts to keep all or part of it in effect.)

PRACTICE TIP: Starting April 1, 2006, FDIC insurance on retirement accounts held in bank accounts, including both conventional and Roth IRAs, rose from $100,000 to $250,000 per account.[1]

People in their fifties and sixties are closer to retirement age than younger people, so they would derive comparatively less benefit from the increased limits if they were not allowed to make "catch-up" contributions. Taxpayers aged 50 and over can contribute an extra $500 per year (over and above the ordinary level of $4,000/$5,000) in the years 2002-2005, and $1,000 a year in the years 2006-2010.

For the years 2002-2006 only, EGTRRA 2001 also provides a tax credit (in addition to any tax deduction which is available) for low-income and moderate-income persons who contribute to IRAs (or 401(k) plans). Qualifying taxpayers have AGI under $25,000 (single persons) or $50,000 (joint returns). The maximum credit is 50% of the first $2,000 of the contribution (for income under $15,000 on a single return, $30,000 on a joint return).

EGTRRA 2001 also makes it easier to shift funds among IRAs, 401(k)s, and employer-sponsored plans (including the plans of non-profit and governmental organizations), but these rules are highly technical, so your clients should consult their tax advisors about proper handling of rollovers between accounts.

But taxpayers who can't take a deduction (because of income and participation in an employer plan, or because their AGI is too high[2]) or who are too old to contribute to a conventional IRA, can use Roth IRAs as part of their investment/retirement planning portfolios, even though conventional IRAs are ruled out.

IRA contributions can be made at any time during the calendar year, and until April 15 of the following year, so individuals making contributions after January 1 and before April 15 should indicate for which year they are being made.

As originally designed, IRAs were supposed to be a pure retirement savings mechanism, and the owner of the account was supposed to use it up during his or her lifetime. Estate planning with IRAs was discouraged. However, several tax-law changes, including a major revision in January, 2001 (see pages 266-268 below) make it much easier to use IRAs as an estate planning tool.

It may seem counter-intuitive that so much of IRA financial planning centers around ways to "stretch out" the distribution. But that's because the account holder can withdraw as much as he or she wants at any time after reaching 59½. There is no excise tax penalty, although distributions from a conventional IRA (or distributions in excess of contributions to a Roth IRA where the funds have not been in the account for five years) do constitute taxable income.

But account holders who do not need more current income, or who are especially eager to enhance the inheritance of their surviving spouse or other heirs, may want to reduce their MRDs and continue to accumulate and re-invest the funds in the account. The January, 2001 changes expand the estate planning options and make the calculation process much simpler.

In addition to this major change, some minor changes in IRA taxation were made by the Consolidated Appropriations Act of 2001 (P.L. 106-554; signed December 21, 2000). This Act makes it clear that distributions from Roth IRAs are not subject to income tax withholding under IRC Section 3405(e)(1)(B)(ii), because it is reasonable to believe that the distributions are not taxable. It also clarifies that, under IRC Section 219(c)(1)(B), contributions made to a spousal IRA on behalf of a nonworking spouse may not be greater than the combined earned income of the spouses. However, this is not a situation that would arise often–individuals with high investment income but very limited earned income seldom set up IRAs. In 2002, the IRS made these rules final, although there were some small changes, making the calculations a little less complex and also making it somewhat easier to distribute benefits to multiple beneficiaries.[3]

ROTH AND OTHER SPECIAL IRAs

The conventional IRA works well for its designed function: allowing non-affluent persons to accumulate a meaningful sum of money for retirement by making steady, affordable contributions, often receiving a deduction from current income tax. However, as discussed below, conventional IRAs are not a very effective estate planning tool, because tax penalties are imposed if the account is not substantially drawn down during the owner's life.

The "back-loaded," "Roth," or "non-deductible" IRA, enacted as part of the Taxpayer Relief Act of 1997, is basically designed for people who don't need another tax deduction, but who want to leave a bigger estate. Non-deductible contributions can be made to a Roth IRA, up to a maximum of $4,000 per person in 2006 (increasing from $3,000 for 2002 through 2004, to $4,000 for 2005 through 2007, and to $5,000 for 2008 through 2010), minus amounts contributed to all other IRAs. The permissible contribution amount is reduced based on the taxpayer's income and phases out entirely at an amount set by the IRS each year.

Amounts can be withdrawn tax-free by any person over age 59½ after a five-year period that begins with the first year an amount is contributed to any Roth IRA. (If a premature withdrawal is made, there is no income tax or penalty on the original amount contributed to fund the IRA, only on its appreciation in value.[4] Furthermore, the calculation is done on a FIFO basis–i.e., it is assumed that the original deposits are withdrawn before the appreciation, even though the tax bill would be higher if the assumption were reversed.) Some states have adopted legislation that is similar to the federal Roth IRA legislation, but others have not. Clients should consult their tax advisor regarding the state-tax impact of funding a Roth account or converting funds from conventional to Roth IRAs.

Although IRS Form 8606 (nondeductible IRAs) must be filed when a nondeductible contribution is made to a conventional IRA (i.e., by a person who is covered by a qualified plan; when the contribution is greater than the permitted amount), the owner of a Roth IRA does not have to file this form every year. The Form 8606 is only required for a Roth IRA if distributions are made before the owner reaches 59½ (or in case of death or disability, or to a first-time homeowner), or before the contributions have spent five years within the account.

Under IRC §408A(d)(4), distributions from a Roth are taxed as if first the distribution is traced back to regular and spousal Roth IRA contributions then to amounts converted from conventional IRAs, then to earnings on the contributions. The regular and spousal Roth contributions are not taxed when they are withdrawn (as long as the age and duration requirements are met), because they were not deducted when they were made. Funds can also be accumulated in a Roth IRA to become part of the estate, because minimum withdrawals are not required during lifetime; the entire account can be accumulated until the death of the account holder.

Financial advisor Gary Schatsky points out that, although the choice between conventional and Roth IRAs is a personal one that must reflect individual factors, there are two lifetime income situations that are especially positive for selecting a Roth over a conventional IRA.[5]

The first is that the account owner expects to be in a higher tax bracket after retirement—and therefore can save income taxes overall by paying taxes now and placing after-tax funds in the Roth IRA.

The second circumstance favoring a Roth over a conventional IRA is that the individual has already made maximum contributions to contributory retirement plans and other tax-sheltered accounts and therefore has to do all further retirement planning with after-tax dollars.

Of course, the situation becomes more complicated when estate planning motivations are added to current income tax planning and planning for post-retirement income.

Other IRA Forms

An Education IRA is not really an IRA because it's not a retirement account. Its name was changed to Coverdell Education Savings Account (ESA) in 2001.[6] In an

ESA, the taxpayer can make a non-deductible contribution of up to $2,000 per year per child, then take the money out tax-free to pay certain higher education expenses. EGTRRA 2001 increased the non-deductible contribution from the previous $500 per year per child and permitted tax-free distributions for certain elementary and secondary education expenses (as well as "higher" education expenses). A Health Savings Account works like an IRA, but is combined with a high-deductible health insurance policy. Funds from the HSA are used to pay medical bills, not retirement costs. A SIMPLE IRA is a pension plan created by a small employer wherein the employer sets up IRA accounts for employees and contributes to them.

THE IRA MARKETPLACE

IRAs and the investment market are intimately connected. Most IRA assets are invested in mutual funds, and IRAs are a critical component in the securities industry, especially its mutual funds arm.

According to the Investment Company Institute, in 2000 total IRA assets were $2.63 billion, $1.23 billion of which was invested in mutual funds and $950 million in brokerage firms (with smaller amounts invested with banks and life insurers). In 2001, of the $2.62 billion total, $1.16 billion was invested in mutual funds and $990 million with brokerages; by 2003, the $3.01 billion total was invested $1.31 billion in mutual funds and $1.12 million with brokerages.

The IRS issued its first report about IRA investments in 2004; by that point, they had only processed figures up through 2000. At the end of 2000, 46.3 million taxpayers held IRAs worth $2.6 trillion. Nearly all of that ($2.4 trillion; 91.5%) was invested in traditional IRAs, versus only $77.6 billion in Roth IRAs. (However, at that point Roth IRAs were brand-new and there hadn't been much time for investors to accumulate assets.) In 2000, 15.1 million people, representing only 9.5% of those eligible to contribute—made IRA contributions, at an average level of $2,412.

Between 2000 and 2005, total IRA assets fluctuated, rising from $2.629 trillion in 2000, dipping to a low of $2.533 trillion in 2002 (after the dot-com crash), then rising to $3.080 trillion in 2003 and $3.475 trillion in 2004 ($3.2 trillion in traditional IRAs, the rest divided among Roth accounts and employer-sponsored plans like SEP and SIMPLE IRAs. Looking at the ways that IRA funds were held, mutual funds lost some ground, holding 47% of IRA assets in 2000, and 43% in 2004. Banks and life insurance companies each held about 8-11% of IRA assets in each year, and securities in brokerage accounts went from 36% in 2000 to 40% in 2003 and 2004.

By mid-2005, the IRA market had expanded to $3.5 trillion (27% of the entire U.S. investment market). The Investment Company Institute reported that 45 million households—more than 40% of all households—had at least one IRA: 37 million own conventional IRAs, 14 million Roth IRAs (the overlap occurs because many households have both kinds). The median value of traditional IRAs was $24,000, and $8,600 for Roth IRAs. More than half of IRA households (54%) have invested their balances in stock mutual funds. In 2003, 5.5 million households made withdrawals from conventional IRAs, with a median amount of $5,000. Almost 17 million households have made rollovers from a qualified plan to a conventional IRA, and almost a quarter of Roth IRAs (23%) include assets converted from a conventional IRA, with a median amount of $10,000.[7]

The Employee Benefit Research Institute reported that in 2003, $338 billion was invested in insurance-funded IRAs, an amount that increased to $379 billion in 2004, so insurers had about 11% of the IRA market in each year. Banks held 8.7% of IRA assets in 2003, but only 7.8% in 2004.[8]

IRA TAXATION

The basic rule is quite simple: each year, the account owner can withdraw any amount from the account, up to 100% of the account, with no upper limit. However, anything withdrawn from a conventional IRA account is taxed as ordinary income, not capital gains. If the account has always been maintained as a conventional IRA, with fully-deductible contributions, there is no need to calculate an exclusion ratio, because no part of the account constitutes a tax-free return of capital.

However, now that there are other options (such as non-deductible contributions, Roth IRAs, rollovers from qualified plans, and transfers from conventional to Roth IRAs), these more complex situations may require exclusion-ratio calculations. Even if the individual continues to work past age 70½, deductible contributions to a conventional IRA may not be made after this date (and, in fact, withdrawals must begin–even if the individual is still working), but Roth contributions can be made at any age.

In most circumstances, withdrawals are considered premature and subject to a penalty of 10% of the premature withdrawal amount that is includable as ordinary income, if the withdrawal occurs before the account owner reaches age 59½ or becomes disabled. However, penalty-free withdrawals are permitted if the money is withdrawn in a lifetime stream of payments. Penalty-free withdrawals are also permitted:

- In a lifetime amount up to $10,000 for a first-time home buyer's expenses of acquiring or fixing up a home (technically speaking, it is possible to be a first-time home buyer more than once, as long as the individual has had no ownership in a principal residence during the two-year period ending on the date of the home purchase; IRA funds can also be used penalty-free to assist a close family member who is a first-time home buyer), and

• For the account owner's higher education expenses, or such expenses of a spouse, child, or grandchild.

A July, 2005 Tax Court decision involved a taxpayer who, before she reached 59½, took two IRA distributions. Some of the money was used to pay down credit card debt incurred to pay her tuition bill for the previous year. The penalty for premature distributions (but not ordinary income tax) is waived when funds are used to pay for higher education (for the taxpayer, the taxpayer's spouse, children, or grandchildren), but the distributions are penalty-free only if they do not exceed the education costs for the taxable year of the distribution. Therefore, the taxpayer was subject to the penalty for money used to pay the prior year's expenses. The same is true if the taxpayer takes out an education loan in one year and uses IRA funds to repay it in a later year.[9]

Although removing excessively large amounts from a conventional IRA does not carry a tax penalty (other than the obligation to pay income tax), FAILURE to withdraw enough is penalized, and so is failure to begin payments on the Required Beginning Date (RBD). The RBD is April 1 of the year after the year in which the account owner reaches age 70½. The minimum required distribution (MRD) is a function of the size of the account and the account owner's actuarially predictable life expectancy. If the actual amount withdrawn from the account in any year after the RBD is less than the MRD, a penalty is imposed equal to 50% of the difference between the MRD and the actual withdrawal, in addition to income tax on the actual withdrawal.

On January 17, 2001, the IRS published crucial regulations dealing with required minimum distributions from IRAs and qualified retirement plans. Because of these new rules, the calculation of the MRD is much simpler, and there is much greater simplicity and flexibility in estate planning. The revised rules make the calculations much easier by designating one simple, uniform table everyone can use to calculate the MRD during lifetime. The base calculation depends only on the owner's current age and the account balance as of the end of the prior year. (The IRA trustee reports the figure to the owner each year.)

The uniform distribution table (formerly known as the MDIB table) assumes a life expectancy or joint life expectancy of 26.2 years for account holders at age 70, 25.3 years at age 71, and so on; the table goes up to age 115, at which point a further

1.8 year life expectancy is assumed! Therefore, the minimum withdrawal for the year in which the account holder is 70 is 3.82% of the account, versus 3.95% for the year in which the account holder is 71, and so on, up to 50% at age 114 and 55.56% at 115 or older.

However, account owners who are married, designate their spouse as beneficiary, and whose spouse actually is more than 10 years younger can use old-law calculation using the spouse's actual life expectancy instead of the basic table to reduce the minimum distribution and accumulate more for inheritance.

The proposals include a new requirement that IRA trustees make an annual report of the MRD to the IRS as well as to the account owner, so it will be easier for the IRS to detect individuals who have failed to take the MRD and therefore are subject to the 50% excise penalty for failure to take the minimum distribution.

The tax picture for Roth IRAs is much simpler. There is no RBD or MRD during the account holder's lifetime. (MRD does apply upon the death of the account holder.) As long as the funds remain within the Roth IRA for at least five years, they can be withdrawn tax-free for qualified distributions (i.e., attainment of age 59½, on account of death or disability and qualified first-time home purchase). It's within the account holder's discretion to retain part or all of the balance within the account, for later consumption or for inheritance.

However, if funds are taken out of a Roth IRA, the question then becomes whether or not they qualify for tax-free status. IRC Section 408A(d)(4)(B) contains the "ordering rules" for analyzing the funds in a Roth account. The withdrawals are analyzed as if they come from non-rollover contributions first (i.e., the non-deductible contributions used to fund the Roth account in the first place), then from conversions from conventional IRAs (starting with taxable amounts), then non-taxable conversions, and finally from the appreciation in value of the Roth account. If there was more than one conversion of the same kind (taxable or non-taxable), the assumption is that the first one in is the first one out. All of the taxpayer's Roth IRAs, if he or she has more than one, are aggregated for this purpose.

IRAs in Bankruptcy

It has long been a principle of bankruptcy law that a debtor's interest in qualified retirement plans could not be reached by creditors before payments were made to the debtor. But the bankruptcy status of IRAs didn't really become clear until 2005.

In its 2005 *Rousey v. Jacoway* decision, the Supreme Court held that creditors cannot reach a bankrupt person's IRAs—these accounts have the same protected status as qualified plans, Social Security benefits, and 401(k) plans. The Supreme Court didn't say whether there was any limit on the size of the IRA that could be protected. At that time, the Bankruptcy Code referred to protection of assets reasonably necessary to the support of the debtor and his dependents, which might call for limits. The status of rollovers was also left unclear by the Supreme Court decision.[10]

Shortly after this decision, Congress passed the Bankruptcy Abuse Prevention and Consumer Protection Act of 2005 (BAPCA; P.L. 109-8, signed April 20, 2005). Under BAPCA § 224(a), both conventional and Roth IRAs, as well as qualified plans, government plans, tax-sheltered annuities, and church plans are excluded from the bankruptcy estate. The exclusion from the bankruptcy estate for conventional and Roth IRAs is limited to $1 million (an amount that will be adjusted for inflation), but the cap can be lifted in the interests of justice. The $1 million cap applies whether or not the debtor has chosen state rather than the federal bankruptcy exemptions, or the size of the state exemptions.

CONVERSIONS, ROLLOVERS AND CONDUIT IRAs

The simplest case is that a person just establishes a conventional IRA account, makes contributions to it throughout his or her working life, and then waits until withdrawals can be made without penalty and is careful to take at least the required minimum amount each year. But there are various other ways that IRAs can be used. For example, a person who changes jobs and receives a distribution from a defined contribution plan would have to include the entire distribution in taxable income for the year—unless he or she rolls over the funds into an IRA or to another qualified plan.

Individuals and married taxpayers filing jointly with AGI under $100,000 can transfer (convert) funds from a conventional to a Roth IRA, at which point the account is subject to the Roth rules. Funds that are converted are treated as taxable income for the year of the conversion. There was a special rule for conversions which occurred in 1998–individuals could spread out the tax on the conversion over a four-year period. Congress did not make the rule available for later years.[11]

A conduit IRA is used to provide relief from the basic rule that all pension funds are taxable in the year of receipt. The general rule could create a serious problem for a person who changes jobs but is not yet eligible to participate in the new job's pension plan (and therefore cannot have the vested pension benefits from the first job rolled over to the second job's plan). The pension funds could be placed into a conduit IRA, then rolled over into the second qualified plan. There is no income tax as long as the individual never receives the funds directly (they are always in the hands of a trustee or custodian)–or even if he or she does receive the funds, but deposits them with a trustee in 60 days or less, and the conduit IRA did not receive any other contributions nor issued any distributions prior to being rolled into the second job's plan. However, if the individual receives the funds to be deposited into a conduit IRA, there is a mandatory 20% withholding on the amount distributed which must be replaced by the individual within 60 days in order to avoid the IRS having deemed the withheld amount to be a distribution.

EGTRRA 2001 makes it somewhat easier to move funds between accounts without using a conduit IRA; however, a conduit IRA must still be used if the individual wants to preserve capital gains and special averaging treatment for the distribution from the pension plan. The new rollover rules are highly technical and tax counsel should be consulted before making such a move.

ESTATE PLANNING WITH IRAs

For many years, IRA estate planning was a contradiction in terms. The tax laws were drafted to make it likely that the account would be depleted or greatly reduced in size during the owner's lifetime. However, Congress has gradually accepted the validity of using the IRA, especially the Roth IRA, as a planning device. Clients making an elder plan should decide what their objective is for their IRA: do they plan to use it during life ("consumption objective") or save it to become part of the estate transmitted to the spouse and other heirs ("estate planning objective")? Of course, it may be impossible to maintain a pure estate planning objective if, for instance, health expenditures become very heavy.

A person with a consumption objective has little planning to do. Each year, he or she simply decides how much to withdraw, bearing in mind that withdrawals from a conventional IRA will be generally taxed as ordinary income, and making sure that the account (in conjunction with other sources of income and assets) will not be depleted during his or her lifetime.

The estate planning objective takes more work. But, if EGTRRA 2001 stays in place, it may greatly reduce the number of estates that will be subject to federal taxation (see Chapter 13), so more clients may simply ignore federal estate tax planning as an objective, and concentrate on purely financial and health planning objectives. The older client should assess whether any funds should be moved from a conventional to a Roth IRA, bearing the tax consequences in mind. For funds remaining in the conventional IRA, the client should take only the MRD each year.

January, 2001 Rules

The IRS Proposed Regulations that were published in January, 2001 eliminate many of the cumbersome, hard-to-use estate planning rules of prior law. Under the proposal, an IRA beneficiary doesn't have to be designated before the account holder's RBD. In fact, the beneficiary can be designated as late as the end of the year after the year in which the account holder dies, so the executor can do post-mortem estate planning. If it is advisable for the overall estate plan, the beneficiary can make a disclaimer of the IRA account (which was not an option under prior law).

The earlier rules had separate, complex schemes for determining the period over which the account balance had to be distributed after the account holder's death. The old rules depended on whether the beneficiary was a spouse, a non-spouse individual, or an entity such as a charity or trust.

Now there is a much simpler scheme, based on distributing the account over the life expectancy of the designated beneficiary (or the oldest beneficiary, if more than one is designated). (If no beneficiary is designated by the end of the year after the year of the account holder's death, distribution is required over the life expectancy of the account holder, calculated using the uniform distribution tables as of the date of his or her death.)

The net result is that in nearly all cases, beneficiaries will be able to take smaller distributions than under the old rules and, therefore, will have less income tax to pay. (Of course, if they want more cash and are willing to pay the income taxes, they can take distributions greater than the minimum.)

The surviving spouse is permitted to treat an inherited IRA as his or her own IRA and have himself or herself named as the owner rather than the beneficiary of the inherited account. However, under the new rules, this election can be made only after the MRD has been made for the year of the account holder's death. Furthermore, the election is permitted only if the surviving spouse is the sole beneficiary of the account and has an unlimited right of withdrawal. But if a trust is named as the beneficiary of the account (and even if the surviving spouse is the sole beneficiary of the trust) the surviving spouse will not be allowed to redesignate ownership of the account. Another option is to roll over the inherited IRA funds into an IRA owned by the surviving spouse.

Although a spouse can roll over the inherited IRA into his or her own IRA, other beneficiaries are not allowed to do this: they must make a trustee-to-trustee transfer instead of a rollover. A spouse can roll over an inherited IRA into his or her own IRA, but other beneficiaries are not allowed to do this. A beneficiary other than a spouse must make a trustee-to-trustee transfer.

If an IRA holder dies without naming a beneficiary, or if the beneficiary has died first, then the account becomes part of the probate estate. If the owner died before the Required Beginning Date, the heirs must withdraw all the money over only five years (as opposed to being able to withdraw it over their lifetimes, if the owner died after the RBD). But charities are not taxed on IRAs left to them.

Inherited Roth IRAs

When the named beneficiary inherits a Roth IRA, he or she will be able to withdraw earnings from the account free of income tax only if the funds have spent the necessary five years in the account. This is true even if the original owner died before the five years have elapsed. However, the heir is entitled to take advantage of any part of the five-year period that passed while the original owner was still alive.[12]

There is an additional tax benefit if the designated beneficiary is the account holder's surviving spouse. The surviving spouse can choose to treat the inherited Roth IRA as his or her own account, and then the five-year period during which funds must remain in the account to be withdrawn tax-free ends on the fifth anniversary for the decedent's IRA or the spouse's own Roth IRA—whichever comes first.

Tax and estate planning expert Noel C. Ice points out that IRC Section 408A doesn't say in so many words that a spouse who inherits a conventional IRA can convert it to a Roth IRA, but it should be possible to do so (if necessary, by rolling over the funds to a conventional IRA, then to the Roth, or by treating the IRA as the survivor's own account). However, the surviving spouse is the only person allowed to roll over an inherited IRA, so a son, daughter, or other relative or friend who inherits an IRA would not be able to do this.

MULTIPLE IRAs

In some instances, a person will have two or more IRAs: perhaps several conventional IRAs with different investment styles; or, after 1997, both conventional and Roth IRAs. The owner of multiple IRAs subject to MRD requirements can take the full MRD from one of the accounts, leaving the others intact, or allocate the MRD among accounts in any desired proportion. On the practical level, it makes sense to withdraw from the IRA that has the worst investment performance, while keeping better-performing accounts intact. However, for this purpose, conventional IRAs can only be aggregated with other conventional IRAs and the same with Roth IRAs.

Roth Conversions and Reconversions

Obviously, it was impossible to use Roth IRAs before they were authorized by the Taxpayer Relief Act of 1997. Thus, taxpayers now face another choice: taking funds out of a conventional deductible IRA and placing them in a Roth. All funds transferred from a conventional to a Roth IRA are deemed taxable income to the account holder, and all such income is taxed in the year of the conversion. (There was a special transition rule, for 1998 only, permitting taxation over a four-year period, but Congress declined to extend the rule.)

Furthermore, taxpayers with AGI over $100,000 (single filers and married filers filing a joint return) are not allowed to convert conventional IRA funds to Roth funds. (Married taxpayers filing separate returns are not allowed to convert a traditional IRA to a Roth IRA.) However, a person frustrated by this provision may have some control over his or her income for the year of the desired conversion.[13]

He or she might switch some investments into low-paying growth stocks, for instance; it might be possible to arrange for payments to be made in installments instead of as a lump sum in the year of conversion. This could also be a factor in deciding whether or not to take a lump-sum pension payout. It could also be a good time to weed losers out of the portfolio, thus generating tax losses that reduce taxable income. However, it could be an argument against profit-taking if high appreciation could foreclose a Roth conversion. An older person who wants to start a small business or consulting practice after retiring from a corporate post might purchase business equipment in the year of the desired conversion. And claim the equipment as a business deduction (up to the tax code' limits).

In August 2005, the IRS published Temporary Regulations (effective August 19, 2005) under IRC § 408A, detailing the tax consequences of conversion. The IRS allows three conversion methods: rollover, account redesignation, and transfer from one trustee to another. The IRS also closed some loopholes, to prevent investors from buying single premium annuities with so-called penalty requirements (that are unlikely to be invoked) that are used to reduce the cash surrender value in the early years, so that an artificially low value can be assigned when the annuity is converted to a Roth IRA.

Under the new rules, the "value" of an IRA converted to Roth form is the fair market value of the annuity, not the cash surrender value assigned to it by the issuer. The FMV would be the purchase price if the annuity was recently purchased. For older annuities with no more premiums due, the value is the price at which the issuer would sell a comparable contract. Contracts with premiums due in the future are valued based on the interpolated terminal reserve plus part of the last premium.[14]

The IRS offered additional guidance in Rev. Proc. 2006-13, 2006-3 I.R.B. 315, providing a safe harbor method that can be used to determine the fair market value of an annuity contract in order to calculate the amount that must be included in gross income as a result of a Roth IRA conversion. The safe harbor is used to determine the value of an annuity contract that has not yet been annuitized when the contract is distributed from a conventional IRA to a Roth IRA as part of a conversion. The annuity's value is the amount credited to the employee's account, plus the actuarial present value of additional benefits (e.g., survivor benefits) that accompany the annuity. The account value must include all front-end loads and other charges imposed in the 12 months before the conversion, and the actuarial present value of additional benefits does not include future distributions.[15]

In 1998, the first year in which conversion was permitted, about $39.3 billion in conventional IRA funds were moved to Roth IRAs. (There was a one-time tax break, since expired, under which the tax liability for the conversion could be stretched out over four years.) In 2005 and later years, taxpayers who are 70 ½ and therefore required to take MRDs from conventional IRAs will still have to pay income tax on their MRDs but will not have to include that income in the calculation of whether or not they are eligible for a Roth IRA conversion. (Remember, only persons with modified Adjusted Gross Income—not counting the amount converted—under $100,000 are allowed to make conversions.)[16]

Converting funds from a conventional to a Roth IRA means the taxpayer will not be required to take MRDs in the future, so more money can continue to grow tax-free. An account owner who thinks that tax rates will go up in the future might want to make a Roth conversion now and pay taxes at lower rates. This could also be a rationale if the plan is to leave the Roth IRA to high-bracket heirs. However, if the taxpayer is in a high bracket and the heirs are expected to be in a low bracket (or the taxpayer thinks tax rates will continue to decline) the Roth conversion increases the overall family tax burden.[17]

Separately Managed Accounts (SMAs) are individual accounts funded with stocks or bonds chosen by a money manager, tailored to a particular investor's needs. In mid-2004, the *Wall Street Journal* reported that they were a popular vehicle for IRA rollovers. The accounts are somewhat more costly for investors than mutual funds, but provide better accommodation to the investor's particular tax situation. The Financial Research Corporation estimates that by 2008, more than $50 billion a year in IRA rollovers will be invested in SMAs. (At the end of 2003, SMAs held $500 billion in assets, 45% in IRA accounts.) SMAs are not for everyone; the minimum for some accounts is $50,000, and some require $100,000.[18]

Theoretically, Roth conversions can only be made from conventional IRAs, not from qualified plans, but in practical terms, funds can be rolled over from a qualified plan to a conventional IRA and then converted to a Roth (minus any required MRDs to be made during the year of the conversion). Remember that rolling over funds from a qualified plan to a conventional IRA defers taxation; taxes are due on the amount converted at the time of the conversion to a Roth IRA.

As a general rule, if a taxpayer who has not yet reached age 59½ (the minimum age at which all IRA withdrawals are generally free from the premature withdrawal penalty) shifts funds from a conventional to a Roth IRA, the premature withdrawal penalty will not be imposed on the conversion.

The taxpayers may then decide that the conversion was imprudent, and recharacterize (i.e., roll some funds back into a conventional IRA). Recharacterization triggers certain tax issues. Because of stock market conditions, some account holders had a motive to recharacterize in 2001 to avert tax problems that could ensue from a conversion in 2000.[19] That's because the bull market peaked in 2000, then declined precipitously. However, taxation on a conventional-to-Roth conversion is based on the value of the account at the time of the conversion.

Let's say that 63-year-old Ellen Kaplan converted a $75,000 IRA to a Roth account in 2006. That would give her additional taxable income of $75,000–but let's also assume that the account's value fell to only $50,000 by early 2007. If she wants to avoid the double-whammy of a big tax bill and a fallen account value, she can file Form 8606 and recharacterize the IRA as a conventional rather than a Roth account. (Recharacterization might also be necessary if Ms. Kaplan's 2006 AGI was to high for a conversion.)

However, only one conversion and one recharacterization is permitted per year. Even in a situation that straddles two years (e.g., conversion in October, recharacterization in December, desired second conversion in January), remember that funds must remain within the conventional IRA for at least 30 days before a second valid Roth conversion can be performed in the subsequent year.

The mathematics of deciding whether to convert conventional to Roth accounts (or how much of the accumulated IRA balance should be converted) are quite sophisticated, and involve some scenarios that are beyond the scope of this book, such as projections of the client's future lifestyle and income tax rate.

Note that a person who converts funds from conventional to Roth accounts, but who continues to make Roth contributions, should segregate the converted funds into a separate account. The separate account should be left untouched for at least five years; distributions during such period are subject to the premature withdrawal penalty (even though such distributions may not be includable in income).

IRA INVESTMENT CHOICES

One effect of EGTRRA 2001 is to allow taxpayers to make larger IRA contributions, and some mid-life and older taxpayers to make extra "catch-up" contributions
to IRAs. The larger the amount invested, the harder it can be to make valid investment choices–especially in an unhappy investment climate.

There are arguments both pro and con as to whether already tax-exempt
investments should be included in tax-deferred retirement accounts. If they're the
best bottom-line values, they should be included; otherwise, their counterparts that
would be taxable outside the retirement context are preferable. If you have separate
growth and income-oriented investments and are satisfied with the performance of
each, it might make sense to put the income-oriented investments into tax-deferred
retirement accounts, while retaining the low-income growth investments outside
the IRA accounts. This is because investment income goes "on top" of the taxpayer's
other income, and is taxed at his or her highest marginal rate.

Wall Street Journal writer Vanessa O'Connell raises another issue: the "tax bomb"
mutual fund that trades stocks both frequently and successfully. The "successful" part
is great, but the downside is investors' exposure to large capital gains distributions
from the fund. In a taxable account, this could be annoying, but the problem doesn't
arise in a tax-free account. She also points out that a low-load or low-fee account is
much more important in an IRA than in an ordinary investment account, because
fees take a heavier toll on an IRA (where the maximum contribution is limited)
than an investment account (where the impact of the fees is spread out over annual
investments that may be much greater than the IRA contribution).[20]

In 2005 and 2006, the financial service industry added new options for IRA
account holders, such as cash management features allowing withdrawals from the
IRA account by check, debit card, or by directing electronic bill payment from the
account, as an alternative to taking scheduled distributions (e.g., $1,000 a month)
and depositing the funds in a checking account. Some commentators were concerned
that by making access so easy, the changes would place account holders at risk of
depleting the account for trivial purchases, and running out of money.[21]

It is not illegal for IRAs to invest in real estate, but so far that is not a popular
choice. About 2% of IRA funds are invested in real estate, in self-directed accounts
that are managed by the account owner and held by a custodian. That amount
doubled between 2003 and 2005. Managing a real estate portfolio while complying with IRA restrictions is difficult. IRA-owned real estate cannot be used as the
account owner's primary residence, business location, or vacation home. Property
purchased from a close relative cannot be placed into a Roth IRA. IRAs can invest

in single-family homes, apartment and office buildings, hotels, shopping centers, raw land, and tax lien certificates.

Another problem is that the account must generate enough income to meet the expenses of property ownership (which involves both the size of the account and the liquidity of its investments)—and must have been large enough in the first place to purchase property! It's permissible for IRAs to be pooled into partnerships to increase the amount available for investment.[22]

A "self-directed IRA" allows the owner to tailor the IRA's retirement portfolio instead of relying on professionally managed investment modes such as mutual funds. The Internal Revenue Code forbids IRA investments in life insurance and collectables, but otherwise leaves open tremendous leeway—which could be enough rope for inexperienced investors to hang themselves with! Some transactions would constitute forbidden "self-dealing" (making a profit on the account before withdrawals are permitted), which could result in the IRS disqualifying the account and imposing heavy penalties. The Department of Labor has a procedure for getting advance approval of transactions that might be controversial. Another problem is that, unlike conventional investments whose value can easily be determined at any time, a self-directed IRA's value might be hard to assess—making it hard to determine what the MRD would be. So that could mean a costly annual appraisal to keep the valuation current.[23]

If the individual does not have enough money to take full advantage of all the tax-deferred investment options available (i.e., conventional and Roth IRAs; annuities; and a work-related 401(k) plan), it then becomes necessary to balance the advantages of each and select one or make an allocation among them. Although EGTRRA 2001 includes taxpayer-friendly IRA provisions, it also does a great deal to make the 401(k) plan an important part of planning for persons entitled to participate in these plans as employees. For many people, the best strategy will be to defer at least part of the salary in a 401(k) plan (although many people will not be able to afford the maximum deferral), perhaps in conjunction with maintaining a conventional and/or Roth IRA.[24]

IRA MISTAKES, AND HOW TO AVOID THEM

Experts have identified many common mistakes that IRA investors make, especially when it comes to some of the complex tax and estate planning issues that IRAs can create.

- In 2004, the IRS added a new requirement that institutions holding IRAs make a report each year—to account owners and the IRS—whether a withdrawal is required.

- When an account owner retires, leaves a job where he or she was covered by a defined contribution plan, or moves an IRA to a new institution, there is a 60-day deadline for moving the money to another tax-deferred account. Failure to miss the deadline means income tax liability on the entire amount—so it's important to check back to make sure that the transfers were made as ordered.

- The IRS has an automatic waiver provision to help taxpayers who made a proper direction but the former employer, bank, or other institution failed to comply with transfer instructions.

- To prevent problems, be sure to comply with the paperwork requirements of the employer's plan or the financial institution holding the IRA, so rollovers and inheritances won't be blocked because of noncompliance with these rules.

- Clients should know what the MRD is for each year, and be sure to take at least that much from the account!

- Persons over 70½ should take their MRDs before making a rollover, because MRDs cannot be rolled over. There's also a risk that both custodians—from the transferor and transferee plans—will report the withdrawal of the MRD so the older person might have to explain why taxes were paid only once with respect to what seems to be two withdrawals.

- Not only must there be a valid beneficiary designation (updated if, for example, the original heir dies or becomes incapacitated, or if it is rendered obsolete by a divorce), the executor or administrator of the estate must be able to find it!

- The heirs of an IRA should be informed about their potential inheritance and its financial and tax consequences, and what practical steps should be taken to make withdrawals and save tax.

- Although it is perfectly possible to inherit a Roth IRA (and in fact a lot of estate plans rely on this), the heirs of a conventional IRA cannot convert these amounts to their own Roth IRA. A spouse can roll over an inherited IRA to his or her own IRA, but a non-spouse heir cannot do this. Nor can several inherited IRAs be combined into a single account. However, since 2001, the IRA rules have permitted heirs to stretch out IRA withdrawals over their own life expectancies instead of cashing out within five years. The inherited IRA must be retitled to show that the original owner has died and the account is now owned by the heir. RMDs are required from inherited IRAs on the same terms as IRAs containing savings from the owner's working life. If there are several heirs (e.g., a person leaves the account to his or her children) then the account can be divided with each heir making withdrawals calculated based on his or her own age and life expectancy. If the account is not divided, the withdrawal schedule is based on the life expectancy of the oldest heir.

- Beneficiaries who are named in the account owner's will, but not in the IRA beneficiary designation, can inherit the account, but will not be allowed to stretch out distributions unless they are designated.

- These rules just explain the tax consequences; there is no requirement that institutions draft their custodial agreements to allow heirs to transfer their interests or stretch out distributions.

- For amounts over $1.5 million left to a grandchild or relative of the grandchild's generation, consult a tax professional about Generation Skipping Tax (GST).[25]

CHAPTER ENDNOTES

1. Fred Schneyer, "FDIC to Cover up to $250K in Retirement Accounts," http://www.plansponsor.com/pi_type10_print.jsp?RECORD_ID=32732 (March 14, 2006). The FDIC's distribution draft of the regulation was posted at http://www.fdic.gov/news/board/06march14reformreg.pdf.

2. The ins and outs of IRA contributions are primarily an issue for working-age clients and therefore outside the scope of this book; for details, see IRS Publication 590, http://www.irs.gov/publications, p590.

3. IRS Notice 2002-27, 2002-18 IRB 814.

4. See Ellen E. Schultz, "Tax Advantages of Roth IRAs Top Annuities," *Wall Street Journal*, October 16, 1997, p. C1.

5. Gary Schatsky, "A Roth IRA Isn't a One-Size-Fits-All Investment," http://www.benefitslink.com/articles/feeds/983479342.shtml (February 26, 2001).

6. See P.L. 107-22 (7/26/2001).

7. Fundamentals (Investment Company Institute Research in Brief) Vol. 14 #4 (August 2005) http://www.ici.org [fm-v14n4.pdf?; Kelly Greene, "How Retirees Are Blowing Their Nest Eggs," *Wall Street Journal*, June 27, 2005, p. R1; Craig Copeland, "401(k)-Type Plan and IRA Ownership," EBRI Notes Volume 26 #1 (Jan 2005), http://www.ebri.org/publications/notes/index.cfm?fa=notesDisp&content_id=3230; SmartPros Editorial Staff, "IRS Income Stats Reveal IRAs for First Time," http://www.smartpros.com/x44568.xml (August 2, 2004).

8. "Insurers Maintain IRA Share," NU Online News Service, January 20, 2006.

9. The case is *Lodder-Beckert*, discussed in Tom Herman, "Tax Report," *Wall Street Journal*, July 20, 2005, p. D3.

10. Christopher Conkey and Rachel Emma Silverman, "High Court Rules IRAs Untouchable," *Wall Street Journal*, April 5, 2005, p. D1.

11. The IRS Restructuring and Reform Act of 1998 provides that the 10% penalty on early withdraw-als from an IRA is also imposed on amounts converted from a conventional to a Roth IRA, then withdrawn in less than five years. If the person who made the conversion dies before the four years elapse, and the beneficiary of the Roth IRA is not the surviving spouse, the amounts not yet recognized in income must be included on the final income tax return for the deceased account holder. See Sidney Kess, "Technical Corrections Bill for Taxpayer Relief," *New York Law Journal*, October 20, 1997, p. 3 and Bryan Schmitt, "New Rules Clarify Roth IRA Choices," *Best's Review* Life/Health Edition (October, 1998), p. 89.

12. Reg. § 1.408A-6, Q&A 7.

13. Such strategies are discussed in Karen Hube and Bridget O'Brien, "Roth IRAs Prompt the Wealthy to 'Earn' Less," *Wall Street Journal*, October 30, 1998, p. C1.

14. Treasury Decision TD 9220, RIN 1545-BE66, "Converting an IRA Annuity to a Roth IRA," 70 *Federal Register* 48868 (August 22, 2005).

15. See Allison Bell, "Feds Offer Valuation Relief," NU Online News Service, December 29, 2005.

16. Jane J. Kim, "Making Roth IRAs More Attractive," *Wall Street Journal*, June 1, 2004, p. D2.

17. Karen Damato, "Some Older Investors May Find Roth IRAs More Attractive," *Wall Street Journal*, January 4, 2005, p. C1.

18. Tara Siegel Bernard, "SMAs Gain Favor for IRA Rollovers," *Wall Street Journal*, August 31, 2004, p. D9.

19. This strategy is discussed in Jan M. Rosen, "How a Costly Conversion Can Be Undone," *New York Times*, February 18, 2001, p. Bus16.

20. Vanessa O'Connell, "Strategies to Try During Roth IRA Rush," *Wall Street Journal*, February 26, 1998, p. C1.

21. Jeff D. Opdyke, "Retirees Get More Ways to Tap IRAs," *Wall Street Journal*, January 10, 2006, p. D2.

22. Vivian Marino, "Using an IRA to Buy Real Estate," *New York Times*, April 17, 2005, p. RE11.

23. Kelly Greene, "You Did *What* With an IRA?," *Wall Street Journal*, October 15-16, 2005, p. B1.

24. See Virginia Munger Kahn, "Roth I.R.A.'s Giving 401(k)'s a Run for the (Retirement) Money," *New York Times*, March 1, 1998, p. Bus21.

25. Kelly Greene, "How Retirees Are Blowing Their Nest Eggs," *Wall Street Journal*, June 27, 2005, p. R1; Kelly B. Spors, "Heir Alert," *Wall Street Journal*, March 28, 2005, p. R6.

Chapter 11

Special Portfolio Issues for the Older Investor

Investment planning is crucial to retirement and post-retirement planning for many reasons. In general, Social Security benefits (even if they continue to be paid as scheduled) are a fairly minor factor in post-retirement security for most people. Once a person retires and chooses an option for payment of quali- fied plan benefits, there is not much the person can do to change or control the adequacy or inadequacy of the pension income. But, as long as the person retains contractual capacity and is interested in doing so, he can respond to market trends and changes in personal needs and preferences by changing his investments. This chapter deals with general investment issues for the senior citizen. Chapter 12 focuses on annuities, a complex type of investment that can perform many func- tions in the elder plan.

Traditional thinking calls for a shift from growth-oriented assets (with con- comitant risk) to income-producing assets for older investors. One simple rule of thumb is to decrease the proportion of equities in the portfolio and increase the proportion of bonds and other income instruments every five or 10 years. The shift from growth to income is, by and large, a sound strategy, but it is not the complete answer. Remember, it is very likely that a person who retires at 65 will still be alive 20 years later, and it is not at all impossible that he or she will be alive *30* years later. This is a fairly long-range planning horizon, and a growth component is important.[1]

Traditional thinking also assumes that having more income is better than having less. Yet, if the older person is a current or potential Medicaid beneficiary, having less income is better because it decreases the spend-down obligation. (See Chapter 6.) Even if Medicaid is not a factor, the older person may be unable to handle funds prudently because of medical or psychiatric factors. Having a small income that one can handle as one likes can be important to self-esteem, whereas having a large income can be counterproductive. Much of this chapter is concerned with the advantages of annuity investments for middle-aged and older investors.

In the 1980's, retirees with fixed incomes often suffered as inflation ran rampant. Inflation is one of the factors that triggered the transition from defined benefit to defined contribution plans. Defined contribution plans are more market-sensitive than defined benefit plans, so they offer the potential for increasing income during periods of high inflation (which is often identified with a booming stock market).

Net borrowers such as businesses tend to prefer low interest rates, but retirees and other net savers can benefit from high interest rates. For example, if the Federal Reserve raises its rate by ¼ of a percentage point, that means an additional $14 billion a year for investors. At the end of the first quarter of 2004, U.S. households and nonprofit organizations had a total of $4.5 trillion invested in certificates of deposit (CDs), money market funds, and savings and checking accounts—5.6% more than in 2003, and 26% more than in 2000 (according to the Federal Reserve). But in 2004, households and non-profits had holdings of individual stocks (rather than mutual funds) of $5.83 trillion—24% *below* the 2000 figure.[2]

It is hard to think of the decade of disco music and Qiana shirts as a golden era, but it did have one characteristic that is a legitimate source of nostalgia. Risk-averse investors could earn double-digit returns on safe money market funds and certificates of deposit (CDs). Today, the returns from comparably safe investments are relatively small. By the late 1990's, retirees were in a paradoxical situation: inflation risk was low, but investment risk was fairly high.

Some older investors missed a lot of the immense appreciation that occurred in the extreme bull market of the late 1990s because they did not invest in the riskier technology and other New Economy stocks, and chose not to (or did not have access to) IPO investments. The advantage is that they also avoided the worst of the crash in 2001, when many stocks lost 90% or more of their value.

Unfortunately, however, even older investors who followed admirable habits of prudence (e.g., investing in only what they knew and understood) and diversification are at risk of being adversely affected by overall market conditions, depressed prices and earnings for mutual funds, and restricted choices in retirement timing (if retirement at the desired time would mean an unfeasibly small pension). It was not just the high-flying tech stocks that declined in the crash – even major blue chip companies lost a lot of stock value. Many corporate bonds also declined in value.

According to a recent Fidelity Viewpoint article, between 1926 and 2003 stocks generated a much higher return than bonds in their best years, and there were five periods of returns over 40%. However, stocks also fell at least 20% in each of the worst years. In contrast, bonds did not score gains as large in the best years—but didn't fall as far in the worst. Between 1926 and 2003, there were 23 years in which the stock market had negative returns; in 21 of those years, bonds had a positive return.[3]

Even among households whose net worth (not including the principal residence) was over $1 million, half or more say they are still progressing toward, but have not achieved, their financial goals. Long-term care insurance is the only product or service that 5% or more of households intend to purchase in the future; but even a 3% penetration represents 185,000 high net worth households (5% is over 300,000 households).[4]

A recent AARP survey of stockholders aged 50-70 showed that 77% had lost money in stocks. Among those who were still working, 20% said their portfolio losses had caused them to postpone retirement. One-third of retirees who had lost money in the stock market had gone back to work full-time or part-time.[5]

DIRECTIONS FOR THE OLDER INVESTOR

Although each client (of any age) must be approached as an individual, there are some patterns that are characteristic of senior citizen investors:

- They are usually intolerant of risk, which is only logical since they do not have much time to make up for mistakes, and they rely on portfolio income for a substantial part of their living and health care expenses.

- They tend to be income-oriented, rather than growth-oriented.

- They are very interested in accumulating an estate, and also extremely interested in avoiding federal estate tax liability.

A good planner will help clients assemble a portfolio that meets their needs for lifetime and estate objectives at a tolerable level of risk, and make sure they understand that stock prices do not inevitably go up.

Interestingly, it may be necessary to steer male and female clients in different directions. In many instances, older male investors may be too willing to undertake unnecessary risks. Alternatively, older female investors may be too risk-intolerant, loading up their portfolios with fixed-income investments that fall behind inflation, thus depriving themselves of critically needed growth that would promote real financial security.[6]

A good planner will also help clients avoid some of the scams that plague all investors, but particularly older investors – whether the con artists operate in cyber-space or in the real world. Elders who are afraid their money will run out (whether or not this fear is well-grounded) are easy prey for get-rich-quick schemes. Lonely, isolated senior citizens are vulnerable to financial elder abuse committed by people who seem to be their friends and appear to genuinely care about them.

According to the Investment Company Institute about 75% of the money invested by individuals in mutual funds (other than employer-sponsored plans) is invested through advisors, often at a cost of 1% of the assets each year. Fifty-five percent of mutual funds are purchased through stockbrokers and other advisors; 5% from fund supermarkets, 16% in retirement plans, 13% institutional accounts, and 12% purchased directly from the fund itself.[7]

A poll by Merrill Lynch Investment Managers shows that both men and women made common investment mistakes (e.g., not balancing the portfolio; keeping losing investments too long). Women, however, reported making fewer mistakes (e.g., investing in a hot stock without doing research; hanging on to losers; making investments without considering tax consequences), and repeated them less often. The survey looked at people who had annual household income and investable as-sets over $75,000. Half of the men, and 70% of the women, had a primary financial advisor. Sixty-two percent of the men and 77% of women had a formal financial plan. Perhaps women were better at learning from their mistakes because they had professional advice.[8]

Two Notre Dame finance professors published a paper in mid-2005, concluding that as investors get older, they tend to adopt one good habit (greater diversification) but, in general, their decision-making powers tend to decline and their portfolio performance tends to get worse as they age. The professors studied a large group of self-directed brokerage accounts and found that the older investors tended to hold more stocks than younger investors, permitting greater diversification, and were less likely to make the common mistake of holding on to losing stocks and selling their most appreciated stocks too quickly. But their overall investment return tended to decline with age: their stock picks tended to fall further and further behind the market average as they got older. The researchers concluded that one effect of aging is reduction in mental flexibility—with respect to investments as well as in other ways—so the older the investor, the lower the investment returns he or she could be expected to earn. The professors' suggestion was that professional advice is especially important as investors age.[9]

Where They Stand

How do today's pre-retirees stack up against older generations? In some ways, the picture is more optimistic, because they have more financial assets, and decades of housing appreciation have given even modest family homes a large price tag. However, in 1983, more than two-thirds of households headed by a person aged 47-64 included someone earning a pension. This was true of less than half of these households in 2001, and current retirement benefits are much riskier for workers than the traditional defined benefit plans. In 1985, almost 115,000 companies had defined benefit plans, a number that fell to about 31,000 in 2003; and many of these plans were frozen, close to being frozen, or were closed to new employees.

Using constant dollars, economist Edward Wolff determined that between 1983 and 2001, the average net worth of older households increased 44% to $673,000, but much of the growth was limited to the richest households. For median households, wealth dropped 2.2%, to $199,900. So, despite close to two decades of a bull market, the average older household actually had somewhat less wealth in 2001 than in 1983.

In 1983, the total net worth of a typical older-worker household (headed by someone aged 47-64) was $204,400 (after debt of $40,500 had been subtracted): a $91,600 home, $4,600 in securities, $31,900 in cash and bank accounts, $3,200 in IRAs and 401(k) plans, $94,700 in accrued pension benefits, and $18,900 "other." In 2001, total net worth for such households had dropped to $199,900 with $43,600 in debt; the home was worth more, at $107,300; investment assets had risen to $11,300; cash and bank deposits had dropped to $21,900; IRAs and 401(k)s were much higher at $37,900; and other assets were about the same at $17,800. But accrued pensions had fallen to $47,400.[10]

So much for assets—what about income? The Employee Benefits Research Institute (EBRI) reported that, using constant 2003 dollars, the median income of the elderly population rose from $11,376 in 1974 to reach a peak of $15,007 in 1999, and then fell to $14,400 in 2003. (The median is the point at which half of the examples are above that level and half are below.)

Social Security was the main source of income for seniors in 2003, providing 41.9% of their income, with 20.6% coming from pensions and retirement plans, 13.9% income from assets, and 21.7% from work earnings. The picture was different for elderly women, who got 50.8% of their income from Social Security (elderly men got 35.5% of their income from this program). Social Security was also much more significant for poor people than for rich people: the highest income quintile of elderly people got 19.5% of their income there, whereas the lowest quintile got 91.2% of their income from Social Security.

In 2003, if we look at just the top 20% of income (because this is the group most likely to do financial planning), seniors with income of $30,000 a year or more looked to Social Security for 20% of their income. Pensions and annuities provided 25% of income, assets 19%, work earnings 34%, and other sources 2%.[11]

INVESTMENT CHOICES FOR THE OLDER INVESTOR

The components of the portfolio, the degree of risk in the portfolio, and the amount of time that can reasonably be spent monitoring the portfolio all depend on the client's preferences, capacity for risk, and the size of the amount under investment. The conventional wisdom is that risk and return move in tandem: the investor endures greater risk in the hope of securing greater return. This is sometimes known as a choice between "eating well" and "sleeping well." Portfolios are usually built based on a pyramid, starting with the safest options, then adding more diversification and risk once it is assured that the individual will have adequate income for lifetime needs, and the surviving spouse (if any) will be provided for.

Therefore, investments work in conjunction with other financial assets. The larger the income deriving from the individual's pension and Social Security, the less current investment income is required for daily needs, and the more likely that the individual can concentrate on growth and creating an estate. However, personal preferences may call for adding extra income for a more luxurious lifestyle, or there may be heavy costs associated with health and custodial needs.

Although the markets offer a baffling variety of investment options, most of them are unsuitable for senior citizen clients of low-to-moderate means. Wealthy and very affluent older clients should have a correspondingly larger planning team, including investment professionals—although it is important for someone (e.g., a family member or fiduciary) to keep an eye on the investment professionals, with respect to both integrity and performance.

Broadly speaking, investments are selected for (1) their growth potential (i.e., the belief that they can be sold at a higher price than they were purchased for), (2) their income potential (i.e., interest, dividends, or other payments made with respect to the investment), or (3) for both reasons.

For example, a person may purchase a coupon bond, intending to hold it to maturity (at which time the face value will be returned) while also receiving regular interest payments. However, the owner also has the option of selling the bond if the price of the bond has risen so much that selling it has become attractive, or the bondholder simply needs additional funds. Some investors like preferred stock because it combines the liquidity of common stock (i.e., the ability to be sold at any time) with the potential for price appreciation, and the opportunity for income in the form of dividends, which must be paid (at a fixed rate) before any dividends can be paid on the company's common stock.

The Baby Boomers are now headed from the end of the accumulation phase to the beginning of the distribution phase, so annuity products will probably take over from asset allocation and lifestyle funds as the leading product category. At the 2005 Financial Advisor Retirement Planning Symposium, popular panels included calculating retirement withdrawal rates and income investing in a low-rate environment.

Suggestions for finding income in a low-interest environment ranged from Real Estate Investment Trusts to short-term bond ladders to searching out non-mainstream fixed income investments. A debate over withdrawal rates arose between Bill Bengen (who pioneered the now-conventional suggestion of restricting withdrawals to 4%) and Jonathan Guyton (who says withdrawals of 5-6% are probably sustainable, although rising life expectancy poses problems).[12]

Most older investors will choose some combination of these reasonably safe, conventional investments:

- *Government Securities.* Perhaps the safest investments are direct federal government obligations, such as Treasury bonds and notes. (The security is a "note" if its maturity date is from one year to ten years; "bonds" have maturities in excess of ten years.[13]) These obligations are backed by the entire financial and taxing power of the United States government. Notably, there are many other kinds of securities issued by federal agencies that are not direct obligations of the federal government, including housing securities issued by the Government National Mortgage Association, the Federal National Mortgage Association, and the Federal Home Loan Mortgage Corporation. These securities are known as "Ginnie Maes," "Fannie Maes," and "Freddie Macs," respectively. Ginnie Maes are the safest of these securities because they are backed by the "full faith and credit" of the United States; the other two types merely have an implicit federal guarantee.

An important trend in mid-2005 was the stress on inflation-linked products, such as municipal bonds, corporate bonds, certificates of deposit, and inflation-indexed

Treasury securities. Some corporate bonds offer monthly income that moves with the Consumer Price Index. The coupon for the bond consists of two parts—a fixed base and a CPI adjustment. Inflation-indexed CDs have a similar two-part return; the first $250,000 of the CD is FDIC-insured.

The federal I-Bond (savings bond) is designed to be an inflation hedge for small investors. According to the Bureau of Public Debt, the earnings rate combines two separate rates: (1) a fixed rate of return, which remains the same throughout the life of the I-Bond; and (2) a variable semiannual inflation rate based on changes in the Consumer Price Index for all Urban Consumers (CPI-U). The Bureau of the Public Debt announces the rates each May and November. (The I-Bond's fixed rate was cut to 3.67% in November 2005.) The semiannual inflation rate announced in May is the change between the CPI-U figures from the preceding September and March; the inflation rate announced in November is the change between the CPI-U figures from the preceding March and September. Buyers who redeem the bond within five years of purchase must forfeit three months' interest.[14]

It's possible to invest in municipal bonds that are exempt from federal tax and inflation-adjusted, although they pay income only twice a year. The downside is that small investors pay higher premiums than institutions—and these products don't perform well if inflation remains under control, so they should be only a component (perhaps 10%) of the portfolio, not the whole portfolio.

For example, a current 10-year TIPS (i.e., inflation-protected Treasury) would only pay a yield of about 1.6% if there were no inflation, whereas the regular 10-year Treasury note pays about 4.2%.[15] When a TIPS bond matures, the investors receive the original investment, plus an additional sum representing an inflation adjustment. The inflation adjustment is taxed each year, even though the taxpayer does not receive the funds until the bond matures or is sold. TIPS are sold in increments of $1,000, and can be purchased directly from http://www.treasurydirect.gov.[16]

When TIPS were first introduced, they could only be purchased through the periodic Treasury auctions. In late 2005, the Treasury made it easier for individuals to buy securities of this type, as well as other Treasury investments, online. Purchases (including purchases of securities as gifts for others) and redemptions of Treasury securities can be done online at the Treasury Direct site.

To open an account, an investor must go to the secure area of the site and provide his phone number, Social Security number, driver's license number, and bank account routing information. Purchases will be directly debited from the designated bank account; redemptions and interest will be directly credited. There are no maintenance fees for the accounts, but a sales charge of $45 per security is imposed. (Of course, TIPS and other Treasury securities can be purchased from a broker, but that will entail a commission.)[17]

The interest rate calculation on Series EE savings bonds changed as of May 1, 2005. The bonds now have a fixed interest rate, which can be re-set every six months for new purchases. Previously, Series EE savings bonds had a floating rate that adjusted every six months equal to 90% of the average market yield of five-year Treasury securities.

PLANNING TIP: For the Savings Bond Calculator to keep track of U.S. Savings Bonds owned by a client, see http://www.publicdebt.treas.gov/sav/sav/htm. The site also contains Savings Bond Wizard software that can be downloaded to manage the savings bond portfolio.

- *Certificates of Deposit (CDs).* The investor deposits funds with a financial institution. The institution agrees to pay a stated rate of interest for the term of the deposit; usually, part of the interest will be withheld if withdrawals are made before the date of the certificate. In other words, a CD differs from a bank account because it is less liquid—and, to compensate the investor for the loss of liquidity, a higher interest rate is paid.

Usually, CDs have a short-to-medium term (e.g., three months to five years). However, in late 2000, the SEC became concerned about potentially abusive "callable" CDs—that is, long-term certificates (perhaps as much as 15 or even 30 years) whose issuers retain the right to retire the securities by repaying the principal. The issuer is likely to "call" a bond if interest rates drop, because the interest rates will be above the then-current market value. (This is true of callable bonds too—the time when the investors really want to keep the securities is exactly the time the issuer wants to call them.)

The SEC's concerns centered on CDs sold by brokers, rather than by banks and thrift institutions. In 1996-1999, for instance, the agency received only a handful of complaints from investors about CDs purchased from brokers. However, in 2000 there were about 300 complaints. By that time, broker-sold CDs had become a major industry with $168 billion in outstanding CDs. The problem with some broker-sold CD's is one of liquidity. For example, a senior citizen investor may not want to invest in anything with a 10-year term because he believes that he might not be around in 10 years. Furthermore, funds might be needed quickly (e.g., for nursing home placement after a stroke). The investor could lose as much as 30% of the face value of the CD by re-selling it in a hurry because there are not a lot of buyers in this thinly-traded market.[18]

• *Corporate and Municipal Bonds.* Bonds can be issued by government entities and agencies or by private-sector corporations. Municipal bonds ("munis") are issued by states, cities, municipalities, and their agencies. The safety of these bonds depends on the issuer's credit (i.e., whether it is good or bad). Traditionally, municipal bonds were a favorite choice of conservative older investors because of their tax-exempt status. However, not all municipal bond interest is free of tax consequences. Thus, it is important to ascertain this status in advance. Some municipal bonds are insured by third-party guarantors, but this guarantee means only as much as the financial soundness of the guaranteeing organization.

• *Coupon and "Zero-coupon" Bonds.* A conventional "coupon" bond makes regular (e.g., quarterly or semi-annual) payments of interest at a stated rate. However, a "zero-coupon" bond is sold at a deep discount (i.e., a reduction in price from face value), and does not make interest payments. Zero-coupon bonds work well for an individual who wants to make a small investment in order to get a larger amount at a scheduled future date. The downside is that zero-coupon bond prices fluctuate more than coupon bond prices. Thus, if an individual desires or needs to sell the bond before maturity, significant losses are possible. "Original issue discount" (OID) is a tax concept which means that the owner of the bond has to pay taxes each year on the interest that was not paid on the zero-coupon bond, but that was accrued (i.e., accumulated but not paid). See IRC Code Secs. 1272 and 1273. (However, OID on tax-exempt bonds is not taxed.) In effect, the owner of the bond has to pay federal income tax each year on the accrual (i.e., accumulation) even though he does not receive cash income from the bond.

• *Mutual Funds.* A mutual fund assembles a portfolio of stocks, bonds, and/or other securities, then sells shares in this portfolio to the public. One advantage of a mutual fund is that it provides diversification and professional management. Sometimes, however, professional managers do not produce returns that are higher than well-publicized measures of the combined performance of certain groups of stocks (i.e., indexes)—hence, the popularity of index funds that invest in all of the securities covered by a particular index (such as the Dow Jones Industrial Average or the Standard & Poor's 500) and, naturally, achieve the same results as the index.

There are a multitude of mutual funds in existence today. Some of them are identified by their objective: aggressive growth; high growth; growth; growth and income; balanced growth; high income; income; tax-exempt income. Others are identified by the sector in which they invest: technology stocks; health care stocks; international stocks; short-term bonds; etc.

In late 2004 and 2005, a number of mutual funds were launched to satisfy investors' interest in gaining a safe income stream. Some of the funds buy stocks that pay dividends; because these funds themselves are exchange-traded (their prices are quoted on a constantly updated basis, like shares of stock), they can pass along more dividend income to investors than conventional mutual funds (which often use dividends paid on their portfolios to pay fund fees; because the market-wide average dividend is 1.7% yield, fees can eat up much or all of that).

A variation on this theme is a fund that invests both in high-dividend stocks and in options to enhance income. Funds like this can be good supplements to, or substitutes for, bond funds (since bond funds provide income but usually don't provide the growth component that is important for retirees facing a planning horizon in the decades).[19]

Although "stable value mutual funds" that invested in high-quality bonds and used insurance contracts to protect net asset value against interest rate changes were popular with retirees, most of them were shut down in late 2004 after regulators challenged their methods of operation. Often, these funds were renamed or merged into other funds. However, the SEC does not regulate stable value funds that are part of an employer plan rather than being sold as retail mutual funds, and over $350 billion was invested in such funds in late 2004.[20]

- *Common and Preferred Stock.* Corporations issue various kinds of securities: common stock; preferred stock (which is "preferred" in the sense that it must pay dividends before the issuing company is allowed to pay dividends on its common stock); rights; warrants; and options. (Options are different ways to give someone the opportunity to speculate (or hedge) on price movements in the stock without actually purchasing the stock immediately).

- *Real Estate.* Most people have some degree of real estate investment in that they own a home. Many other kinds of real estate investments are possible, including: buying raw land and developing it, or holding it for sale to a developer; investing in commercial properties; buying real estate-oriented securities such as Ginnie Maes; investing in real estate limited partnerships; or investing in real estate investment trusts (REITs), or real estate mortgage investment conduits (REMICs). REITs and REMICs assemble portfolios of real property and mortgages, respectively—in effect, they resemble real estate mutual funds.

- *Precious Metals and Collectibles.* "Hard assets" include precious metals, artwork, and collectibles. These are not income-producing assets and, in fact, can cost money for conservation and security. The investor hopes to identify "bargains," then hold them for personal enjoyment with the ultimate goal of selling them at a profit. These are not very liquid investments. It is not always easy to find a buyer when one is wanted and sales are usually subject to high commissions (auction houses impose commissions on both buyers and sellers).

Very Small Investor

A client who has only one major asset (e.g., a home), receives only a pension and Social Security, and has a small amount of money saved does not need, and would not benefit by, a complex investment plan. A better strategy would be to invest some or all of the savings in a commercial annuity, a charitable annuity (if the individual is religiously or charitably minded), or an income- or growth-and-income-oriented mutual fund with a good track record and low expenses.

A new option that came on-stream in 2004 was the "personal pension" investment fund, which is designed to supplement or replace lost pension benefits. In effect, these are deferred annuity products, that call for annual deposits in return for a promise of post-retirement income (e.g.,$3,000 a year deposited by a 40-year-old in exchange for the promise of $10,200 a year from age 65 onward). Because these are long-range investments, the crucial factor to consider is the financial soundness of the insurer; and the impact of fees and surrender charges can be heavy on a small investment. These products can be either fixed or variable annuities (see Chapter 12 for further discussion).[21]

Small Investor

A client with somewhat larger savings may benefit from investing in several (say, two to five) mutual funds. It often makes sense to select all of the funds from the same mutual "fund family," as long as it:

- Has a good reputation and track record;

- Offers a wide variety of funds satisfying various objectives;

- Does not impose excessive fees, charges, and commissions; and

• Provides useful disclosure information in easy-to-understand form.

The small investor should choose funds that provide a low-to-moderate risk level, and that offer genuine diversification in that they respond differently to different market conditions. If all the funds invest in similar securities with similar objectives, there is no point in having all of them. It makes far more sense to guard against a downturn in the *stock* market by investing in some *bonds*, or bond funds. Within the stock sector, investing in emerging growth stocks should be balanced with investing in higher-capitalization, more stable "blue chip" stocks.

In the past, small investors usually had some money market funds and/or bank CDs because of the safety and convenience of these investments for small portfolios. Unfortunately, under current conditions their rate of return is still somewhat low, but they could be recommended to small investors who are extremely intolerant of risk.

Medium Investor

An individual with more funds to invest, and who has adequate insurance coverage (to protect the surviving spouse in case the investor dies at a time when the portfolio has a low value), would probably begin by creating a diversified mutual fund portfolio. He might want to add a commercial or private annuity to the portfolio (see Chapter 12).

With this basic program in place, the investor would probably want to add some investments in individual securities. He might buy Treasury bonds or notes, rather than just investing in bond funds. He might also invest in particular stocks, not just in stock funds. A mutual fund allows an investor who otherwise could afford to invest in only one or two stocks to invest in a broad portfolio of stocks. However, an investor who can afford to buy stock in a dozen or so companies may prefer simply to buy those stocks individually.

At this level, the investor (or advisor or fiduciary acting on the investor's behalf) will probably engage in more active trading. At lower levels of investment, it is probably not worthwhile to trade a lot because the fees, commissions, and taxes involved in selling 100 shares of stock at a profit of $2.00 a share tend to overwhelm the profits. However, if the profits are greater, or the number of shares involved significantly larger, active trading makes more sense.

It should be noted that municipal bond income is taken into account when computing income taxes on Social Security benefits (see Chapter 9), which may make municipal bonds somewhat less attractive than they would otherwise be to this group of investors.

The successful moderate investor may be at risk of having a federally taxable estate, especially if he owns a valuable home. Therefore, he should implement basic estate planning measures (see Chapter 13) such as a gifting program, credit shelter trust, and/or QTIP trust. It is possible that there will be no tax due on the first estate because of the marital deduction, but there can be a significant risk of a tax problem with the second estate.

Large Investor

As noted above, the large investor will probably have a multi-person team responsible for investment choices. (Sophisticated portfolio management techniques are beyond the scope of this book.) Certain high-risk/high-opportunity investments that might otherwise be suitable for large investors (such as options and futures) are probably unsuitable for older investors because of the possibility of having to turn the portfolio over to a fiduciary at some point in the future.

A large investor will no doubt be in the top income tax bracket, so tax-exempt investments may gain in attractiveness. In this bracket, however, the impact of the alternative minimum tax (AMT) must be considered. Naturally, estate planning will be critical because it is extremely likely that there will be a taxable estate for both spouses unless planning steps are taken (see Chapter 13). A complex, multi-trust estate plan may be necessary, perhaps in conjunction with a giving program and significant charitable bequests (outright or in trust).

BOTTOM-LINE FACTORS

The initial choice of investments, particularly investments chosen to re-balance a portfolio or in response to changing market conditions, must take into account the impact of costs and fees on overall investment performance. For instance, a "full-load" mutual fund purchased through a broker will have an initial "load" (fee) that may be as high as 8%. A "low-load" fund purchased directly from a mutual fund family may impose an initial fee as low as 1%. (Although initially there was a sharp distinction between "load" and "no-load funds," mutual funds have increased the amount, variety, and number of fees that they charge, so true no-load funds are rare.) Technically speaking, a "12b-1" fee—which is not a load, but a fee imposed to cover a fund's marketing costs—functions about the same way from the customer's perspective.

Once an investment has been purchased, there may be ongoing fees for maintenance of the account. Certainly, when an investment that is a capital asset is sold at a profit, there will be capital gains tax liability—and, generally, there is no ability to "roll over" the gain and escape taxation by buying another security.

PRACTICE TIP. Many mutual funds offer the convenience of check redemption (i.e., the account owner can write checks on the account to any payee). But this is a taxable transaction, and the account owner will have to calculate the capital gain or loss on the transaction. This is not a simple matter if the $5,000 check to the home health care agency actually constitutes a redemption of 468.22 shares, 137 of which were purchased at $9 a share, and 77 of which were purchased at $12.13 a share.

Another convenience offered by many mutual fund families is "switching" between accounts (i.e., moving $10,000 from a technology fund to an income oriented fund). However, it is common for the fund family to impose fees on switches, or to limit the number of switches per year that can be performed without a fee. Make sure that your clients are aware of the cost of shifting assets within a fund family. Furthermore, these switches are also taxable events in that securities have been sold at either a profit or a loss.

Taxes and expenses are vital considerations in determining the final yield of an investment (i.e., the amount that is actually available for the client to spend, reinvest, or leave to heirs). A return that appears high may shrink a good deal when taxes and expenses are considered. If the choice is between a taxable and a tax-free investment, the calculation is as follows: subtract fees and costs from the tax-free investment; subtract fees, costs, and income tax (at the marginal rate, i.e., the taxpayer's top tax bracket) from the taxable investment, and compare. If necessary, adjust the figures to correspond for differences in risk level.

Typically, mutual funds will reconfigure their portfolios near the end of each year, resulting in many sales of assets and, consequently, capital gains distributions to fund owners. When a mutual fund changes managers, the new manager often changes the investment direction, which can also result in heavy capital gain distributions. Some fund owners choose to sell their fund shares before this happens, to avoid the tax hit. In the year 2000, many funds also took profits at other points in the year, resulting in other capital gains distributions during the year. This was especially irksome for some investors whose fund shares had lost a great deal of value by the end of the year, and who still had a heavy tax bill due to redemptions by other shareholders.

PLANNING TIP: Shareholder reports issued by mutual funds may give advance warning of major redemptions, which could be a cue for selling fund shares to prevent the capital gain pileup.[22]

On the other hand, clients should not worry too much about small differences in return. If one person invests $5,000 in a mutual fund that scores top performance for the quarter in its class, and someone else invests $5,000 in a comparable mutual fund that scores only average performance for the class, the two will likely end up with very similar returns. It probably would not make sense for the second investor to dump the disappointing fund and reinvest in the leader because next quarter the rankings may be reversed.

TAILORING THE PORTFOLIO OVER TIME

In many instances, persons who have retired recently are still active and vigorous and they may take an especially strong interest in hands-on portfolio management. They may need some gentle guidance to avoid serious errors. Over time, it is typical (though not universal) for interest in active investing to decline. A shift from a portfolio that is primarily invested in individual stocks and bonds to one with a predominance of mutual funds might be appropriate.

The financial planner should also pay attention to changes in the client's level of activity, ability to communicate with others, or his interest in life in general. Negative changes should be discussed with other members of the planning team and/or members of the client's family to determine whether intervention is required, or if incapacity planning steps should be taken.

If the portfolio might have to be turned over to a fiduciary one day, bear in mind that the attorney-in-fact, guardian, or trustee is likely to be a family member, who in turn is unlikely to be a financial professional. For a smooth transition, the investment plan should be flexible, fairly simple, and so well documented that the fiduciary can pick up the reins immediately.

Although, as noted above, moving the entire portfolio into income investments is probably poor strategy, it is often a good idea to alter the equity-income balance of the portfolio as the client ages. A typical allocation at age 60 would be 60-70% stock and 30-40% bonds and other income instruments. Perhaps, at age 70, the same individual would prefer a 50-50% split, or even a predominance of income instruments.

It should also be noted that many individuals drop from a high to a lower tax bracket as they age, so taxable investments may become more attractive than tax-exempt investments. Also, municipal bond income may be a tax preference item for alternative minimum tax purposes, and in any event, it can result in taxability, or increased taxability, of Social Security benefits (see Chapter 9) – another factor that could argue in favor of holding more taxable investments.

If the stock market declines, or the older client is afraid that it might, then reducing the risk level of the portfolio might be a good idea. Once again, a shift from small-cap stocks to more stable, higher-yielding utility stocks could be called for. Alternatively, switching funds within a mutual fund family to more balanced, less risky funds, investing in bonds or bond funds rather than stocks, or even shifting part of the portfolio into money market funds or other cash equivalents could be the proper move. On the other hand, an older investor with a strong interest in enhancing the size of the estate to be transmitted to his heirs might view a time of market uncertainty as an excellent opportunity for bargain-hunting, trusting that the value of the stocks will increase in time (without generating significant taxable capital gains for the heirs due to the "step-up" in basis – see Chapter 13).[23]

The senior citizen's portfolio often requires wise investment of lump-sums, such as pension payouts, home sale gains, and life insurance proceeds. Sometimes the proceeds can simply be allocated in the same proportion as the rest of the portfolio. In other plans, purchase of an immediate annuity (see Chapter 12) can be an excellent way to generate needed income without generating a large amount of effort in managing the portfolio. In still other instances, lump-sums should become the subject of a giving program to reduce the potentially taxable estate, and/or as part of a Medicaid plan.

Last, but not least, there may be events beyond the investor's control that affect the investment plan. For instance, someone may buy bonds intending to hold them to maturity, but the issuer of the bond may exercise a right to "call" the bond (i.e., to repurchase it after a particular date at a stated price, or according to a price schedule set out in advance). And, of course, as soon as a bond matures, the owner will have to have a strategy for re-investing the principal from the initial investment.

INCOME TAX, INCLUDING CAPITAL GAINS TAX: INVESTMENTS

Dividends paid on corporate stock are ordinary income (see Code Section 61(a)(7)). A dividend is a payment that is made to shareholders because of their stock ownership deriving from the corporation's current or accumulated earnings and profits. Distributions made by a corporation from sources other than earnings and profits are generally not taxed as dividends. Instead, they are first applied to reduce the owner's adjusted basis in the stock. Once adjusted basis reaches zero, any remaining distribution is taxed as gain, usually as a capital gain.

Amounts paid or credited to life insurance policyholders are not taxed as dividends if they serve as partial refunds of the insurance premium (see Code Section 316(b)(1)). But dividends that exceed the consideration paid for the policy are taxable as dividends.

Throughout much of the history of United States taxation, capital gains (which are, broadly speaking, gains generated from sales of investment assets) have received preferential treatment. The theory is that the economy as a whole will benefit if people have an incentive not only to save instead of consuming, but to invest in securities rather than simply retaining all their savings in bank accounts. Interest earned on bank accounts, or on taxable bonds, is taxed at ordinary income rates and does not receive preferential treatment. However, there was a period of time when capital gains and ordinary income rates were identical, or at least not significantly different.

The Taxpayer Relief Act of 1997, as amended by the Internal Revenue Service Restructuring and Reform Act of 1998, dramatically altered the taxation of capital gains, generally in a downward direction favorable to most investors. And under the Jobs and Growth Tax Relief and Reconciliation Act of 2003 (JGTRRA), most long-term capital gains (generally those on capital assets held more than one year) are currently taxed at a maximum rate of 15%. That is almost half of the top income tax bracket.[24] Senior citizens who are asset-rich but have a fairly low income and, therefore, are in the 15% income tax bracket qualify for a lower capital gains rate of 5% (in 2006 and 2007, decreasing to 0% in 2008). Taxpayers in the 10% income tax bracket (established under EGTRRA 2001) also qualify for the 5% capital gains rate.[25]

Therefore, for some taxpayers in fairly low brackets—including many retirees—the difference between capital gain and ordinary income rates will be fairly modest. Thus, risk-averse investors can choose bonds, even taxable bonds, or high-dividend stocks instead of growth stocks, thus increasing their current returns with a fair degree of safety, and without encountering a very large additional tax cost.

The complex rules for capital gains transactions can require especially sophisticated record keeping to monitor which shares (and other assets) were purchased or otherwise acquired (e.g., through reinvestment of dividends) at which time. There are also many situations in which it may be necessary to sell some assets to pay expenses, or it may be desirable to give or sell some assets for other purposes. In either case, a decision has to be made which assets should be sold or donated. If the senior citizen client will have to pay capital gains tax on the gain, then the best choice might be the assets that have appreciated the least. On the other hand, if the capital gain can escape taxation, then the better choice might be the asset that has appreciated the most.

Code Section 1211 provides that capital losses are deductible in any year only to the extent of gains. The excess of the loss over the gain (net short-term or net long-term capital loss), can offset ordinary income on a dollar-for-dollar basis, up to $3,000 a year. (The limit is $1,500 for married taxpayers filing separate returns.) Losses greater than the limit can be carried forward to later tax years.

Interest from corporate bonds is taxed as ordinary income. Interest on municipal bonds, other than certain private-activity bonds or other atypical bonds, is tax-exempt under Code Section 150. (See IRC Sec. 149 for classifications of municipal bonds that are not tax-exempt.) Interest paid on Treasury bonds is taxable for federal purposes, but exempt from state and local income taxes. Interest on United States Savings Bonds is taxable.

A "stripped" bond has been divided into an underlying right to have principal repaid and a series of interest coupons; the two components are traded separately. Code Section 1286 treats stripped bonds and coupons like zero-coupon bonds, and original issue discount (OID) is taxed each year.

CAPITAL GAINS TAX: HOMES

The Taxpayer Relief Act of 1997 (TRA '97) replaced former Code Section 121 (i.e., the one-time capital gain exclusion for the sale of a home after age 55) and Code Section 1034 (i.e., rollover of gain when a more expensive home was purchased) with a single new provision, Code Section 121. Under this provision, a person of any age can generally exclude up to $250,000 in home sale capital gain from taxable income. A married home seller who files a joint return can exclude home sale gain of up to $500,000.

To qualify for this tax break, the property must have been the principal residence of the owner for two of the five years preceding the sale, or one of the five years preceding the sale if the sale was occasioned by the owner's entering a nursing home. A 1998 amendment permits a partial exclusion from capital gains taxation if the home was owned for less than the two-out-of-five years required for a full exclusion. This issue is discussed in more detail in Chapter 7.

INVESTMENT AND DISINVESTMENT PLANNING

Pre-retirement planning is largely concerned with accumulation of additional assets. The best case scenario is that investment income, in conjunction with Social Security benefits and the individual's pension, will be more than ample for a comfortable lifestyle, and the capital can also be kept intact for inheritance by the spouse, children, or other heirs. Unfortunately, many people fail or are unable to save enough to satisfy this scenario; or they are excellent savers and investors, but encounter a high-cost health situation or other crisis. In that case, the question becomes how to plan for "disinvestment", drawing down on the capital without completely exhausting the fund.

A simple rule of thumb is that the fund will never diminish if the principal sum remains invested and only the investment appreciation is withdrawn. One factor to keep in mind in choosing investments is how easy it is to set up a withdrawal schedule or to make withdrawals or redemptions as desired—including whether there are fees associated with the withdrawal.

A wealthy client will have enough assets to generate ample income, so that the portfolio will remain more or less intact to be inherited by the surviving spouse and perhaps by children and grandchildren, with provision for charities. But even a large estate can be depleted by health care costs that run over $100,000 a year for several years. Less affluent clients have to be concerned that their funds not run out before they die. If they have not been good at saving, or if they have saved a meaningful portion of their income but encountered investment losses, they may have to reduce their lifestyle to make sure that their money lasts throughout their lifetimes.

The traditional rule is that if the retirement fund must last for 30 years, withdrawals must be limited to 4.1% a year—or even less, if a bad stock market year early in retirement depletes the account before withdrawals are taken. One reason for having a lot of equities in the portfolio is their historically validated potential for appreciation. However, the *Wall Street Journal's* financial columnist, Jonathan Clements, pointed out that a person who is willing to cut back on withdrawals in bad years (which requires continuing mental capacity as well as the self-discipline to spend less) can probably withdraw as much as 6.2% a year without running out of capital. Clements suggests tactics such as: reducing discretionary spending in any year following a year in which there was a portfolio loss for the year as a whole; selecting low-cost funds; not selling funds that have heavy losses (because that just locks in the loss); and considering adding immediate annuities to the mix to boost income. The example given is a $600,000 portfolio with a 3% inflation rate and 6% withdrawal rate. In the first year of retirement, the portfolio owner can take out $36,000 the first year, $37,080 the next year, and $38,192 in the third year. Dividends and interest taken in cash should be treated as withdrawals when calculating safe levels. Clements interviewed CERTIFIED FINANCIAL PLANNER™ practitioner Jonathan Guyton, who said that historic rates of return for an 80% stock/20% bond portfolio could support a 6.2% annual withdrawal rate; a more conservative 65% stock/35% bond portfolio could support a 5.8% withdrawal.

However, even before Hurricane Katrina, the twenty-first century hasn't been very kind to retirees' financial planning. Clements asked T. Rowe Price Group for analyses of three retirement strategies for a hypothetical couple who retired at the end of 1999, when they were both 65, starting out with $500,000 in savings. The hypothetical couple had 40% of their investments in U.S. stock, 10% in foreign stocks, 35% in intermediate-term bonds, 10% in cash, and 5% in real estate securities.

If the couple had withdrawn 4.5% of the portfolio each year with automatic inflation increases, taking out $22,500 the first year and the same amount plus inflation adjustments, the portfolio would have dipped below $400,000 by the end of 2002. It would have recovered somewhat by 2004, but still would have been worth only $457,000.

What if the couple had taken out $25,000 the first year, but had not increased their withdrawals in any year in which the portfolio had fallen below its opening value? They would have lost 2.3% on their investments in 2001 and lost 7.1% in 2002; by the end of 2004, their nest egg would have been down to $445,000.

If the couple had just taken out 5% at the beginning of each year of what the portfolio was worth then, their income would have dropped from $25,000 in 2000 to $19,900 in 2001, then back up to $22,300. At the end of 2004, their portfolio would not have been intact—it would have fallen from $500,000 to $463,000. If the couple had insisted on keeping their nest egg intact, they would have been able to take out only $15,500 in their first retirement year under the first strategy, and would have been able to withdraw only 3.2% under the second strategy, and 3.5% a year under the third.[26]

A 5.5% withdrawal rate from a $1 million retirement fund would produce $50,000 a year, and a broker or financial planner might charge 2-3% of portfolio value per year. Clements recommends that the total fees for advisers and mutual funds not exceed 1.2% of portfolio value per year. He suggests that to save taxes, an older investor should accumulate enough cash within taxable accounts to cover living expenses for three years. At retirement, the dividends and interest on the taxable account should be low enough to permit shifting funds from a conventional to a Roth IRA. The conversion would be taxable, but should happen at a low bracket. The Roth account would continue to grow tax-free, and the smaller IRA would also have a smaller required minimum distribution than the original account before the conversion.[27]

Another approach is to have larger withdrawals in the earlier years of retirement, when the older person is more active and inclined to travel, buy consumer goods, or otherwise engage in hobbies and recreation. With the very significant exception of health care, the older people get, the less they tend to spend. Therefore, an initial withdrawal rate of 6% rather than the conventional 4% might be sustainable for the early years of retirement. Len Reinhart of the "Managed Money" column visualizes three distinct stages: (1) early retirement and high consumption; (2) a second stage where seniors tend to revert to activities they enjoyed before retirement; and (3) the last phase begins when health problems both limit seniors' activities and increase their spending needs.[28]

The Society of Actuaries has posted a "Retirement Probability Analyzer" (see http://www.SOA.org) that adds pension assets, expected return on investment, and the effects of an immediate annuity to increase the sophistication of the calculation of how long retirement assets will last. However, because this was designed as a professional tool for actuaries, it can be harder to use than some of the less complex models. Their example is a 65 year old woman who has $300,000 invested (50% in stock, 30% in bonds, and 20% in cash savings), and wants $40,000 a year in retirement income. If she doesn't change her investments, her money could run out at 73. If she uses $50,000 of investment funds to buy an immediate annuity, her income rises to $3,413 a year but could run out at 72. But if she purchases a $50,000 immediate annuity and lowers spending to $25,000 a year, her money could last to age 83.[29]

THE ROLE OF THE FIDUCIARY

The older client may have appointed an agent under a durable power of attorney who has full power over all of the older person's assets, or limited powers that include some degree of investment management. Perhaps the client has placed funds into a trust, and the trustee must find suitable investments. Or, a court may have appointed a guardian to manage the property of an incapacitated person.

What an agent, trustee, and guardian have in common is that they are all fiduciaries (i.e., they are all subject to a legal duty to safeguard someone else's property). Fiduciary authority can be created by contract (e.g., a durable power of attorney or trust instrument), or by court order (with respect to a guardianship).

Fiduciaries are required to act in the best interests of the principal. They are forbidden to engage in self-dealing (i.e., promoting their own interests at the expense of the principal). They are also required to act prudently, which involves taking care of the principal's funds (and, if possible, making the funds grow) while avoiding excessive risks that could reduce the principal's capital.

In many instances, the instrument appointing the fiduciary, when read in conjunction with state law, explains what is permissible and what is forbidden for fiduciary investments. In doubtful cases, it makes sense for the fiduciary to petition the court for authorization of a transaction that might give rise to liability.

Fiduciaries are required to balance the need to generate additional income and to create additional value against the obligation to invest prudently for the preservation of principal. The safety of the capital must be preserved. It is not enough to simply choose investments—the fiduciary must also monitor their performance, remove assets that have failed to perform at a satisfactory level, and substitute more appropriate investments when necessary.

The traditional approach to controlling investments by fiduciaries was to create a "legal list" of extremely safe investments, such as United States government obligations and first mortgages on valuable property. A few states still forbid fiduciaries to engage in any investment outside the "legal list." Other states use the "legal list" as a guideline, but permit other prudent investments.

The modern approach to trust investing is to discard the "legal list" entirely, but retain the duty of prudence. A fiduciary acts prudently by using the degree of attention, skill, and care that a reasonable person would use in investing his or her own money. In additional to legal list investments, government-related financing devices (such as Ginnie Maes), and state bonds on which there has been no recent history of default, will probably be deemed prudent. Municipal bonds are probably prudent, especially if they are insured by a third-party guarantor or adequately secured (such as by sufficient tax revenues). Blue-chip stocks and highly-rated corporate bonds are also probably prudent.

On the other hand, direct investment in real estate (as distinguished from high-quality mortgages or mortgage pools) is probably not prudent unless the property is immediately salable and the fiduciary has the expertise to manage the property and place it on the market. Unsecured loans to corporations or individuals are probably not prudent; nor are investing in business start-ups, or selling trust or guardianship property in exchange for an unsecured note instead of cash or a secured obligation considered prudent. Investing in high-tech stocks, other speculative stocks, options, futures and commodities are almost certainly imprudent.

The prudence of an investment transaction depends on factors such as:

- The research done by the fiduciary prior to investing;

- The rating assigned to the investment by recognized rating authorities;

- Whether the fiduciary acted on advice from an attorney, broker, or other professional;

- Whether the investment was part of an overall pattern of diversification (among prudent investments only, of course); or

- The fiduciary's attention to tax planning and cushioning the impact of inflation.

The fiduciary often has to balance several interests—not just the current trust beneficiary (who usually desires additional income), but also the trust remainderman (who will be harmed unless the principal is preserved and, preferably, augmented). In addition, a guardian may have to think about the ward's spouse or other dependents of the ward.

Guardianship law has not squarely confronted Medicaid planning. Under traditional principles (still adhered to by some probate judges in guardianship cases), the fiduciary's duty is to increase the ward's income, on the theory that more income is better than less income. Other judges will allow a guardian to carry on a ward's pre-existing pattern of benefiting relatives or charities, or maintaining a structured gifting program, but will not allow creation of a new pattern. The judicial treatment most favorable to the ward is the theory that the guardian can do anything that the ward could have done personally. Thus, the guardian can engage in tax-saving or Medicaid-oriented transactions if they would have been done by the ward before he became incapacitated, or if they are in the ward's best interests.

OLDER INVESTORS "ONLINE"

Although some older people are afraid of, or distrustful of computers, others have embraced the technology enthusiastically. A surprising number of older people are now using the Internet to gather investment information and to discuss it with other investors, as well as to buy securities directly. About seven million people over age 55 used the Internet in 1998, and of this group, two-thirds are college graduates, one-third have an advanced degree, almost one-quarter have household income over $100,000, and more than one-quarter have a portfolio worth at least $250,000. Almost one-fifth not only obtain investment information through the Internet, but are also active seekers of trading information.[30] (Note that including people aged 55-64 may distort the picture of senior citizens in general, because this younger group is typically healthier, more affluent, and more active.)

It is very common for recent retirees to take an extremely active interest in money management and investing. In a sense, they become full-time investors as a substitute for their prior careers. In a more negative sense, investing can become a substitute for gambling—another financially risky pastime that attracts a disproportionate number of senior citizens. Older people frequently need less sleep than they did in their younger days, so the ability to chat on an investment forum at 2:00 a.m. is valued by some senior citizens. The ability to trade at deeply discounted commissions is attractive to frugal older people.

Unfortunately, much of the "information" available on-line is naive, misguided, foolish—or outright fraudulent. Furthermore, individuals who are lonely, anxious about their financial future, or declining in capacity are particularly vulnerable to manipulation and are unduly willing to believe anything they read on a computer screen. An important part of incapacity planning is monitoring the older individual's transactions to see if they reflect declining capacity or victimization. If necessary, the amount of capital that the individual can manage directly should be reduced or durable powers of attorney, trusts, and other management mechanisms should be brought into play.

CHAPTER ENDNOTES

1. See Joseph D'Allegro, "Insurers Say Seniors Should Keep Some Risk in Their Investments," *National Underwriter Life & Health*, August 10, 1998, p. 7.

2. Aaron Lucchetti, "Rising Interest Rates Have Many Cheerleaders," *Wall Street Journal*, June 29, 2004, p. C1.

3. George A. Fischer and Shawn M. Verbout, Fidelity Viewpoint, "The Case For Investing in Fixed Income" at: http://personal.fidelity.com/products/fixedincome/pdf/fiwhitepaper.pdf.

4. This information comes from the 2004 Phoenix Wealth Survey. See Walter Zultowski, *National Underwriter Life & Health*, Week in Life & Health 2004 Issue #38.

5. Barbara Whitaker, "After the Storm, Rebuilding the Nest Egg," *New York Times*, April 12, 2004, p. G2.

6. Judith Burns, "Gender Gap in Retirement Investments is Cited, With Women Too Conservative," *Wall Street Journal*, June 20, 1997, p. A5A.; Defined Contribution Plan Distribution Choices at Retirement at: http://www.ici.org/pdf/rpt_distribution_choices.pdf.

7. Karen Damato, "Uh, No Thanks for Your Advice," *Wall Street Journal*, May 14, 2004, p. C1.

8. Colleen DeBaise, "When Investing, Women Tend to Err Less Often Than Men," *Wall Street Journal*, April 20, 2005, p. D2.

9. The paper, George M. Korniotis and Alok Kumar's "Does Investment Skill Decline Due to Cognitive Aging or Improve With Experience," http://papers.ssrn.com/sol3/papers.cfm?abstract-id=767125, is discussed in Mark Hulbert, "Aging Brings Wisdom, But Not On Investing," *New York Times* December 4, 2005 Business p. 6.

10. Mary Williams Walsh, "Healthier and Wiser? Sure, but Not Wealthier," *New York Times*, June 13, 2004 Business, p. 1.

11. "Income of the Elderly Population: 2003," EBRI Notes Volume 26 No. 1 (Jan 2005), at: http://www.ebri.org/publications/notes/index.cfm?fa=notesDisp&content_id=3230.

12. Dorothy Hinchcliff, "The Retirement Boom," *Financial Advisor* Magazine, June 2005 (accessible through http://benefitslink.com; no www).

13. Treasury securities are sold at regular auctions and are redeemable at maturity at face value. If the buyer's purchase price was below the face value, a refund will be granted to the purchaser for the difference between the purchase price and the face value. This amount will generally be taxed as original issue discount (OID). On the other hand, if the buyer's purchase price is higher than the face value (because Treasury securities were paying higher rates than the market rate for comparably safe securities), then the purchaser has paid a "premium," which can be amortized over the life of the security (reducing its basis by the amortized premium deducted each year). The 30-year Treasury security, which was discontinued in 2001, was reintroduced in 2006.

14. See http://www.treasurydirect.gov/indiv/research/indepth/ibonds/res_i_faq.htm.

15. Jennifer Saranow, "Savings Bonds Lose Their Allure," *Wall Street Journal* , April 13, 2005, p. D2.

16. Jane J. Kim, "Wall Street Pushes Inflation Protection," *Wall Street Journal*, May 5, 2005, p. D1.

17. Erin E. Arvedlund, "Investors Can More Easily Buy Treasurys Online," *Wall Street Journal*, October 1, 2005, p. B4.

18. Ruth Simon and Ann Davis, "Regulators Probe Sales by Large Brokers of 'Callable' CDs as Investors Complain," *Wall Street Journal*, December 20, 2000, p. C1.

19. Tom Lauricella, "New Ways to Get Growth and Income Pop Up As Aging Investors' Needs Shift," *Wall Street Journal*, September 23, 2005, p. C1.

20. Christopher Oster, "Popular Funds For Retirees Are Nearly Dead," *Wall Street Journal*, October 14, 2004, p. D1.

21. Tom Lauricella, "The Latest Pension Substitute," *Wall Street Journal*, March 11-12, 2006, p. B1.

22. Karen Damato and Ken Brown, "Capital-Gains Payouts Hit Investors Early," *Wall Street Journal*, August 25, 2000, p. C1.

23. Karen Hube, "Vulnerable Retirees Need to Maintain Their Cool," *Wall Street Journal*, August 31, 1998, p. C1.

24. Under EGTRRA 2001, the top income tax rate was scheduled for incremental reduction as follows: 39.1% in 2001; 38.6% in 2002-2003; 37.6% in 2004-2005; and 35% in 2006-2010. JGTRRA 2003 accelerated the reductions that were scheduled to occur in 2004 and 2006. Thus, for 2003 and thereafter, the top income tax rate was lowered to 35%. This provision was effective for taxable years beginning after December 31, 2002.

25. A rate of 18% was available for gains on assets that were purchased after December 31, 2000 and held for five years or more before the sale or exchange. An even lower rate of 8% applied after 1999 to property held more than five years before the sale or exchange and sold by an individual in the 15% income tax bracket (or the new 10% bracket, as discussed above). Under JGTRRA 2003, the 5-year holding period requirement, and the 18% and 8% tax rates for qualified 5-year gain were repealed. When the 15% and 5% rates for capital gains "sunset" (expire), the 5-year holding period requirement and 18% and 8% rates will, once again, be effective. IRC Secs. 1(h)(2), 1(h)(9), as repealed by JGTRRA 2003; Act Sec. 107, JGTRRA 2003.

26. Jonathan Clements, "Burning Through Money in Retirement: A Tale of Three Withdrawal Strategies," *Wall Street Journal* April 27, 2005, p. D1; "Retirees Don't Have To Be So Frugal: A Case For Withdrawing Up to 6% a Year," *Wall Street Journal*,, November 17, 2004, p. D1; and "Another Number to Fret About: The Key to Retirement is Your Withdrawal Rate," *Wall Street Journal*, March 10, 2004, p. D1.

27. Jonathan Clements, "To Afford Retirement, Cut Your Taxes, Fire Your Broker, and Get a Part-Time Job," *Wall Street Journal*, June 2, 2004, p. D1.

28. Ilana Polyak, "New Advice to Retirees: Spend More At First, Cut Back Later," *New York Times* September 25, 2005, Business p. 5; Paul B. Brown, "What's Offline," *New York Times*, June 2, 2005, p. C5.

29. Kaja Whitehouse, "Tool Tells How Long Nest Egg Will Last," *Wall Streeet Journal,* August 31, 2004, p. D2.

30. David Barboza, "On-Line Traders: Older, Wiser and Richer," *New York Times,* December 20, 1998, Section 3 (Business), p. 1.

Chapter 12

Annuities

THE BASIC CONCEPT

The basic annuity concept is very simple. Someone who has a large sum of money, but who wants continuing income, transfers the funds to a commercial issuer (usually an insurance company) or a private person. The annuity issuer promises to provide a continuing stream of income payments. The payments can be promised for life, the joint lives of two people, a number of years, or a number of years with refund provisions if the annuitant dies before the term ends. The more payments that must be made based on the deposit of a sum of money, the smaller each individual payment will be.

There are many reasons why annuities are useful in the elder care financial plan. A person whose judgment is somewhat impaired might be capable of administering each month's income and paying bills, but incapable of managing large principal sums. Even a mentally sound person might concede limited investment expertise, so that professional management of an annuity could provide a larger monthly income and better lifestyle. Annuities receive quite favorable tax treatment. Persons in mid-life may achieve better total after-tax return by investing in annuities than in mutual funds.

In many ways, annuities and IRA accounts are similar; in fact, the taxation of distributions from IRAs depends on Internal Revenue Code Section 72, the annuity section. An important difference is that no tax deduction is available for investing in annuities, while conventional IRA contributions can generate tax deductions and/or credits. (Contributions to Roth IRAs are not tax-deductible.)

A taxpayer who does not qualify for an IRA deduction, who finds the tax savings attributable to the potential deduction a trivial factor in planning or who has already made the maximum IRA contribution, may find an annuity an attractive investment option.

When capital gains and ordinary income tax rates were essentially the same, deferred annuities had a clear advantage over mutual funds and investments in individual securities: tax liability was also deferred for the annuities. Tax deferral works much like compound interest. Compound interest allows the investor to earn "interest on interest" while tax deferral allows the entire pre-tax amount, not just the reduced after-tax amount, to appreciate. Under current law, capital gains rates can be lower than ordinary income rates, so some clients will be deterred from purchasing annuities by the requirement of paying tax, when it finally falls due, at ordinary income rates. The tax deferral and convenience of annuities must be balanced against their often-higher fee structure and reduced ability to be taxed at capital gains rates.

As Chapter 8 (Retirement Planning) shows, the traditional defined benefit pension plan maintained by employers is legally required to make a joint and survivor annuity the basic payment method for married retirees. However, these traditional plans are now greatly eclipsed by 401(k) plans and other defined contribution plans. Few defined contribution plans even offer an annuity as a payment option, and even where this option is available, it is unpopular.

Some kinds of annuities, especially variable annuities, have been criticized as products that are marketed too aggressively, sometimes to vulnerable older people who buy unsuitable products that carry excessive fees and restrictions. As usual, moderation must be exercised. Instead of placing all their assets in just one annuity product, sensible older investors should diversify their portfolios in this respect as well. Furthermore, they should tailor the provisions to their needs: a heavy surrender charge, for example, is very counter-productive if funds are needed to pay for long-term care after a stroke or hip fracture. A surrender charge that phases out after fifteen years or more is unlikely to be survived by a 75-year-old purchaser![1]

As Chapter 8 shows, there has been a transition from retirement based on receiving an annuity from an employer's defined benefit plan to retirement based on receiving the balance from a 401(k) or other defined contribution plan. Although many people say they want guaranteed income, annuity sales remain low.

Of retirees who were entitled to a lump sum under their defined benefit or defined contribution retirement plan, only 9% took an annuity; 23% took installment payments of income (not guaranteed for life), 37% rolled over their balance to an IRA, and 14% took a lump sum. Looking at defined benefit retirees, 49% of those who knew an annuity was available took it, but overall only 16% got their benefits in annuity form. (It is possible that survey recipients who said they received installment payments actually did obtain an annuity but did not know how to describe it.) Furthermore, in 2003, less than 1% of individual deferred annuity assets were annuitized ($11.1 billion), and $5.3 billion in individual immediate annuities were sold. 47% of those buying an immediate annuity or annuitizing a deferred annuity in the 2000-2001 period bought for a term of years (usually less than 10 years), but that represented only 26% of the dollars annuitized.[2]

AmeriSave, a pension reform proposal introduced in the House of Representatives in 2005, includes tax credits for businesses that give 401(k) owners the option to annuitize their plan balances when they retire. If the program passes, part of the 401(k) balance tax-free after retirement, as long as it was taken in annuity form. Congress wants to encourage annuity investments because of worries that too many people will run out of money if they spend too much of a lump-sum payout, or invest it poorly.[3]

CLASSIFYING ANNUITIES

A closer look at annuities shows that the simple basic concept supports many variations:

- When will the first annuity payment be made? If it is due as soon as the annuity is purchased, the annuity is immediate; if it is scheduled for the future (e.g., post-retirement), the annuity is deferred. Deferred annuities are divided into an accumulation period, during which appreciation is not taxed; and a payout period, when the payment stream begins (and a portion of each payment will become subject to income tax).

- What determines the span over which the issuer will make payments to the owner?[4] If it is a certain number of years, such as 10 or 20, it is a term certain annuity. (Payments are made to the designated beneficiaries if the annuitant dies before the end of the term.) If it is the lifetime of the annuitant, it is a life annuity. If it is the lifetime of both the annuitant and a designated beneficiary (usually the spouse), it is a joint and survivor annuity. A further complication is that the benefit might be cut in half after the first death (joint and 50% survivor annuity), continue at the original level (joint and 100% survivor annuity), or fall anywhere in between.

- Although many annuities are purchased with a single lump-sum payment (i.e., are classified as single premium annuities), multiple premium annuities are possible. A scheduled multiple premium annuity contract includes a schedule of payments in specific amounts to be made by the annuity purchaser, whereas a flexible premium contract permits the purchaser to control the timing and amount of premium payments.

• Is the rate of return set in advance, responding to interest rates (fixed annuity) or subject to change based on market forces (variable annuity)? Many hybrid forms are possible. For instance, the rate may be guaranteed at its initial level for a certain period of time, then permitted to float.

• How much control does the purchaser have over the investment of the account? Typically, variable annuities permit the investor to select among several mutual fund-like accounts investing in different types of securities with different risk levels, as well as a fixed account with a guaranteed return. In contrast, the issuer manages the funds invested in fixed annuities.

• Is a charge imposed for surrendering the annuity? A frequent provision is a "back-end" charge that starts out fairly high, is reduced each year, and phases out after seven years. There may be other charges as well, such as an investment management fee.

• Is there an insurance element and, if so, what is its effective cost? Most annuities include a death benefit provision of some type. For example, there may be a guarantee that the account of a variable annuity will be re-valued to the minimum guaranteed amount if the market value of the account is lower than this amount should the account holder die during the accumulation phase.

• The NAIC has a modified guaranteed annuity model regulation.[5]

• Who regulates it? Variable annuity products are considered securities, so the person selling them must have a securities license.

SUITABILITY

One concern is that potential buyers will be pressured into purchasing products that are inappropriate for their needs. Because annuities often represent a large portion of an older person's portfolio—or, in fact, become the person's only investment and a major source of income—unsuitable products can be a real danger. Therefore, the NAIC has a Life Insurance and Annuities Suitability Model Act and Model Regulation covering products sold based on a licensed insurance professional's recommendation.

The purpose of suitability requirements is to obligate the professional to find out the potential purchaser's income, assets, health and financial status, and possible needs for future liquidity that could result in incurring surrender charges.

The National Association of Securities Dealers (NASD) has proposed Rule 2821 (Sales Suitability). The rule tightens the sales standards for variable annuities, requiring the broker-dealer or salesperson to have a reasonable basis, premised on a five-point evaluation process, for believing the variable annuity is suitable for the customer. The salesperson is required to make reasonable efforts to learn about the customer's age, income, financial status and needs, existing portfolio and investment style, risk tolerance, tax bracket, and liquidity needs. Under the rule, the producer's supervisor must review the deal under various cost and investment criteria, and must acknowledge in writing that the deal was reviewed. Broker-dealer firms must give their salespersons adequate training to fully understand variable annuities.

Industry groups such as the American Council of Life Insurers (ACLI) opposed the rule, on the grounds that existing suitability rules are adequate and there is no objective empirical proof that a new rule is needed, because variable annuity sales have not given rise to many complaints to securities regulators.

In response to financial services industry concerns, the SEC gave broker-dealers four additional months to comply with the SEC regulation applying to variable annuity (and variable life insurance) sales by financial planners and discretionary brokerage accounts. The rule was originally slated to go into effect October 24, 2005, but the deadline was extended to January 31, 2006. The regulation makes broker-dealers subject to the SEC's requirements for investment advisors whenever they provide financial advice to customers as part of a financial plan.[6] Robert Glauber, chairman of the National Association of Securities Dealers, suggested in early 2006 that current regulation is not applied equally: consumers who buy annuities should be entitled to the same degree of protection, and to make decisions on the basis of the same quantum of disclosures, whether they buy fixed, variable, or equity-indexed annuities.[7]

FACTORS IN THE ANNUITY PAYMENT

Usually, the size of each benefit payment under a fixed annuity will be the same, and will be determined at the time of the initial benefit payment, based on the earnings of the funds deposited in the account (minus the fees charged by the company issuing the annuity). Variable annuity payments can fluctuate with market factors, although there may be a guaranteed "floor" below which benefit payments will not fall.

The more payments the issuer has to make, naturally, the smaller each individual payment will be. The more risk the issuer takes, the smaller the payments will be. Therefore, payments will be smaller for a joint-and-survivor annuity than for a single-life annuity. In the same vein, payments will be smaller for a term certain (e.g., 10 or 20-year) annuity if payments will be made to a designated beneficiary after the initial owner's death than if the payments stop if the owner dies during the term and there is no refund feature.

A single person would be more likely to select a lifetime-only annuity than a married person concerned with the financial welfare of the surviving spouse. The married individual would be more likely to prefer a joint-and-survivor annuity (unless the other spouse is already amply provided for). Someone who is concerned about outliving other income sources would tend to prefer a life or joint and survivor payment, unless these payments are too small to meet the financial objective. In that case, it might make sense to assume the risk of outliving the income in order to make sure that current expenses can be paid for at least a few years.

ANNUITY FEES

Although the company issuing the annuity has the opportunity to benefit from the "float" on the invested funds, it also has expenses related to marketing and administering the annuity. Thus, fees of various kinds are imposed, depending on the annuity contract. The various fees reduce the amount that will eventually be available to the owner of the annuity (or his or her heirs). The longer the investment horizon, the greater the potential impact of fees.

A contract fee is a defined amount, either charged when the annuity is issued or billed to the annuity each year. A transaction fee is imposed on each transaction, such as additional premiums added to an account that permits additions. A percentage of premium charge is deducted from each premium and could be expressed as a sliding scale that diminishes over time, or is inversely proportional to the amount invested in the account.

Charges may be imposed for withdrawals (reducing the annuity balance) or surrenders (removing the entire balance and terminating the annuity). Typically, these charges begin at a fairly high level to discourage premature depletion of the annuity, but decrease each year until they phase-out, usually between the seventh and tenth year. Depending on the terms, the percentage could be calculated on the entire value of the contract, the premiums paid to purchase the contract, or the amount withdrawn.

Penalty-free withdrawals might be permitted in hardship situations, such as nursing home institutionalization or terminal illness. Or, the account might permit a certain number or dollar amount of withdrawals without charge, but impose a charge on additional withdrawals or withdrawals in excess of a particular percentage of account value. A "rolling" charge on a multiple-premium annuity applies to funds that can be traced to each premium, running from the date of deposit of the premium to the date of withdrawal or surrender.

It is conventional to waive the surrender charge when a death benefit is paid on an account that has not yet annuitized. In an annuity with a "bail-out" option, there is no surrender charge for surrendering a contract that fails to live up to its own stated minimum interest rate. If the annuity is structured to include a "market value adjustment," the cash surrender value may go up or down based on whether interest rates at the time of surrender are higher or lower than at the time of purchase. (This is intellectually similar to the rise or fall in the value of bonds, depending on whether their interest rate is higher or lower than prevailing market rates.) A group of variable annuities was introduced a couple of years ago that does not impose surrender charges on withdrawals.[8] This type of annuity might be attractive to cost-conscious customers who fear that they may need to take money out of their annuity accounts.

Although most annuities can be maintained as an investment for the rest of the owner's life, some annuity contracts stay in force only for a particular number of years (i.e., equity-indexed annuity contracts, discussed below). With this type of annuity, at the end of the term the contract expires unless, during the permitted "window," the owner takes steps to renew the contract or exchange it for another type of contract. Typically, surrender charges do not apply to annuities that expire by their own terms and are not renewed.

Another cost factor is the premium taxes imposed by some states on annuity accounts. These taxes may be deducted from each premium as it is paid to the issuer, at the time of withdrawal, once the account annuitizes, or when death benefits are paid.

THE ANNUITY MARKET

In 2004, total annuity sales, according to LIMRA, were $218 billion, but only $5.3 billion of that came from immediate annuity sales. The National Association of Variable Annuities reported that in 1993, there were $399 billion in variable annuity assets, an amount that rose to $993 billion in 2004 and over $1.12 trillion in 2005.[9] LIMRA reported 2004 immediate annuity sales almost doubled between 1999 and 2004 (when they reached $5.6 billion). Deferred annuity sales rose from $156.6 billion in 1999 to $212.4 billion in 2004. Another 2005 trend was insurers' offering annuities as 401(k) options—with "sweeteners" in the form of reduced early withdrawal penalties. (Plan sponsors are often dubious about adding deferred annuities as an option, taking the position that the fees and early withdrawal penalties are too high, and double tax deferral is unnecessary.)

If, instead, one looks at whether the annuity is fixed or variable, in 2005 and 2006, fixed annuities were at a serious disadvantage versus variable annuities. In fact, September, 2005 was the first time in five years that banks sold more variable than fixed annuities. A year earlier, banks sold $1.4 billion worth of variable annuities, a figure that rose to $1.9 billion in September, 2005, but fixed annuity sales dropped from $2.2 billion (September 2004) to $1.6 billion (September 2005). Investors often found CDs more attractive than fixed annuities, because the CDs did not have fees and did not require locking in funds for as long as a fixed annuity would.

In effect, fixed annuities are only attractive if long-term interest rates are high; in 2005 and early 2006, long-term rates were quite low. A rule of thumb is that fixed annuities sold by banks need to pay at least 2% more than bank CDs for fixed annuities to attract the interest of buyers. Bank annuity sales continued to decline; in December, 2005 sales were 15% lower than a year earlier. Variable annuity sales fell by only 7%, but fixed annuity sales fell 22%. For 2005 as a whole, $133.4 billion worth of variable annuities were sold, 1.2% higher than the 2004 figure. In the fourth quarter of 2005, nearly two-thirds of premium flows for variable annuities came from qualified retirement plans.[10]

MetLife's Personal Pension Builder allows the investor to lock in an interest rate for sums invested. At retirement, the deferred annuity converts to an immediate annuity, with payments based on the rates prevailing at the time of the investment. (A traditional annuity uses the rates in effect at the time of the conversion.)[11]

Worries about the effect of possible Social Security cutbacks are motivating insurers to target annuity marketing to women (who are likely to depend heavily on survivor benefits). Some successful strategies have included marketing to small groups of women who bring friends to talk about retirement planning. Some companies offer "streamlined" annuities with simple features that are easy for purchasers with limited investment experience to understand.[12]

PLANNING TIP: There are plenty of web resources about annuities, including www. annuity.com and www.totalreturnannuities.com for price quotes and calculators for annuities; www.totalreturnannuities.com/annuity-variable/variable-annuities.html and the National Association of Variable Annuities site, www.retireonyourterms.com for planning tips; and www.ambest.com for ratings of annuity issuers.

DEPLOYING A LUMP SUM

There are many contexts in which an older person comes into possession of a lump sum but is unable or unwilling either to manage the money personally or turn over management to a broker or other financial advisor. From the older person's view, it is possible that this advisor might misappropriate funds or make honest but misguided choices. One example of a lump sum that an older person might come into is if, after due consideration of Medicaid consequences, the older person sells the family home and moves to other accommodations. In most cases, no capital gains tax will be due on the sale, so the entire amount can be invested. Lump sums may also be encountered as a result of a pension payout, an inheritance, or as life insurance death benefits for which settlement options are not elected.

If the goal is to arrange a secure lifetime income stream, a single premium immediate annuity is a good choice.

In early 2005, to purchase a single-premium annuity paying $1,000 per month for life from a company with a Best rating of A or better, a 55-year-old man would pay between $179,003 and $191,278, with an average of $184,661. A 65-year-old man would pay between $148,045 and $160,719, with an average of $153,450. Because of longer life expectancies, women pay more: an average of $195,691 (and a range of $189,448-$201,692) at age 55, and an average of $166,588 (range of $161,243 to $171,957) at age 65. As a rule of thumb, a 65-year-old man would pay about 13 times the annual benefit to buy a single-premium annuity.[13]

TYPES OF ANNUITIES

Fixed Annuities

The National Association of Insurance Commissioners (NAIC) defines a fixed deferred annuity as one that earns interest during the accumulation period at a set rate or based on a methodology set out in the annuity contract and subject to an interest-rate floor.[14]

Several interest rates are used with respect to fixed deferred annuities. The current interest rate is the rate credited to a contract at a particular time, subject to a guarantee that it will be maintained until a stipulated date. Some issuers offer an initial rate that is a "bonus" rate, i.e., more favorable than the renewal rate that will take over a defined time after purchase. The renewal rate is often indexed, i.e., calculated based on an objective factor such as prime rates. It is not necessarily true that a single interest rate will apply to the entire contract. The contract may specify adjustments to the interest rate for each premium payment or for time periods during which premiums are paid.

The immediate fixed annuity is another option, where the income payments begin as soon as the annuity is purchased. This is a comparatively small piece of the annuity market, and one that some commentators believe is undeservedly obscure. In 2004, only $5.3 billion in immediate fixed annuities were purchased, versus $53.2 billion in mutual funds. Many retirees shy away from immediate annuities because they are afraid they will die prematurely, wasting much of their investment. That is one reason why guarantees are popular, even though they reduce the monthly income from the annuity investment.

Jonathan Clements suggests that immediate annuity purchasers should concentrate on their own income needs, not potential disappointment for their heirs. Clements predicts that pure longevity guarantees will be offered in the future, products that provide monthly income if the purchaser survives to a stated age. He suggests purchasing a lifetime income annuity only from a top-rated insurer; only if the purchaser's health and family background suggest survival well into the 80s; and postponing the purchase if the investor believes that interest rates will rise in the future. Because of the risk structures, an investor can get more income from a conventional annuity by deferring the purchase until his or her seventies, but new annuities that defer income until age 80 are cheaper if purchased further in advance.

His August, 2005 article profiles new products: MetLife's retirement income insurance that locks in units of $1,000 of income for life starting at age 85. The product can be purchased at age 65 with a single premium of $33,800. Full or partial withdrawals of annuity value can be made. The purchaser's heirs receive the investment plus 3%. Clements says that most investors would do better by investing the $33,800 in a tax-deferred fixed annuity, then using it to purchase an immediate annuity at 85.

New York Life's step-up annuity pays $10,000 a year between ages 65 and 85 then the payment jumps to $40,000 (although after 20 years of inflation, $40,000 might not have much remaining buying power!) An annuity of this type would cost $158,844 for a 65 year old man and $187,215 for a 65 year old woman. For a man, that costs only about $30,000 more than a $10,000 per year annuity that has a level payment with no step-up; a woman would pay about $45,000 more for this feature.[15]

Fixed annuities have an important role in elder care planning that may not even be noticed by the planning client. They are an important tool used by employers to fund pension plans.[16] Plan investment managers are fiduciaries, constrained to secure the best investment returns consistent with a very low acceptance of risk. Generally speaking, fixed annuities do not fluctuate in response to market forces and so offer predictability. They can also be "laddered," i.e., different maturities can be combined in a single plan in order to lock in rates for various durations.

Another important role is as a mechanism for Individual Retirement Annuities (IRAs) into which pension funds are rolled over. Generally, more than 90% of fixed annuity contracts accept IRA rollovers.

According to Beacon Research Publications Inc., which reviewed 213 fixed annuity products offered by 47 insurers in the second quarter of 2005, 77% of sales came from contracts with one-year guarantee periods (down somewhat from 82% the same period a year earlier). Market-value adjusted fixed-rate annuity products with shorter guarantee periods represented 40% of sales, up from 36% a year earlier. A market-value adjusted fixed annuity pays a declared rate of interest for a specified period. There is some interest rate risk when the holder withdraws assets during the contract term, because the market value reflects changes in the specified benchmark index. Book value fixed annuities also pay a stipulated rate of interest for a specified period, but without market value adjustment on withdrawals. Generally, when fixed annuity buyers prefer one-year rates, it is a signal that rates are high or buyers expect them to rise in the future. Fixed annuity buyers' preference for multi-year contracts would show that the multi-year rates are too high, or that buyers expect interest rates in the economy as a whole to be stable or to fall.[17]

Equity Indexed Annuities

The equity indexed annuity (EIA) is a counterpart to index funds that try to reduce risk by duplicating the performance of the entire market or an entire sector of the market. This type of annuity is generally not considered to be a security. Therefore, an equity indexed annuity can be sold by persons who do not have a securities license and buyers do not have to be given the full range of securities disclosures before they purchase.

Equity indexed annuities were very popular in 2005; in the first half of the year, $13.8 billion (up almost 50% from the previous year) was invested in EIAs. 2004 sales were $23.4 billion—up two-thirds from 2003. Bank sales of equity indexed annuities nearly tripled between 2004 and 2005, and the bank share of total EIA premiums rose from 5% to 7%. The number of annuities available to purchasers rose from 140 in 2004 to 242 in 2005. EIAs were attractive because of their guarantee of return of principal, combined with the chance to earn market-based returns; conservative investors who want higher rates than traditional fixed annuities might wish to turn to EIAs.

But this attractiveness also bears its own risks. The SEC and the NASD have expressed concern about whether investors received adequate disclosure, or whether they were being given the impression that they could benefit by stock market gains but did not undertake any risk.[18] Critics charged that EIAs were too complex, placed investors' funds at high risk, and were weighted down by excessively high commissions. A number of major insurers declined even to offer EIAs. According to MassMutual Financial Group, between 1973 and 2003, EIAs earned annual returns of 5.8%, well below the 8.5% that could have been earned by investing in an S&P 500 index fund, and looking even worse in comparison to the 12.2% potentially earned by investing in the entire S&P 500 and reinvesting dividends. A number of lawsuits have been filed alleging that EIAs have been sold deceptively, or to unsuitable purchasers.[19]

The difference between a variable annuity and an equity indexed annuity is the way it responds to market changes. The investor in a variable annuity divides his or her investment among several accounts and is permitted to switch several times a year if his or her investment preferences change. Equity indexed annuity investments are controlled by the issuer who guarantees a floor interest rate (typically, 3%) but also promises to return a specified percentage of the gain in the chosen index (e.g., S&P 500) to investors. The percentage, such as 70%, is called the participation rate and can be fixed for the entire term of the annuity contract or changeable at stated intervals. The calculation could be based on simple or compound interest. The contract might also include a cap amount that limits the upside potential. Usually, the computation does not include dividends on the stocks comprising the index. Yet another approach is to compute the change in the relevant index then subtract an administrative fee before crediting the investor's account.

Equity indexed annuities use several methods to adjust account values, including ratcheting (also called annual reset), high-water-mark, and point-to-point. The annuity is enhanced each year of an annual reset based on changes in the value of the index at the start and end of the contract year. High-water-mark adjustments are based on changes in index value during the term, usually as of anniversary dates of purchase of the annuity, measured by the difference between the highest value of the index during the term and the initial value. Point-to-point adjustments are made based on the ending and beginning values of the relevant index.

As a general rule, the annual reset generates the lowest participation rate and is the most likely to be subject to a cap on upside appreciation. But it might offer the best results during a period of significant fluctuations in the index. Furthermore, interest is credited each year whereas interest is only credited at the end of the term using high-water-mark or point-to-point methodologies. Thus, surrender of the annuity in mid-term could result in loss of interest for part of the term.

Interest is credited to annuity accounts at the end of a specified term, which can be anywhere from one to ten years, but usually is either six or seven years. A variation is to make calculations based on a series of consecutive terms. At the end of each term, there is a window period when withdrawals will be permitted without penalty.

An equity indexed annuity could be a good choice for an individual who wants the steady income of a fixed annuity, but also believes that the market as a whole will go up (thus influencing the index), but prefers to invest in the market as a whole, not individual securities. But, as the discussion above shows, these are complex products, with the eventual return responsive both to the design of the individual annuity and to outside market factors.

There are significant differences among equity indexed annuities. It's simplistic to choose merely on the basis of participation rate because that is not the only determinant of the actual value of the annuity to its owner. Furthermore, even if the owner fully intends to maintain the annuity and avoid withdrawals or surrenders this objective may be frustrated by a sudden need for cash.

Variable Annuities

The variable annuity, unlike the fixed annuity, is a security product so only persons holding a securities license can sell it. During the accumulation period, the premium (net of charges) is invested in accordance with the account owner's directions. Several choices, including a guaranteed account, are offered. The payments from a matured variable annuity might be either fixed (as defined by the contract at the outset) or variable (responding to market conditions at the time of annuitization).

The entire balance of the variable annuity can be withdrawn in a lump sum or annuitized using one of the typically available settlement options. Some contracts allow "commutation," or surrender of the contract in exchange for the present value of the expected future payment stream. If the owner of a straight single-life annuity dies before his or her predicted life expectancy, in effect part of the value of the account will be forfeited, because the insurer has no obligation to make any payments to the heirs of the deceased owner.[20]

The cost of a variable annuity includes:

- Surrender charges, which usually will phase down until the surrender period ends;

- Mortality and expense risk charges, usually about 1.25% of the account value each year;

- Administrative fees, either an annual fee of about $25-$35 or a small percentage of the account's value each year (e.g., 0.15%); and

- Fees and charges for optional features such as extra income protection or long-term care benefits.

Morningstar reports that in 2005, average annual expenses for variable annuities (fund expenses and insurance expenses) were 2.08%--much higher than the average of 1.34% for mutual funds, and the variable annuities were also subject to loads on subaccounts, surrender charges, and annual contract charges (e.g., $25/year).[21]

In the late 1990s, new ways to pay out variable annuities emerged. For instance, a fixed immediate life annuity offers regular income for life in exchange for a one-time payment. Immediate life variable annuities also guarantee life income, but the level of income responds to the performance of the mutual fund investments underlying the annuity. The annuity purchase rate for a fixed immediate annuity depends on mortality expectations, age, and the interest rate guaranteed; it may also depend on the purchaser's sex. Calculations for the immediate variable annuity depend on an assumed interest rate such as 3, 5, or 7% (the annuitant may be given a choice). The initial payment is calculated as if the annuity were fixed, whereas later payments depend on whether the actual investment result is better or worse than the assumed interest rate.[22]

The *Wall Street Journal*'s Clements gives an example of a tax-deferred variable annuity with living benefits for a 60-year-old couple who want to invest $100,000 in an annuity. If they purchase an immediate fixed annuity with lifetime benefits, www.immediateannuities.com quotes income of $6,084 a year for their joint lifetimes. According to Morningstar Inc., by 2006 nearly all (over 85%) of variable annuity contracts offered living benefit guarantees. For example, a $100,000 investment in Minnesota Life's MultiOption Advisor would guarantee $5,000 annual income for life; the guarantee would increase to $5,500 if withdrawals did not begin until age 70, or $6,000 for withdrawals delayed to age 80. Payments can also increase for favorable investment performance, but are not reduced if investment return drops. Prudential Life's Lifetime 5 also promises a minimum 5% annual income stream, with withdrawals based on the highest value of the account's investments over a 10-year term. The typical annual charge for living benefits riders is about 0.6% of the amount invested.[23]

A Guaranteed Minimum Income Benefit (GMIB) gives the owner and spouse the choice each year to either withdraw 6% of the initial amount or invest the 6%, increasing the income base. After 10 years, the owner can swap the variable annuity for an immediate annuity. The size of the annuity is governed by the highest value on any anniversary date (minus withdrawals taken after the high point of income). The initial income base is guaranteed, and the owner can always convert to an immediate annuity of that size. In the $100,000 example, the couple could get $5,020 a year from age 70 until the second spouse's death. However, a variable annuity with GMIB could have annual costs as high as 2.5-3% of assets. Such high costs could be made up for with good results from stock investments.[24]

The variable annuity market has attracted some adverse interest from securities regulators. In Notice to Members 99-35, the NASD warned about the responsibilities of selling variable annuities, and made 16 suggestions as to what registered representatives should discuss with their clients before a variable annuity purchase. In February, 2001, NASD accepted a $112,000 settlement of charges against four issuers (Prudential, First Union Brokerage Services Inc., Allmerica Investments Inc., and Lutheran Brotherhood Securities Corp.).[25]

The allegations involved misleading advertising and violations of the suitability rule (by failure to collect enough information about the customer's needs and financial assets). The sanctioned firms said that the violations were technical in nature and did not involve financial harm to their customers.

The NASD issued an investor alert on variable annuities in the wake of this investigation stating that exchange or replacement of annuity contracts is generally not a good idea. The NASD is concerned about the potential for "churning" (i.e., transactions that generate additional commissions for a broker but do not benefit the investor). It is also concerned because, in some cases, a surrender charge will be imposed and the exchange will trigger a new period during which surrender charges can be imposed. (Variable annuity commissions are typically twice those paid on mutual fund sales.)

The NAIC's Model 250, the Variable Annuity Model Regulation, can be found online at www.naic.org/documents/committees_models_variable_annuities.pdf. The latest proposed amendments require the use of the Annuity 2000 Mortality table (or any other post-1996 table approved by the NAIC) instead of the 1949 Mortality Table. Variable annuities (but not immediate annuities or deferred annuities already in pay status) must provide nonforfeiture benefits, e.g., paid-up annuities, cash surrender benefits, or death benefits, calculated based on a net investment return of 7% a year.

The SEC's Web site includes buyer's guides, "Variable Annuities: What You Should know," and "Variable Annuities and Variable Life Products: Questions to Ask." The agency notes that because a variable annuity is a security, its prospectus offers valuable information about the investments available within the annuity and how to allocate among them.

Some variable annuities give the option of choosing a "stepped up" death benefit, a minimum based on a larger amount than the total of the investor's purchase payments net of his or her withdrawals. (There is an additional charge for this feature.) Some variable annuities are linked to long-term care insurance benefits. Many variable annuities provide a guaranteed minimum income level—for example, if the annuity owner's investment choices have not panned out well. The annuity seller imposes an additional charge for such protection. The SEC warns investors to consider whether financial features that they select might be available elsewhere at lower cost.

The SEC suggests considering the following in conjunction with a variable annuity purchase:

- Will the money be needed quickly? Variable annuities are long-term investments, and are not very liquid because of surrender charges and tax costs.

- Is the product affordable out of current income or investment funds? The SEC warns that it is financially unwise to mortgage one's home to buy variable investment products; the SEC has a complaint hotline at (800) SEC-0330 if a salesperson exerts pressure to encumber the investor's house.

- Is the product intended for a tax-favored retirement account? The SEC's position is that "double deferral" is not worth the high cost of variable annuity investing.

- Is the recommendation personally tailored or do all clients get the same advice?

- Is a proposed 1035 exchange worthwhile to the customer, or is the new guaranteed death benefit lower than the old one, the annual fees are higher, and the surrender charge and/or surrender period may be greater; if so, the exchange subtracts rather than adding value.

- Does the potential purchaser understand the financial and tax implications of the purchase?

The SEC advises customers who have complaints about variable annuity sales practices to contact the National Association of Securities Dealers (NASD);

a database of NASD local offices can be found at www.sec.gov. The SEC itself has an online complaint form for questions or complaints, or investors can write to the Office of Investor Education and Assistance, 100 F Street NE, Washington, DC, 20549-0213.

Late in 2005, an NAIC committee voted in favor of changes to the standards for variable annuities that have performance guarantees. (The whole NAIC was not able to vote, because the Fall 2005 annual meeting had to be cancelled because of Hurricane Katrina.) Under the new standards, the capital requirements for guaranteed variable annuity products will have to combine standard scenarios and principles-based analysis of risk, to make sure that the reserves will be large enough to support payments no matter how the market moves.[26]

Combination Products

The financial services industry is evolving various combinations of annuities with other planning tools.

Because of the predictable needs of older investors, combinations of annuities and long-term care benefits have been suggested. A white paper published by the Pension Research Council says that there are many reasons why life annuities are not as popular as they could and perhaps should be. The annuity purchase is irrevocable, which can deter potential purchasers who place a high value on having liquid assets—or those who expect to need immediate cash to pay health bills. Commercial life annuities aren't indexed for inflation, so some potential purchasers fear that they will be trapped with an inadequate fixed income. Of course, a life annuity without guarantees ends when the annuitant dies, which is unacceptable to persons with an estate planning motivation.

The combination of annuity and LTCI policy could be attractive by offering liquid funds for care, and also protecting the inheritance because an insured person does not have to spend down assets (or at least not as many assets) to qualify for Medicaid. The combination is also psychologically attractive because the annuitant "wins" by living a long time, whereas the LTCI insured "wins" by becoming severely disabled and requiring a lot of care! A common objection to purchasing stand-alone LTCI is that potential buyers are afraid of forfeiture if they never require long-term care; a combination product offers investment value. Furthermore, the same premium can cover both the situation of healthy aging, with a need for income that continues for a long time, and the situation of age-related disabilities that shorten the life expectancy but increase the need to pay for care.

Long-term care benefits from an annuity product can be arranged in various ways. Many annuity providers will allow withdrawals to pay for LTC and will not impose the normal surrender charge. Some annuities permit immediate annuitization of deferred benefits, or increase the payment available under an immediate annuity, based on a showing that the individual needs assistance with Activities of Daily Living. The most elaborate method of coordination uses cash value from the annuity to provide long-term care benefits (for example, for two years, subject to a 90-day elimination period) with riders available to continue the long-term care benefits for an additional period of years. The money used to pay for LTC is treated as a withdrawal from the annuity.

At press time, both the House and the Senate had passed separate retirement plan reform bills, so a conference committee was appointed to iron out the differences and come up with a single bill for the President's signature. The House version of the bill included provisions for favorable tax treatment of combination annuity and LTCI products, to encourage purchase of such products.

The bill makes it clear that qualified LTCI benefits provided under a combination product would receive the same favorable tax treatment as benefits under a stand-alone LTCI policy that satisfied the Internal Revenue Code rules. Charges paid for insurance coverage would not be considered withdrawals from an annuity contract containing gains, so they would not be taxed (unless withdrawals were taken in the full amount of the contract, when the contract had a tax basis greater than zero). The bill allows tax-free exchanges between combination products (life/LTCI and annuity/LTCI).

The Treasury Department supports the House bill and the tax uniformity it would create (i.e., each part of a combination policy would get the same tax treatment as a stand-alone annuity or LTCI policy).[27]

Other combination strategies are possible. Hersh Stern of Totalreturnannuities. com suggests that deferred annuity investors back-stop their plans against inflation by buying a smaller annuity than they planned for, putting the additional funds into a separate investment account. Later on, the investment proceeds can be used to purchase an additional annuity, which will make larger payments because the now-older person has a shorter life expectancy.

"Retirement income insurance" is MetLife's deferred annuity that delays withdrawals until late in retirement. A 55 year-old man who purchased such an annuity in 2004 for $25,000 would receive a guaranteed $22,000 a year by delaying withdrawals until age 85.[28]

STRATEGIES FOR THE DEATH BENEFIT

One approach to life insurance planning is simply for financial advisors to assist their elder clients in selecting an appropriate life insurance program. Then, the elder clients can keep their investment decisions separate from their insurance decisions. However, savvy clients often like combination products, especially if there is a tax advantage to be gained. Before mid-1998, some claimed that the variable annuity death benefit was essentially valueless because the stock market would never decline enough to force the value of variable annuity accounts below the death benefit. The events of that year proved them wrong, as did earlier unpleasantness in 1997.

A strategy that can work if the stock market declines is to withdraw funds from the variable annuity account, leaving in enough to keep the account open. The death benefit is defined as at least the principal minus withdrawals, so this strategy operates as a form of unofficial life insurance.[29]

Throughout the variable annuity industry, the average "mortality and expense risk" (M&E) fee is about 1.25% of assets per year. However, some companies offer both a basic death benefit and an optional, higher-cost enhanced benefit. A rising-floor death benefit re-calculates the value of the death benefit regularly (it could be anywhere from annually to every six years). A stepped-up benefit re-adjusts the death benefit to equal the market value of the annuity account, rather than the initial investment. The death benefit might even be generously defined as the highest of the current contract value or the value of the contract as of any anniversary of the purchase.[30]

Some advisors suggest that it makes sense to divide a large variable annuity investment between two or more accounts with differing risk profiles. That way, if one account (usually the riskier one) drops in value, the death benefit can be used to make up for the loss. The overall result, in the somewhat unlikely case that the account holder dies before the accounts recover value, can be better than if there were only one account, which lost less and therefore got a smaller death benefit.[31]

ANNUITY OR ?

Clearly, then, a commercial annuity bears a striking resemblance to an Individual Retirement Account (IRA), but it also resembles a mutual fund or Certificate of Deposit (CD). What determines which should be selected when an older client wants to make an investment?

- *Size of investment*: Contributions to an IRA account are limited and a penalty tax is imposed on excess contributions. Persons who invest in annuities, CDs, or mutual funds are not constrained by such a limit and can invest on any schedule.

- *Possible tax deduction*: Depending on the client's income and compensation situation, part or all of the maximum annual contribution to a conventional IRA may be deductible for income tax purposes. Roth IRA contributions, annuity contributions, and funds used to purchase mutual fund shares are not deductible.

- *Tax on accumulation*: Funds within an IRA (conventional or Roth) or annuity account accumulate on a tax deferred basis, but mutual fund shareholders are taxed each year on distributions from the account. (Distributions from the account are not necessarily the same amount as the appreciation in the account's value.) Some of the mutual fund distributions will be taxable at ordinary income rates, others at capital gains rates. Naturally, the taxpayer's income tax bracket will determine the value of the distinction between capital gain and ordinary income taxation.

- *Tax accounting*: Even a premature withdrawal from a Roth IRA is treated as if it were made first as a non-taxable return of capital and only subsequently from income. Thus, there is no income tax or premature withdrawal penalty on a premature withdrawal that does not exceed the actual contributions made by the taxpayer. But annuity withdrawals are taxed as if the taxable appreciation was withdrawn first and the premature withdrawal penalty applies to the portion of the withdrawal that is taxable.[32]

- *Liquidity limitations*: A penalty income tax is imposed on withdrawals from an IRA account or annuity before the owner reaches age 59½ (unless he or she is disabled, or other special conditions apply). There is no penalty when mutual fund owners withdraw funds from the account (i.e., sell some of their shares), but they do have to pay income tax (usually at capital gains rates) on any profits earned by selling shares. In addition, many annuities impose surrender charges on withdrawals at least until the funds have remained in the account for seven to ten years.

- *Mandatory withdrawals*: A penalty tax is also imposed on conventional IRAs if the owner fails to withdraw the mandated minimum amount each year. There is no minimum required withdrawal from Roth IRAs (during lifetime), mutual fund accounts, or annuities. It is perfectly permissible for the owner of the account to permit most or all of it to accumulate for inheritance by his or her heirs.

- *Tax on distributions*: In general, the amounts withdrawn from a conventional IRA account represent ordinary income. Withdrawals from a Roth account are generally tax-free as long as the funds remained in the account for at least five years. Mutual fund distributions are taxed as either capital gains or ordinary income depending on the nature of the transaction at the level of the mutual fund. Annuity payments are part tax-free return of capital and part ordinary income. Even though some of the annuity income stream comes from capital transactions, the annuity owner is not allowed to take advantage of capital gains tax rates on such payments.

- *Tax on switches*: Internal Revenue Code Section 1035 permits certain tax-free exchanges of insurance products (including annuities). However, a person who switches between mutual funds (even mutual funds in the same family) will be taxed on any profits on the sale of one fund and cannot "roll over" the gains to the second fund.

- *Fees and costs*: Variable annuities have an insurance aspect which is absent from mutual funds. According to VARDS, total fees for the average variable annuity in 2001 aggregated about 2.3% of assets. Both types of investment have some kind of investment and management fee. Some mutual funds have up-front loads (not present in variable annuities) but most variable annuities have surrender charges which are less common in mutual funds.[33]

- *Estate inclusion or exclusion*: Under appropriate circumstances the designated beneficiary of a deceased person's IRA can defer taxation of the inheritance.[34] There are no corresponding provisions for mutual funds or annuities. If the account owner has "annuitized" for life there will be nothing to go into the estate, i.e., nothing subject to estate taxation but also no benefit to heirs. Under IRC Section 2039, the present value of any amount payable to heirs under a joint-and-survivor annuity or under a term-certain is included in the taxable estate of the deceased account owner. (Note that EGTRRA 2001 repeals the estate tax in 2010 for one year.)

- *Security*: Which investment is most likely to make payments as promised? What is the availability of government or other safety mechanisms if the issuer fails?

- *Personal preference*: Which investment makes the client feel most secure? For instance, even though the death benefit feature of annuities is seldom triggered, it provides comfort to many older investors who are afraid that, at the time of their death, the value of their annuity may have declined beneath its initial value.

Probably, the older client should begin by investing in the appropriate housing. This may be a free-standing home, a retirement community or a continuing care retirement community (CCRC) unit, or some other living arrangement that suits the client's financial profile, tax bracket, Medicaid plan, and estate plan. Next, the older client should address any security needs by having a sensible portfolio of life and health insurance (including long-term care insurance, if desired and affordable).

Afterward, the first move is probably using highly tax-favored mechanisms such as 401(k) plans and IRAs and then investing. A deferred annuity can be an especially compelling investment because of its potential to defer taxation on appreciation. An immediate annuity can be an appropriate investment for a retiree whose main interest is in a continuing income stream that does not require active investment monitoring.

Experts have shown how adding annuities to the portfolio improves the older client's ability to satisfy financial objectives. TIAA-CREF found that 71% of pre-retirees are worried about their ability to maintain a reasonable standard of living for the rest of their lives. More than two-thirds of plan participants (69%) consider guaranteed monthly retirement income very important, but 61% also want a payout option that lets them maintain control over their savings. Forty-nine percent want protection from loss of annuity value if they die before their predicted life expectancy (which could explain why annuitization is not popular).

Yet only 31% of workers with retirement plans are very confident of their ability to manage investments once they retire, and only 19% were very confident about their ability to make good decisions about annuitization. The author of this report points out that annuitizing half, or even a quarter, of assets, makes it much more likely that the individual can maintain the target level of income.

A retiree with a conservative portfolio consisting of 20% stock, 50% bonds, 30% cash has a 33% chance of being able to withdraw 4.5% of the initial balance (with inflation adjustments) for 30 years. Putting 25% of the portfolio lifts the probability to 53%, and annuitizing 50% raises the probability to 80%.

In a more diverse portfolio (40% each stock and bonds, 20% cash), the investor has a 76% likelihood of maintaining a 4.5% withdrawal rate with no annuity,

85% with 25% of the investment value annuitized, and 95% if half is annuitized. An ACLI study found that 22% of the owners of immediate annuities consider it one of the best financial decisions they ever made, and 60% think it was at least a good decision.[35]

The Wall Street Journal's Jonathan Clements, a proponent of fixed annuities, suggested a fixed-annuity strategy in late 2005. Under this plan, an affluent 65-year-old with a $1 million retirement account might split the $1 million in half, using $500,000 to buy inflation-indexed Treasury bonds, the other half to buy a life annuity with guaranteed payments for 15 years. The annuity would pay close to $26,000 in the first year, with the payout rising in response to inflation. If the bond portfolio is kept intact, by the time the investor reaches age 80 the bonds would be worth $673,000 in 2005 dollars. However, the investor might be reluctant to tie up half of his $1 million fund at the time of retirement. Clements suggests purchasing an inflation-adjusted annuity each year in the amount of $23,300, with the rest of the retirement fund in Treasuries. By age 80, the 15 annuity purchases would generate income of about $26,000 a year; the bonds would be worth $686,000, about $13,000 more than if the investor had chosen the half-and-half strategy. Furthermore, if the annuity purchase is an annual event, it can be adjusted upward or downward (for example, if health care costs were especially high during the year).[36]

DOUBLE DEFERRAL: PROS AND CONS

About half of variable annuities are sold for use in IRAs or corporate retirement plans. The other half are sold as alternatives to investments in mutual funds and individual securities. In fact, in 2004, about 60% of all annuity sales went to qualified plans. One viewpoint is that annuities are a poor choice to fund retirement accounts that are already tax-deferred, especially if the annuity will be surrendered quickly enough to be subject to a heavy surrender charge.

The opposite viewpoint is that annuities are an insurance product as well as an investment product and the availability of a death benefit offers some hedge against market risk, in that it provides security for the account holder's heirs even if the investor dies when the market value of the annuity is at a low ebb. Further, it may be easier and less costly to shift between annuity sub-accounts than to sell mutual fund shares and re-invest in another mutual fund. Market factors are also crucial: at a particular point in time a fixed annuity may simply offer a higher rate of interest than the taxable mutual fund that might be selected instead.[37]

The National Association for Variable Annuities reported in March, 2006 that 70% of the financial advisors they surveyed thought that combining income guarantees and insurance benefits made it a good idea to use annuities in IRAs and qualified plans. Sixty-one percent called living benefits an important reason to use annuities in retirement planning; 66% pointed to guaranteed income.[38]

In September 2005, a class action was filed in federal court in Georgia, charging improper variable annuity sales for use within IRAs. A class was certified, and 120,000 persons who purchased variable annuities from Pacific Life between August 19, 1998 and April 30, 2002 were notified of the suit. According to the plaintiffs, variable annuities were sold to customers rolling over funds from 401(k) plans to IRAs, and the customers were not informed that double deferral is not necessary. The defendant, Pacific Life, denied the charges. The industry view is that variable annuities can be helpful even for retirement accounts, because variable annuities offer death benefits and guaranteed retirement income; they are not merely a tax planning vehicle.[39]

The major financial service companies responded to criticism by reducing their fees. Fidelity Investments introduced new variable annuity products with low maintenance fees and no charge for early redemption (although one of the products does not provide a death

JUMBO SHRIMP

An annuity that is not annuitized, like a jumbo shrimp, may seem like a contradiction in terms. Yet the majority of annuity purchasers withdraw the funds from their accounts in one or more installments, rather than leaving the funds in place to create an income stream. In fact, in any given year, only about one percent of annuity owners actually begin to receive payments.[40]

Why? It could be because they believed that a variable annuity offered a better return than a comparable mutual fund or individual security but they now want to withdraw funds to re-invest in a more favorable opportunity or that they need the money for some other reason. Yet again, they could be concerned that they will die after a straight life annuity goes into pay status but before they have recovered the full amount deposited with the result that their heirs will not receive anything deriving from the annuity investment. They might discover that, because they live in a Medicaid "cap" state, additional income from the annuity is perilous to their Medicaid plan. They could dislike the fact that, once they select an annuitization option, they will not be able to alter it to respond to market conditions or changing needs but will simply receive the benefit as stipulated.[41]

Insurers are responding to the reluctance to annuitize by offering more flexible options. There is a trend among an increasing number of companies to allow the chance to "commute" (take the remaining funds in a lump sum), for instance.

Or, the insurer may allow a lump sum withdrawal of part of the sum, with the rest converted into a payment stream.

INCOME TAXATION OF ANNUITIES

As noted above, Internal Revenue Code Section 72 governs annuity income taxation.[42] Annuity taxation starts with a simple principle. The investor gets back his or her capital tax-free, but must pay income tax on the portion of the payment that represents investment income built up before the annuity entered pay status. But since the tax code is involved, the simple rule soon gathers complexity.

It should be noted that, for income tax purposes, annuities are either qualified or nonqualified. Nonqualified annuities are purchased with after-tax dollars and therefore, as mentioned above, the portion of each payment attributable to principal is received tax-free. In contrast, the entire payment from a qualified annuity, including the part that can be traced back to the initial investment, is taxable. Qualified annuities, which generally are used to fund qualified retirement plans, are subject to limitations on the amount that can be invested initially and specify the age at which withdrawals must begin.

The central concept in nonqualified annuity taxation is "investment in the contract." The net cost of the annuity includes everything the annuity owner paid for the contract minus any non-taxable amounts received under the contract before the annuity starting date or date of first payment.[43] This net cost is the maximum that can be recovered without paying tax. Once the entire net cost is recovered, the whole annuity payment (not just part of it) will be subject to income tax.

Refunds

The refund concept doesn't apply to a life annuity or a joint life annuity, but a term annuity (e.g., payments for 10 or 20 years) may include a refund feature in case the annuitant dies before the term ends. The net cost of such annuities has to be reduced to account for the value of the refund feature. (Generally, as the net cost goes down, the amount that might be taxable goes up.) In some instances, the value of the refund feature is considered to be zero, so there will be no effect on the taxation of the annuity benefits. In other situations, the refund feature does have a value for tax purposes. The value depends on IRS actuarial tables (see IRS Publication 939 (General Rule for Pensions and Annuities) for details).

Expected Return

Once the net cost of the annuity is known, the next hurdle is calculating the expected return which is the total payments that can be expected based on the terms of the annuity contract. For a fixed period annuity (for a term of years), the expected return is simply the number of fixed payments times the amount of each payment. For example, a ten-year annuity paying $500 a month would have an expected return of $600,000 (120 x $500).

The expected return for a single life annuity is the amount of the annual payment multiplied by a "multiple" found in the IRS actuarial tables. For example, the multiple for a man whose annuity starting date is closer to his 66th birthday than to his 65th or 67th birthday is 19.2. In other words, it is expected that payments will be made for 19.2 years, so the expected return is 19.2 times the payments for one year.[44]

The IRS defines "temporary life annuities" as those where payments are made for life or until a specified period ends, whichever is shorter. The IRS has actuarial tables for this situation.

For joint and 100% survivor annuities (i.e., the payment is not reduced after the first death), expected return is based on the combined life expectancies of the two annuitants. Adjustments are required if the annuity is reduced. In that case, expected return is calculated separately, based on payments that will be received during the joint life expectancies of both plus reduced payments that will be received during the predicted period of survival.

Income Tax Calculation

An exclusion percentage is determined by dividing the investment in the contract (as adjusted for refund features) by the expected return. This percentage of every regular payment is tax-free. The rest of each payment is taxable. If the payment level subsequently increases, the entire increase is taxable.

However, once the entire net cost of the annuity (for this purpose, calculated without a reduction for any refund feature) has been recovered, typically, because the annuitant has exceeded his or her predicted life expectancy, then all further annuity payments are taxed as ordinary income.

On the other hand, if the annuitant dies prematurely, so that some of the net cost remains unrecovered at death, the "leftover" net cost can be claimed as a deduction on the annuitant's final tax return.

Income Taxation of Variable Annuities

The income tax issues are even more complex for variable annuities because there is no certainty about the size of each payment. One thing is clear: any withdrawals made before the annuity starting date are fully taxable as ordinary income (up to the amount of gain in the contract). In other words, even though the annuity is an investment, withdrawals are not taxed at capital gains rates.

The basic method described above is used to calculate the exclusion percentage for the annuity. However, since the investment nature of the variable annuity means that each benefit payment will not necessarily be the same amount, the exclusion percentage is calculated by dividing the investment in the contract by the number of years over which the annuity benefits will be paid.

It is also possible that, in a time of low returns on the variable annuity, payments for a particular year could be lower than the amount that could be received free of income tax. In this situation, the tax-free portion of future payments can be re-calculated to make up for the shortfall.[45]

Transfer of Annuities

Like other investment assets, an annuity can be given away, sold, or exchanged. As a general rule, the sale of an annuity results in ordinary income, not capital gains, taxation to the seller. The amount of taxable income is equal to the sale price less the net premium cost of the annuity.

However, there is no gain or loss on the exchange of one annuity for another annuity with the same annuitant. Nor is gain or loss taxable if the reason for the exchange is the insolvency of the company that issued the annuity.

CHANGES IN MEDICAID TREATMENT OF ANNUITIES

Before the enactment of the Deficit Reform Act of 2005 (DRA '05; see Chapter 6 for more discussion), the general Medicaid rule was that the purchase of an actuarially sound annuity would not be considered a transfer, because the purchaser exchanged a sum of money for an equivalent income stream in an arm's length transaction representing fair market value. In a state that provides Medicaid benefits to the "medically needy," excess resources can be used to purchase annuities and, if the annuitant requires long-term care, the income stream from the annuity can be spent down to pay for the nursing home resident's financial obligations. Annuities are also used in planning for the community spouse.

According to a GAO report published in September, 2005, the use of annuities in Medicaid planning costs the Medicaid system close to $200 million a year.[46] For this reason, and because of the need to reduce Medicaid costs, the use of annuities in Medicaid planning has been restricted. See Chapter 6. DRA '05 has added additional rules to prevent abuse of investment annuities. (Retirement annuities and annuities purchased with balances from conventional or Roth IRAs are not subject to the new rules.) The purchase of an annuity by, or on behalf of, someone who has already applied for long-term care Medicaid will give rise to transfer penalties. Medicaid applicants who purchased annuities on or after February 8, 2006 must disclose the purchases, and a penalty period will be imposed unless the state Medicaid agency is entitled to the remainder of the annuity to recoup its Medicaid expenditures on behalf of the annuitant. The state agency can be named as secondary beneficiary if the annuitant has a community spouse or minor, blind, or disabled child who is named as primary remainder beneficiary.

An actuarially sound annuity are exempt from transfer penalties if the annuity is irrevocable; non-assignable; and makes equal payments throughout the term. These provisions were adopted to prevent abuses via "balloon annuities" that made small payments throughout the term, with larger payments later (that were more likely to be inherited by the remainder beneficiary than received by the elderly annuitant).

PROTECTING VULNERABLE CONSUMERS

In March, 2005, the Oklahoma Department of Insurance adopted Senior Protection in Annuity Transactions Regulation (effective until July 14, 2006) to protect vulnerable senior consumers. It raises issues that might become the target of regulation in other states.

This Regulation covers both fixed and variable annuities sold to individuals (rather than used by employers as part of a pension plan). It is a violation of the regulation to make recommendations about annuities that are fraudulent or contain misrepresentations to induce consumers to replace their annuity holdings. An insurer or agent who recommends that a senior consumer buy an annuity must have reasonable grounds for believing the annuity is a suitable purchase, based on information provided by the consumer about his or her financial situation (including annuities and other investments the consumer already owns, and his or her tax bracket) and needs. Events described as "seminars" or "classes" must also be described in their advertising as "insurance sales presentations" if that is their purpose. Seniors who receive at-home visits from life insurance or annuity salespersons must be given written notice of their right to terminate the home visit and complain to the insurance department if they are pressured or other abusive practices take place. Compliance with the NASD Conduct Rules on suitability will constitute compliance with the Regulation.[47]

The NAIC has a Senior Protection in Annuity Transactions Regulation, which has been adopted by eight states, including Colorado, Connecticut, Florida and Utah.

The regulation mandates annuity issuers to maintain data showing suitability of the annuity for the individual purchaser. Insurers are required to supervise agents' recommendations to make sure that suitability rules are not violated. Some insurance commissioners seek to extend the suitability provisions of this regulation to all consumers, not just those over 65, but the financial services industry position was that it has not been documented that younger consumers face the same kinds of problems in choosing suitable annuity products. At its Spring 2006 meeting, the NAIC's Life Insurance and Annuities Committee adopted a proposal to require suitability review for annuity buyers of all ages.[48]

Several states already regulate annuity sales. New Jersey's Senior Citizen Investment Protection Act of 2005 limits the duration during which surrender charges can be imposed on annuities to 10 years. (Utah and Washington already had similar provisions in effect.) In California, "twisting" is a crime (inducing surrender and replacement of an annuity merely to generate a commission for a salesperson) punishable by a fine and imprisonment. Another dozen states are considering their own legislation to prevent financial abuses.[49]

Without admitting liability the Bank of America settled charges brought by Massachusetts securities regulators and agreed to let thousands of elderly investors withdraw without penalties from variable annuities. The regulators investigated whether investors were pressured into buying annuities without understanding fees and tax consequences. Variable annuity customers who were at least 78 in the 2003-2004 period can liquidate their accounts without surrender charges (although the settlement does not alter the tax consequences of surrender.)[50]

ESTATE TAXATION OF ANNUITIES

The estate tax implications of single life annuities are simple: there aren't any. The annuity ends at the annuitant's death, so there is nothing to be included or taxed in the estate. However, IRC Section 2039 does create estate tax consequences for joint and survivor annuities. The estate of the first annuitant to die may have to include the value of the benefit that the survivor will receive. Section 2039 also requires estate inclusion in some cases when the decedent died before the first annuity payment, but there was a guarantee feature to prevent the decedent's interest from being entirely extinguished.

The value of the survivor's interest that is included in the decedent's estate depends on whether the annuity is pension-related or was purchased as an investment. For investment annuities, the value equals what it would cost the surviving annuitant to buy a comparable annuity as of the date of the decedent's death. For other annuities, such as pensions paid in joint and survivor form, the valuation depends on the present value of the survivor's right to annuity income.

For the years 2002-2009, the number of federally taxable estates may be reduced because of EGTRRA 2001, the tax reform legislation passed in May, 2001. EGTRRA 2001 also eliminates estate tax completely for the year 2010, and perhaps repeal will be extended or made permanent. Certainly, in the interim, some clients may take the chance that estates that would have been taxable pre-EGTRRA 2001 will be relieved of federal tax by the new provisions (and that the new law will stay on the books and, possibly, be extended).

CHAPTER ENDNOTES

1. Joseph B. Treaster, "S.E.C. To Increase Scrutiny of Some Annuity Sales," *New York Times* June 15, 2004 p. C2; Jonathan Clements, "A 'Conservative' Investment That Comes At Too High a Price: Variable Annuities," *Wall Street Journal*, January 21, 2004, p. D1.

2. Eric T. Sondergeld, Mathew Greenwald, "Public Misperceptions about Retirement Security," (LIMRA International) (2005), www.limra.com/reports/publicmisperceptions.pdf.

3. Jeff D. Opdyke, "Incentives to Buy Annuities Gain Push in Congress," *Wall Street Journal*, August 25, 2004, p. D2.

4. This discussion assumes that the owner of the account is the annuitant – the person who receives annuity payments – but other scenarios are possible: someone could purchase an annuity that makes payments to or for the benefit of someone else (such as the purchaser's spouse or child); or the account could be surrendered before annuity payments begin.

5. See www.naic.org/documents/committees_models_255-3.pdf.

6. Arthur D. Postal, "Carrier Group Continues to Fight NASD VA Proposal," National Underwriter Life & Health, The Week in Life & Health, National Underwriter Online News Service, September 20, 2005, and "SEC Delays Enforcement of Investment Advisor Rule," National Underwriter Online News Service, September 13, 2005. The rule is available at Release No. 34-52046A at www.sec.gov, or at www.nasd.com.

7. Allison Bell, "Official Calls for Annuity Regulation Summit," NU Online News Service, January 9, 2006.

8. Linda Koco, "No-Surrender-Fee VAs Hit the Street," *National Underwriter*, Life and Health/Financial Services Edition, December 28, 1998, p. 13.

9. Erin E. Arvedlund, "Variable-Annuity Charges Decline," *Wall Street Journal*, September 17-18, 2005, p. B3; Jeff D. Opdyke, "Incentives to Buy Annuities Gain Push in Congress," *Wall Street Journal*, August 25, 2004, p. D2; Christopher Oster, "Some New Ways to Preserve Your Retirement," *Wall Street Journal*, Nov. 18, 2004, p. D1.

10. Angela Pruitt, "Allure of Fixed Annuities Fades," *Wall Street Journal*, March 8, 2006, p. D4; "Bank VA Sales Overtake Bank FA Sales," NU Online News Service, December 14, 2005 and "Banks See Annuity Sales Decline in December," NU Online News Service, March 9, 2006 and "VA Sales Up Slightly in 2005: NAVA," NU Online News Service, March 9, 2006.

11. Kaja Whitehouse, "Annuities, Meet 401(k)s," *Wall Street Journal*, August 15, 2005, p. R5.

12. Colleen DeBaise, "Financial Firms Use a Soft Touch in Pitching Annuities to Women," *Wall Street Journal*, October 4, 2005, p. R4.

13. Robert D. Hershey, "An Annuity with a Twist: Pay Just Once, Then Collect," *New York Times*, Jan. 23, 2005, p. Bu8.

14. The NAIC issues a *Buyer's Guide to Fixed Deferred Annuities*. Purchasing information is available at www.naic.org.

15. Jonathan Clements, "Longevity Insurance: New Products Attempt to Solve an Age-Old Problem," *Wall Street Journal*, August 10, 2005, p. D1.

16. See Jeremy Alexander, "Fixed Annuities Play Major Role in Pensions," *National Underwriter*, Life and Health/Financial Services Edition, September 28, 1998, p. 21.

17. National Underwriter Life & Health The Week in Life & Health, "Fixed Annuity Buyers Split on Durations," September 20, 2005.

18. Eleanor Laise, "Popular Annuity Can Be Tricky," *Wall Street Journal*, October 15-16, 2005, p. B4; No by-line, "Bank Indexed Annuity Sales Swell," National Underwriter Life & Health, The Week in Life & Health Online News Service, October 5, 2005.

19. Jonathan Clements, "Why Big Insurers Are Staying Away From This Year's Hot Investment Product," *Wall Street Journal*, December 14, 2005, p. D1.

20. See Bridget O'Brian, "Bet Your Life: How to Weigh Payout Choices," *Wall Street Journal*, June 16, 1997, p. C1.

21. "Variable Annuities: What Are They and Do They Make Sense?" www.totalreturnannuities.com/annuity-variable/variable-annuities.html.

22. Nancy M. Kenneally, "Some VAs Zero in on 'Income Stabilization,'þ" *National Underwriter*, Life and Health/Financial Services Edition, October 16, 2000, p. 8.

23. Colleen DeBaise, "Insurers Add a Twist to Annuity Offerings," *Wall Street Journal*, January 5, 2006, p. R3.

24. Jonathan Clements, "An Annuity That's Worth a Second Look: Retirement Security—But At a Price," *Wall Street Journal*, September 28, 2005, p. D1.

25. Marcy Gordon, "Insurers to Settle Annuity Cases," AP Online, February 15, 2001. In 2005, several lawsuits were filed against attorneys, sellers of annuities, and agents charging deception and abuses of annuities combined with living trusts, e.g., Stein v. AmerUs Group Co., No. 05-CIV-2391 (filed in the Eastern District of Pennsylvania on May 19, 2005): see www.estateattorney.com/fltas~1.htm.

26. Jim Connolly, "NAIC Oks Guarantee Proposals," National Underwriter Online News Service, October 14, 2005.

27. Tim Hill, "Annuity/LTC Combos: The Total Is Greater Than the Sum of the Parts," www.milliman.com/pubs/Annuit%20-%20LTC%20combos.doc; Arthur D. Postal, "Treasury Voices Support for LTC Annuity Rider," NU Online News Service, March 13, 2006 and "Treasury Gives View on Pension Bill," NU Online News Service, March 8, 2006.

28. Christopher Oster, "Some New Ways to Preserve Your Retirement," *Wall Street Journal*, November 18, 2004, p. D1.

29. Ellen E. Schultz, "Stock Loss in Variable Annuity Can Be Used to Lift Insurance," *Wall Street Journal*, November 11, 1997, p. C1. *Wall Street Journal* writer Ellen Schultz gives the example of a variable annuity account initially funded with $100,000, but whose value has declined to $75,000. Withdrawal of $74,000 from the account would be treated as a non-taxable return of capital (although the impact of surrender charges would have to be considered); the benefit paid to the heirs of the account holder would be $26,000 if he or she died with the $1,000 account still open.

30. Bridget O'Brian, "Annuities Firms Market the Death Benefit," *Wall Street Journal*, July 14, 1997, p. C1.

31. Ellen E. Schultz, "Variable-Annuity Tip Finds Two Better Than One," *Wall Street Journal*, September 26, 1987, p. C1.

32. Ellen E. Schultz makes this point in "Tax Advantages of Roth IRA Top Annuities," *Wall Street Journal*, October 16, 1997, p. C1. Her conclusion is that Roth IRAs offer a better tax "play" to eligible taxpayers than annuities do.

33. Jeff D. Opdyke, "Shifting Annuities May Help Brokers More Than Investors," *Wall Street Journal*, February 16, 2001, p. C1.

34. Treas.. Reg. §1.401(a)(9)-1. For more information see Chapter 8.

35. Paul Yakoboski, TIAA-CREF Policy Brief, "Annuitization: What Individuals Say, What Individuals Do," www.tiaa-crefinstitute.org/research/policy/pol030105.html.

36. Jonathan Clements, "Retirement on the Installment Plan: A Less-Risky Way to Buy Annuities," *Wall Street Journal*, November 23, 2005, p. D1.

37. Compare Danny Fisher, "Why Put IRA Money Into a Fixed Annuity?" *National Underwriter*, Life and Health/Financial Services Edition, September 28, 1998, p. 12 and David Shapiro, "Annuity Vs. Mutual Fund: Fairer Comparisons," *National Underwriter*, Life and Health/Financial Services Edition, August 3, 1998, p. 21 with Ellen E. Schultz and Bridget O'Brian, "Annuity Buyers May be Overdosing on Tax Deferral," *Wall Street Journal*, July 28, 1997, p. C1.

38. Rebecca Moore, "Study: Annuities Add Value to Retirement Plans," (March 15, 2006), www.plansponsor.com/pi_type10_print.jsp?RECORD_ID=32739.

39. The case is *Cooper v. Pacific Life;* see Steve Tuckey, "Suit Questions Sale of Annuities to IRA Holders," NU Online News Service, September 20, 2005; Erin E. Arvedlund, "Variable-Annuity Charges Decline," *Wall Street Journal*, September 17-18, 2005, p. B3.

40. See Elizabeth MacDonald, "Annuity Firms Seek to Update Mortality Data," *Wall Street Journal*, May 4, 1998, p. C1.

41. Karen Hube's "Annuity Companies Pitch 'Annuitization'o Recover Their Appeal," *Wall Street Journal*, June 8, 1998, p. C1 addresses these issues.

42. Excellent guidance about applying the rules in various situations can be found in IRS Publications 939 (General Rule for Pensions and Annuity) and 575 (Pension and Annuity Income).

43. The annuity starting date is the first day of the first period in which an amount is received as an annuity.

44. See Reg. §1.72-9, Table V.

45. IRS Publication 939 (4/2003), p. 7.

46. GAO Report, "Medicaid: Transfers of Assets by Elderly Individuals to Obtain Long-Term Care Coverage," GAO-05-968 (September 2005), www.gao.gov/cgi-bin/getrpt?GAO-05-968.

47. See www.oid.state.ok.us/www2.oid.state.ok.us/Notices/Legal%20Notices/EME%20050905.pdf.

48. See Jim Connolly, "NAIC May Expand Scope of Suitability Rules," NU Online News Service, January 18, 2006, "NAIC Panel Eyes Broader Suitability Model," NU Online News Service, February 23, 2006 and "NAIC Committee Oks Suitability Expansion," NU Online News Service, March 6, 2006.

49. Jeff D. Opdyke, "Under Pressure, Insurers Push Rules on Annuity-Sales Tactics," *Wall Street Journal*, August 11, 2005, p. D2 and "Annuity Sales Face Crackdown by Regulators," *Wall Street Journal*, August 4, 2005, p. D1.

50. Valerie Bauerlein, "Bank of America Agrees to Settle Annuities Case," *Wall Street Journal*, July 14, 2005, p. D2.

Chapter 13

Special Estate Planning Issues for the Older Client

The Economic Growth and Tax Relief Reconciliation Act of 2001 (EGTRRA 2001) repeals the estate tax for one year in 2010. For the years 2002 to 2009, EGTRRA 2001 provides a phase-in under which larger and larger estates are exempt from estate tax, and the top estate tax rate is reduced. However, because EGTRRA 2001 expires at the end of 2010, in 2011 the Internal Revenue Code reverts to its pre-EGTRRA 2001 status.

EGTRRA 2001 leaves most of the Internal Revenue Code estate tax rules intact, so the basic principles of estate tax planning are modified but retain viability. Furthermore, it has always been true that estate **tax** planning has always been only part of estate planning.

Whether or not there is an estate tax, and whether or not a particular person's estate will be subject to it, nearly all clients will require an estate plan that is coordinated with lifetime planning to assure not only fair provision for the client's needs, but for the needs of the client's surviving spouse and children (if any) and for transmission of family businesses and other forms of wealth. For older clients, coordination of estate and incapacity planning is especially important.

Although certain basic estate planning concepts are applicable to all, there are also special issues that should be taken into account when elderly persons make an initial estate plan or modify an existing plan. Paradoxically, it can be hard to find the right moment to discuss estate planning with clients. To young, active clients, the entire subject seems impossibly remote (although it is often possible to get clients to understand the importance of maintaining adequate life insurance to protect growing families). To older clients, on the contrary, the subject may seem all too relevant and thus too threatening, with planning put off to "some other time."

Unfortunately, however, "some other time" might never arrive. Even if the older person is still alive, the person must have mental capacity to be allowed to make a will, set up a trust, or modify existing legal instruments and beneficiary designations. Some of these tasks can be performed by an attorney-in-fact (person authorized by a power of attorney, see page 369) or a guardian, but in most states making a will is considered inherently personal, so guardians are limited in their estate planning powers. It may be impossible to create a necessary document, or to update a document that no longer reflects current statutes.

How does elder estate planning differ from estate planning in general? In general, most estate planning clients are married, and taking care of the spouse is a very important planning objective. Yet, in the elder care context, a high concentration of widowed and never-married clients is found. In most estate plans, increasing the amount of funds available to the surviving spouse helps the surviving spouse. But if the survivor is elderly, reducing the available funds might be better–if the survivor is incapacitated and unable to handle money, and especially if the survivor has already made or might make a Medicaid application in the future.

Because federal law allows an unlimited marital deduction, estate tax on the estate of the first spouse to die can be eliminated completely by leaving the whole estate to the spouse. This simple approach (sometimes called an "I Love You Will") doesn't always work in the long run. Apart from Medicaid and capacity questions, it can create a "second estate problem." If the widow or widower dies without having remarried, the estate may be quite large (especially if the inherited assets have appreciated significantly), but there is no marital deduction available. The overall tax bill may be larger than if the survivor had received a smaller sum; or if other planning devices (such as the credit shelter trust; see page 346) had been used wisely to plan the first estate.

The older client's estate plan has to strike a delicate balance. There must be funds for current and continuing needs, especially medical and care needs. However, if a Medicaid plan is underway, it will be necessary to divest assets that are "excess" in the Medicaid context. This can also work well with the estate plan, where the objective is to reduce the estate, preferably below the taxable level. But in most instances, receiving Medicaid benefits will subject the estate to claims by the Medicaid agency after the recipient of benefits dies (see page 148)–so a decision will have to made whether receiving Medicaid benefits is more worthwhile than transmitting assets to future generations.

PRACTICE TIP: If the decedent did not leave a will, or if there is a will but no detailed inventory of assets, checkbook registers, bank and investment statements, and tax returns are helpful in cataloging assets. Each state has an office for unclaimed property and the state Comptroller's Office has records of inactive bank and brokerage accounts.[1]

The parents of disabled people face additional planning problems. In earlier years, people with disabilities often had a short lifespan; today, it is much more likely that they will survive their parents. Several insurance companies and brokerage houses have special divisions to deal with the challenges of estate and other planning for disabled children. For example, if the disabilities are entirely physical, the disabled person may be able to manage an inheritance, but a developmentally disabled or mentally ill person would not. Any gifts, trusts, or bequests to disabled persons must be carefully planned to avoid disqualifying the person for Supplemental Security Income or Medicaid.[2]

BASIC ESTATE PLANNING OBJECTIVES

An estate plan is a way to transmit wealth to other people, and across generations, in accordance with the client's wishes–while reducing the amount of taxes that must be paid (both during life and on the estate itself). The typical estate plan uses a will to govern transmission of assets at the testator's (will creator's) death. Many estate plans use trusts, both for tax reasons and for convenient long-term management of assets. Life insurance makes it possible to create an "instant estate" for a person who has family responsibilities but few financial assets. Even affluent people benefit by the use of life insurance, because it receives favorable tax consideration. Combining devices (e.g., life insurance trusts) often enhances the power of each separate planning device.

This chapter refers to the "potentially taxable estate," because in the real world the vast majority of estates are not subject to federal estate tax–because they're too small; because of the marital deduction; because of charitable and other deductions. An important theme of estate planning is using giving programs and other devices to reduce the estate below the federally taxable level–without creating further tax problems later.

An additional problem arises for estates larger than the generation-skipping exemption ($2 million in 2006). The exemption is equal to the amount exempt from estate tax in 2004 to 2009 and the generation-skipping transfer tax (GSTT) is repealed for one year in 2010. The GSTT is imposed on certain gifts and other transfers made to a grandchild or person of the grandchild's generation, but not on transfers to persons of the transferor's own generation or one generation younger.

PRACTICE TIP: Although these issues are beyond the scope of this book, both trusts and estates are potential payors of income tax. Most trusts are "grantor trusts," whose income will be taxed to the grantor (even if someone else receives the income). However, some trusts must pay tax on their own income, and the income tax rules for trusts are less generous than those available to individuals. Under some circumstances, the beneficiary rather than the grantor or the trust is taxed. Allowing a trust to "accumulate" income (save it up from one year to the next) can add useful flexibility for meeting beneficiaries' needs–but greatly multiplies the trust's accounting problems! Invasions of principal also create problems in allocating between principal and income.

Simple estates are frequently settled in the year of the decedent's death; but a more complex estate may linger on for one or even more years. As it generates income on the decedent's assets, it has the potential to become a taxpayer.

If a person owns real estate in more than one state, probate is required not only in the state of domicile, but in each state where real property was owned. This requirement of "ancillary probate" can often be avoided by putting ownership of the out-of-state real property into a trust.

According to estate planning attorney James Lange, one useful strategy is to divide investments into three categories: regular taxable accounts; tax-deferred 401(k)s and IRAs; and Roth IRAs. The after-tax dollars should be spent first, followed by the IRA and then the Roth. The Roth comes last, because there is no obligation to take minimum distributions, allowing more funds to be kept intact for the heirs, who can then get a lifetime stream of tax-free income. However, this is not always practical, because many employer plans only allow ongoing 401(k) withdrawals by a surviving spouse. Other heirs would have to cash out the plan (and pay tax immediately).

A parent who is afraid his or children will not use their inheritance wisely might prefer to spend IRA and 401(k) balances themselves in retirement, leaving their children the stocks and mutual funds that were held in taxable accounts. That way, the children get a basis step-up (unless of course the estate tax rules are revised to eliminate this feature!) when they sell the inherited assets. What to do with real estate depends on individual priorities. For example, older persons who seldom use second homes and don't like the responsibilities of being a landlord should consider selling the properties. But people of advanced years or facing serious illness might prefer to retain real estate to give heirs access to the basis step-up, because so many real estate properties have appreciated significantly since they were purchased by the older generation.[3]

State Death Taxes

Although this discussion revolves around federal estate tax, it should be noted that most of the states impose their own estate taxes. If an older person is contemplating a move to another state, one factor in choosing a new home is whether it is a high- or low-tax state–definitely including its estate tax. A few states have "inheritance" taxes (imposed on the heirs, for the privilege of inheriting) rather than or in addition to "estate" taxes (imposed on the estate itself, for the privilege of passing along assets).

Before EGTRRA 2001, the majority of the states had what is called a "sponge tax," i.e., their tax was defined as the maximum amount that can be used as a state death tax credit against federal estate taxation. IRC Section 2011(a) gave the formula for crediting state death taxes against the federal tax obligation.

EGTRRA 2001 changed the treatment of state death taxes. In 2005, the **credit** for state death taxes is repealed, but estates can take a **deduction** for state death taxes.

State death taxes are imposed by the state that was the decedent's "domicile" at the time of death, so disputes can arise about people who had more than one home or apartment. A person has only one domicile, no matter how many residences the person has. Domicile is a fairly complex concept, involving not just the intent to reside in one state rather than another, but the strength of the connection with the state (including where bank accounts were maintained, which state issued the driver's license, and where the person was registered to vote).

Since EGTRRA, the significance of state taxes in estate planning has expanded significantly. Many revenue-hungry states have increased their estate and/or gift taxes, sometimes to an extent that the burden is substantial. Some states had an estate tax that was scheduled to expire, but have re-enacted the tax. Some states have "decoupled" their estate taxes from the federal system, and a number of those states continue to tax estates above $1 million, because the "decoupled" states have much lower exemptions than the federal system.

A few states do not have estate taxes. Some states have constitutional provisions that make it difficult for the legislatures to change their estate tax rules—which could be a factor in choosing domicile, because it doesn't help to move to a low-tax state if it becomes a high-tax state before the planning client dies!

EGTRRA 2001

Under present-day law, estate taxes and gift taxes are supposed to work together. If a person dies without having made any nonexempt lifetime gifts, the estate qualifies for the entire unified credit. On the other hand, nonexempt lifetime gifts reduce the unified credit; if the entire credit is used up, gift taxes have to be paid during life. (Most gifts to spouses and most gifts to charities are exempt from gift tax. There is also an annual exclusion of $10,000, as adjusted for inflation, per donee. If a married person's spouse agrees to join in the gift, the annual exclusion goes up to $20,000 per donee (with inflation adjustments). By the way, gift tax liability has to be used to reduce the unified credit. The taxpayer doesn't have the option of paying gift tax immediately in cash in order to preserve the unified credit for later use.

People usually focus, not on the unified credit itself, but the amount of money that can be sheltered from estate and gift taxation by applying the unified credit. EGTRRA 2001 provides for substantial increases in the estate tax amounts. These are the figures for the years 2001 to 2011 (the estate tax is repealed for one year in 2010):

Year	Estate Tax Max. Amount Protected	Unified Credit
2001	$675,000	$220,550
2002-2003	$1,000,000	$345,800
2004-2005	$1,500,000	$555,800
2006-2008	$2,000,000	$780,800
2009	$3,500,000	$1,455,800
2010	NA	NA
2011	$1,000,000	$345,800

However, the amount protected from gift tax by the unified credit is only $1,000,000 in 2002 to 2011. Furthermore, the gift tax is not repealed in 2010.

EGTRRA 2001 also reduces the top estate and gift tax rate.

Year	Top Tax Rate
2001	55%*
2002	50%
2003	49%
2004	48%
2005	47%
2006	46%
2007-2009	45%
2010	35%**
2011	55%*

* plus 5% additional tax on estates over $10,000,000 to recapture lower marginal tax rates

** gift tax only

The generation-skipping transfer tax (GSTT) rate is also reduced because it is equal to the top estate tax rate above. And, as noted above, the GSTT exemption is equal to the amount exempt from estate tax in 2004 to 2009. The GSTT, like the estate tax, is repealed for one year in 2010.

Under pre-EGTRRA 2001 law, merely receiving an inheritance was not an event subject to income tax. However, if the inheritance took the form of property rather than money, and the heir sold the property instead of keeping it, any profit on the sale would be subject to income tax. For many heirs, the impact was reduced because their "basis" (the tax value of the property used to compute the amount of taxable profit) was calculated as of the time of the decedent's death (or six months after death, if the alternate valuation date was elected). In many cases, the inherited property had appreciated in value significantly since it was acquired by the decedent–but the appreciation would escape taxation because of the increased basis at death.

However, EGTRRA 2001 provides that, when the estate tax is repealed for one year in 2010, heirs will get a "carryover basis" (i.e., be taxed as if they had the same basis as the decedent had when he or she acquired the property), and therefore is more likely to be subject to income tax on the profits. Each estate gets a total $1.3 million exemption from this requirement–so $1.3 million in property can be given a "stepped-up" basis instead of a "carryover basis." An additional $3 million in transfers to the surviving spouse can also qualify for the basis step-up.

EGTRRA 2001 imposes additional record-keeping and reporting requirements in 2010 for lifetime gifts and property transferred at death, because of the need for a transferee to know the basis of any property received by gift or inheritance.

THE GROSS ESTATE

The first step in calculating estate tax is determining the "gross estate"; then various deductions are allowed. If the remaining estate is large enough to be taxable, then the applicable tax rate is applied.

Any tax is then reduced by various credits (including the unified credit referred to above).

The problem is that, for tax purposes, the gross estate excludes some important items that would, according to common sense, seem to belong in the estate; yet it includes some equally important items that would seem not to belong there, such as some items that were given away. Furthermore, the "probate" estate–the amount that is subject to the jurisdiction of a probate court–is different from either the gross or the taxable estate. Joint property is excluded from the probate estate, but part or all of it (depending on the circumstances) might have to be included in the gross estate.

The Internal Revenue Code provides, in sections noted here, that the following items must be included in the gross estate:

- Property in which the decedent had an interest at the time of death, such as unpaid salary and bonuses, dividends on stock the decedent owned at the time of death, the decedent's business interests in partnerships and closely-held corporations (§2033).

- Transfers of insurance made less than three years before death (§2035).

- Transfers with a retained life estate (§2036).

- Transfers to someone else, on condition that the transferee survive the transferor, if there is a meaningful chance that the property will revert to the transferor–what counts is the likelihood at the moment before death (§2037).

- Revocable transfers during life, such as "living trusts" (§2038). This section also requires that, if a parent or grandparent sets up a Uniform Gifts to Minors Act or Uniform Transfer to Minors Act account for a child or grandchild, and serves as custodian of the account, the property will be included in the donor/custodian's estate if he dies while the child is still a minor.

- Certain joint and survivor annuities (§2039); see page 347 for more about this.

- Jointly owned property (§2040).

- General powers of appointment (§2041).

- Life insurance proceeds (§2042).

For estate tax purposes, the gross estate is reduced by creditors' claims against the estate; funeral and estate administration expenses; charitable bequests; the marital deduction; and state death taxes (in 2005 to 2009; see above). State death taxes paid act as a credit until 2004 (and after 2010): that is, within limitations, each dollar paid to another jurisdiction reduces the federal estate tax liability by one dollar. A credit is available for foreign death taxes.

THE MARITAL DEDUCTION AND THE SECOND ESTATE PROBLEM

Any married person can leave his entire estate to his spouse, and there will be no gift tax on interspousal gifts, and no estate tax on the spouse's inheritance–even if the gift or inheritance is in the millions or tens of millions of dollars. But it would be short-sighted to plan a very large estate using nothing but the marital deduction. After all, sooner or later the surviving spouse will die. In some cases, the surviving spouse will have remarried, and will be able to repeat the process–but often, the survivor will die unmarried.

Depending on the size of the estate, the survivor's needs, the investment climate, and how well the inheritance was invested, the estate may have fallen below the taxable threshold–or may be much larger, as a result of good investment choices. At this point, then, there may not only be a taxable estate, but one that is large enough to be taxed in the highest estate tax bracket, not just the lowest bracket. True, the estate tax has been deferred (one reason that the estate could grow), but now it's time to pay the price.

To avoid this second estate problem, the bequest to the surviving spouse can be limited; gifts to charities can be used to reduce the estate; a lifetime giving program can get assets (especially appreciated assets) out of the estate; or a credit shelter trust (see below) can be created. If the second estate is likely to be fairly small, the surviving spouse might choose to enter a retirement home or Continuing Care Retirement Community (see page 377); if a substantial entrance fee is required for admission, but this fee does not create an equity interest in a particular residential unit, the funds can be effectively removed from the potentially taxable estate.

Many couples engage in "estate splitting": that is, because it's impossible to tell which will die first, they use interspousal gifts (which are free from gift tax) to divide their assets more or less equally. That way, there will be two estates of roughly equal size (preferably each small enough to escape taxation), not one large and one small estate.

Another approach to the second estate problem is to use second-to-die insurance (see page 38) to provide funds to pay the taxes, without reducing the bequests. This approach solves the problem of having to predict which spouse will die first, because the insurance becomes payable when both spouses have died, in whichever order.

THE RIGHT OF ELECTION

The basic rule of estate planning is that people can do anything they want with their property. There are also some basic exceptions to the basic rule: joint property passes automatically to the other joint tenants, not by will. It's legal to disinherit your children, but there are limitations on disinheriting a spouse. The "right of election" is a surviving spouse's right to challenge a deceased spouse's will that leaves nothing, or less than a statutory share (usually one-third to one-half of the estate[4]) to the survivor. The result of the challenge is automatic: the probate court is obligated to give the statutory share to the surviving spouse, at the expense of the estate plan set out in the will. It has nothing to do with the surviving spouse's needs, financial condition, or even ability to manage money.

In general, the right of election belongs to the surviving spouse. The surviving spouse can decide to exercise it or forego it (if, for instance, the couple's children need the money more; or the survivor anticipates a significant second-estate problem if the right is exercised). A pre-nuptial or post-nuptial agreement can be used to surrender the right to exercise the right of election in the future. For our purposes, there is an important exception to the rule: making a Medicaid application involves a commitment to exercise the right of election, even if exercising the right and inheriting the funds means loss of Medicaid benefits. (See page 172 for more about this issue.)

CREDIT SHELTER/BYPASS TRUSTS

The credit shelter trust (also called the bypass trust) is one of the bedrock estate planning tools; in fact, many smaller estates can be handled very adequately merely by drafting simple wills for each spouse, planning for incapacity, creating a credit shelter trust, and leaving all assets over and above the credit shelter trust to the spouse. (Some plans also leave the credit shelter trust to the spouse.[5])

Until 1997, it was simplicity itself to define the optimum size of the credit shelter trust: $600,000, the largest estate that would automatically be exempt from estate taxation. Today, the optimum amount is found in the table on page 342: the maximum amount that can be sheltered by the current level of unified credit. Any kind of trust can be used as a bypass trust; unlike the QTIP trust discussed on page 352 below, there is no requirement that the surviving spouse receive all (or, indeed, any) of the trust income.

To see how the bypass trust works, consider a fairly small taxable estate. When the first spouse dies, the estate is divided into two parts: a credit shelter trust and either another trust or outright inheritances. There's no tax on the credit shelter trust, because it is protected by the unified credit. Also, amounts passing to the surviving spouse are free of estate tax.

Assume that the surviving spouse inherits the credit shelter trust, and keeps it more or less intact (but withdraws enough so that it never gets larger than the amount that can be sheltered by the prevailing unified credit), leaving it to a son or daughter. When the second spouse dies, the credit shelter trust is still free of estate tax; only the balance of the estate might be taxable.

The two trusts are often called the A Trust (or marital trust) and B trust (credit shelter or exemption equivalent trust). Life insurance can be used to fund the B Trust if that trust is not needed to produce current income for its beneficiaries. Choosing variable universal life insurance for this purpose can create the potential for both cash accumulation and tax deferral.[6]

ESTATE PLANNING FOR RETIREMENT BENEFITS

In many instances, senior citizens will already be getting retirement benefits when they make or revise a will. In the simplest case, it's not necessary to make an estate plan for pension benefits received after retiring from a job, because the benefits are received in joint and survivor annuity form, and payments continue after the death of the retiree (to the surviving spouse) or surviving spouse (to the retiree). But many other, more complex, situations occur, especially in connection with pensions received in lump-sum form, IRAs and other self-funded plans, and nonqualified benefits. Furthermore, it is quite legitimate for clients to differ in their objectives for their retirement funds. Some want to consume the funds for current needs; others want to accumulate them to become part of the estate.

If an employee dies before the first pension payment is made, the plan must generally do one of two things: either distribute the employee's whole interest in the plan within five years after the employee's death; or make the first payment within one year, and continue the payments over the lifetime of the designated beneficiary.

The basic pension payment form for married persons is the "joint and survivor annuity": i.e., payments are made as long as either spouse is alive. IRC Section 2039 provides that, when the first spouse dies, the decedent's estate includes the present value of the survivor annuity payments that will be made to the other spouse. However, the amount passing to the surviving spouse generally qualifies for the marital deduction.

It sometimes makes sense for the nonemployee spouse to agree to payments being made only for the first life. This increases the amount of income available during the first spouse's life (because the fewer the payments the employer expects to make, the larger each payment will be) and could reduce second death estate tax consequences (because there are no survivor benefits paid to the surviving spouse)–but, of course, should only be elected if the survivor can be expected to have adequate funds after the first spouse's death. Sometimes life insurance is purchased with the increased payments received during the first spouse's life, and the life insurance proceeds could be made available to the surviving spouse if desired.

Choice of Beneficiary

Before the Taxpayer Relief Act of 1997, married people with large pension benefits had a real incentive to choose their spouse as beneficiary of pension plan death benefits, because the 15% excise tax on excess accumulations was imposed unless virtually all of the assets remaining in the plan at the employee spouse's death went to the survivor. Today, the excise tax has been repealed, so in certain estate plans, it makes sense to select a nonspouse beneficiary (e.g., a child or grandchild, a charity, the decedent's own estate, or a trust).

Once again, this should not be done if the surviving spouse will genuinely need the money. Even if the survivor can spare the funds, there are real tax advantages to naming the surviving spouse as beneficiary. Death benefits that go to the surviving spouse qualify for the marital deduction in the first spouse's estate (although they might create a second-estate problem). The surviving spouse (but no other beneficiary) is allowed to take lump-sum death benefits and roll them over into an IRA, thus escaping taxation.

Making an irrevocable beneficiary designation is considered a taxable gift (and of a future, not a present interest, so the annual exclusion is unavailable). Interspousal gifts are free from gift tax. However, if there is a subsequent divorce, and the person is no longer a spouse, an irrevocable designation will remain intact.

As noted above, payments of the "qualified preretirement survivor annuity" (QPSA) required when an employee dies before receiving a pension can be made over the "lifetime" of the beneficiary. Under earlier rules, a revocable trust was deemed not to have a life expectancy, and therefore the entire pension would have to be distributed over five years. But IRS regulations provide that if a trust is named as beneficiary, the pension can be paid out over the life of the beneficiaries of the trust. It's OK to name a revocable trust as beneficiary of the QPSA, as long as the trust is drafted to become irrevocable when its grantor dies. The IRS and the pension plan must be given copies of the trust document, or at least a complete and accurate list of trust beneficiaries; and, after the employee dies, the executor of the employee's estate must give the pension plan a final list of the trust beneficiaries no later than nine months after the death.

Planning For and With IRAs

As discussed in greater detail in Chapter 10, IRS rules now greatly simplify estate planning for qualified plan benefits and IRAs, by permitting the designated beneficiary to be changed; by making the rules generally uniform for all beneficiaries instead of having separate rules for spouses (some special provisions are still available), individuals other than the spouse, and entities (such as trusts or charitable organizations).

There are now really only two lifetime options: to make calculations based on tables that assume that the beneficiary is 10 years younger than the account owner; or to make calculations based on the actual life expectancy of the account owner's spouse, if he or she is in fact more than 10 years younger than the account owner.

Under prior law, persons who were very interested in "stretching out" withdrawals from the IRA (that is, taking small amounts each year in order to leave more to the beneficiary) but did not want to pay the excise tax penalty were allowed to make an annual recalculation reflecting the greater life expectancy of people who had already demonstrated longevity. The final rules simplify this calculation–in effect, conceding that it is legitimate to treat an IRA (or qualified plan benefits) as an estate planning tool as well as a source of current income after retirement.

Nonqualified Benefits

A company gets tax benefits by maintaining "qualified" pension and welfare benefit plans for its workers, but at a heavy price. The plan must benefit all eligible workers, without discrimination in favor of the highly-compensated, and contributions generally must be made each year, even if the company needs the money for other things. Therefore, some companies do not provide qualified plans; or they supplement the qualified plans with plans that offer generous benefits to top management. Such "nonqualified" plans are perfectly legal, but do not provide the company with as many tax benefits.

Some nonqualified plans either guarantee a certain number of payments (even if the highly-compensated executive has died in the interim) or provide for payments to survivors. Deferred compensation that is paid after the executive's death generally becomes part of the gross estate. Not only do these payments have estate tax implications, they are also income in respect of a decedent (IRD) which must be included in income by the person receiving such payments. (The person who inherits these funds is entitled to an income tax deduction equal to any extra estate tax generated by the inclusion of the funds in the estate.)

TRUSTS IN ESTATE PLANNING

A trust is an arrangement under which the owner of money, securities, or other property (usually, but not always, income-producing property) transfers ownership and control of the property to a trust.[7] The original owner of the property is known as the grantor, creator, or settlor of the trust. The principal or corpus of the trust is the total sum of the trust's assets and accumulated income. The trust is managed by one or more trustees; sometimes the grantor is the trustee, or one of the trustees. Inter vivos ("living") trusts are created by contracts; testamentary trusts are created by wills.

The terms of the trust generally call for the trust to exist for a certain number of years, or for a person's lifetime or the joint lifetime of more than one person. During this trust term, income is paid to beneficiaries named in the trust (or described as a class, such as "all my grandchildren then living"). Or, the trustee can be given the discretion to accumulate the income instead of distributing it, or to distribute the income among a class of beneficiaries as the trustee sees fit. (This last variation is known as a spray or sprinkle trust.)

The trustee may also have discretion to invade the principal of the trust–to distribute part of the corpus. Often, discretion is limited by an "ascertainable standard" such as the health and support needs of the beneficiary (because this keeps certain amounts out of the estate that would otherwise be included). But see page 154 for Medicaid problems with ascertainable standard language in trusts. Finally, when the term of the trust ends, the remaining corpus (plus any accumulated income that was not distributed) goes to the remainderperson(s) named in the trust.

As a general rule, the more control the grantor has over the trust after its establishment, the more likely the trustee is to be liable for income tax on the income the trust earns, and the more likely the trust is to be included in the trustee's estate. It is also possible that the trust itself will be taxed on trust income, or that the beneficiary will be taxed. The "kiddie tax" requirements reduce the value of income-shifting within the family by providing that the unearned income of a minor under 14 is generally taxed at the parent's highest tax rate.

If the trust is revocable, the grantor retains the power to terminate the trust, alter its terms, or get back part of the corpus. The grantor of an irrevocable trust surrenders these powers (although even then, there may be a legal mechanism for ending the trust or revising its terms).

The IRS has published regulations clarifying the definition of "grantor."[8] Under these rules, if Mary Jones funds a trust on behalf of Sally Smith, both of them will be treated as grantors. But a person who creates a trust but does not make any gifts to the trust, or who nominally funds a trust but is immediately reimbursed for the funds placed into the trust, is not considered a grantor.

In practical terms, very small trusts usually don't work, because the legal fees for setting up the trust, the problems of transferring assets into the trust, and the continuing costs of management outweigh the benefits.

Trusts are discussed at many places in this book: in incapacity planning, and as a Medicaid planning tool (see page 152), for instance. See the chapter on the family home (page 191) for a discussion of PRTs and QPRTs–trusts that take title to homesteads and vacation homes. The life insurance chapter considers the advantages of placing policies into an irrevocable life insurance trust (ILIT). But perhaps the classic use of trusts is as an estate planning tool. Revocable trusts are included in the estate, because of the grantor's degree of control over the corpus; but, under the right circumstances, irrevocable trusts can be used to get funds out of the estate.

One effect of the estate tax changes made by EGTRRA 2001 will probably be to reduce the number of new trusts created, because more estates will be able to avoid estate tax even without the use of trusts. However, remember that trusts were in existence long before the U.S. estate tax (and long before there was a United States, for that matter!) because trusts serve important functions for managing assets for incapacitated persons and minors; for carrying out complex estate plans; and for making assets "unavailable" under Medicaid rules. Therefore, at least some of your clients should consider maintaining their existing trusts, or setting up new ones.

Note that, transfers of funds into trusts in 2010 will be treated as taxable gifts, unless the trust is a "grantor trust" that is deemed to be wholly owned by the grantor or the grantor's spouse. If this provision survives, trust planning could carry some additional gift and income tax costs.

Living Trusts and Probate Planning

Revocable living trusts are extremely popular, and are the subject of many books and planning seminars. To the elder planning team, living trusts are a valuable adjunct to the incapacity plan, with the caveat that living trust corpus remains available for Medicaid purposes. To the estate planner, living trusts are a useful though perhaps over-hyped device for avoiding probate, with the caveat that living trust corpus becomes part of the potentially taxable estate.

The executor of the estate and the trustee of a qualifying revocable trust can elect to treat the trust as part of the estate for income tax purposes, so the trust won't have to calculate and file a separate income tax return.[9]

The probate process can be prolonged and expensive, and in rare instances the fact that a will is a public document can lead to disclosure of embarrassing facts. Therefore, a living trust can be a useful part of the plan for a large estate to minimize these problems. Probate fees usually increase with the size of the estate, so reducing the size of a large probate estate can be productive. However, the estate would have to be pretty large–setting up and maintaining a trust costs money. Furthermore, in larger estates, federal estate tax is a more important factor than probate costs.

Even people who decide against living trusts can take steps to cope with probate problems. Life insurance can be used to provide liquidity until the estate is settled. Each spouse should maintain a separate bank account with enough funds for several months' living expenses (because joint accounts are often frozen during the probate period). The actual court fees for probate are a given, but overall expenses can be reduced by making sure that all relevant records are easy to find, so that expensive attorney time is not consumed in detective work.

Assets that pass outside the probate process are sometimes called "will substitutes." They include jointly held real estate; joint bank or brokerage accounts; IRAs and pension plans where a beneficiary has been named; and bank accounts in trust for a named beneficiary. Ownership is automatically transferred to the other joint owner or the named beneficiary when the joint owner/account holder dies. These will substitutes should not be forgotten when the estate plan is made (they can determine if the provision for the surviving spouse is adequate, for example)–but it's important not to try to dispose of them by will, because the disposition will probably be ineffective, and a time-consuming, expensive lawsuit will probably be needed to settle the issue.

Qualified Terminable Interest Property (QTIP)

Amounts left outright to the surviving spouse reduce the deceased spouse's taxable estate for federal estate tax purposes, because they qualify for the marital deduction. However, there are many possible legal forms other than outright ownership, including life estates and various kinds of trusts. For estate tax purposes, a QTIP is qualified terminable interest property–less than outright transmission of ownership that still qualifies for the marital deduction.

Although some other variations are possible, the basic QTIP is a trust that benefits the surviving spouse. During the surviving spouse's lifetime, the spouse must receive all the income from the trust (nobody else can get any of it, and the income can't be accumulated–it has to be distributed). At least one income payment must be made every year; usually quarterly payments are made.

The QTIP provisions require all the income of the trust to go to the surviving spouse, but don't require that principal go to the surviving spouse, so a trust can be a valid QTIP whether or not the surviving spouse[10] and/or the trustee is given the power to invade the principal on behalf of the spouse. However, no one can have the power to appoint the principal to anyone other than the surviving spouse during the spouse's lifetime.

Another possibility is to make the decedent spouse's IRA payable to a QTIP trust for the surviving spouse, with the provision that the surviving spouse gets either all the income of the trust, or the minimum distribution required from the IRA, whichever is larger. This is a valid QTIP, because the survivor gets at least all the income from the trust, and possibly more.[11]

When the surviving spouse dies, the corpus of the QTIP trust passes to whomever the deceased spouse designated–not according to the will or directions of the surviving spouse. However, because the trust was excluded from the estate of the first spouse to die, it must be included in the estate of the survivor. (In other words, QTIP trusts don't solve the second-estate problem.)

There can be many reasons for leaving a spouse less than an outright interest in money or property. In the elder planning context, it's important to note that the survivor's capacity may be limited or diminishing. The spouse may be able to handle income responsibly, but not to make decisions about investing large sums of capital. However, the IRS has ruled that a trust is not a QTIP, and not eligible for the marital deduction, if the trust calls for reduction or cessation of income when the surviving spouse becomes incapacitated.[12] (Nor can a QTIP stop income if the surviving spouse remarries; the spouse has to get trust income for life.)

QTIPs work well in general where the spouse who owns property wants the eventual ownership to pass to someone else (such as to his children). This is an especially strong rationale in the case of divorced and remarried persons who want to provide lifetime income for the current spouse, while making sure that the property eventually passes to the children of the first marriage. Also, the surviving spouse may receive Medicaid benefits, or be contemplating a Medicaid application–with the result that additional income is less detrimental to the plan than additional assets.

Although the trust is drafted while the grantor spouse is still alive, technically the trust doesn't become a QTIP until the executor of the grantor's estate makes an irrevocable election, on the federal estate tax return (IRS Form 706), to treat part or all of the trust as a QTIP.

A partial QTIP election might be better than a full one, if the surviving spouse is in poor health and might die soon, creating a second estate problem if the spouse is likely to die soon. In that circumstance, a smaller estate–and thus a nontaxable estate or one subject to lower estate taxes–would be preferable. If this is done, invasions of principal for the benefit of the surviving spouse can be charged to the QTIP trust, not the nonQTIP trust–with the result that the survivor's eventual taxable estate will be reduced.

Split-Interest Charitable Trusts (CLATs, CLUTs, CRATs and CRUTs)

Outright charitable giving can be very satisfying, and generous givers can get the satisfaction of being thanked in person, being elected to prestigious boards of directors, participating in gala social events, and the like. Lifetime gifts (with some limits) generally qualify for an income tax deduction. If the taxpayer contributes appreciated property to the charity (rather than selling the appreciated property and donating part or all of the proceeds), it will generally not be necessary to pay capital gains tax on the appreciation.

Furthermore, the income-tax charitable deduction is generally measured by the fair market value of the asset, not the donor's basis–so a large amount of otherwise taxable income can be offset by the deduction.[13] All outright gifts to public charities are exempt from gift tax, no matter how large the gift. However, sometimes it is inadvisable to make very large lifetime gifts, because it is quite possible that the funds will be needed, e.g., for long-term custodial care.

By the same token, outright bequests to charity qualify for the estate tax charitable deduction, and can eliminate estate tax by reducing the size of the estate below the potentially taxable level. (This can be an especially productive avenue for single people, who cannot take advantage of the marital deduction, and may not have close family members they particularly want to benefit.) But very large bequests may imperil the financial security of survivors.

One incentive for people to give more to charity is giving them a way to benefit the charity while still retaining personal or family financial benefits–and, in fact, that's exactly why the Internal Revenue Code includes provisions for irrevocable "split-interest" trusts, such as charitable lead trusts and charitable remainder trusts.

These arrangements are split-interest because the charity derives payments from the trust property for a defined term, at which time it reverts to the grantor or the beneficiary selected by the grantor (charitable lead trusts[14]), or they make payments to the grantor (or beneficiary selected by the grantor) for life or for a term of years, at which time the remainder passes to the charity (charitable remainder trusts). For instance, an older individual who has plenty of assets (including illiquid or highly appreciated assets that would generate an immense tax liability if sold) but requires more income and is charitably inclined might place some assets into a charitable remainder trust, and benefit by the additional income.

Split-interest trusts are classified into several categories; the most common are annuity trusts and unitrusts. The difference between them is the way that they define the payout that must be made to the beneficiary.

In an annuity trust, the beneficiary is entitled to a set percentage of the initial value of the corpus of the trust, paid every year: e.g., 6% of a trust set up with $100,000. The percentage does not change based on the actual current value of the trust or its investment success, with the result that it may be necessary to dip into capital to satisfy the payment obligation (and, if this happens often enough, the remainder may end up with a good deal less than the grantor originally intended). On the other hand, if the trust's rate of appreciation is greater than the payment obligation, the trust will grow in size, and the remainder will be larger than originally intended. Nor will the beneficiary get greater payments because of the trust's greater income; it's a risk the grantor takes.

In contrast, the payout under a unitrust does fluctuate; it is defined as a set percentage of the current value of the trust when the payout is made (e.g., 6% of whatever the trust is worth on a particular date of the year). As a practical matter, then, a CRUT should be funded with publicly traded securities or other assets that are easy to value. Under a CRAT, the beneficiary knows exactly what the payment will be; a CRUT beneficiary's payment is uncertain.

Another difference is that unitrusts can be drafted to accept additional deposits after the trust is first set up. This can be a worthwhile drafting technique for the next few years, as the estate tax unified credit exclusion continues to phase upwards. That is, the trust can be set up with a present value amount for noncharitable beneficiaries that does not exceed the maximum credit shelter amount, and then additional funds can be deposited to keep the trust at a level equal to the maximum credit shelter. (In other words, the charitable trust is used as a credit shelter trust; this strategy won't work in a plan where there already is a credit shelter trust. Also, keep in mind that the credit shelter amount will be much greater for estate tax purposes than for gift tax purposes from 2004 to 2009, so greater contributions to unitrusts protected by the unified credit can be made at death than during life.)

The term of a charitable remainder trust can be a term of years (but not over 20 years) or the life or lives of the annuitant(s). Although most charitable remainder trusts are inter vivos trusts (because the grantor wants to get personal benefits!), it is possible to set up a CRT by will, benefiting one's spouse or other heirs.

The choice between a CRAT and a CRUT, for a person already determined to set up a charitable trust, depends on the grantor's projections for future inflation and future appreciation in the value of the trust assets. The unitrust would probably work better for someone who is willing to accept some uncertainty and anticipates inflation- or appreciation-related increase in the value of the fund, or for someone who wants to continue adding to the credit shelter amount in the trust as the unified credit increases (see above). Naturally, the selection of an irrevocable trust must be made after serious thought, because there is no possibility of dissolving the trust or increasing the payout percentage.

The grantor has discretion to determine the annuity amount or percentage, but the Internal Revenue Code sets a minimum and maximum range that is permitted. The minimum percentage payment under either a CRAT or CRUT is 5% a year of the initial corpus, or of the current value of the corpus, respectively. For trusts either created or added to after July 28, 1997, a trust can generally qualify as a CRAT or CRUT only if the charity's remainder is worth at least 10% of the trust value, and the annual payout to the beneficiary must be no more than 50% of the trust value.

In the gift tax context, the gift to the charity in a CRAT or a CRUT is not the entire corpus of a charitable remainder trust—only the present value of the charity's remainder.

If the grantor is also the beneficiary of the annuity or unitrust, initially the trust assets will be included in the grantor's estate (because of the retained life estate). An estate tax charitable deduction will be available for the actuarial value of the interest passing to charity.

Charities are allowed to maintain "pooled income funds"—in effect, big trusts made up of contributions from individuals who can't or don't want to contribute enough to set up their own trusts. Pooled income funds can provide a stream of payments (based on the fund's income), much like charitable remainder trusts.

Trusts as IRA Beneficiaries

See page 348 above for basic estate planning strategies with IRAs. As seen many times in this book, estate planning strategies can often be combined, sometimes creating significant leverage. This is also true of naming a trust as the beneficiary of an IRA. The trust must be created before it can be named as beneficiary—and before the account holder reaches 70½. The trust must be irrevocable, or become irrevocable no later than when the IRA account holder dies. The IRA custodian or trustee must be given a copy of the trust or a list of the beneficiaries and their rights under the trust. As long as these requirements are satisfied, many kinds of trusts can become IRA beneficiaries, including QTIP trusts and bypass trusts.

A revocable living trust could be created, to be divided into two irrevocable trusts on the account holder's death, at which time the maximum amount that can be sheltered by the then-current unified credit is deposited into one trust and the rest is distributed into the other trust, which is a QTIP.[15]

Another option is to name the spouse as the primary IRA beneficiary, but make a trust the contingent beneficiary. This often makes sense in a small estate, where it's possible but not certain that there will be enough nonretirement assets to fully fund a credit shelter trust. When the IRA owner dies, the question then becomes whether the credit shelter trust will be fully funded; if not, the surviving spouse can disclaim part of the IRA, which then goes into a trust which becomes a credit shelter trust.

Dynasty Trusts

A spendthrift trust is one which prevents the creditors of the beneficiary from getting access to the trust corpus. The creditors can claim each income payment as it is made, but they can't unlock the principal. Traditionally, it has been held that no one can set up a spendthrift trust for his own benefit, only for the benefit of someone else (usually a sibling, child, or grandchild who is financially irresponsible or suffers from a disability). However, in the late 1990s, Alaska pioneered a new type of trust, and several other states have adopted similar provisions.

These trusts are unusual in two ways. First, they allow self-settled spendthrift trusts, so the trusts can be protected against creditors—including former spouses after a divorce. So far, the courts have not ruled on the Medicaid implications of these trusts, but they may work in that context. Second, they eliminate the "rule against perpetuities": most noncharitable trusts have to end within three or four genera-tions[16]; these trusts can go on much longer, allowing family wealth to accumulate without estate taxation.

Creditors' rights are very significant to estate planning. A transfer to a trust is incomplete (and therefore has no gift tax consequences) as long as the grantor's creditors can reach the entire corpus of the trust. The downside is that the entire trust corpus must be included in the estate of the grantor. If a trust, such as an Alaska-type trust, is exempt from creditor claims, it may escape inclusion in the estate under this rationale (but would be includable if the grantor retained certain interests, such as a life estate).[17]

Dynasty trusts, also called perpetual and legacy trusts, can extend the number of generations that wealth can be kept within the trust. At least 20 states, including Alaska and Delaware (the pioneers in trusts of this type), Florida, South Dakota, and Wyoming, allow dynasty trusts. In fact, in Wyoming and Utah, a trust can last

1,000 years, a Florida trust can last 360 years. Dynasty trusts are irrevocable, so they can be used to protect assets against creditor claims in case of lawsuit, bankruptcy, or divorce.

A rule of thumb is that it probably requires at least $1.5 million to make such a trust worthwhile (to justify the expenses of creation and ongoing management), although with a steady 7.0% annual growth rate, a $1 million dynasty trust would grow to $867.7 million in 100 years. The market for these trusts has continued to grow: according to a study done by Merrill Lynch and Cap Gemini, for example, the number of people in the United States with financial (non-housing) assets over $1 million went from 2 million in 2002 to 2.27 million in 2003 (a 13.5% increase).[18]

LIFE INTERESTS, REMAINDERS, LEASE-BACKS, AND OTHER INTRAFAMILY TRANSACTIONS

The ownership of an asset can be divided among several people at the same time–or split among several people at different times. The simplest example is the gift or sale of a remainder subject to a life estate. That is, the original owner of property transfers the ownership, but retains the right to use the asset for the rest of his life. The typical case is giving ownership of the family home to a child, while retaining the right to live in the house for life. This technique might be used if the asset is expected to continue appreciating in value; the purpose is to remove the appreciation from the estate.

In this instance, the owner gives away the remainder (the right to inherit the property after the life estate ends), and keeps the life estate. Therefore, there has been a gift to the remainder person, and the gift tax on the gift will reduce the unified credit available when the donor eventually dies. (See pages 341-342, above, for more about the unified credit.) A gift of a remainder with retention of a life estate will cause the property to be subject to estate tax.

The value of the gift is the present value of the remainder interest, which is actuarially determined based on the donor's life expectancy (using IRS tables). Present value is less than the full value, because of the "time value of money"–the right to get $1 five years from now is worth less than $1. In other words, the gift can be made at a discount–and a lot of taxes can be saved by getting the remainder out of the estate if the property appreciates significantly after the gift. A gift of a remainder with retention of a life estate will generally be valued as a gift of the entire property, except for certain transfers in trust.

In response to increased life expectancies, the IRS periodically revises its actuarial tables for valuing annuities, life estates, remainders, and reversions. These tables should be consulted whenever actuarial values must be computed for tax purposes. (The Health Care Financing Administration has its own, separate set of tables that must be used to calculate actuarial values for Medicaid purposes.)

A remainder is the right to receive property after someone else's interest in it has ended (for instance, the right to inherit a home after one's grandmother occupied it for life). A reversion is the right to take back property–for instance, property might revert back to its grantor if a particular person dies without heirs.

Sometimes it makes sense for ownership of a senior citizen's asset (such as a home: see page 182) to be transferred, while the senior citizen continues to make use of the asset. While it's true that outright gifts can remove assets from the potentially taxable estate, they can also be taxable events in and of themselves, or transfers that are inconsistent with a Medicaid plan. In that case, it may make sense to sell the asset to children or other potential heirs, but lease it back from them; or to make a gift, but make the gift subject to a lease-back. (Gift tax is not due until a gift is completed–until there are no strings attached to it.) Frequently, such transactions are structured as installment sales, because the younger generation often lacks funds to make an outright, lump-sum purchase. An installment sale can be attractive to a senior citizen who wants more current income, but wants to divest assets from the estate.

In some instances, intrafamily loans make sense, such as when the younger-generation member needs money to buy a home, pay medical bills, or pay tuition bills for children. But for the transaction to be treated as a loan, rather than as a gift, the parent must have a rational expectation of repayment; there must be signed notes; it helps if there is a set payment schedule–which the younger generation member actually adheres to–and if the agreement calls for market-rate interest, which is actually paid.[19] The lender should report interest as income; in fact, making a no-interest or below-market-rate loan actually constitutes a gift of the interest that was foregone.

Self-Canceling Installment Notes (SCINs)

The self-canceling installment note (SCIN) is another intrafamily financial planning option. The usual structure is an installment sale by parents to children, with the additional feature that the note representing the transaction includes the provision that it will be canceled if the seller-parent dies before all the payments have been completed. The asset is removed from the parent's estate; the child gets possession of the asset–although with the somewhat ambivalent factor that the child can get the asset at a discount if and only if the parent dies before the installment payments have been completed. (The odds are that the payments made during the seller's lifetime will end up in the seller's estate–unless they are spent; and if the asset has appreciated, the parent will have to pay capital gains tax on the profit, unless the SCIN involves a family home for which capital gains can be excluded.)

The desired estate planning result will be obtained only if the SCIN is a legitimate transaction, so the IRS will require that the buyer pay somewhat above the normal market price for the asset, because the self-canceling feature is an additional benefit that is worth money. The transaction will be disregarded if the SCIN's term is longer than the seller-parent's life expectancy, or if the seller was terminally ill at the time of the transaction.

SPECIAL PROVISIONS FOR SMALL BUSINESS AND FAMILY FARMS

Estate planning for family businesses and family-owned farms can be difficult for many reasons. Stock in most large corporations is liquid and freely traded: that is, at any time, you can find a buyer, and there are standard, published prices for the shares. Neither of these is generally true for closely-held businesses. In many cases, it takes a long time to find someone who wants to buy the shares; there may be no market at all. This would not be a tragedy if the intention is to keep ownership in the family, and if there are younger-generation family members interested in and qualified to keep it running. However, without good estate planning, a deceased business owner may have an estate large enough to be taxable, but without enough nonbusiness assets to pay the estate taxes without depriving the survivors of funds they need to live on.

The Internal Revenue Code includes some relief provisions, and the rest of the problem can be solved by good planning. For one thing, the value of the estate could drop between the date of death and the date administration of the estate is completed, leaving a large estate tax liability and little money with which to pay it. The executor of an estate can make an election (but can't change back, after the election is made) to value the estate as of an "alternate valuation date," six months after the date of death–but only if the effect of the election is to lower the value of the estate and the estate tax.

Illiquid estates can also elect to pay their estate tax in installments, so that they avoid the need to sell farm land or closely-held securities to pay the taxes. IRC Section 6166 allows the estate to pay only the interest on the estate taxes for four years and nine months after the decedent's death, and to stretch out payments of the actual taxes over a ten-year period on the portion of the estate tax attributable to interests in a closely-held business (the value of the interests must exceed 35% of the adjusted gross estate). Installment payment relief is not automatic; the executor has to apply for it. If the IRS turns down the application, the estate can use the IRS' own internal appeal procedure, or go to Tax Court and ask for a court order authorizing installment payments. (It isn't necessary to pay the full estate tax first and then get a refund.)

Furthermore, Section 6166 allows estates to pay interest on the tax at very low interest rates: 2% for the first $1 million as indexed of value over and above the amount sheltered by the unified credit, and only 45% of the IRS' normal interest rate on underpayments for the balance. However, the executor can no longer claim an income tax or estate tax deduction for payment of interest under Section 6166.

Perhaps paradoxically, the IRS and the courts recognize several reasons to discount the value of a gift or bequest of closely-held business stock: blockage and minority interest and lack of marketability. The paradox comes from the fact that a blockage discount is available when the block of stock transmitted is so large that its disposition will distort the stock price. The minority interest discount is available for transmission of a block of stock that is so small that its recipient will not be able to influence corporate policy. In other words, a discount is available based either on the transmission of a very large or a very small percentage of corporate shares. Although the facts of each case are different, a 30-35% discount is usually recognized for the combined factors of minority interest and limited marketability. The estate claims a valuation for its assets and, if challenged, has to be able to back up its valuation methods.

Estate Freezes and Chapter 14

The "estate freeze" was a traditional planning technique. In its simplest form, a business owner who wanted to retire would recapitalize the corporation. The owner would get preferred stock; the people who were supposed to inherit the business would get common stock. The corporation would then possibly declare generous dividends, providing retirement income for the initial owner. Meanwhile, the appreciation in the value of the company would go to the younger generation and would be removed from the estate of the older generation member.

Chapter 14 of the Internal Revenue Code (Sections 2701 to 2704) limits this device by providing, first of all, that the preferred interest must yield dividends or interest proportionate to its value based on current market rates. If it doesn't, then the value of the preferred interest retained by the parent is deemed to be $0; in other words, a taxable gift of the entire transferred interest has been made, not just a gift of common stock valued at the parent's original interest minus the parent's retained interest.

Many businesses use buy-sell agreements not only to handle the practical task of making a transition to a new generation of owners, but to establish the value of the stock for gift and estate tax purposes. IRC Section 2703(a) says that an agreement can establish tax value only if it is a bona fide agreement, with terms comparable to those that would be negotiated in an arm's length transaction–not just a device for transferring property within a family.

Real Estate Valuation

How much is farmland, or land used in a family business worth–what it can bring in based on the family's use of it, or a higher theoretical valuation if the land were developed? IRC Section 2032A allows valuation based on actual use (however, the maximum reduction in value is limited to $750,000 as indexed–the figure for 2006 is $900,000) not potential development, as long as the property was used for five of the eight years before the decedent's death as either a family farm or in a trade or business carried on by the decedent or his family. The property must have been left to a family member who will carry on the family business or farm. Tax benefits are generally recaptured if the property is no longer family operated.

GIVING PROGRAMS

If the older client is in reasonable health, and there is some prospect of estate taxation but the estate is not in the multimillion dollar league, a structured giving program can be an excellent estate plan, or an excellent tool within a larger estate plan. Properly planned gifts can reduce the estate below the taxable level, or at least reduce the tax cost of a large estate.

Don't forget that these gifts constitute transfers for Medicaid purposes. Therefore, unless there are ample funds and insurance to pay for care, and the client is unwilling or unable to make an effective Medicaid plan, consider doing a modified "half-a-loaf" plan (give some assets, but retain assets for the penalty period that will start at the time of the Medicaid application). Because Medicaid doesn't have to conform to tax rules, you can't assert a charitable deduction or annual exclusion when applying for benefits.

Some gifts are subject to gift tax, thus reducing the amount of unified credit available when an individual dies; other gifts are exempt. All gifts between spouses are generally free of gift tax. A person can give $10,000 per year per donee (adjusted for inflation; the 2006 figure is $12,000) free of gift tax, or $20,000 per year per donee (as adjusted--$24,000 for 2006) if the giver's spouse agrees to join in the gift. This is a purely formal requirement–it's OK for all the funds for a split gift to come from one spouse.

The annual exclusion expires each year–it is not permitted, say, to give $5,000 to a particular donee in one year, then give $15,000 the next year to make up for the unused annual exclusion in the earlier year. There is no legal requirement that gifts be made consistently from year to year or even that gifts be repeated: it's up to the donor to decide when and to whom gifts are made. To qualify for the gift tax annual exclusion, the gift must be made to a person, not an institution; and the gift must be of a "present interest," not a right to receive something in the future.

EXAMPLE: In 2006, Stephen Bannion's assets are worth about $3,100,000; his wife Marta's assets are worth about $900,000. Therefore, it is possible (although not certain) that one or both of them will have a taxable estate. It depends on when they die, how much they spend in the interim, and whether their assets appreciate or depreciate. One simple step they can take is for Stephen to make gifts of about $1,100,000 to Marta. The interspousal gift is free of gift tax, and equalizes the two estates at about $2,000,000 each, reducing the implications of the uncertainty as to which will die first because each has a nontaxable estate in 2006–although the survivor may very well have a second estate problem. If they also agree to "gift-split" each year, they can reduce the estate by, for instance, giving at least $20,000 each year to each of their three children, giving them the potential to get $60,000 or more out of the estate each year. They can also make gifts to their grandchildren, to other relatives, and to friends, as well as charitable gifts.

PRACTICE TIP: See the Planned Giving Design Center, http://www.pgdc.net/, a site that provides extensive and frequently updated information about all kinds of charitable giving programs.

Benefiting Children and Grandchildren

In most (though not all) cases, the focus of a married person's financial and estate plan is taking care of the surviving spouse; benefits to children and grandchildren are subsidiary. However, if it's clear that the surviving spouse will be taken care of, or if the financial needs of the younger generations are especially great, or if a giving program is in order, then children and grandchildren become natural recipients.

There are obvious problems with making large cash gifts to minors. Even if they are in fact very responsible people, and won't squander the money on motorcycles (or worse), they have legal disabilities that limit the extent to which they are allowed to handle funds. The states have coped with this problem by adopting various versions of the Uniform Gifts to Minors Act (UGMA) and Uniform Transfers to Minors Act (UTMA). Although they have technical differences, the acts share a common purpose: creating a simple, inexpensive way to make gifts to minors.

The money or property is placed into a special custodianship account; an adult, usually the parent,[20] serves as custodian. As soon as the minor reaches adulthood (usually age 18, but age 21 in some states; state law may also give the donor the election of keeping the account intact until the child reaches 21), the funds belong absolutely to the minor.

PLANNING TIP: This can be a problem if the donor would prefer to impose tighter control–many grandparents are unhappy about the prospect of a possibly immature 18- or even 21-year-old getting a large sum of money and spending it on a motor-cycle–or worse. For large sums of money, the answer is to establish a trust, which can keep the funds tied up long after the minor reaches adulthood, and can impose other conditions. However, where small sums are involved, or where even a comparatively large sum is used to benefit several grandchildren, then UGMA/UTMA, with all its flaws, is probably a better choice than a trust.

UGMA/UTMA gifts qualify for the gift tax annual exclusion, even though they may seem like future interests in that the child doesn't get access to the funds until attaining majority.

Another special gift tax rule says that there is no gift tax on an expenditure of any size used to pay directly for someone else's education or health care expenses. (Payment must be made directly to the educational institution or health care provider, not given to the student or patient who then uses it for the appropriate purpose.) There's no limitation on the number of people whose expenses can be paid. Nor does the money have to flow down to a younger generation: it works just as well for adult children who pay doctors, nursing homes, and others who provide care to their elderly parents.

Yet another special gift tax rule applies to the "2503(c) trust" (Section 2503(c) is the governing Internal Revenue Code section). A 2503(c) trust provides that both principal and income of the trust can be used for the minor's benefit; once the minor reaches age 21, the remaining corpus goes to the minor. A permissible alternative, if it is not desirable to give control of the entire trust to a 21-year-old, is to give the minor a 30 to 60 day period after reaching age 21 during which the former minor can make withdrawals; the amount not withdrawn can be kept in trust for several more years. The trust must provide that, if the beneficiary dies before reaching 21, the trust's assets must be distributed to the estate of the minor.

Valuing Gifts

Valuation is not a problem for cash or for readily marketable securities, but can be extremely contentious for other assets (for instance, real estate, artworks, or shares in a closely held business). A charitable gift of over $10,000 in close corporation stock, or over $5,000 of other property for which current price quotes are not readily available requires an appraisal by a professional. The donor must complete IRS Form 8283 (Noncash Charitable Contributions) and attach it to the income tax return on which the charitable deduction is claimed. For artworks worth $20,000 or more, a copy of the actual appraisal itself must be attached to the Form 8283.

PRACTICE TIP: The donor should retain color photos or slides of the artwork in case the IRS wants to see them–but the photos or slides need not be included with the tax return.

The Tax Reform Act of 1997 encourages filing of a gift tax return reporting gifts, even if no gift tax is due. For gifts made after August 5, 1997, the IRS cannot challenge the value of any gift for estate tax purposes once the gift tax statute of limitation has expired if the donor has shown the gift on a gift tax return, or disclosed it on a statement to the government.

If the taxpayer fails to submit some of the necessary information, the statute of limitations for revaluing the gift doesn't start running until the date the taxpayer amends the return to provide the necessary information.[21]

PRACTICE TIP: Although it is not necessary to file a gift tax return for gifts lower than the annual exclusion (for 2006, the figure is $12,000), it may be a good idea to file a gift tax return anyway, for gifts of hard-to-value assets such as stock in family businesses. That way, the valuation is on record and might become immune to IRS challenge.

JOINT PROPERTY IN THE ESTATE

As noted above, jointly owned property with rights of survivorship doesn't become part of the probate estate, but that doesn't mean that it escapes estate taxation. For federal estate tax purposes, the most important question is generally whether joint property is owned by a married couple, or by anyone else (e.g., brothers and sisters who inherit shares in family real estate).

For married couples, 50% of the value of joint property is included in the estate of the first spouse to die. This rule is applied no matter which spouse actually bought the property, or whether one spouse contributed all the money to buy the property. The 50% included should qualify for the marital deduction.

Then, when the survivor dies (unless the survivor has disposed of the property in the interim), 100% of the value of the property is included in the survivor's estate.

This is one reason why the "second estate" problem can be so acute. The surviving spouse does get a stepped-up basis in the inherited joint property.

For joint property owned by anyone other than a married couple,[22] inclusion in the estate generally depends on who paid for the property. The entire value of the property is included in the estate of the first joint tenant to die–except to the extent that the survivor(s) can prove that the survivor(s) paid part of the purchase price. Then, part or all of the value of the property is potentially included in the estate of the surviving joint tenant(s) when each one dies. In other words, joint property is potentially subject to multiple estate taxation.

However, if joint owners acquired the jointly owned property by gift or inheritance, at the first owner's death the property is treated as if each had contributed a proportionate part of the purchase price.

STRATEGIES FOR APPRECIATED AND DEPRECIATED ASSETS

Generally, $1 in cash or a cash equivalent is worth $1; but for most other investments, at any given time they may be either appreciated (worth more than their adjusted basis) or depreciated (worth less than their adjusted basis). The tax consequences of this fact can affect not only how many shares of stock or a mutual fund, how many bonds, how much real estate a person will buy, sell, or exchange; when the person will transact; but also which assets will be selected for sale or exchange, which will be retained, and which will be placed into trust or donated to charity. Furthermore, the older person may have a clear intention to benefit a relative or friend, while being uncertain about whether to make a lifetime gift or leave a bequest.

There are obvious practical differences between a lifetime gift and a bequest. Lifetime gifts immediately become unavailable to the donor. Funds intended to be bequeathed can still be used by the potential testator if the testator needs them (or if feelings about the potential donee change!). Lifetime gifts can be given when the donor can be thanked personally; bequests are colored by the sadness of a loved one's death. However, many affluent older people have a significant concern with estate planning. Properly handled lifetime gifts can remove assets from the potentially taxable estate, whereas most bequests (other than those to spouses or charities) cannot be carried out until the estate's debts are paid and its estate tax liability settled.

The basis of a lifetime gift is a carryover basis: that is, the donee has the same basis as the donor–the donor's purchase price for the asset, with whatever adjustments are permitted. See page 343, above, for EGTRRA 2001 changes in the treatment of the basis of inherited assets when the estate tax is repealed for one year in 2010.

Therefore, the basis of a lifetime gift is known in advance (as is the timing of its receipt), whereas the basis of an inheritance is uncertain and its timing is uncertain and generally not under the testator's control. One simple answer is to give or devise appreciated assets, but to sell depreciated assets (using the tax losses to offset other income), then give or leave the proceeds of the sale.

PLANNING TIP: A similar analysis should be used if the older person has to make a significant expenditure. In that case, it's probably best to use savings or cash equivalents first, because there are no capital gains implications. But if assets have to be sold, then it's probably best to sell depreciated assets and spend the proceeds (using the tax loss to offset other income).

It's probably better to sell assets whose capital gains will be tax-free (e.g., home sale proceeds up to $250,000, or $500,000 for a married couple) instead of fully taxable capital gains; and it's probably better to have taxable capital gains than a corresponding amount of taxable ordinary income, because capital gains rates are slightly lower.

Tax factors aren't everything, of course. In practical terms, it may be better to keep living in the family home than to sell it, even if there is no capital gains tax to be paid. Some assets are highly liquid, and can be disposed of at any time with low brokerage and other fees; other assets are illiquid, and even the process of disposition is costly. If a person needs money in a hurry, the person can't rely on illiquid assets, so the person has to use cash, cash equivalents, and freely tradable securities as a source of funds.

The recipient's tax concerns are the flip side of the donor's or testator's. If the donee or heir of real estate intends to inhabit the property, or the donee or heir of securities intends to hold them or live on their income instead of selling them, the basis is fairly irrelevant. But in many cases, a person who receives a gift or inheritance puts it on the market as soon as possible—and therefore faces capital gains tax as soon as the sale is consummated. Therefore, the lower the basis, the greater is the tax liability.

How much does this matter in the elder care plan? Probably, the older person will be more concerned about his own tax position than the position of recipients of his bounty, but this is one of the issues in the "who is the client?" question. A potential donor who is exceptionally generous may be willing to put the potential heir's tax position ahead of his own, but this is probably uncommon.

DISCLAIMERS AND POST-MORTEM PLANNING

Sometimes an inheritance is a "white elephant"–a valuable object that actually creates more disadvantages than it's worth. It would be an insult to return a real white elephant to the person who gave it, but the Internal Revenue Code permits heirs to "disclaim"–refuse to accept an inheritance. The effect of a qualified disclaimer that satisfies the rules is that, for tax purposes, the individual never received the inheritance; it is not treated as if the person got the inheritance but returned it to the estate. In effect, disclaimers can be used for postmortem estate planning, because the funds or property pass as if the disclaimant had died first.

A qualified disclaimer must:

- Be written, not oral

- Be made before the disclaimant has received any benefit from the inheritance

- Shift the property to someone else; the disclaimer doesn't count if the disclaimant ends up receiving the property in another role. As an exception, a surviving spouse can disclaim an interest that qualifies for the marital deduction yet receive the property in another way that does not qualify for the marital deduction.

- Be made within nine months of a lifetime gift, or nine months of the date of death for a bequest

These are the tax rules for disclaimers: for Medicaid purposes, a disclaimer is a transfer of assets and is likely to have negative consequences.

The regulations for post-death distributions of IRA and qualified plan accounts (see page 348) change prior law: opening up greater planning opportunities, by allowing disclaimers by the person originally named as beneficiary, and transfer to an alternative designated beneficiary of the account even after the death of the IRA account owner or employee.

PLANNING TIP: Be sure to follow all the steps set out in the various Internal Revenue Code provisions for post-mortem estate planning. One case required valuation as of the date of death, not the alternate valuation date, for an estate whose estate tax return was filed more than 18 months after the extended due date.[23]

INCAPACITY PLANNING

Historically, the court system had very few tools for dealing with incapacity. After a hearing, a conservator could be named to take care of an "incompetent" person's property, or a guardian to take responsibility for the incompetent "ward's" well being. The problem was that a declaration of incompetency was not only psychologically shattering for the ward, but caused the ward to lose many civil rights. Thus, courts were reluctant to make the finding in borderline cases—leaving vulnerable people without help, and leaving their financial affairs in limbo.

Therefore, the modern guardianship procedure evolved. The modern theory is that it is not necessary to have black-and-white categories of "competent" and "incompetent"; but for some elderly or disabled people, some degree of "incapacity" exists. If the individual admits that incapacity is present, or if it is proved by a hearing, then the court will appoint a "guardian of the person" and/or "guardian of the property."

The court's guardianship order will spell out which powers are retained by the ward (person for whom a guardian is appointed), and which have been transferred to the guardian. The guardian will have only those powers specifically awarded by the court. Sometimes the court will find that a full-scale appointment is not necessary, but will appoint a limited purpose guardian for a single task, such as getting the elderly person admitted to a nursing home or continuing care retirement community, or setting up a trust.

PLANNING TIP: Testation (making a will or codicil) is usually considered so inherently personal that the guardian will not be allowed to do it, although a guardian of the property can handle day-to-day financial tasks and probably will be allowed to make transfers that save income and estate taxes. That means that the will is essentially "frozen" as soon as the senior citizen becomes a ward, so it should be drafted in general and flexible enough terms that it will not require constant retailoring to fit every year's new tax laws.

Most of the states allow advance designation of a guardian; any person who still has capacity can designate a trusted person to serve as guardian if one is ever needed. This allows the elderly person to pick the guardian he finds most acceptable; it also reduces the duration and expense of the guardianship proceeding.

PRACTICE TIP: The designated guardian (like the DPA agent, discussed below, or the trustee of a trust) must retain capacity even after the principal loses it, and must be expected to retain capacity throughout the ward's life. Therefore, selecting a spouse or sibling may be a poor idea if such person is at risk of the same illnesses and conditions that beset the principal.

DURABLE POWER OF ATTORNEY

The durable power of attorney (DPA) is a simple yet powerful tool, recognized in all 50 states, for incapacity planning. A power of attorney is a designation of someone else (whether a person, a business, a law firm, or a financial institution) as "agent," otherwise known as "attorney in fact," to carry out anything from one very specific task to complete management of the "principal's" financial affairs. A power of attorney is durable if its terms provide that it will remain in effect even after the principal becomes incapacitated. (An ordinary power of attorney ceases to be valid if and when the principal loses capacity.)

A power of attorney is "springing" if it does not take effect until a certain event occurs. In the elder planning context, this usually means a determination of incapacity confirmed by a doctor, or by two doctors. Springing powers of attorney are good to the extent that they allow hesitant senior citizens to sign a power of attorney that they would otherwise be uncomfortable with. They're bad, to the extent that it can be quite difficult for the agent to exercise a springing power of attorney, because financial institutions or contracting parties may be dubious that the event has actually occurred and the agent actually is legally entitled to act on behalf of the principal.

A simple workaround is for the older person to sign an ordinary DPA, but allow an attorney or other trusted person to hold onto it, not notifying the agent until the condition has occurred. However, this technique places the principal at the mercy of the good judgment (and memory!) of the person holding the DPA document in escrow.

The state laws about DPAs contain a list of statutory powers that automatically belong to the agent unless the principal actually refuses to grant them. In a few states, a DPA is only valid if it uses the official form. Most states do prescribe an official form, but let principals draft their own forms or customize the basic form. Note that, even if the state law automatically gives agents the power to handle tax matters, the IRS has its own Power of Attorney form, which should be filled out and signed at the same time as the basic DPA.

An important decision is whether or not the agent should be given the power to make gifts of the principal's property. This is a complex question. The ability to make gifts can safeguard the elderly person's Medicaid plan. However, if the agent has the power to make gifts (especially gifts to the agent), there is serious potential for abuse. If large enough gifts are made, the principal's estate plan will be destroyed, because there won't be enough left in the estate to carry out the plan (unless the gifts follow the same proportions as the dispositions in the will). Furthermore, some states actually forbid agents from making gifts to themselves.

The basic tax rule is that gifts made by a DPA agent are removed from the principal's estate only if the agent was explicitly granted the power to make gifts under the terms of the document. Sometimes this rule can be averted if making gifts is one of the basic powers of agents under state law; but it's better to make this point clear and save trouble in the future. This rule is embodied in many decisions.[24]

In many cases, the durable power of attorney with a power to make gifts will also be a general power of appointment for tax purposes, because the agent will be able to appoint the principal's property for the benefit of himself, his estate, his creditors, or the creditors of his estate. So, if the agent dies before the principal, all of the property covered by the DPA will be included in the gross estate of the agent, based on the agent's holding a general power of appointment. The test is the amount over which the decedent had power, not the size of appointments or whether any appointments were ever made at all.

PRACTICE TIP: If this is a problem, then draft the DPA denying power to appoint to self, estate, or creditors. If giving the agent the power to make gifts on behalf of the principal is an important part of the plan, perhaps the principal could purchase additional life insurance on the agent's life that will cover any estate tax liability that occurs if the agent dies before the principal.

In some states, the probate court will accept the argument that the presence of a durable power of attorney, plus trusts to administer an incapacitated person's funds, will make it unnecessary to appoint a guardian at all. However, in states that do not take this position, get advice from an experienced attorney about the interaction between the DPA and guardianship. In some states, the DPA retains all of its force; in others, the agent has to report to the guardian, and the guardian, not the agent, has primary responsibility for managing the incapacitated person's financial affairs. (For many smaller estates, there is no practical difference among these alternatives, because the same small pool of family members is tapped by the court to serve as guardian, and have already been named as agents and trustees.)

PRACTICE TIP: The privacy rules under the Health Insurance Portability and Accessibility Act (HIPAA) can create problems for persons serving as agents under Durable Powers of Attorney for Health Care, and for agents under "springing" Durable Powers of Attorney. The agent can get into an infinite loop, where privacy rules deny the agent access to the information needed to prove that incapacity has occurred. Therefore, powers of attorney should be drafted to provide an advance HIPAA waiver so the agent can see medical records.[25]

SUMMARY

Even if federal estate tax is not a consideration, it's important for the client to have an estate plan to take care of the client's family and dispose of property in accordance with the client's wishes. The larger the estate, the more significant tax planning becomes—and the more worthwhile it is to use multiple, complex, or expensive legal devices. A small estate can be handled with a simple will, enough life insurance to provide liquidity and "fill the gaps" in the provision for the surviving spouse—and an incapacity plan such as a durable power of attorney and advance designation of a guardian.

Of course, in the year 2010, no estates will be taxable—and between now and then, many estates will not be taxable even though they might have been under pre-EGTRRA 2001 law.

As the estate becomes larger, the risk of a second estate problem becomes greater, and more protective devices are needed. Estate splitting is an easy way to reduce the problem. Creation of a credit shelter trust becomes worthwhile, whether it is left to the surviving spouse or is left to the children or other heirs, while the surviving spouse receives the balance of the estate. A QTIP trust can provide useful income for the survivor, but will be included in the survivor's estate. A split-interest charitable trust is another useful way to combine tax planning with generating additional current income. Properly handled, life insurance in trust can be an inexpensive and tax wise way to create major benefits for survivors.

Special situations call for special estate planning: disposing of interests in the family business, for instance. Or, the testator/trust creator may have an especially complicated dispositive scheme, which cannot be handled adequately with simple devices.

In the upcoming years, estate planners will face additional challenges, because the amount that can be sheltered by the unified credit will continue to change (and the estate tax is repealed for one year in 2010). It generally makes good sense to draft documents referring to the maximum amount that qualifies for the unified credit, rather than specifying a dollar amount. Of course, alternative dispositive provisions must be made for a decedent dying in a year in which there is no estate tax.

Any good estate plan must respond to changes in the law; but when the client is a senior citizen, there is an additional risk that the client will decline in capacity, and it may become impossible to make necessary amendments to documents. The plan may also have to accommodate involvement by DPA agents and guardians, in addition to the original client and the client's spouse.

CHAPTER ENDNOTES

1. Jennifer Friedlin, "After Writing a Will, You Still Have I's To Dot," *New York Times*, January 2, 2005, Business p. 7.

2. Colleen DeBaise, "Parents of Disabled Face Financial-Planning Hurdles," *Wall Street Journal*, April 13, 2005, p. D2.

3. Jonathan Clements, "What to Leave Behind: Choosing Assets That Will Benefit Your Kids Most," *Wall Street Journal*, June 29, 2005, p. C1.

4. States differ in their approach to the statutory share. Some of them allow the spouse to take a share only of probate assets; others allow a share of all the decedent's assets, including items such as insurance and living trusts. However, some of them also allow the provision for the surviving spouse to be less than an outright inheritance–putting funds into trust for the surviving spouse can satisfy the requirement.

5. If the spouse benefits both under a QTIP and under the bypass trust, the spouse should take money out of the QTIP trust first and preserve the bypass trust as much as possible, because the QTIP trust will be included in the spouse's estate; the bypass trust will not.

6. Brett W. Berg, "Ideas for Managing Wealth in B Trusts With Life Insurance," National Underwriter Week in Life & Health 2004 Issue #19.

7. This is a funded trust; an unfunded trust can also be created, and its terms set down, with the intention that funding will occur at a later time, e.g., when the grantor dies and insurance proceeds on the grantor's life become available.

8. Treas. Reg. §1.671-2(e)(1).

9. IRC Sec. 645.

10. If the survivor is given the power to withdraw principal from the trust, it is usually limited by what is called a "five or five" power, i.e., the maximum that can be withdrawn each year is the greater of $5,000 or 5% of the trust. This is done to assist the surviving spouse's planning, because IRC Section 2514 provides that if the power of withdrawal is more generous than "five or five," and the surviving spouse doesn't exercise the power in a particular year, the money that was not withdrawn from the trust is a taxable gift to the remainder persons of the trust.

11. Let. Rul. 9738010.

12. TAM 9645006.

13. This is generally true only of contributions to public charities, not private foundations; and there is a limitation calculated based on the taxpayer's "contribution base"; but the clients of most readers of this book will not be in a position to make contributions large enough to encounter the limitation.

14. CLTs are somewhat less common than charitable remainder trusts. There is no limit on the duration of the charity's annuity or unitrust interest. If the trust earns more income than is needed to pay the annuity or unitrust amount to the charity, the excess income can be accumulated for the noncharitable remaindermen. The gift or bequest to the noncharitable beneficiary is the discounted present value of the remainder.

15. See Roy M. Adams, "Ask the Expert," *Trusts & Estates* (March, 1998), p. 71.

16. Technically, noncharitable trusts generally have to end no later than the time that the grantor's youngest living descendant named in the trust would reach age 21; in practical terms, until the grantor's youngest grandchild or greatgrandchild reaches adulthood.

17. For more information, see Douglas Blattmachr and Jonathan G. Blattmachr, "A New Direction in Estate Planning: North to Alaska," *Trusts & Estates* (September, 1997), p. 48; Jonathan Blattmachr, Richard Thwaites, and Howard M. Zaritsky, "New Alaska Trust Act Provides Many Estate Planning Opportunities," *Estate Planning* (October, 1997), p. 347; Donald F. Cady's "Alaska Trusts: Cool Idea or Merely a Snow Job?" *National Underwriter*, Life and Health/Financial Services Edition, January 4, 1999, p. 7.

18. Rachel Emma Silverman, "Building Your Own Dynasty," *Wall Street Journal*, September 15, 2004, p. D1.

19. See *Miller v. Comm.*, TC Memo 1996-3.

20. If the donor, e.g., a grandparent, serves as custodian, and dies while the donee is still a minor, the custodial account will be included in the donor's estate, possibly frustrating the estate planning purpose for establishing the account in the first place.

21. Rev. Proc. 2000-34, 2000-34 IRB 186.

22. If one of the spouses is not a U.S. citizen, the nonmarital rules are applied.

23. *Est. of Eddy v. Comm.*, 115 TC 135 (2000).

24. See, e.g., *Est. of Swanson v. U.S.*, 2000-1 USTC ¶60,371 (Ct. Cl. 2000).

25. Kaja Whitehouse, "Privacy Rules Snarl Estate Planning," *Wall Street Journal*, November 6, 2004, p. D3.

Chapter 14

Housing and Care Alternatives

Access to appropriate, high-quality care is an essential part of the elder plan. Care is available in a confusing variety of settings, by a wide range of providers, and often at a wide range of prices and payment sources. Some of the alternatives involve substantial investments of money. Many care settings voluntarily provide, or are legally obligated to provide, voluminous financial disclosures. The planning team can provide tremendous benefit to elderly clients and their families by assessing and explaining these disclosure documents, and by offering an objective determination of the comparative financial, tax, Medicaid, and estate planning implications involved in making a selection.

The choice has immense implications. Some financial decisions are hard to reverse for several reasons: refunds are unavailable; the care provider has either engaged in deliberate fraud, or has failed financially despite good intentions; or, there simply are no suitable alternatives for the older person's changed needs.

Furthermore, the concept of "transfer trauma" is well-recognized in the social sciences. The mere act of moving from one residence or nursing home to another can be risky, or even fatal, for a frail elderly person–even if, objectively speaking, the quality of care is better in the second setting. The more confused the elder is, the more likely that transfer trauma will occur. Even for a strong, healthy elderly person, making multiple moves is not only inconvenient, it is also expensive.

PRACTICE TIP: Buying a home or renting an apartment is always stressful. The stresses are even more severe when seniors have to leave a home with decades of memories, or seek specialized housing for needs they may find it emotionally hard to acknowledge. The Senior Advantage Real Estate Council (a realtors' group) has certified almost 12,000 real estate agents and brokers since 1997 as Seniors Real Estate Specialists. The designation requires a two-day training course and an exam.[1]

According to Virginia's Genworth Financial Inc., the average cost of a year of long-term care in 2005 was $72,240. Costs were 20% higher in urban than non-urban areas—40% higher in high-cost states like California, New York, and Minnesota. Costs for a private room ran from a low of $41,600 a year, in rural Missouri, to $191,400 a year in Alaska. Genworth found that the average cost of spending a year in a private room in an assisted living facility (ALF) was $28,800; home health care cost an average of $18.67 an hour, and homemaker services cost an average of $16.67 an hour.[2]

The majority of senior citizens are homeowners. Traditionally, they entered retirement mortgage-free, although an increasing percentage of them still have mortgage debt. See Chapter 7 for a discussion of senior homeownership, including reverse mortgages and other ways to use housing equity to pay for medical care and other needs.

Yet, senior homeowners are at risk: predatory lenders, home improvement frauds, or abuses in second mortgages, home equity loans, and reverse equity arrangements.

A slightly more exotic planning option involves providing for present and future care needs by using funds (e.g., from investments, a lump-sum distribution from a pension plan, or the sale of the family home) to purchase entry into a Continuing Care Retirement Community (or "CCRC," see below) in which the resident does not receive an equity interest in the residential unit. In that case, future care is provided for irrespective of the client's medical condition (which might make it impossible to qualify for long-term care insurance, "LTCI"), and without the limitations of Medicaid planning. Furthermore, funds that could trigger estate taxation are removed from the estate. (Purchasing a unit that comes with an equity interest will not accomplish this because the estate will include the value of the unit, which might appreciate over time, thus making the problem worse rather than better.)

THE CONTINUUM OF CARE

Our society recognizes that "one size fits all" works better for t-shirts than for elder care. The concept of the continuum of care is best described as a series of services that can be combined in many ways to suit differing needs. Usually, a person enters the continuum of care with a small need for services, but over time the individual's need for services will increase and, ultimately, it may be necessary to provide care in a more specialized, intensive medical setting.

The base of the continuum of care pyramid is care in the home and in the community. Services can be rendered at home by the few physicians who make house calls, professional nurses, lower-skilled home health aides who provide personal care, and by homemakers who provide non-medical services such as cooking and cleaning. In this context, personal care means vital services that do not require professional training (e.g., feeding a person who cannot eat independently, bathing a person with limited mobility, helping a person dress, pushing a person's wheelchair). Home delivery of meals is an important service that can make the difference between continued independent living and the need for institutionalization. (See Chapter 5 for a discussion of Medicare coverage of home care, and Chapter 6 for Medicaid home care.) Although it is possible to purchase a LTCI policy that pays benefits only for institutional care, most insureds choose a policy that combines institutional and home care benefits.

Services can be rendered outside the home, but within the community. For instance, senior centers provide companionship and, perhaps, meals and social services. Adult day care centers usually serve a somewhat more impaired population. They may also provide screening and other health services, or specialized services for demented persons.

If remaining at home is no longer desirable or feasible, there are many kinds of specialized housing for the elderly. Some of them, such as retirement communities, are oriented toward leisure and recreation. See www.PrivateCommunities.com for information about dozens of retirement and golf-oriented communities. Other facilities designated as shared housing, congregate housing, enriched housing, Assisted Living Facilities, etc., target the needs of individuals for whom a medical setting is inappropriate (and excessively expensive), but who cannot live entirely independently either. These settings provide some services, such as congregate meals, transportation, or assistance with taking prescribed medications, but do not offer nursing care or medical services.

The life-care community, or Continuing Care Retirement Community (CCRC), attempts to make the full continuum of care available. At first, new residents live in conventional housing units and have access to social and recreational activities. However, nursing care is also available on-site and, if necessary, residents can move into assisted living or nursing home units within the same complex (or nearby, subject to transfer agreements).

There are also several kinds of facilities that are operated and licensed as health care rather than housing facilities, including Skilled Nursing Facilities (SNFs) qualifying for Medicare reimbursement (see Chapter 5) and facilities with a custodial orientation. Medicaid refers to its participating nursing homes as "nursing facilities."

Medicaid formerly had separate rules for SNFs and Intermediate Care Facilities (ICFs), but now has a single set of rules. Depending on local law, there may also be lower-level facilities (e.g., Health-Related Facilities, or HRFs) that offer a less intensive level of medical services.

Some questions for analyzing any potential housing or care situations include:

- Does the facility consider itself residential, medical, or both?

- Is the facility required to have a state license? If so, what kind of license? What are the licensing requirements, and is the facility in good standing with regulators?

- Is the facility subject to financial disclosure requirements (see Chapter 5)? CCRCs, for instance, must provide prospectuses to potential entrants.

- Are there minimum requirements for entering the facility? An individual cannot simply reserve a bed at a nursing home, even if he or she wants to. Instead, an individual has to suffer at least a minimum level of disability, as measured by a standard assessment process.

- Is there a maximum level of disability that the facility can handle (in practical terms), or is allowed to handle (in legal terms)? Typically, Assisted Living Facilities (ALFs) laws allow a facility to have only residents who are healthy enough to leave by themselves in a fire or other emergency.

- Is there a requirement for a deposit or other lump-sum payment prior to entry? If so, how much is it, what is its tax status, and under what circumstances are refunds available?

- Do community residents receive an equity interest in their unit?

- Does residence at the facility, or care provided by the facility, qualify for reimbursement from Medicare, Medicaid, and/or the potential resident's own LTCI policy?

Older persons' abilities – or, more accurately, disabilities – are often measured on the basis of ADLs (Activities of Daily Living) and IADLs (Instrumental Activities of Daily Living). Activities of Daily Living are bedrock capabilities, such as being able to move from bed to chair, being able to remain continent, to use the toilet, and to dress or bathe oneself. Instrumental Activities of Daily Living are socially significant activities with a lesser physical component – for instance, the ability to manage money, shop, or use a telephone.

Senior citizens can suffer problems with physical illness, cognitive deterioration, or both. Frustratingly, a person whose cognitive disability is so severe that he might endanger himself or others, might nevertheless be in good shape physically – perhaps strong enough to harm a nurse or aide if he becomes agitated. The problem is that an Alzheimer's patient (or other cognitively disabled person) might unpredictably do any of the following: wander and be unable to find the way home; leave water running until it causes a flood; ingest household chemicals thinking they are food; cause a fire by leaving an empty pot on a stove burner; or create many other dangerous situations.

The Census Bureau reports that in 2000, there were 33 million seniors living in the community—94% of this age group—so far more seniors encounter housing issues than nursing home issues. The Centers for Medicare and Medicaid Services (CMS) says that home care spending rose 23%, from $42.7 billion in 1997 to $52.5 billion in 2002.

Threatened evictions and other housing-related problems raise questions about when family members and social service agencies should get involved, and when placement in a facility is necessary. Even residents in senior housing may experience discrimination, if it is believed that their usage of home care detracts from the "active adult" image of the development.

The Federal Fair Housing Act allows the eviction of tenants who pose a direct threat to the health and safety of others; the question becomes whether a particular eviction suit is based on reasonable suspicion or bigoted attitudes about the aged. Under the Fair Housing Act, it is illegal to ask health questions until and unless a tenant requests a specialized health service or facility.[3]

THE CONTINUUM OF PAYMENT

It is vital that senior clients have access to quality medical care and other services that they need, but access probably will not begin, and certainly will not continue, unless the means for payment are in place.

Under the current system, the basic source of payment for long-term care is out-of-pocket spending by elders and their families. However, there are many other potential payors, and one of the planning team's tasks is to sort out which payor is responsible for paying what.

Unless care needs are very limited, "the continuum of payment" means "the continuum of paying a lot of money!" According to MetLife's 2004 survey, the average private-pay rate for a nursing home private room was $192 per day ($70,080 per year), and for a semi-private room, it was $169 per day ($61,685 per year). At that time, there were 18,000 nursing homes, with 1.6 million residents, more than 90% of them senior citizens, and about half (46.5%) "old-old" (85 or over). The average length of stay is 2.4 years; 72% of nursing home residents are women; and three-quarters of nursing home residents are dependent in three or more ADLs. The survey found that close to 38% of senior citizens have a severe disability and nearly half (47%) of persons over 85 suffer from dementia. The average hourly rate for home health aides was $18 per hour. MetLife found that more than 1.3 million patients received home care from 7,200 agencies. About two-thirds of home care patients were women; 70% were senior citizens; and more than half had limitations in at least one Activity of Daily Living.[4]

Early in 2005, Genworth Financial reported slightly different cost figures, finding that the average annual cost of long-term care, whether received in an institution or at home, was $72,240, with costs 20% higher in urban than in rural areas. Their 2004 cost figure for a semi-private nursing home room was $179 a day, or $65,200 a year—13% more than 2003; a semiprivate room was almost as expensive, averaging $158 a day. However, in the highest-cost state (Alaska) nursing home care cost almost five times as much as in lowest-cost rural Missouri ($41,600 vs. $191,400). Genworth reported an average cost of $18.67 per hour for home health care services and $16.67 an hour for homemaker services.[5]

As Chapter 5 shows, once the necessary deductibles and co-insurance payments have been satisfied, or if the senior client is a managed care beneficiary, Medicare will assume a major role in paying hospital and doctor bills. It will cover up to 100 days of post-hospital recuperation in a skilled nursing facility, but will not cover any custodial, long-term care. It will also provide part-time or intermittent home care to homebound beneficiaries, especially if they are recuperating after a hospitalization or a skilled nursing home stay. However, if an older person is covered by an Employer Group Health Plan (EGHP), in most instances the EGHP, not Medicare, is supposed to be the primary payor (see Chapter 5).

Medicaid is supposed to be a payor of last resort, so if services can be covered under both Medicare and Medicaid, Medicare is supposed to pay first. The Balanced Budget Act of 1997 made health care providers very unhappy by allowing providers to be paid at the Medicaid rate (which is almost always lower than the Medicare rate) when providing care for "dual eligibles" (senior citizens eligible for both Medicare and Medicaid.)

So far, long-term care insurance (see Chapter 4) is not a major factor in paying for long-term care, but that should change as more and more policyholders age and require services. Naturally, LTCI policies provide benefits according to their own terms, so policy selection involves selecting the correct mix of benefits as well as choosing the most cost-effective policy from a quality insurer.

Many states have non-Medicaid programs that provide services to elderly and disabled persons, such as: senior centers; adult day care; home care; housekeeping and chore services; home-delivered meals; caregiver training; and respite care (which provides a part-time or temporary substitute caregiver to relieve some of the stress of caregiving). Many of these programs are funded under the federal Older Americans Act (OAA), so a good place to find out about them is the nearest "single state agency" delegated to handle OAA matters. Similar programs are frequently offered by religious and charitable organizations. Although these programs are usually paid for out-of-pocket by the person receiving the services (or his or her family), it is typical for the fees to be set on a sliding scale so that less affluent people pay less.

HOME CARE

There are two important but basic questions that must be asked when setting up a home care plan. First, does the senior citizen want to stay home? Second, if so (which is usually the case), how realistic is the desire? "Home" is a very emotive word, and most people have a strong desire, even a willingness to make sacrifices, in order to remain in their home and in the community in which they are accustomed to living.

Depending on the older person's needs, wishes, family situation, financial situation, insurance coverage, and eligibility for insurance and government benefits, home care can be a small-scale, informal process or a full-scale deployment of resources from many directions. Home care has its own continuum, from a little bit of help from family and friends to the equivalent of nursing home care provided at home by skilled professionals with assistance from para-professionals.

See Chapter 5 for a discussion of Medicare coverage of recuperative home care for a home-bound person who has recently been hospitalized.

Home care usually involves two components: (1) the health and personal care of the older person; and (2) the housekeeping and home maintenance tasks. The distinction is important because it determines which health care professional can perform those services, their eligibility for reimbursement, and their income tax status. For example, a professional nurse might make periodic visits to the elderly to assess their health status and to perform skilled services (such as wound care and giving injections). A physical therapist might visit to help a stroke patient regain mobility.

Those professional visits could be supplemented by less skilled personal services, such as bathing the elder, giving him a shampoo, seeing that he takes prescribed medications, or feeding him if he is immobile. Under appropriate circumstances, a person who qualifies for Medicare home care can get some household services performed by a home health attendant, but household services are not covered unless they are needed in conjunction with skilled professional and personal services.

Although it was traditional for doctors to make house calls, the tradition died out as medical care became more dependent on technology. However, a small number of doctors and nurses (armed with portable devices like computers and EKG machines) are beginning to make house calls to chronically ill elderly patients who have problems getting out of the house to receive care. Case managers, hospital staff, social workers, and neighbors make referrals of homebound seniors who need the services.[6]

Home care, like penicillin, is a valuable remedy but not a panacea, and it is not without risks. Home care works well when it promotes the happiness of a person who does not want to leave a beloved home, but does not work when a person is trapped in a dilapidated, unsafe home in a dangerous neighborhood. It is difficult to supervise what goes on in home care. In the best case, a skillful, compassionate worker not only performs hands-on care, but also recognizes when medical assistance is needed. In the worst case, a poorly trained worker fails to recognize emergencies (or even inadvertently creates them by making mistakes), shows up for work late (or inconsistently), neglects the elderly person, or even steals from or abuses the elderly person.

A frequent assertion is that home care is an economical alternative to institutionalization. This is true only if the person's home care needs are fairly light – imagine the cost of employing several full-time workers, or even the three shifts of workers needed for around-the-clock care of a demented or very physically debilitated person. Sometimes institutionalization actually saves money because of economies of scale and because the cost of the institution replaces both health care costs and ordinary living costs such as rent and food. That does not make home care either good or bad, only a tool that works in some situations and not in others.

A trend is developing in both the United States and Europe[7] for home care to be controlled by consumers, not home health agencies or social service departments. Under that model, the health care consumer (or his or her family) hires, trains, supervises, and fires the home health care worker, perhaps receiving some government subsidies to help pay for the care. (The U.S. experience is that younger, disabled people show more interest in self-managing home care than do frail, elderly people.)

According to the study, when they have a chance, home health consumers often hire family members and friends–so some of the informal, unpaid care they were already receiving is transformed into paid care. There still is not enough research to show if consumer-controlled care is better by objective measures, but consumers are often more satisfied with the care when they feel they have more control. However, if agencies control the care, there is more scope for credentialing, training, and supervision, all of which are hard to achieve when consumers manage the care.

Employment Issues

What if there are no family members or friends available to provide care, but the person needing the care is not homebound (ruling out Medicare services), not eligible for Medicaid, and there are no available state-run or voluntary programs that meet the person's needs? In all probability, the older person will hire someone on a part-time or full-time basis as a companion or housekeeper. Although enforcement is sparse, employing an individual creates legal obligations. The employer must go through the Form I-9 process of ascertaining either that the employee is a citizen, or that he or she is a legal immigrant permitted to work in the United States.

Household employees are subject to the so-called "Nanny tax" rules and are, therefore, subject to FICA (Social Security/Medicare) tax if they earn more than $1,500 a year in 2006 (indexed annually).[8] The employer must either pay the entire FICA tax (15.3% of wages), or pay one-half of the FICA tax and withhold the other half from the worker's wages. However, instead of the complex procedures for reporting and remitting tax that regular employers are subject to, household employers can simply report and remit the FICA tax with their own tax return (Schedule H). (Federal unemployment tax (FUTA) is also due if the employee's cash wages are greater than $1,000 in any calendar quarter. The FUTA tax equals 8/10 of 1% of the first $7,000 of the household employee's wages.) Household employers are not legally obligated to withhold federal income taxes on employee wages. A household employer should withhold federal income tax only if the employee requests withholding and the employer agrees to do it. See IRS Publication 926 for details on taxes on household employment.

Who is the "employer" of the home health worker or housekeeper? If the senior citizen or family member hired the worker directly, then clearly the parent or child is the employer. However, if the worker was provided by a home health agency, the question becomes more complex. If the agency provides the worker and controls what the worker does and how the worker does it, then the home health worker is an employee of the home health agency and the agency is responsible for employment-related taxes. If, despite the agency's involvement, the family controls what the worker does and how it is done, then the family member is the official employer.

PRACTICE TIP: If any of your clients employ home health workers, clarify this point. "Gee, I thought the agency was taking care of it" is not a valid defense. People who fail to remit FICA taxes are personally liable for the failure. The penalty can be as much as 100% of the unpaid taxes.

Some state Medicaid agencies have an option known as "vendorization." This is a situation under which a person who applies for Medicaid home care, and who already has a successful working relationship with a home care worker, can get the worker qualified for Medicaid reimbursement.

Another option that is usually more convenient, but also more expensive, is to hire a Home Health Agency (HHA) to coordinate the care plan and to provide care. The HHA will screen workers (it is a legal requirement that potential workers' names be checked against a database of convicted criminals and elder abusers), assign them, supervise them, and handle all of the tax paperwork. Furthermore, the agency has many workers so a substitute can be assigned if the client and worker do not get along well, or if a particular worker is ill or on vacation.

It is usually the case (but not always) that Medicaid and insurance reimbursement will be unavailable for paid services rendered by relatives. Check with an experienced elder law attorney to see if there are regulations that allow the hiring of a relative.

RETIREMENT COMMUNITIES AND SENIOR HOUSING

A large market sector exists to provide housing units (for sale or purchase) suitable for the needs of the active elderly—people who do not yet have serious medical needs, but who want features such as golf courses, excellent security, and easy-to-care-for housing.

When the twenty-first century began, construction of housing for the elderly dropped sharply (in part because there had been excess capacity added to this sector). By 2005, it began to increase again. In mid-2005, the *New York Times* profiled Senior Lifestyle Corporation's Chicago development for the middle-income active elderly. The company owns three tiers of housing to meet various levels of service needs. The new development charges $1,800 a month for a one-bedroom apartment including several meals and twice-a-month housekeeping services. Staff is limited, however, so the target population is the active elderly. Senior Lifestyle's high-end project charges $2,800 a month and up for a one-bedroom apartment, with meals and services included.[9]

Many senior housing complexes were developed in suburban or rural areas; a current trend is to build rental units in urban areas suitable for active adults. These apartments do not provide health care or supportive services; the target market is people who want to sell their houses in order to rent a high-quality, easy-to-care-for unit. (This sector is sometimes described as "independent living" for seniors, in contrast with "assisted living" projects.) Usually, the developments are garden-style rather than high-rise, with large apartments to accommodate a lifetime of accumulated possessions. The units are intended for active seniors, but are prepared for health needs with features such as bathroom grab bars, tubs large enough for a removable chair, emergency alarms, and door levers instead of knobs (in case arthritis makes it hard to turn doorknobs). Sometimes meals are included in the package, but health care is not. Both for-profit and not-for-profit developments exist within this sector; the cost depends on location, services, and the nature of the project.[10]

In 2002, 4,566 senior apartment units were built, a number that increased to 8,789 in 2003 (the figures come from the American Seniors Housing Association). In 2003, the number of new ALF units rose 69% (to 6,147). The ALF sector was overbuilt in the 1990s, resulting in a glut, so it took a long time for building to pick up again.[11] Another development in housing construction for older people is to build smaller housing complexes featuring larger and more luxurious homes for over-55 active adults, for example, two-story houses of 2,500-2,700 square feet. In mid-2004, several complexes were being developed at prices starting in the mid-$400,000 range.[12]

Developing upscale housing units for the elderly (e.g., $3,105 to $7,430 in monthly charges at Hyatt's Classic Residence in Palo Alto, California, over and above entry fees of $500,000 to $4.5 million dollars) has become a thriving part of the housing market. According to David S. Schless, president of the trade group American Seniors Housing Association, institutional investors are once again willing to invest in this sector of the housing market. Capitalization rates for senior housing average 9%, nearly twice as much as the average 5% return on conventional apartment development.[13]

COMMUNITY ALTERNATIVES

A wide range of services and care settings exist at the lower end of the continuum of care, coping with elderly people who are at risk if they live entirely alone, but who do not require a full-scale medical setting. According to the AARP, although there is a clear preference for "aging in place" instead of moving to another area or entering specialized housing or an institution; whether this is a realistic ambition depends on community resources. Census Bureau figures show that although 17% of younger people move every year, this is true of only 5% of the over-55 population. One-eighth of people over 50 do not drive, and those who do not drive are six times as likely as those who do drive to forego pleasant or even desirable activities for lack of transportation. Non-drivers usually make walking their predominant mode of transportation, so a community where walking is unsafe is unsuitable for their needs.[14]

In 2006, the New York Times profiled Beacon Hill Village, a nonprofit organization in Boston that coordinates home care and community services for dues-paying members to help them age in place. The dues ($550 a year for an individual, $780 for a household) cover assistance with shopping, information and referral, and group exercise classes, as well as 10-50% discounts on services such as home care and home repair coordinated by the program. Members of the "virtual retirement community" have the reassurance of knowing where to go for help if a problem arises. A similar project, Princeton, New Jersey's Community Without Walls, links elders residing in the community who hold meetings and create networks of fellow community members who can help with, for example, a ride to a medical appointment.

Glacier Circle, in Davis, California, was described as the first housing development for the elderly planned and developed entirely by its residents. Glacier Circle's residents have their own townhouses, built around a courtyard, but share a communal living room, dining room, and kitchen. This design was chosen to enhance the feeling of community among the residents. The development also includes a studio apartment designed to be made available at a low rent to a nurse who can care for community members. An estimated 80 or more communities nationwide offer "co-housing" for elders who do not want to be isolated but who also do not want to live in an institutional setting.[15]

This is a hard sector to quantify or even describe because there are many alternatives, and not all of them are subject to state licensure or any kind of regulation. Possibilities include:

- *Home-sharing* – where a more able-bodied person moves in and provides companionship and perhaps some assistance with chores.

- *Adult foster care* – where an impaired adult becomes a paying "boarder" in a household that might also have a small number of other foster residents; the "hosts" may be reimbursed by state programs in some circumstances.[16]

- *Group homes* – homes for several physically or mentally disabled persons, under the supervision of one or more paid staff members.

- *Adult homes, domiciliary homes, personal care homes, rest homes* – names for various kinds of residences (which may or may not require state licensure or qualification for reimbursement) providing some degree of supervision and services to persons who are basically capable of self-care with some help.

Often, these facilities operate with little or no state supervision; thus, they offer little protection for residents. There have been some reported scandals (e.g., financial improprieties or physical abuse of vulnerable residents). Many residents of these facilities get SSI (federal and state Supplemental Security Income) and/or other forms of disability benefits. A federal law called the Keys Amendment (an amendment to the Social Security Act) requires the states to create and enforce standards for housing operations where a significant number of SSI recipients live. (The standards are supposed to deal with admissions, residents' rights, sanitation, safety, etc.)

Another option, adult day care (also called adult day programs) combines worthwhile activities for an impaired elderly person with respite for the caregiver. There are about 3,400 adult day care programs nationwide, serving some 150,000 senior citizens. The programs vary in the scope of services they provide. Some of them offer a measure of health care, such as physical, occupational, and speech therapy and assistance taking medications. Others are more socially oriented. The programs also vary in the populations they serve: some of them are for the cognitively impaired, others for the cognitively intact. Typically, the program lasts for part of the day, several days a week.

In 2002, the average cost of adult day care was $56 a day. This was much lower than the cost of hiring a home health aide for eight hours ($149), a private room in an Assisted Living Facility (ALF; that would cost $77 a day) or a private room in a nursing home ($179 a day). However, the services are not the same, and adult day care is only suitable for a person who can live in the community with little or no assistance.[17]

PRACTICE TIP: The National Adult Day Services Association Website, www.nadsa. org has a checklist for choosing a center. Adult day care locations can be found at www.eldercarelink.com and www.eldercare.gov.

Even elderly tenants in conventional apartments may have some special entitlements. Check to see if they are entitled to rent rebates, homestead tax rebates, protection against excessive rent increases and eviction, or entitlement to remain as tenants without purchasing their apartments if the building becomes a co-op or condominium.[18]

ASSISTED LIVING FACILITIES

There are many elders who would be at risk if they lived entirely alone, without supportive services or assistance with basic activities such as mobility and continence. Yet, they do not need, or want, to pay for full-scale nursing care either (even if they could be admitted to a facility). Furthermore, the more pleasant and home-like a setting is (and the less restrictive and "institutional" it is), the more attractive it will be to potential residents. That is the rationale for the development of Assisted Living Facilities (ALFs). These are predominantly developed by religious organizations or the private sector, especially by hotel chains. The assisted living philosophy calls for promotion of autonomy and catering (where possible) to residents' preferences.

The definition of an ALF is not very precise. Many of these facilities are considered private housing developments and are not subjected to any form of licensure or regulation. In October, 2004, MetLife released its survey on the assisted living market, noting that this is not an easy area to research, because at least 26 names (e.g., "board and care," "sheltered housing," and "congregate housing") are used for these facilities. MetLife found that there are more than 36,000 ALFs nationwide, with about one million residents in 910,000 housing units. Most facilities are fairly small, with 25 to 125 units. The typical resident is an 83 year old woman who has problems with 1.7 of the 6 Activities of Daily Living (ADLs).

The average price MetLife found for an ALF in 2004 was $2,524 a month, or $30,288 a year. The corresponding 2003 figure was $2,379 a month, or $28,548 a year. Usually the base price for ALF residency includes two or three meals a day, ADL assistance, help taking medication, laundry, housekeeping, and maintenance, and social and recreational activities. Residents are often charged additional fees for services such as dementia care, meals delivered to the unit, extra laundry service, or expanded personal care.[19] In 2005, MetLife found an average cost of $2,905 a month, $34,980 a year—a hefty 15% increase over the 2004 figure. Costs ranged from a low of $1,642 a month (Jackson, Mississippi) to $4,629 a month in Boston.[20] In 2006, the MetLife Mature Market Institute returned to the subject, finding that close to two-thirds of ALFs offer specialized care for residents with dementia, but that half of the facilities imposed additional fees rather than setting their fees to cover dementia care. The range for the additional cost ran from $50 to $3,000 a month, with a $1,000 monthly increase typical. Close to three-quarters of home health agencies trained their staff to handle dementia care.[21]

The National Center for Assisted Living's *State Regulatory Review 2005* said that 37 states use "assisted living" as the term for licensing these facilities. The 2005 review, available online at www.ncal.org/about/2005_reg_review.pdf, gives state-by-state data on important topics such as the information assisted living facility owners are required to disclose to potential residents; the kind of care provided by facilities; who is suitable to live in an ALF—or can be forced to move out; staffing requirements; physical and life safety requirements imposed by the state; special requirements for Alzheimer's units. The review also gives contact information for state regulators in case planners want to research a facility and see if it has been cited for deficiencies.

One constraint on profits is that the industry is under pressure to accept sicker applicants or to allow residents to "age in place" as their condition deteriorates; the more care a resident needs, the higher the facility's expenses. When the first statutes were passed regulating ALFs, the facilities were only permitted to accept and retain fairly healthy residents. However, several states have passed laws allowing ALF residents to remain in the facility as their health deteriorates (because moving itself can cause "transfer trauma" which is deleterious to the health of the frail elderly). Sometimes the facility offers additional services (at a charge over and above the regular charge); residents may also hire home health agencies to provide the additional services.[22]

Regulators in several states have investigated Alterra Healthcare Corporation, the largest ALF operator in the United States, alleging quality-of-care problems. Alterra has about 475 facilities and 22,000 residents in 28 states, including 150 specialized Alzheimer's facilities. The allegations involve inadequate staffing or inadequate training of staff; failure to give residents their prescribed medications and supplements; failure to detect when residents wander; and inadequate fall protection.[23]

The American Association of Homes and Services for the Aging defines assisted living as providing and/or arranging for meals, personal and supportive services, health care, and 24-hour supervision to residents in a group facility. The Assisted Living Federation of America's formulation "is a special combination of housing, personalized supportive services and health care designed to respond to the individual needs of those who need help with Activities of Daily Living but do not need the skilled medical care provided in a nursing home."

Depending on the geographic area and the extent of services provided, an ALF can be a luxurious but high-cost alternative. A rule of thumb within the housing industry is that residents of newly-constructed senior housing will spend 80% of their income on housing and allied services, and they will need an annual income of $50,000 to support an ALF lifestyle.

PLANNING TIP: The National Aging Information Center (run by the federal Administration on Aging) has an online "bibliography" of information about the assisted living sector: www.aoa.gov/prof/notes/notes_assisted_living.asp. Both industry and consumer organizations have made checklists available online for selecting ALFs; it's interesting to compare their viewpoints! See, e.g., the Consumer Consortium on Assisted Living, www.ccal.org, the American Association of Homes and Services for the Aging, www.aahsa.org/advocacy/assisted_living/default.asp; and the American Seniors Housing Association, www.seniorshousing.org/site/ housing/index_assisted.html.

Most ALF residents pay privately (out-of-pocket) for their stay at the facility.

In 2005, the states of Alaska, Arizona, Arkansas, California, Colorado, Connecticut, Delaware, Florida, Georgia, Hawaii, Idaho, Indiana, Iowa, Kansas, Maine, Maryland, Massachusetts, Michigan, Minnesota, Missouri, Montana, Nebraska, Nevada, New Hampshire , New Jersey, New Mexico,, North Carolina, North Dakota, Oregon, Rhode Island, South Dakota, Texas, Vermont, Washington, and Wisconsin had some degree of Medicaid coverage of ALF services, under at least some circumstances.

Between 1998 and 2000 alone, Medicaid funding for ALFs increased 50%. In some instances, Medicaid rates are competitive with private-pay rates, and operators in markets with excess capacity may be willing to accept Medicaid funding to fill their beds. However, a greater Medicaid role in ALF funding could lead to the same kind of detailed and perhaps pettifogging regulation that nursing facilities also face. Another potential source of frustration for the industry is payment delays; it is not uncommon for nursing facilities to wait three to six months for reimbursement.[24]

Although the first generations of LTCI policies sold do not cover assisted living, viewing it as a form of housing (i.e., a personal expense) rather than as a form of medical treatment, some later policies cover assisted living under the heading of "innovative benefits." An increasing number of insurers have realized that it makes more sense to pay a smaller amount for ALF costs, promoting the happiness of the insured person, than to make expensive institutionalization the only route to insurance reimbursement.

ALFs are subject to some federal regulation, but states are primarily responsible for regulating and monitoring ALFs. States vary in their treatment of ALFs. Some states consider ALFs to be board and care facilities, whereas others use terms such as Residential Care Facility, personal care home, enriched housing, sheltered care facility, or home for the aged. All of the states except Kentucky license ALFs (and even Kentucky has a voluntary certification program).

The prospective resident will sign a contract prior to moving to an ALF. There is no government-prescribed or industry standard ALF contract, so careful review by the planning team is especially important. An optimum contract would cover items such as:

- What services the facility offers;

- The extent and degree of available services;

- Which services are covered under the basic fee;

- The optional services available, and the extra charges for those services;

- The number of staff, and the qualifications for the staff;

- Staff coverage at night and on weekends;

- The facilities available for coping with medical emergencies and for transferring residents to hospitals; and

- Refund provisions.

However, in practice, contracts often fail to cover important issues and might even require the potential resident to relieve the facility of liability (e.g., if a person decides to remain in the facility despite experiencing deterioration in his or her physical condition).

There are at least two quality control initiatives for the assisted living sector – the American Health Care Association's Quality Initiative for Assisted Living, and the Assisted Living Quality Coalition. (Created by AARP, the Assisted Living Facilities Association, the American Association of Homes and Services for the Aging, and the Alzheimer's Association.)

In August, 1996, the Assisted Living Quality Coalition published a paper entitled "Assisted Living Quality Initiative: Building a Structure That Promotes Quality." The coalition's recommendations include:

- Choosing a facility that accepts and adheres to guidelines issued by the National Assisted Living Quality Organization (an independent industry association);

- Insurers and other third-party payors should support quality by providing reimbursement for private rooms for all ALF residents who want them;

- Building codes should be reformed so that ALFs can conform to the codes and provide safety in emergencies without "breaking the bank";

- Residents, their families, and advocates should be included on each facility's internal quality assessment team; and

- Facilities should create a database of quality indicators (such as improvement, or at least non-deterioration, in the functional status of residents), so that facilities can be compared and a facility's performance over time can be assessed.

CONTINUING CARE RETIREMENT COMMUNITIES

The terms "life care community" and "Continuing Care Retirement Community" (CCRC) are broadly similar, although some state statutes use one term rather than the other; there may also be technical differences in the way the two terms are applied. Nevertheless, the basic theory is that a developer constructs a community containing residential units, community and recreational facilities and varying levels of medical care, up to skilled nursing. Most people who move to the community are fairly healthy when they arrive, and so they will move to residential units and take advantage of the recreational opportunities. Over time, they may need home care that will be administered within their units, or they may have to move to the facility's nursing unit.

Continuing Care Retirement Communities use a team approach in identifying residents' needs and keeping them healthy and functional as long as possible (e.g., by monitoring arthritis, high blood pressure, and other chronic conditions). According to the GAO, that approach is effective in maintaining residents' health, but it is not necessarily effective in reducing overall health costs.[25]

According to the GAO, approximately 350,000 people lived in about 1,200 CCRCs as of the beginning of 1997. (The American Seniors Housing Association, a trade association for CCRCs, has a much higher estimate of about 2,700 facilities nationwide.) The average CCRC had about 300 residents, most of them living independently in housing units. The GAO visited 11 CCRCs, finding that entry fees ranged from $34,000 (studio apartment) to $439,600 (two-bedroom home). In addition to the entry fee, single people and couples had to pay monthly charges of $1,383 and $4,267, respectively.

Thirty-six states have some degree of CCRC regulation; unfortunately, that leaves 14 states that do not. (It is interesting to note that regulation is usually handled by a state's insurance department, not its department of public health. The focus of enforcement is on the kind of disclosure usually found in a securities prospectus, information that is usually not provided in a typical doctor-patient relationship.)

Furthermore, state regulation may be porous. There may be no requirement that facility operators keep entry fees in escrow (so that they will be available if refunds are called for), and reserves for operating expenses are not always mandated. In the best case scenario, residents either never need a nursing home bed, or they find one available when they need it. In one worst case scenario, the facility underestimated the number of nursing home level beds that would be available, or filled beds with non-residents to earn extra money, leaving residents unable to access the necessary level of care. Nursing home beds in CCRCs will probably not be Medicaid-participating, so if residents need to pay extra fees for nursing care, but run out of money, they probably will not be able to get Medicaid reimbursement.

Some facility operators are unscrupulous and deliberately exploit residents. However, it is far more likely that financial problems, including facility bankruptcy, will be caused by the facility operator's inexperience or inability to estimate future costs. Residents may be forced to pay additional fees, or to leave facilities that are being closed down in conjunction with a bankruptcy.[26]

Factors to consider in assessing a brochure or contract include:

- The sponsor's track record;

- The financial history of the project, and projections for the future;

- Whether the actuarial assumptions about residents' longevity and care needs are reasonable;

- What happens to residents who need a nursing home level of care when all the nursing home beds are full;

- The conditions for canceling the contract and getting a refund (e.g., whether the refund may be deferred until someone else buys the unit);

- When, and how often, housekeeping and laundry services are provided; and

- The extent to which the sponsor can raise fees, or cut back on services, if it runs into financial trouble.

Determine whether your state publishes an official state consumer guide to CCRCs. These guides can be an excellent resource for potential residents and their families (and a convenient source of information about where to reach regulators to file a complaint).

PLANNING TIP: The Deficit Reduction Act of 2005 makes it harder to combine prepayment for a CCRC with Medicaid planning, so this factor should be taken into account if a client intends to become a CCRC resident but expects to be able to access Medicaid benefits later.

NURSING HOMES

Too many caregivers think they have only two (or perhaps three) alternatives to consider: (1) do nothing; (2) maybe "have Mom move in with us"; or (3) "put Mom in a nursing home." Nursing home placement is often seen by elders, and perceived by caregivers, as an act of hostility and abandonment. Certainly, inappropriate institutionalization is bad for everyone – bad for elders who feel imprisoned, bad for the institutions that care for residents who really do not belong there, and bad for Medicaid, insurance companies, and out-of-pocket payors who pay for a higher level of care than is required.

Senior citizens and caregivers who have access to a qualified planning team should have a greater degree of insight into the continuum of care, and should be able to understand the resources available in the senior citizens' community.

However, not all institutionalization is inappropriate. Sometimes the senior citizen has such intensive health care needs that a medical setting is required. Furthermore, especially in rural areas, it might be theoretically possible to put together a plan of home care and community services, but the plan might not work as a practical matter because there are not enough agencies and workers in the area, or because the distances to be covered are too great. Another common reason for moving to a nursing home is a change in the availability of care from family members. The death of a caregiver spouse (particularly the wife) may make it impossible for the survivor to remain at home any longer. A child or in-law who formerly provided care may move away, get a new job or a more demanding job, have to care for a spouse, or assume increased child care responsibilities – once again, making it necessary for the elder to be placed in a nursing home. In those circumstances, it must be understood that a nursing home is the best choice for care, and the focus will then be to pick the best available facility.

Placing a parent in a nursing home is, in some respects, like enrolling a child in his or her first choice of colleges. An individual needs a rational plan for paying for it all, but money is not the only factor. Whereas college admission revolves around factors such as GPAs, SAT scores, and extracurricular activities, nursing home admission depends on "assessment" – a standardized test used to determine the elder's degree of physical and cognitive disability, and the areas in which assistance will be required. As a general rule, unless the assessment score is higher than the cut-off level (i.e., unless the applicant is seriously ill), nursing home admission cannot occur.

Some nursing home developers are responding to criticisms of the industry by stressing community in smaller, more home-like facilities. In the 1960s, when Medicaid funds first became available, many large nursing homes were built, modeled after hospitals. Today, the generation of Depression survivors has mostly died off, and residents now entering nursing homes are more consumer-oriented. For example, Beverly Enterprises is renovating 39 of its 351 institutional-style homes, retraining staff and dividing 100-bed units into 24-bed "neighborhoods," and replacing hospital-style delivery of meals on trays with more sociable group meals in a dining room.[27]

The Nursing Home Market

In 2002, there were about 16,500 nursing homes in the U.S., with 1,768,686 residents.[28] AARP has published a compilation of state long-term care data every other year since 1992—most recently in 2004. The organization found that people over age 50 represented 27.9% of the U.S. population in 2002, and this number is expected to grow to 33.4% of the population in 2020. Senior citizens were one-eighth of the population in 2002, with one-sixth predicted for 2020; people over 85 were 1.6% of the population in 2002, 2.0% predicted for 2020. One-fifth of senior citizens have limitations in mobility or ability to care for themselves; one-ninth have cognitive or mental limitations. In 2004, the percentage of senior citizens living in nursing homes ranged from 1.6% in Alaska to 7.3% in North Dakota.

AARP found that in 2003, one-third of all Medicaid spending was for long-term care, and Medicaid paid at least part of the bill for two-thirds of nursing home residents. For every two Medicaid beneficiaries in a nursing home, one senior citizen or disabled younger person received Medicaid home care under a waiver (an arrangement where Congress allows a state to rewrite some of the Medicaid rules).

In 2002, Medicare paid skilled nursing homes $265/day, whereas Medicaid paid regular nursing homes only $118.[29]

Factors in Choosing a Nursing Home

An individual who has already qualified for Medicaid and who needs to enter a nursing home is given no choice in picking a nursing home. That person must enter the first Medicaid-certified nursing home within a certain geographic radius of the home or hospital that has an available Medicaid bed. (Nursing homes are allowed to, and generally do, have separate waiting lists for private-pay and Medicaid patients.)

In contrast, a private-pay patient can select any nursing home that he or she wishes. However, since high quality nursing care is always in demand, the best facilities may have a long waiting list, and it might be impossible to enter the preferred home at the time that institutionalization is required. To a certain extent, it is possible to plan and reserve a bed in advance, but it is impossible to predict when a stroke, heart attack, or hip fracture will occur, or when it will become evident that a person is cognitively impaired, and not just mildly forgetful.

If a subsequent Medicaid application is contemplated, it makes sense to choose a facility that participates in Medicaid. The federal laws regulating nursing homes make it unlawful to evict a resident merely because the payment method changes from private-pay to Medicaid. Federal legislation signed in March, 1999 also protects Medicaid residents from being evicted after a nursing home terminates its participation in the Medicaid system. "Private-pay" contracts are also unlawful; the facility is not allowed to require new residents to agree *not* to apply for Medicaid, or *not* to apply for a certain period of time. A person who satisfies the Medicaid requirements has a legal right to get those benefits and, therefore, the right to apply for those benefits even if the facility's financial interest is better served by the patient paying privately for a longer period of time.

Nursing homes are not allowed to impose a contractual requirement that the residents' relatives make donations to the facility, or use their own funds to guarantee that the resident's bills will be paid. (However, if the resident's son or daughter has access to the resident's funds in a joint checking account, or has been named as trustee, attorney-in-fact, or guardian, then it is entirely appropriate for the son or daughter to use the resident's money to pay for the care.)

PRACTICE TIP. The Centers for Medicare & Medicaid Services (CMS) maintains a current, on-line database of all Medicare and Medicaid-certified nursing homes in the United States, and any enforcement actions against them, as well as their assessment surveys. The address is www.medicare.gov/NHCompare/home.asp. Also see www.healthgrades.com, which provides ratings of nursing homes, hospitals, doctors, and health plans for consumers who want to make wise choices. Although the nursing home information is based on CMS's data, the Healthgrades site adds additional search features and has a point system for classifying the severity of nursing home deficiencies.

Short-Term Placements

More and more nursing homes allow short-term stays, not just to give caregivers a breathing space, but so potential residents can get a good look at the facility. In 2004, the *Wall Street Journal* reported that costs ranged from $70-$200 a day for these "auditions," with the highest costs for dementia care. Sometimes a short ALF stay is used by people who are ready for discharge from a hospital and do not qualify for Medicare skilled nursing care, but who do not feel ready to return home (especially if they live alone).

Because the mean rate of occupancy at ALFs is now about 85%, many facilities have extra beds, and about 50% of the people who try out a facility end up moving there. Although health insurance probably will not pay for these stays, long-term care insurance will probably cover the stay, as long as the senior citizen is cognitively impaired or needs assistance with at least two ADLs. But check the policy—a limitation of 21 days for respite care per year is common.

The federal Administration on Aging makes some grants to fund state and local agencies that provide respite care, and the California Family Caregiver Alliance makes matching grants of up to $3,600 per year for respite (although with a tremendous waiting list); your clients or their parents might qualify.

PRACTICE TIP: For information on short-term stays, see, e.g., www.aegisal.com; www.emeritus.com; www.sunriseseniorliving.com/Home.do (sites maintained by providers of care); The Family Caregiver Alliance (www.caregiver.org); the ElderCare Locator, www.eldercare.gov (more general) and the National Respite Locator Service, www.respitelocator.org.[30] Most ALFs have at least some provisions for short-term try-out stays, although this alternative is not promoted; it tends to emerge when a potential resident tours. Fully-rented communities would be least likely to allow a short-term stay. In contrast, a facility with many vacancies might offer a discounted rate or a "summer special" for elderly people visiting their children and grandchildren, or might make a specialty of short stays for respite care.[31]

Nursing Home Bill of Rights

Since 1987, federal law has provided protection for residents of nursing homes that participate in Medicare and/or Medicaid (most nursing homes do). Nursing homes have a legal obligation to protect and promote residents' rights, including:

- Participation in medical decision-making, including free choice of physician;

- Freedom from physical, mental, and financial abuse; facilities are not allowed to use physical or chemical restraints for their own convenience, but only when they are actually medically necessary to protect the resident;

- The right to join in resident and family groups, and to express grievances without suffering discrimination;

- Access to state and federal survey reports about the facility;

- Advance notice of the cost of the facility's services;

- The right to be taken care of under a written plan of care supervised by a physician; and

- Freedom from arbitrary transfer or discharge. Residents can be discharged if they are dangerous to other residents, if the facility cannot safely meet their needs, or if there is no source of payment for the resident's care. However, a facility that participates in Medicaid violates federal law by discharging or transferring a resident simply because the resident has switched from paying privately, or using LTCI to pay for care, to having his or her care paid for by Medicaid.

Reviewing the Nursing Home Contract

The contract should spell out which services are included in the basic price, and which services are optional "extras" provided at additional cost. (Nursing home residents and their relatives are often shocked to discover that although they pay substantial amounts of money for nursing care, some very simple items and services are not provided.) The contract should reflect compliance with applicable state and federal laws, and should *not* include any invalid provisions. For instance, it is unlawful to require residents' relatives to guarantee payment, or to require residents to refrain from applying for Medicaid.

Problem Facilities

Ironically, medical improvements and increased knowledge of, and access to, home care have only made it harder to operate nursing homes. The problems of caring for a few dozen sweet little old ladies with minor medical problems are infinitesimal compared to managing a large facility, over half of whose residents are severely demented and most of whom have complex medical problems that would have been fatal only a few decades earlier.

At the other end of the spectrum, nursing home residents are a very vulnerable, and often isolated, population. Most residents never have any visitors at all, much less constant visits from highly involved relatives and friends who could spot deficiencies in the facility and complain vigorously. Since the majority of nursing home days are paid for by Medicaid, those rates are critical to the facilities' financial operations. Operators who believe they are being underpaid by Medicaid may be tempted to cut corners. (Remember, most nursing homes are profit-making operations, and most for-profit nursing homes are part of a chain. Consequently, administrators are under constant pressure not only to enhance stockholder value, but to keep up with other units in the chain.)

Although nursing homes have been subject to nationwide quality standards, and the state survey and certification process has been standardized since the federal law OBRA '87 (Omnibus Budget Reconciliation Act), there are still many facilities with serious and even dangerous quality problems. The federal rules for regulating nursing homes require state employees, working under contracts with the federal government, to inspect nursing homes (an average of once a year) to see if there are deficiencies in complying with federal rules. Then federal officials are supposed to check up on the state inspectors by going to at least 5% of the homes to verify the findings of the state inspectors. However, states are very short of health funds, and there is a temptation to cut corners by reducing the number of inspectors.

Between 1997 and 2003, the percentage of nursing homes that were not found to have any deficiencies dropped from 21.6% to 9.5%, and the average number of deficiencies per facility found during nursing home inspections went from 4.9 to 6.9. The percentage of facilities cited for violations that could create immediate jeopardy for residents dropped, from 30.6% to 16.6%, suggesting that more violations are being cited overall, but they are less serious. In the period running from 2000-2002, federal surveyors found harmful or dangerous violations in 22% of the nursing homes where state surveyors did not report violations. In 2002, 18% of nursing homes were cited after surveys for one or more violations that actually harmed residents or that put residents in jeopardy, although there were dramatic state-to-state variations: only 3% of Delaware facilities, but 42.7% of Connecticut facilities, were cited.

The number of nursing homes given civil penalties for deficiencies fell 18% between 2000 and 2003, and the number of homes fined went down 12% in this period; the number of nursing homes that were not allowed to get paid for accepting new Medicare of Medicaid patients was cut nearly in half. However, this probably reflects less stringent inspection, not better nursing home conditions.

The Long Term Care Community Coalition found that from 2002 to 2005, state health inspectors routinely failed to find problems at New York nursing homes that were found in follow-up federal inspections. And New York is one of the better states, ranking only 39th in the number of deficiencies found per nursing home. The nursing home industry in New York was a $10 billion-a-year industry (for 12,000 nursing home beds), and 78% of the revenue came from Medicaid.

PRACTICE TIP: The Nursing Home Compare segment of the www.medicare.gov Web site includes inspection reports, but these reports should be viewed with some skepticism, because the Inspector General's office for the Department of Housing and Human Services said that information was missing or inaccurate for about one-fifth of the nursing homes.[32]

In 2005, when HHS' Office of the Inspector General studied fines for nursing home deficiencies, it found that penalties are usually imposed at the low end of the range; it took an average of 14 months for appealed cases, and six months even for cases that were not appealed, for fines to be collected. In 2000 and 2001, $81.7 million in nursing home penalties were theoretically imposed, but by the end of 2002, only 42% had been collected.[33]

Congressional investigators found that at least 59% of nursing homes surveyed were cited for fire safety deficiencies in their most recent inspections, and most nursing home residents are limited in their ability to respond to emergencies. Many homes refused to install sprinklers and smoke detectors for cost reasons (20-30% of nursing homes do not have sprinkler systems). The nursing home industry supports imposing a federal requirement of sprinkler systems, but only if the federal government contributes toward the estimated $1 billion cost and allows three to five years to install them instead of mandating immediate compliance. The GAO concluded that oversight of fire safety in nursing homes is inadequate; many nursing homes are not constructed to prevent the spread of fire and smoke; few of them have fire drills; and even if deficiencies are detected, penalties are seldom imposed.[34]

The problem has not gone away. A 2006 report by the GAO accused state inspectors of making unrealistically optimistic reports for political reasons, and ignoring serious or even dangerous conditions within the facilities they inspect. In addition to fire safety violations, the deficiencies that went unreported and uncorrected included falls and avoidable bedsores. According to the GAO, even when states receive complaints from nursing home residents or their families, investigations are often delayed rather than pursued promptly. Inspections that are supposed to be made without notice are performed on a predictable schedule, allowing facilities to "clean up" temporarily and then return to sloppy or even dangerous practices after the inspection. The GAO also found major differences among the states: more than half the nursing homes in Connecticut, but only 6% of homes in California, were cited for deficiencies. No doubt some of the difference was due to actually differences in quality of care, but some of it must have reflected differences in the rigor of the inspections.[35]

There is not very much litigation about nursing home negligence, because the cases are hard to prove and recoveries are usually low (because of the short life expectancy of nursing home residents, and because their injuries or deaths do not cause substantial loss of income). Another factor is that so many nursing home residents receive Medicare and/or Medicaid benefits, and these programs are entitled to a lien if recipients obtain a tort judgment. After the lien for past benefits is satisfied and legal fees are paid, there may not be much left over for the injured person. Ironically, if there is a significant amount left over, it could be treated as excess assets impairing future eligibility for Supplemental Security Income and Medicaid!

However, a few law firms make a specialty of handling these cases. There have been some exceptional cases resulting in large jury verdicts: in 2001, for example, an Arkansas jury awarded $78.4 million to the estate of an 88-year-old nursing home resident who died after being left without food or water. The Arkansas Supreme Court upheld the nursing home's liability in 2003, but reduced the verdict to $26.4 million. New Jersey has a strong pro-nursing-home-resident statute, and injured nursing home residents are allowed to sue for violations and can recover their fees and costs as well as damages.

In 2001, Jury Verdict Research found that, nationwide, half of the jury awards in all nursing home negligence cases were higher than $192,997. Half of the plaintiffs asked for a quarter of a million dollars or more; half of the defendants offered $45,000 or more to settle the case. The greatest average damages were awarded in cases of physical or sexual abuse of nursing home residents ($376,500), followed by $275,000 for claims of improper medical treatment, $150,000 for negligent supervision claims, and $125,000 for premises liability claims. Texas and Florida impose statutory curbs on damages in nursing home negligence cases. Across the whole country, 60% of plaintiffs win damages in nursing home suits that are tried (i.e., are not dismissed or settled)—whereas only 1/3 of medical malpractice plaintiffs win their cases.[36]

The Tenth Circuit upheld a $1,300 a day penalty against a nursing home that allowed a resident to develop bedsores because the failure to satisfy the federal standards had the effect of harming the patient.[37]

In a California case from 2000,[38] the daughter of a nursing home resident (who also served as her mother's conservator) sued nursing home operator Beverly Enterprises under California's Elder Abuse and Dependent Adult Civil Protection Act. The Act says it is illegal for a custodian to deprive an elderly or dependent adult of the goods and services necessary to avoid physical harm or mental suffering.

The jury instructions given by the trial judge referred to state statutes and state and federal regulations about nursing home residents' rights. The jury awarded $365,000 in compensatory damages and close to $100,000 in punitive damages, based on a finding that the defendants acted with malice, oppression, or fraud.

The defendants objected to using the state and federal regulations to define the standard of care in nursing homes. The appeals court held that the jury instructions did not mislead or prejudice the jury. The appeals court also approved the use of duly authorized state and federal regulations to set the standard of care that determines whether elder abuse has occurred.

A 2000 case from Massachusetts[39] involves a nursing home abandoned by its owner. The facility was placed under court supervision to protect residents' safety. The court-appointed receiver has the power to order the sale of the nursing home, but only under court supervision, after the court has determined that selling the home is a better choice than shutting down the home and relocating its residents.

COPING WITH PROBLEMS

There are a wide range of problems connected with housing situations. They can be caused by a mentally incapacitated person's fears or misperceptions (e.g., a person who has misplaced an object accuses the home care worker of stealing it, or a diabetic nursing home resident whose candy bars have been confiscated says the home is "starving" him or her), or by flagrant abuse of vulnerable residents, or anything in between. Sometimes, through no fault of the provider, the housing situation simply is no longer suitable for the older person's changed needs. The remedy is to find a more suitable setting bearing in mind the potential for "transfer trauma."

The Medicare Part D prescription drug program (see Chapter 5) will create many problems for the 1.5 million seniors who are year-round nursing home residents (in any year, 3.5 million seniors spend some time in a nursing home). Nursing home residents take a lot of prescription drugs—an average of eight prescriptions each—but many of them are unable to leave the home to collect prescriptions, and are cognitively impaired and unable to make an intelligent choice among drug plans. Even before Part D was developed, there were supply companies that specialized in serving nursing homes, but not all Part D plans will have contracts with these companies.

The unstated assumption behind Part D is that senior citizens are sophisticated and able to reach drugstores and make informed purchase decisions. More than a third of nursing home residents suffer from dementia, and at least one-fifth have trouble swallowing, so they cannot take pills—which would be a problem if they sign up for a Part D plan whose formulary does not include liquid forms of the drugs the nursing home residents need. Pharmacy benefit managers say they do not have experience with nursing homes; nursing homes say they are unprepared to counsel their residents about insurance. The majority of nursing home residents receive Medicaid, but Medicaid coverage of prescription drugs ended when Part D was implemented, so all of those patients needed new prescriptions, with increased risks of medication errors and adverse reactions to changes in drugs.[40]

All states maintain ombudsman programs for resolving complaints and disputes. Some of the programs are limited to nursing facilities, but others have a broader scope. Resort to these programs is free, but since they are bureaucracies, a speedy response is not always possible.

Furthermore, all states have protective service programs that investigate situations in which vulnerable people are at risk. If necessary, the protective service programs can provide services, or have a guardian appointed for someone who is either incapable of self-care or who is being abused. Again, these programs are free and are publicly supported.

In the private sector, Geriatric Care Managers (GCMs) can do a great job of investigating and solving problems since they are objective professionals with a large database of information about local resources. They can make sure a home health worker is replaced if there is a personality conflict, or they can recommend a better agency if there are problems with the agency itself. They can also advise senior citizens and their families about service availability (e.g., caregiver training, respite for caregivers, home delivered meals, Alzheimer's day care), making recommendations, and assisting with the application process.

CHAPTER ENDNOTES

1. Vivian Marino, "As the Population Ages, Brokers Discover A New Specialty," *New York Times*, June 19, 2005, p. RE 14.

2. Trevor Thomas, "Survey: LTC Costs More Than $72,000 Per Year," *NU Online News Service*, 1/13/05.

3. Motoko Rich, "Independent Living Is Exposing Elderly to Eviction Threat," *New York Times*, February 15, 2004, p. A1.

4. MetLife Market Survey of Nursing Home and Home Care Costs (September 2004), www.metlife. com/WPSAssets/16582885811106064631V1FNursing%20Home%20Home%20Care%20Costs. pdf.

5. Trevor Thomas, "Survey: LTC Costs More Than $72,000 per Year," NU Online News Service, January 13, 2005.

6. Andrea Elliott, "The Doctor Will See You ...at Home" *New York Times*, December 30, 2004, p. B1.

7.   This trend is described by Jane Tilly, Joshua M. Weiner and Alison Evans Cuellar in "Consumer-Directed Home and Community Service Programs in Five Countries: Policy Issues for Older People and Government," October 2000, Urban Institute.

8.   IRC Secs. 3121(a)(7)(B), 3121(x); SSA Notice, 65 Fed. Reg. 63663.

9.   Terry Pristin, "The Gray Middle Market," *New York Times,* June 29, 2005, p. C9.

10. See, e.g., Jennie Green, "Older, and Living in Manhattan," *New York Times,* January 9, 2005, p. RE9, comparing the features available at a number of Manhattan developments.

11. Ray A. Smith, "For Rent: New Apartments for Healthy, Independent Seniors," *Wall Street Journal,* March 31, 2004, p. B1.

12. Antoinette Martin, "For Over-55's, Bigger Homes, Smaller Developments," *New York Times,* May 30, 2004, Real Estate p. 7.

13. Terry Pristin, "Hot Niche in the Rental Market: Housing for the Elderly," *New York Times,* February 15, 2006, p. C6.

14. Kelly Greene, "Neighborhoods Lack Adequate Resources for Aging Population," *Wall Street Journal,* May 5, 2005, p. D4.

15. Lisa Belkin, "A Virtual Retirement Home," *New York Times Magazine,* March 5, 2006, p. 91; Patricia Leigh Brown, "Growing Old Together, in New Kind of Commune," *New York Times,* February 27, 2006, p. A1; Jane Gross, "Aging at Home: For a Lucky Few, a Dream Come True," *New York Times* February 9, 2006, p. F1.

16. George James, "Home and Not Alone: A Foster Care Program for Grown-Ups," *New York Times,* November 29, 1998; includes a resource listing for New Jersey foster care programs. The article notes that foster care is an economical alternative; adult foster care costs $40 per day versus a Medicaid nursing home daily rate of $92. The article estimates that 100,000 elders live nationwide in foster care placements. About half the states had active foster care programs, and eight more had limited programs.

17. Hillary Chura, "A Little-Known Reprieve From Providing Care," *New York Times,* August 20, 2005, p. C5.

18. There may also be special housing assistance projects within the Legal Aid system or court system to assist elderly tenants. See Janelle Nanos, "Agencies Join Forces to Aid Older Tenants," *New York Times,* February 12, 2006, p. A44.

19. MetLife Market Survey of Assisted Living Costs (10/04), www.metlife.com/WPSAssets/18794494171106064943V1FMetLife%20Market%20Survey.pdf. According to Genworth Financial, the average 2004 cost of a private room in an ALF was $28,800: see Trevor Thomas, *Survey: LTC Costs More Than $72,000 Per Year,* NU Online News Service, January 13, 2005.

20. "Assisted Living Costs Soar," NU Online News, October 31, 2005.

21. MetLife press release, "More and More Assisted Living Facilities, Nursing Homes Providing Alzheimer's Care, Some With Additional Costs, According To Metlife Mature Market Institute Study" http://www.metlife.com/Applications/Corporate/WPS/CDA/PageGenerator/0,1674,P250%257ES794,00.html (February 6, 2006). The cost findings are summarized at www.maturemarketinstitute.com in the "What's New" area of the site.

22. Ann Davis, "Assisted Living' Firm Prospers by Housing a Frail Population," *Wall Street Journal,* January 15, 2001, p. A1.

23. Barry Meier, "States See Problems with Care at Chain of Centers for Aged," *New York Times,* November 26, 2000, p. A1.

24. Information from Fred W. Tanner, www.seniorlivingsolutions.com, appearing in "Medicaid in Assisted Living," *BAL Weekly,* December 13, 2000, and from a telephone conversation with Ed Sheehy of the Assisted Living Federation of America, who quoted State Assisted Living Policy 2000.

25. GAO/HEHS-97-36, "Health Care Services: How Continuing Care Retirement Communities Manage Services for the Elderly," January 23, 1997.

26. Michael Moss, "For Retirees, Moving Into 'Continuing Care' Offers No Guarantees," *Wall Street Journal*, October 8, 1998, p. A1, offers some sobering warnings.

27. William Hamilton, "The New Nursing Home, Emphasis on Home," *New York Times*, April 23, 2005, p. A1.

28. Centers for Disease Control, *Health, U.S., 2004*, Table 113, www.cdc.gov.

29. AARP, "Across the States: Profiles of Long-Term Care 2004, assets.aarp.org/rgcenter/post-import/d18202_2004_ats.pdf.

30. "Taking a Vacation at a Nursing Home," *Wall Street Journal*, June 16, 2004, p. D1.

31. Jane Gross, "Test-Driving a Retirement Community (Yes, You Can) *New York Times*, July 14, 2005, p. F1.

32. Al Baker, "New York Said To Be Lax Inspecting Nursing Homes," *New York Times*, May 16, 2005, p. B4; Robert Pear, "Penalties for Nursing Homes Show a Drop in Last 4 Years," *New York Times*, August 6, 2004 p. A11.

33. Bernadette Wright, AARP Public Policy Institute, "Enforcement of Quality Standards in Nursing Homes," (May 2005), www.aarp.org/research/longtermcare/quality/fs83r_homes.html; AARP, "Across the States: Profiles of Long-Term Care 2004, assets.aarp.org/rgcenter/post-import/d18202_2004_ats.pdf.

34. Robert Pear, "Nursing Homes Are Faulted for Fire Safety Weaknesses," *New York Times*, July 16, 2004, p. A18.

35. Robert Pear, "Nursing Home Inspections Miss Violations, Report Says," *New York Times*, January 16, 2006, p. A9.

36. Charles Toutant, "Firms Make Niche of Nursing Home Negligence Suits," *New Jersey Law Journal*, 9/10/04 (available at www.law.com).

37. Robert Pear, "U.S. Toughens Enforcement of Nursing Home Standards," *New York Times*, December 4, 2000, p. A21.

38. *Conservatorship of Gregory v. Beverly Enterprises, Inc.*, 95 Cal. 2d 336 (Cal. Ct. App. 2000); the relevant statute is Welfare & Institutions Code §15610.07.

39. *Attorney General v. M.C.K. Inc.*, 736 N.E.2d 373 (Mass. 2000).

40. Robert Pear, "New Medicare Drug Plan Is Raising Difficult Issues for Nursing Home Patients," *New York Times*, December 5, 2004, p. A38.

Chapter 15

Case Studies and the Coordinated Plan

Art Linkletter wrote a book, "Old Age Is Not for Sissies." Financial planning for old age is no cakewalk either. Of course, as a planner you know that every client not only has an individual fact situation but also individual priorities and preferences, and you are prepared to cope.

The situation is even more difficult when you participate in elder planning. You may be dealing with just one person—or a large, articulate and fractious family, each member of which has a separate agenda! And that is just on the client side. On the professional side, the planning team may include a lawyer, an accountant, a geriatric care manager, medical personnel, and perhaps others.

Furthermore, your recommendations must work now, and continue working in the future, although in the interim, market conditions are likely to change, the legal rules are likely to change, medical science is likely to progress, and your client might or might not experience deteriorations in physical and/or mental health. So your plan must provide for a take-over by a guardian, agent under a Durable Power of Attorney, trustee, or concerned family member or friend acting informally.

Every case will present itself differently. Sometimes you will be able to offer a cornucopia of choices, so the client can select the best. At other times, you will only be able to inform a vulnerable person that there is only one option available.

HYPOTHETICAL PLANS

These brief scenarios raise some of the problems that might be brought to a financial planner by a client. In some of these situations, the tax and estate planning considerations are paramount, while in others, they are of secondary (if any) importance. Understandably, a healthy client will put less emphasis on planning measures for future ill health than a client already suffering from physical and/or cognitive problems will place on dealing with the existing problems and obtaining the necessary care.

1. Lewis and Milla Bolkowski

Lewis Bolkowski, age 67, knows that it is time to turn over the reins of his car dealership, although he is not quite ready to quit working. His son, Dennis, and the dealership manager, Carlton Jackson, have agreed to pay $250,000 to Lewis in five $50,000 installment payments, and to give Lewis a five-year consulting agreement under which he is paid $40,000 per year. Lewis' compensation is a legitimate business expense because Lewis will continue to work as an executive of the company with significant responsibilities. (If he dies or becomes incapacitated in the interim, the balance of the $250,000 will have to be paid, but the consulting payments will end.) Milla Bolkowski, age 63, earns $50,000 per year as purchasing administrator for a manufacturing company, and plans to keep working until her health problems (arthritis and heart disease) make it impractical to continue.

The Bolkowskis own a $350,000 home and have a portfolio in the $750,000-$1,000,000 range. Although their insurance agent has quoted them a price of about $10,000 per year for long-term care insurance (LTCI) policies for both of them, they believe that the premium is, in fact, a good bargain because Medicaid is not a possibility for them. Furthermore, the Bolkowskis know that in five years (or sooner, if Milla must stop working at her current annual salary of $50,000, and start receiving her pension of $27,000 per year), their income will decrease significantly. Consequently, they plan to "live beneath their income" and to continue their investment program. They know that they can expect over ten years (perhaps even over twenty years) of longevity, so they want to continue to invest in growth stocks. However, they are also seriously considering shifting some funds into a deferred annuity that will provide income when the consulting and buy-out payments end.

Whether estate taxes will be due depends on what level the estate tax exclusion has reached. Let's say, for the sake of argument, that Lewis dies in 2008 and Milla dies in 2014. If EGTRRA remains in its present form (and of course Congress could make further modifications in the estate tax structure), Lewis' estate will be tax-free if it is under $2 million (which it probably will be). Milla, on the other hand, would face estate tax on an estate exceeding $1 million (because after EGTRRA's sunset, that will be the level of the unified credit), and unless she remarries, she will not have access to the unlimited marital deduction.

If she is very concerned about the possibility of estate taxation, perhaps the Bolkonskis should get some second-to-die life insurance—or she should concentrate on reducing her estate through health care spending and a lifetime giving program to family, friends, and charities. Clearly, however, they are affluent enough to require professional estate planning. It might make sense to set up credit shelter trusts and perhaps a QTIP trust. (In any event, their estate planning attorney will advise them about this decision.) Perhaps one of the trusts should be set up to manage assets in case of incapacity. Naturally, each should have a durable power of attorney. However, keep in mind that it probably makes more sense for Lewis to designate Milla as his attorney-in-fact than vice versa because Lewis is older than Milla, and is at a greater risk of losing capacity sooner than Milla will.

Because these individuals are still working, it probably makes sense for them to remain in their present home. However, a viable alternative is for them to find a luxury retirement community and move there. Even if the community provides only housing and leisure services, if they have adequate LTCI they can have their health needs taken care of through insurance benefits, rather than by living in a health-oriented setting.

2. Jane Pergolesi

Jane Pergolesi, age 71, was sorrowful but not surprised when her husband, Alex, at age 76, succumbed to the cancer he had been battling for years. Jane inherited a large, somewhat run-down house worth about $200,000, a joint savings account of $65,000, and received the proceeds from her husband's $100,000 life insurance policy.

Prior to his death, Alex received $2,000 per month in pension payments. Since this pension was payable in joint-and-50% survivor annuity form, Jane will now receive only $1,000 a month. (Although Jane held paid jobs sporadically, she does not have a pension of her own.) When Alex was alive, he received $700 a month in Social Security benefits and Jane received $350 a month as his spouse; now she will receive a widow's pension of $700 a month. In other words, she has a monthly income of $1,700, plus earnings on the savings account (possibly $300 a month). Thus, while Jane is far from affluent, she is not destitute either. Clearly, estate planning is not much of a problem for her, but she may have some problems in paying for health care. After careful consideration, Jane decided to buy a Medicare Part D policy; it currently costs $30 a month, although she is aware that the premium could rise in the future.

Jane decides to take the life insurance proceeds in the form of a settlement option, yielding another $6,000 per year in income ($500 per month) bringing her income up to $2,500 a month. Her main asset is the house. It so happens that her son, Dan, is unemployed. Dan suggests that he, his wife, and their three children move in with Jane. Dan is confident that he can fix up the house and increase its value. Of course, he expects that Jane will leave the house to him, or transfer it to him during her lifetime.

Jane agrees to the move since she does not want to live alone right now. Her health is reasonably good and she is mentally acute. She thinks it might be fun to have her lively young relatives around—and it is comforting to know that her son and daughter-in-law would be able to summon help if she ever needed it, or they could take care of her at home if her ability to function declined. However, she is not positive that this arrangement will work out, so she is not ready to enter into any formal agreements. If it does work out, she will consider signing a formal care contract, and if Dan stays around long enough to be a "caregiver child" (see Chapter 6), Jane will consider transferring ownership of the house to him, perhaps subject to her own life estate.

In case the living arrangement does not work out, Jane is gathering information about reverse mortgages (see Chapter 7) as an extra source of income that will not impair her Medicaid eligibility. Her housing equity is below $500,000, so she will not be disqualified for Medicaid on the basis of excess housing equity, although she is likely to have excess assets, as discussed in Chapter 6. She is also considering the purchase of an actuarially sound, immediate annuity with part of her savings—once again, with the goal of receiving extra income without having to make a transfer for Medicaid purposes. But, as Chapter 6 shows, annuity planning requires extra care after DRA '05.

Since Jane does not want to trust her entire financial future to only one of her children, as part of her incapacity plan she grants a durable power of attorney to her daughter, Dottie Lynn Asher, and makes an advance designation of Ms. Asher as her guardian, should she ever need one.

3. Elizabeth and Timothy Hodge

Elizabeth Hodge, age 72, suffers from mental problems that might be due to early-stage Alzheimer's disease, as well as several moderately severe physical problems. Timothy Hodge, also age 72, is cognitively intact, but has leukemia, which is fairly well under control. Timothy's vision and hearing are also limited.

The Hodges own a condominium unit that is worth about $200,000. Elizabeth receives a pension of $1,500 per month, Timothy's pension payments are $3,000 per month, and their Social Security benefits total $1,500 per month. Thus, they have $6,000 per month to work with, plus income from $100,000 in savings and investments.

Elizabeth owns a LTCI policy with benefits of $100 per day for care provided in an institution, and $50 per day for home care. Timothy does not have LTCI and certainly would be a poor candidate to purchase it at this time, given his age and physical condition. An important first step is to rule out non-Alzheimer's causes of Mrs. Hodge's problems–for instance, she might benefit from antidepressants or treatment of high blood pressure. However, if Alzheimer's is diagnosed, the question becomes whether she can be cared for appropriately and safely at home. She probably fits the Medicare definition of "homebound," so she could qualify for some home health assistance from Medicare. In addition, state agencies or charitable organizations may provide services for those with Alzheimer's, such as adult day care.

A geriatric care manager (GCM) should be consulted about how to structure the home health plan, balancing professional services with non-skilled services, such as housekeeping and personal care. The GCM can also advise the Hodges about which local home health agencies are best. Unfortunately, Elizabeth's home care will probably cost more than $50 per day, so there will be a need to make co-payments. The home health worker can also help Timothy by taking care of tasks that would tax his visual or communicative abilities.

However, an "assessment" of Elizabeth's condition may result in a high enough "score" to justify institutionalization. Again, it is quite likely that the $100 daily benefit will not be adequate for actual needs. Medicare will probably do a fairly good job of caring for Timothy's leukemia (including providing hospice services if his condition becomes terminal).

4. Donald and Myra Jennings

Donald Jennings is 71 years old; his second wife, Myra, is 54. Donald is retired, receives a pension of $38,000 per year, and also receives $12,000 per year in Social Security benefits. Myra is the assistant headmistress of a private school, earning $75,000 per year. She will have access to a pension ($40,000 per year) in another seven years, if she chooses to retire, based on her long period of employment with the same school.

No children were born to Donald and Myra, but Donald has three children by his first marriage, and Donald adopted Myra's son by her first marriage. The couple has five grandchildren.

Their portfolio, including IRA accounts, is worth $1 million and generates $60,000 of income (because they have chosen to use a high-growth strategy and have reinvested much of the income from the portfolio). Their income may be increased, if needed, by taking the income currently, instead of reinvesting it. (After all, they are already paying income tax on it). They can also sell a portion of the portfolio, or shift the allocation of assets to obtain more income.

Since their income is $185,000 per year, they are an atypical couple in that they are able to pay for extensive long-term care out of their current income. (Note, however, that their income will diminish after Myra retires.) This also means that they probably will not want to jump through the hoops required to establish a Medicaid plan for an affluent couple—obstacles that increased after the passage of DRA '05.

Depending on Donald's health status, it may be worthwhile for him to buy LTCI (keeping in mind that Donald and Myra have plenty of cash to pay premiums). However, it is crucial that Myra obtain such coverage. The sad statistical fact is that Myra will probably be a wealthy widow. If Donald dies at age 79, and Myra dies at age 83, Myra will have survived Donald by 21 years–with two decades worth of income and potential health care needs to be provided for.

It would not be surprising if Donald lived until 2010 (the year of estate tax repeal)–and Myra will probably live for at least 25 more years. So it is very difficult to predict what the estate tax rules will look like at the relevant time. They will probably need to re-draft their wills and estate plans several times to keep abreast of statutory changes.

Given the couple's profile, estate planning assumes a role in their long-range planning. There is a risk that, without planning, Donald will have a taxable estate (not taking into account the marital deduction), and it is almost certain that Myra will encounter a taxable "second estate" problem based on the build-up of income on her inheritance. Therefore, at least basic estate planning steps are vital.

One option is for Myra and Donald to each place some assets into trust. If they want to keep their Medicaid planning options only, they should favor the "income-only" trust form (which forbids invasion of principal). This type of trust, in conjunction with a durable power of attorney, can also provide major protection in case of incapacity. Alternatively, each should have a credit shelter ("bypass") trust. Given Myra's status as second wife, it might also make sense to make some provision for her in the form of a QTIP trust, in which she receives income for life, but after her death the principal reverts to the children of Donald's first marriage. Purchase of a second-to-die life insurance policy might also be prudent under this plan.

Donald and Myra should also consider a gifting program. Each year, Donald, with Myra's consent (or vice versa) can make "split-gifts," giving $24,000 to each donee without incurring gift tax. (This is the 2006 level.) Potential donees include the children and grandchildren. They may also wish to give to their favorite charities, perhaps in the form of a charitable remainder trust that would generate some extra lifetime income for them. Until the $3.5 million unified credit is fully phased in, the Jennings may prefer to use a charitable remainder *unitrust*, rather than a charitable remainder *annuity* trust, because the unitrust allows them to place additional funds into the trust (to keep pace with the increasing unified credit). Charitable remainder annuity trusts do not allow additional deposits after they are funded.

Although it probably would not be suitable now, moving to a *non-equity* continuing care retirement community could be a good choice in the future. If a suitable facility can be located, such a move might be worthwhile because these facilities combine a comfortable (or even luxurious) housing unit with a promise of nursing care on-site, if and when required. The non-equity feature allows removal of funds from the taxable estate, whereas the value of an equity interest would remain within the estate.

5. Steve and Jill Florian

The Florians are house-rich in comparison to their somewhat limited income. Steve Florian, age 70, is a retiree with a pension of $16,000 per year and Social Security benefits of $8,000 per year. He has had two mild heart attacks, and has moderately severe arthritis. Jill Florian, age 66, is also retired, but her pension is only $5,000 per year. She is diabetic and has had a cataract operation. Her own Social Security benefit would be lower than her spouse's benefit of $4,000 per year, so she draws the spouse's benefit instead. That gives the Florians a basic sum of $33,000 to work with (plus $4,000 in investment income; see below). The availability of long-term care insurance is something worth exploring, but given their ages, health, and income, they might find it hard to secure affordable coverage.

Steve and Jill's major asset is their home, which they have owned for many years and have lovingly improved. The Florian's residence is presently worth about $600,000; their cost basis is $200,000. Of course, if they choose to sell the home, the $400,000 capital gain would be excluded from taxation due to the $500,000 exclusion for married couples filing joint returns. Their IRAs, savings accounts, and investments are fairly limited ($60,000), yielding $4,000 per year in additional income. They should consider liquidating their entire portfolio in return for an immediate annuity that provides an easily manageable income stream.

The Florians live in a state that has not chosen to increase the amount of housing equity that can be retained without forfeiting Medicaid eligibility. Therefore, they will not be able to qualify for Medicaid until they reduce their home equity below the $500,000 level—as well as satisfying all the other requirements. They can use a reverse mortgage or home equity loan to get the equity below $500,000.

Assuming that the Florians live in a "medically needy state," and not a "cap" state, whichever spouse applies for Medicaid will probably have a spend-down obligation, even after transferring the "community spouse income allowance" to the healthy spouse.

For Medicaid purposes, a good move would be for Steve and Jill to place their savings into an income-only trust. Trusts below $50,000 are usually too small to be worth the trouble and costs of administration, but a $60,000 trust, though small, is feasible. Another option is a charity's "pooled fund." If neither of them ever applies for Medicaid, they can still benefit from the income, and the trust principal can be left to the surviving spouse.

It is very unlikely (but possible) that federal estate tax problems will arise, because the first spouse to die will probably have an estate below the federally taxable level. Either Steve or Jill will probably want to leave most of the estate to the surviving spouse, so the marital deduction will shelter the estate of the first to die. If they are very concerned about estate tax, they may want to make some lifetime gifts to reduce the estate below the taxable figure. For this couple, the probability of making a Medicaid application is greater than ending up with a taxable estate. Consequently, care should be taken to avoid making gifts that might fall into the "look-back" period and, thus, create a penalty period of Medicaid ineligibility.

In this plan, estate planning is sacrificed to Medicaid eligibility. If Steve and/or Jill do receive Medicaid benefits, both the income-only trust and the homestead (after the death of both spouses) will be vulnerable to estate recovery (see Chapter 6). However, the estate recovery will be reduced by the obligation to repay any reverse mortgage or home equity loan they have taken to reduce their home equity.

6. Georgia Hailey

Georgia Hailey was widowed at age 66. For a few years afterward, Mrs. Hailey's daughter, Patricia Dawkins, visited her occasionally and telephoned once or twice a week. When Mrs. Hailey was 71, Patricia noticed that the once immaculate home was becoming run down, and her mother sometimes seemed confused or sounded vague over the phone. Patricia nagged until her mother consulted an internist, who diagnosed moderate hypertension and prescribed medication that was helpful, but also caused some unpleasant side effects. Patricia encouraged her mother to hire a neighboring high school student to do chores and heavy cleaning, and Mrs. Hailey agreed.

At about this time, Patricia decided that she needed to keep a closer watch over her mother, so she started driving her mother to church and running errands. When Mrs. Hailey was 72, Patricia observed that her mother's vision had deteriorated somewhat, and that her hands trembled. The new internist in Mrs. Hailey's HMO eventually referred her to an ophthalmologist, who recommended cataract surgery, and a neurologist, who diagnosed a mild case of Parkinson 's disease. Medicare covered most of the costs of the surgery, and the cost of the neurologist. Patricia urged her mother to apply for Medicare Part D, but Mrs. Hailey took one look at the top brochure on the pile that Patricia got for her, and said, "That's too difficult—I can't be worried about that." So Mrs. Hailey continues to pay out of pocket for her medications.

The cataract surgery was performed on an outpatient basis. Since Mrs. Hailey did not satisfy the definition of "homebound," she was not eligible for Medicare home care. At this point, Patricia hired a Geriatric Care Manager (GCM). Patricia's brother, Peter, who lives 500 miles away, contributed most of the GCM's fee. The GCM recommended a local home health agency, which sent a worker to Mrs. Hailey's home twice a week for four-hour intervals to see that Mrs. Hailey was functioning well. This worker also cleans the house and helps Mrs. Hailey bathe. Patricia continued her Sunday visits, and took over responsibility for shopping, some of the cooking, and helping her mother pay bills.

At present, Mrs. Hailey is doing fairly well at home. Patricia cannot increase her hands-on caregiving because of her obligations to her job and to her husband and children. Peter Hailey has agreed to contribute $200 per month toward the cost of his mother's medications and home care, but cannot afford to contribute much more. Patricia and the GCM, Nina Roskova, have researched local housing options, but have not found any high-quality, affordable congregate housing or assisted living facilities. Everyone hopes that the home care plan will continue to be satisfactory.

There could eventually be a problem if it is no longer safe for Mrs. Hailey to remain at home by herself, but her condition is not bad enough to qualify her for nursing home admission. Patricia's husband and teenage children do not want Mrs. Hailey to move in with them. Patricia hates to admit it, but she really does not want this either. Peter Hailey lives far away, in a one-bedroom condominium. He is single and owns a small business that consumes his time and income, so he is an unlikely candidate to be a hands-on caregiver. A move to an Assisted Living Facility is possible, but that would involve moving away from the suburb where Mrs. Hailey has spent most of her life, and the whole family, spending as much as they could afford, could just about cover the cost of a year or two in an ALF. Cost increases, or additional longevity, would exhaust the family's financial as well as emotional resources.

ISSUE SPOTTING: ANALYZING ACTUAL CASES

This is a checklist of some factors to consider when determining the needs and desires of your clients, and when discussing strategies with the other members of the planning team:

Marshalling Assets

- Based on the client's own reports, what is the value of:

    - the family home

    - the investment portfolio

    - the insurance portfolio

    - the IRA/401(k) accounts?

- Is there any reason to doubt the client's veracity or accuracy? If so, what do you estimate the true values to be?

- Are there any assets of which the client is unaware?

- If the client is still employed, what is his/her income? Spouse's income?

- If retired, what is his/her Social Security benefit? Spouse's benefit?

- How much income does the client currently receive from his/her investment portfolio?

- Is the client entitled to income from any other sources (e.g., pensions from former employers other than the most recent employer, veterans' benefits, disability benefits)?

- Does the client own personal property of significant value (e.g., artwork, silverware, antiques)? Has the property been professionally appraised?

Insurance

- How much life insurance does the client have?

- For term insurance, when does the term expire? Is the insurance renewable? What would it cost to continue or convert the coverage?

- For whole life insurance, how much is the death benefit? The cash value? What accelerated death benefit provisions does the policy have?

- Is the client insurable, rated-up, or uninsurable for additional coverage?

- Is the type of coverage suitable, and the amount of coverage adequate? What are the alternatives if additional coverage is needed, but is unavailable or unaffordable?

- Does the client have Medigap insurance? If so, is it the appropriate form? Are changes in Medigap coverage required in light of the introduction of Medicare Part D? Is the coverage cost-effective, or would switching to another insurer or another policy be helpful?

- Does the client have long-term care insurance (LTCI)? If so, what benefits are provided? Is the policy qualified? What are its tax implications? Is a change in coverage warranted?

- If the client does not have LTCI, does he/she want it? Is he/she insurable? What do you advise, and what does the client want with respect to daily benefits, duration of coverage, services covered, etc.? What would such a policy cost with/without inflation protection and nonforfeiture protection?

- If the client wants LTCI but does not think it is affordable, are there options for funding premium dollars (e.g., receiving contributions from the children, selling part of the investment portfolio, tapping the home equity)?

- Should LTCI be purchased to provide funds for private payment during a Medicaid penalty period, or if it seems clear that DRA '05 changes rule out future Medicaid eligibility?

Investments

- Are the client's assets allocated appropriately for his/her age, income-tax bracket, investment, and estate planning objectives?

- What additional investments should be made in the future?

- Would shifting part of the portfolio into an immediate annuity be appropriate, to provide professional management and lifetime income?

- Does the portfolio have enough growth elements to deal with the projected life expectancies of the client and his/her spouse?

- Is the portfolio adequately documented so that a fiduciary could readily begin managing the investments, if necessary?

- Does the portfolio offer opportunities for profit-taking?

- What are the tax consequences of selling investments now?

- Will the client be eligible for the reduced rate for certain capital gains (after 2005)? How will this affect investment plans?

Capacity Issues

- Does the client possess full mental capacity, or has there been some cognitive decline?

- Are there medical options for improving alertness and memory?

- Does the client have a durable power of attorney? If so, does the agent know that he/she has been named as agent? Is he/she willing to serve in that capacity?

- Does the agent have gifting (and self-gifting) powers? Should these powers be added or removed?

- Has the client designated a guardian to be appointed if necessary?

- If there is no existing guardian designation, is a guardianship proceeding appropriate? If so, who should file the petition, who should be named as the guardian (for the person and/or their property), and what powers should the guardian be given?

- How would appointment of a guardian affect the operation of the financial plan?

- In planning for gifts, transfers, and bequests, have capacity issues of the recipient(s) been considered?

Housing Issues

- Is the client's home safe and appropriate for his/her needs for the foreseeable future?

- Has the home been "elder-proofed" (e.g., have additional lights been added, loose rugs secured or removed, doorways widened for use with a wheelchair or walker, alarm and security system installed or expanded)?

- If the client still has a mortgage, would it be wise to pay off or reduce the mortgage?

- How much could the client raise through home equity loans or reverse mortgages? Would this be a wise step, in light of the plan as a whole?

- Does the client have excess housing equity in the Medicaid sense (i.e., over $500,000, in general; over the additional amount permitted by the state, subject to a federal limit of $750,000)? If so, at what point would it be wise to "shed" some housing equity through home equity loans or reverse mortgages?

- Does it make sense for the client to live with a son or daughter, or for a son or daughter to move into the client's home?

- Is there space for home-sharing, or for a live-in companion or home health worker?

- How far away is the client willing to move?

- What is the availability, within this radius, of specialized apartments for the elderly? Retirement communities? Assisted-living facilities? Continuing care retirement communities? Nursing homes?

- Which of these facilities have the best reputation for quality? Which ones are the most attractive? If they are subject to inspection requirements, have the inspection reports uncovered problems?

- How does the client feel about moving to specialized housing, or to a medical facility?

- If the client is opposed to moving, and wants to remain at home, is this a realistic desire in terms of safety and affordability of home care?

- What are the costs (e.g., entry fee, ongoing payments, payments for supplementary services) of the various housing options that are not only suitable for the client's needs, but also attractive to the client?

- Does the client receive an equity interest in the housing unit?

- Is the housing facility eligible for insurance, Medicare, or Medicaid reimbursement? Is any part of the cost tax-deductible?

- What refund provisions are available if the client is dissatisfied and wants to move out?

Health Care Planning

- Does the client know the reputation, services, and pros and cons of the local medical practices, hospitals, and home health agencies?

- Does the client have a Geriatric Care Manager (GCM)?

- Does the client have an emergency response alarm system at home?

- Does the client get Medicare benefits through the conventional system, or through managed care (Medicare Advantage)? Would a change be better for the client?

- Does the client receive prescription drug benefits under retiree health coverage? If so, does this offer a better deal than Medicare Part D? If not, the client probably should enroll in Part D. Because retiree health benefits are so uncertain, even a client with good retirement benefits might opt for Part D instead.

- Which of the available Part D plans offers the best coverage for the client's needs (e.g., coverage of drugs that the client is already taking)?

- Part D enrollees will definitely need to budget for their monthly premiums, but may realize substantial savings—cash that can be used to meet other needs, or can be invested.

- Does the client have any advance directives (e.g., living will; durable power of attorney for health care (health care proxy); instructions concerning "do-not-resuscitate" orders and artificial nutrition/hydration; anatomical gift forms)? Do these forms reflect both local law and the client's feelings about life support in cases of permanent unconsciousness? If so, are the forms complete, current, and in conformity with state law? Are the patient's doctors aware of these instructions and willing to comply with them? Does the designated proxy decision-maker know that he or she is the proxy, does he or she understand the senior citizen's wishes, and is he or she willing to carry them out (even in the face of opposition)?

Estate Planning

- How likely is it that the client will have a federally taxable estate (or that the client's spouse will have a federally taxable second estate)?

- How is the estate plan handling the uncertainty of the EGTRRA planning environment?

- Is the client already using trusts for incapacity planning? If so, how do these trusts fit into the estate plan?

- Is it worth creating one or more revocable living trusts for probate avoidance purposes, or for professional asset management purposes?

- Should income-only trusts be created for Medicaid planning purposes?

- Should title to the family home be placed into trust?

- Does each spouse have a credit shelter trust? Should the spouse or someone else be the beneficiary of the credit shelter trust?

- Is a QTIP trust a logical addition to the estate plan?

- Is the client's will complete, current, and flexible enough to operate if the client is incapacitated at a time when tax laws are being amended?

- Does the client wish to make major donations to charity, and if so, should they be made during lifetime (outright gifts or in trust) or by testamentary bequests?

- If you believe that your client will receive Medicaid benefits, how do you think Medicaid estate recovery will affect the estate plan?

Income Tax Planning

- Are the client's Social Security benefits taxable?

- Is the client a dependent of a caregiver child?

- Is the caregiver child entitled to an income tax deduction?

- Is the client entitled to a long-term care insurance (LTCI) premium deduction?

- Has the client received benefits under a LTCI policy? Are the benefits taxable?

- Is the client entitled to the larger standard deduction for taxpayers age 65 (or older), and/or the credit for the elderly?

- Has the client incurred enough medical expenses, unreimbursed by Medicare or Medicaid, to be able to deduct those expenses?

Medicaid Planning

- What kind, and amount, of home health care can be covered under your state's Medicaid plan?

- Has your state taken advantage of the option, under DRA '05, to expand Home and Community-Based Services? If so, what are the qualifications for the program? Is there a waiting list?

- Is your state a "cap" or a "medically needy" state?

- In a "cap" state, can any measures be taken to restrict your client's income?

- Can your client set up a trust for the excess income to preserve Medicaid eligibility?

- What asset transfers have your client and his/her spouse made within the past five years (DRA '05 made the look-back period five years for all types of transfers, not just irrevocable trust transfers)?

- Do you predict that your client, or the client's spouse, will need nursing home care within the foreseeable future? If so, when?

- What are your client's non-exempt assets?

- Should ownership of the homestead be changed to prevent estate recovery?

- Should the client use otherwise-available funds to fix up the homestead?

- If your client made an immediate, non-exempt transfer of all non-exempt assets, how long would the penalty period be? How would the client cope with the change in methodology (the penalty period now begins at the time of the Medicaid application, not at the time of the transfer)?

- If your client is married, how much could be transferred to his/her spouse as a "Community Spouse Resource Allowance"? How much could be transferred each month as a "Community Spouse Income Allowance"?

- If you live in a "medically needy" state, how much must your client "spend-down" each month for nursing home care (or for home care that follows the nursing home financial eligibility rules)?

- Should your client start making "half-a-loaf" transfers now?

- Should your client place assets into an income-only trust?

- Can your client use LTCI to cover the payment obligation during the penalty period?

- What is your client's fall-back plan if the state where he or she lives further reduces Medicaid long-term care services, or changes financial eligibility rules so that your client will not be able to qualify?

THE ELDER-FRIENDLY PRACTICE

Experienced elder planners have developed some techniques for making it easier to communicate with senior citizens, and for optimizing their office arrangements for working with the elderly, as listed below:

- Use more written communications for older persons whose hearing is impaired, and more oral communications (for instance, a cassette recording of you reading a document) for those individuals with visual limitations.

- Make large-print versions of all documents available.

- If clients need a little extra time to think things over, schedule another appointment, and make sure they have written documentation of all the issues.

- If possible, locate your office near public transportation (since not all senior citizens still drive), or near a senior center (where specialized transportation may be available).

- Older people often find it easier to get up from a hard chair than a deep, cushiony one.

- Try to locate your office in a handicap-accessible building, or add your own ramps and widen doorways so cane and wheelchair users can easily get through them.

- If you can manage them, home and hospital visits can be real practice-builders.

- The phenomenon of "sundowning" is well known in elder care: many people who start out the day fairly cogent may become more and more confused as the day goes on. So the earlier in the day you can schedule your elder planning appointments, the easier it may be for your clients to grasp what you are saying.

- Sometimes a temporary or long-range change in medication can clear up mental confusion, so work with the patient's doctor if an especially important transaction must be carried out.

SUMMARY

Not every issue will arise in every case. Some of your clients will need help with only one or two simple issues, and you will be able to answer their questions and solve their problem fairly quickly. Other clients will present far more complex problems such that even maximum deployment of products and services will resolve only part of the problem. You will be able to manage some clients' situations by yourself, while other clients will call for the skills of a full team. Some situations can be happily resolved in a short period of time, others can be unhappily resolved in a somewhat longer period of time (e.g., the death of the client and the administration and closing of the estate), and other situations may require years of continued attention to changing needs. Health care costs continue to increase, while many seniors face reductions or loss of pension benefits they expected, and are at risk depending on stock market forces. As the Medicare and Medicaid programs grow larger and more expensive, senior citizens may face ongoing contractions of public benefit eligibility.

Personal preferences are also significant—even if you have two cases with virtually identical fact situations, you may discover that your clients, after receiving appropriate advice, choose completely different strategies. In some plans, staying at home is the client's top priority, and tremendous amounts of money and effort will be devoted to that objective, whereas other plans will revolve around an immediate move to a new housing or medical facility. Some caregivers are willing to devote endless hours to caring for a parent or in-law, including performing the most personal of tasks; certain caregivers will even go so far as to learn sophisticated nursing skills. There are other cases in which no caregiver is available or willing to provide hands-on or financial assistance.

Elder planning involves more than dollars and cents. You will be deeply involved in the lives of families, as well as single or widowed people who may have few other meaningful contacts with the community. Elder planning can be much more psychologically demanding than business planning where "only" money is involved, but it can also be extremely satisfying to know that you are making a real difference in the lives of senior citizens and their families.

Index